£16.95

£11.25

59

D1493334

ALPHONSE DE LAMARTINE

Alphonse de Lamartine

A POLITICAL BIOGRAPHY

William Fortescue

CROOM HELM
London & Canberra

ST. MARTIN'S PRESS
New York

© 1983 William Fortescue
Croom Helm Ltd, Provident House, Burrell Row,
Beckenham, Kent BR3 1AT

British Library Cataloguing in Publication Data

Fortescue, William
    Alphonse de Lamartine.
    1. Lamartine, Alphonse de 2. France —
    Politics and government — 19th century — Biography
    I. Title
    944.07'092'4   DC269.L/

    ISBN 0-7099-1254-4

All rights reserved. For information, write:
St. Martin's Press, Inc., 175 Fifth Avenue, New York, N.Y. 10010
First published in the United States of America in 1983

Library of Congress Card Catalog Number: 82-42927

ISBN 0-312-02138-0

Printed and bound in Great Britain
by Billing and Sons Ltd, Worcester.

CONTENTS

PREFACE

M. de Lamartine est une des figures de notre temps les plus intéressantes à étudier.
— *Journal du docteur Prosper Ménière* (Paris, 1903), p. 64

La vie de Lamartine est si riche qu'elle n'a pas fini d'être écrite.
— Marquis de Luppé, *Les Travaux et les jours d'Alphonse de Lamartine* (Paris, 1948), p. 7.

For much of his life Alphonse de Lamartine made an important contribution to French literature and politics. In the 1820s he was (with Victor Hugo and Alfred de Vigny) one of the three leading French Romantic writers; he became a major political figure in France during the 1830s; throughout the brief but critical Revolution of 1848 he played a crucial role in government; and some of his historical works were among the most popular literary publications of his time. In addition, his ideas and attitudes are extremely revealing on currents of French thought and opinion between the Restoration Monarchy and the Second Empire; and he is an interesting example of an intellectual significantly involved in politics.

While the published literature on Lamartine is very extensive, much about his life and work remains to be discovered, and there have been few satisfactory works of synthesis. In French there are numerous biographies, including those by Jean Des Cognets (1913), Paul Hazard (1925), André Lebey (1929), Jean Lucas-Dubreton (1930), Louis Bertrand (1940), Henri Guillemin (1940), Jacques Castelnau (1943), the Marquis de Luppé (1943 and 1948), Gonzague Truc (1968), and Maurice Toesca (1969). In addition, a large, and growing, number of articles and longer studies are concerned with Lamartine. Only two biographies of him exist in English, however, a romantic account of his life by Lady Margaret Domville (1882) and a solid two volume work by H. R. Whitehouse (1918), which is now necessarily out of date. Moreover, Lamartine's political career has received surprisingly little detailed scholarly examination in French or English, apart from two studies by Pierre Quentin-Bauchart (1907 and 1913). This political biography, therefore, attempts to fill a gap, though as it focuses on Lamartine's political career it does not aim to cover all aspects of his long, varied and productive life.

Preface

I owe a special debt to my first teachers in French history, Professor Richard Cobb and Professor James Leith. Professor Douglas Johnson originally suggested that I should tackle Lamartine, and he was my research supervisor at University College, London. Over the years I have accumulated many other debts. The research for this book could not have been undertaken without the financial assistance provided by the Scottish Education Department, the research fund of the University of Kent at Canterbury, the Sir Ernest Cassel Educational Trust, and the British Academy. Many people have been generous with their help and advice, including Dr Stephen Bann, Dr Roger Bullen, Mr Antony Copley, M. Antoine Court, Mr Ian Frazer, Mlle Marie-Renée Morin, Dr Pamela Pilbeam, Professor David Pinkney, Mr Roger Price, Dr Graham Thomas, M. Paul Viallaneix, and Dr Theodore Zeldin. I am particularly grateful to Mrs Irene Collins for her painstaking critical appraisal of the entire manuscript, to Mrs Pamela Duesbury for her typing and editorial skills, to M. Fernand Letessier for his exhaustive knowledge of all matters relating to Lamartine, and to my wife Clare for her efforts to improve my literary style. My greatest debt is to the British Library, and to its astonishingly rich collection of materials on nineteenth-century France.

1 POETRY, POSITION AND POLITICS, 1790-1830

J'aurais un grand désir et surtout un grand besoin d'être placé.
— Lamartine to his uncle François-Louis de Lamartine,
11 November 1815

In a generation of Frenchmen among whom brilliant talents and remarkable lives were not uncommon, Lamartine remains outstanding for his extraordinarily complex personality, his exceptional and varied abilities, and his unusually rich and productive career. Lamartine himself once claimed he possessed two distinct personalities, 'l'homme de coeur' and 'l'homme de bon sens'. He also suggested his life could be divided into two quite separate periods, the first devoted to poetry, the second to politics.[1] The familiar conflict between reason and emotion was certainly present in his character, though there was much else — a remarkably pronounced self-preoccupation, a strong desire for public approval and success, and a willingness to service his needs and ambitions by hypocritical behaviour and the exploitation of others. Equally, a new phase in his life, in which politics predominated over poetry, did begin about 1830. However, many connections existed between his literary and political activities, and he deliberately used the former to promote the latter. A study of his early life can help to explain how his complex personality developed, how he sought, and achieved, success in a variety of fields, and how he laid the foundations for his future political career.

The society in which Lamartine achieved his first significant public successes was that of Restoration France, when (except for the Hundred Day episode) France was successively ruled by Louis XVIII (1814-24) and Charles X (1824-30), the younger brothers of Louis XVI. According to the Charters of 1814 and 1815 they ruled as constitutional monarchs in conjunction with a two chamber legislature. This parliament reflected and reinforced France's domination by a small élite, largely composed of those who had emerged from the Revolutionary and Napoleonic periods as substantial landowners. Membership of the Chamber of Peers, which rose from 154 in 1814 to 365 in 1830, was initially by royal appointment and thereafter hereditary (apart from members of the Royal Family and Princes of the Blood, who were peers by right of birth). Those appointed included *ancien régime* aristocrats, prominent figures in Napoleon's former élite, and

Roman Catholic bishops and archbishops. The Chamber of Deputies (membership fluctuated between 258 and 430) was elected by a property franchise which restricted the number of electors to approximately 70,000 males aged 30 years or over, and the number of possible parliamentary candidates to approximately 15,000 of the wealthiest Frenchmen aged 40 or over, out of a total population in 1814 of about 27 million. No organised political parties existed, though those in politics were usually either conservatives or liberals. Conservatives tended to look back nostalgically to pre-Revolutionary France, to support the Bourbon dynasty and monarchical authority, and to share in the Roman Catholic revival that occurred after 1814. Liberals tended to believe in parliamentary sovereignty, traditional liberal freedoms, and the separation of the Catholic Church from the French State. Conservative-liberal conflicts normally characterised French politics throughout the Restoration.

The domination of Restoration France by a small élite took various forms. At a local level, wealthy and well established families asserted their ascendancy through their pre-eminent social position, and through their influence in institutions such as learned societies or academies and in the administrative councils of the town and the department. In a wider context, patronage by members of the élite was often of enormous importance: it could determine social acceptance, literary and artistic success, and appointments and promotions in government service. For at least part of the year, leading members of the élite usually lived in Paris, the pre-eminence of which had been reinforced by the centralisation of the Revolution and Napoleon. In Paris the Court held no monopoly over the élite's social life, due to constraints on the royal finances and the personal inclinations of Louis XVIII and Charles X. Instead, much élite social activity revolved around the private *salons* of a select number of socially prominent women. Since the élite of Restoration France was so relatively small, since the opportunities for self-advancement were so relatively restricted, and since personal contacts and recommendations were so all-important, such *salons* played a vital social, political and intellectual role. Entry into and success in Paris *salons* depended upon a variety of factors including personal introductions, aristocratic status, individual charm, and intellectual distinction. The same factors were often important for those seeking official and public success.

Lamartine was not ill-equipped to succeed in such a society. His parents, Pierre de Lamartine (1750-1840) and Françoise-Alix des Roys (1766-1829) were both aristocrats, though, like so many members of their class, they did not possess noble titles. In 1651 Lamartine's paternal great-great grandfather, Estienne de Lamartine, had purchased the post of *secrétaire du roi*, which conferred hereditary aristocratic status. Estienne's descendants in the main line consolidated their aristocratic claims by marrying heiresses and acquiring *terres nobles*. On Lamartine's mother's side, the des Roys could trace their descent back to the sixteenth century. They belonged to the provincial *noblesse de robe*, but were connected with several important noble families.[2] On his father's side, Lamartine also inherited a distinguished record of military service to the Bourbon monarchy. His paternal grandfather had risen to the rank of captain in the armies of Louis XV, and had won the much coveted Cross of Saint-Louis at the battle of Fontenoy. Similarly, his father was commissioned into a cavalry regiment in 1769 and promoted captain in 1788. Through his mother Lamartine had a more personal link with the Bourbons, but with the Orléans branch: her father, Jean-Louis des Roys, had served as *intendant des finances* to Louis XVI's cousin, the duc d'Orléans (father of the future Philippe-Egalité), from 1772 until the duke's death in 1785, while her mother had been a *sous-gouvernante* to the Orléans family from the birth of the future King Louis-Philippe in 1773 until 1778.

By the time of Lamartine's birth (21 October 1790), the Lamartines had been rooted in the Mâconnais district of Burgundy (in what became the department of Saône-et-Loire) for more than two hundred years. Extensive landowners, they owned the estate of Monceau near Mâcon, a large town house in Mâcon, the estate of Montculot near Dijon, and property in the Jura. Pierre de Lamartine was the youngest of three sons and had three sisters. But he alone married and, although he and his wife had six children who survived, they had only one son, their eldest child Alphonse-Marie-Louis de Lamartine. Consequently Lamartine became the heir presumptive to the bulk of the Lamartine estates, which were to make him one of the richest landowners in Saône-et-Loire.

The Revolutionary period between 1789 and 1799 left few French families, particularly French aristocratic families, completely untouched. In many cases it profoundly influenced future political loyalties and future economic and social status. During the Revolution Pierre de Lamartine demonstrated his staunch royalism: he resigned his officer's commission to avoid swearing an oath of loyalty to the Constitution of 1791; and on 10 August 1792 he took part in the unsuccessful defence of the Tuileries Palace. Subsequently he managed to escape from Paris, but was arrested as a political suspect in October 1793, and imprisoned in first Mâcon and then Autun. After his release at the end of October 1794 he settled with his family near Mâcon in the village of Milly, where in his marriage contract he had been given a substantial house. A further move came in 1801, when Pierre bought for 80,000 francs the *château* and estate of Saint-Point, about twelve miles from Mâcon — the money coming from the sale of his father's property in the Jura. Thus Pierre de Lamartine, like many provincial aristocrats, through loyalty to the Bourbons suffered during the Revolution. But neither Pierre nor his brothers emigrated, and they all survived the Revolution still possessing most of their former wealth.

It is clear that, while Lamartine owed his social status to his father, his mother exercised a greater influence on his early personal and intellectual development. Having been brought up in the two main residences of the Orléans family, the Palais-Royal in central Paris and the *château* of Saint-Cloud between Paris and Versailles, Lamartine's mother had lived in one of France's premier households at an impressionable age. She had also come under the sway of the comtesse de Genlis, *dame d'honneur* to the duchesse de Chartres (later duchesse d'Orléans) and principal governess to the Orléans children from 1777. The comtesse was a remarkable woman, who, during a long and adventurous life, became an important theorist on education and a prolific authoress. She apparently quarrelled with Lamartine's grandmother.[3] Also she was publicly reputed to have been the mistress of the duc de Chartres, and her radicalism during the Revolution and *ralliement* to Napoleon would have distanced her politically from the des Roys and Lamartine families. Nevertheless, the comtesse de Genlis probably impressed Lamartine's mother by her interest in education, her adaptation of Rousseau's educational ideas, her defence of Christianity against the scepticism of the *philosophes*, and by her belief that moral principles could be inculcated through suitable literature.

About 1781 Lamartine's mother had entered the chapter house of Saint-Martin de Salles, near Villefranche-sur-Saône in the Beaujolais, though like many French aristocratic women who entered chapter houses at this time, she took no vows there. However, for approximately eight years she lived as a member of a religious community, and she certainly became a devout Catholic. In her surviving letters and the journal she kept after her marriage, she reveals herself as a sensitive, well educated and deeply religious woman. She met her husband while he was visiting one of her sisters at the same chapter house. Their marriage (7 January 1790) was evidently an affair of the heart, and they remained devoted to each other. By upbringing she was more cosmopolitan and sophisticated than her husband, whose attitudes and way of life were typical of those of a rather obscure minor provincial aristocrat; and, while his world centred on his properties and Mâcon, hers embraced (although distantly) aristocratic Paris society and the intellectual ferment of the Enlightenment.[4]

At an early age Lamartine was read to by his parents. His mother, concerned to bring up her son a devout Catholic, read him parts of the Bible, Fénelon and *The Imitation of Christ*. She and her husband also introduced him to Homer, Tacitus, La Fontaine, Bernardin de Saint-Pierre, and Voltaire's tragedies. The Bible came to exercise a very profound influence on Lamartine, providing him throughout his life with literary, intellectual and spiritual inspiration. He also became an admirer of Fénelon, and *The Imitation of Christ* remained one of his favourite books. With Homer and Tacitus Lamartine encountered classical civilisation, a study of which was then an indispensable part of education. Bernardin de Saint-Pierre, particularly his *Paul et Virginie* (1787), would have given Lamartine a literary introduction to nature, the sea and exotic lands, while La Fontaine's fables and Voltaire's tragedies would have introduced him to poetry and drama. Lamartine's parents thus contributed to their son's intellectual development by arousing his interest in reading, by giving him a strongly Christian and Catholic upbringing, and by introducing him to poetry, classical writers and some contemporary literature. Through reading aloud to him they may also have encouraged him to attach importance to the sound of words.

When the time came to send Lamartine to school, the choice of a suitable establishment presented problems. No local school existed; the Revolution had severely disrupted education in France; and the Napoleonic *lycées*, founded in 1802, were to be considered too Bonapartist by his father and too militarist by his mother. Eventually it was decided to send Lamartine to the Institut Puppier, a private school in Lyons, where some of his mother's relations lived. From March 1801 until the summer of 1803 he was a boarder there, spending holidays at home. He disliked the school, and in December 1802 made an unsuccessful attempt to run away. As a result Lamartine's mother persuaded her husband and brothers-in-law that her son's education should be continued by the Jesuits, who were renowned for their pedagogic ability and whose colleges had long been patronised by the French aristocracy. The Jesuits had been expelled from France in 1764 and suppressed by the Pope in 1773. They continued, however, to maintain an unofficial existence; and, under the name of the Fathers of the Faith, in January 1803 they had re-established a college at Belley, a village in Savoy not far from Chambéry and the lake of Le Bourget, which were to have important associations for Lamartine.

In October 1803 Lamartine was admitted to the new school, and an important phase began in his intellectual and personal development. Jesuit teachers tended to be concerned with inculcating religious piety, fluent oral and literary expression, intellectual liveliness, and a competitive spirit. Lamartine's Catholic upbringing must have been reinforced by the religious atmosphere of the college at Belley, and his lessons in literature, philosophy and rhetoric were doubtless not unimportant for the future writer and orator. He certainly developed both respect and affection for several of his teachers, who sharpened his intellect and broadened his education. In particular, at Belley Lamartine was introduced to one of the most important literary works of the Napoleonic period, Chateaubriand's *Génie du christianisme* (1802), which affirmed the alliance between Christianity and liberty and which gave literary and intellectual stimulus to the French Catholic revival. At Belley, too, Lamartine achieved academic distinction. While his progress in ancient Greek and mathematics was unremarkable, he won first prizes in French and Latin composition and in Latin verse.[5] He also began to write poems, two of which, 'Le Rossignol' and 'Cantique sur le Torrent de Tuisy', have survived.[6]

On a personal level, at Belley Lamartine developed important friendships with three of his aristocratic fellow-pupils, Aymon de Virieu,[7] Louis de Vignet[8] and Prosper Guichard de Bienassis.[9] Virieu became his closest friend and confidant, and their extensive correspondence is extremely revealing on Lamartine's ideas, motives and opinions. Vignet and Bienassis never enjoyed a comparable intimacy with Lamartine, and after about 1820 he maintained rather irregular contact with them. But they were on friendly terms for at least ten years after leaving Belley, and Bienassis in particular remained a faithful if distant friend until he died. In surrounding himself with a small group of friends in whom he confided, Lamartine was behaving in a manner that was to be repeated throughout his life. His conduct at Belley was equally characteristic in other respects. The Jesuit Fathers reported to his parents that he was intelligent, imaginative and quick to learn, but also inclined towards superficiality, unwilling to apply himself, and dangerously engrossed in the pursuit of pleasure. His mother noted that at Belley, although adequately provided with pocket money, he always seemed to be in financial difficulties and that he regularly suffered from headaches and fevers, possibly symptoms of a chest complaint which troubled him for most of his life.[10] One reason for his financial problems was that while at Belley he fathered by a servant girl an illegitimate son, whom he supported. The affair, the first of many, seems to have been concealed remarkably effectively.[11]

Lamartine left the college at Belley at the age of seventeen (January 1808) before completing his studies, since it was thought that Belley was bad for his health. There then began a period in Lamartine's life during which he suffered from intense and frequent boredom. As he himself later confessed, 'Ennui was then the dominating factor of my life, the incurable disease of my spirit.'[12] His family's uncompromising royalist traditions meant that a career in the army, administration or diplomatic service was unthinkable so long as Napoleon ruled France, although Napoleon was then at the height of his career and the Empire offered numerous opportunities for young men of birth, education and ability. It was apparently equally unthinkable for this son of a provincial aristocrat to go into commerce. Thus on leaving school he had no regular occupation and no purpose in life, except a restless search for distraction and entertainment. Pierre de Lamartine gave surprisingly little guidance or assistance to his only son. For his mother Lamartine always showed a very deep affection, and he was the constant object of her love, anxiety and concern. Yet her devout Catholicism and strict moral principles were probably somewhat inhibiting; she gradually ceased to share in her son's intellectual interests and emotional problems; and she viewed his literary aspirations with grave misgivings — possibly because one of her brothers had been an unsuccessful poet, and had committed suicide in 1804.[13] Family life at Milly, Mâcon and Saint-Point, with five sisters, three maiden aunts, a domineering uncle, and a small circle of local families, was evidently stifling and restricting. Lamartine withdrew into himself, went for long solitary walks and rides, and frequently suffered from boredom and melancholy.

Avenues of escape were limited, but for Lamartine literature offered one of the most obvious and important. His correspondence indicates what he was reading.[14] Like most young men of his class and education, he acquired a solid grounding in the classics of ancient Greece and Rome. But, untypically, he virtually ignored the medieval period, read few sixteenth or seventeenth century works, and concentrated on recent French and English literature. Much that he read clearly contributed to his development as a Romantic writer. Particularly significant seems to have been the influence of Ossian, Rousseau and Chateaubriand. The poems attributed to Ossian enjoyed a considerable vogue in France and helped popularise many of the characteristics of French

Romantic literature: a literary style that deliberately appealed to the imagination and the emotions, a love of nature in its wilder aspects, a sense of the mysterious in Man and the universe, an all-pervasive mood of melancholy, and a disenchantment with the transitoriness of life and with the vanity of human affairs. Rousseau became briefly almost a cult figure for Lamartine: he read his works with emotional fervour and made special pilgrimages to places associated with him (May 1810, September and October 1811). On Lamartine and other French Romantics Rousseau exercised a very profound influence: his self-preoccupation, self-analysis and self-revelation, his portrayal and defence of love as a physical passion inspired by a divinely implanted human instinct, his alienation from and disillusion with society, his love of solitude and nature, belief in God's presence in nature, and striving for mystic union between Man and God, all became essential elements of the French Romantic creed. Chateaubriand was the first important French Romantic prose writer. His harmonious literary style, imaginative, reflective and introspective approach, and strong attachment to his family, territorial and religious roots, seem to have particularly influenced Lamartine.

Another avenue of escape for Lamartine was to leave the home environment. There were visits to friends — to Bienassis and Virieu, who both lived in the Isère between Lyons and Chambéry and who introduced Lamartine to various works of the *philosophes*, and to another friend, Clériade Vacher, who lived in the neighbouring department of the Allier.[15] Vaguely intending to study law, Lamartine spent a month with his uncle, the abbé Jean-Baptiste de Lamartine, at Dijon. Twice he visited Lyons to stay with Mme de Rocquemont, a cousin of his mother's; in January 1810 he was despatched there again by his family, following an affair with the daughter of a local doctor. This time he lived alone, ostensibly learning English but in fact gambling, writing poetry, visiting the theatre, and going for 'poetic, botanical and philosophical walks' in the country.[16] He ran into debt and had to borrow from friends and his English teacher. Also he claimed that while in Lyons he indulged in 'charming follies' at night with 'mistresses of a sort'.[17]

Lamartine's succession of affairs had begun at school and continued until his marriage, at the age of thirty, in 1820. Tall, handsome and attractive to women, he clearly sought and easily gained female admiration and sexual pleasure, but his affairs can also be explained by his ennui, restlessness, sense of adventure, and egotistical exploitation of others. Back in Mâcon, he apparently fell seriously in love for the first time: he wanted to marry Marie-Henriette Pommier, daughter of a local *juge de paix*.[18] To distract him from another undesirable match, François-Louis de Lamartine arranged that his nephew should be admitted (19 March 1811) to the Academy of Mâcon, which he had helped to found in 1805. Like many such academies which had developed in provincial France during the eighteenth century, its membership of aristocrats, landowners and officials regularly held intellectual and scientific meetings. The Academy of Mâcon enabled Lamartine to meet important local figures and provided him with a useful literary forum. Soon a more effective distraction was found for him. A daughter of Mme de Rocquemont, together with her husband, La Haste, were going to visit the commercial house of Vassé de Rocquemont et Cie in Leghorn, and it was decided that Lamartine should accompany them. In private letters to Virieu and Bienassis Lamartine professed an extreme reluctance to leave Henriette, but also revealed his excitement at the prospect of a journey to Italy. For him Italy was a land of beauty, history and romance, with an outstandingly rich cultural tradition. Conveniently enough, the whole of Italy was then under French administration.

On 1 July Lamartine left Mâcon to join the de La Hastes in Lyons.[19] Setting out from Lyons in mid-July, they travelled together to Florence, from where Lamartine proceeded alone to Rome. After a month in Rome, spent sight-seeing and learning Italian, he went on to Naples which he had reached by early December. As a solitary tourist he visited the local sights, but soon turned to other distractions (including gambling and perhaps prostitutes), thus rapidly spending the money given by his family and borrowed from friends. Probably in order to economise, he moved in January 1812 to the house of Antoine Dareste de La Chavanne, the brother of Mme de Rocquemont and director of a royal tobacco factory in Naples. In this house Lamartine fell in love with a servant girl called Mariantonia Iacomino. The details of this affair are obscure.[20] However, the time spent with Mariantonia in Naples formed one of his life's most idyllic periods; memories of this Neapolitan romance inspired many of the poems he published after 1820; and the affair lived on in his imagination, to be inaccurately but movingly described in *Les Confidences* (1849), *Graziella* (1852), *Antoniella* (1867) and in his *Mémoires inédits* (1870). Lamartine left Naples and Mariantonia at the beginning of April and by early May had returned to Mâcon. There he faced a cold reception from his family, who deplored his extravagances. Their alarm would have been greater had they known of his infatuation with a servant girl and new-found taste for foreign travel. He had also acquired a lasting affection for Italy.

During his absence, Lamartine's family had persuaded the prefect of Saône-et-Loire to appoint Lamartine mayor of Milly, and on his return he was duly installed in this post. Lamartine's family hoped, thereby, to interest him in local affairs and gain him exemption from military conscription. His duties as mayor of a small village turned out to be light, and once more he sought the usual distractions. 'I am looking for a mistress to sleep with', he confided to Virieu, 'because that is the only way I can calm my imagination and my nerves . . . I am so unimaginably bored that I am ill.'[21] He soon found a mistress in Nina de Pierreclau, a local landowner's wife.[22] By her he had another illegitimate son, Jean-Baptiste-Léon de Pierreclau, born in March 1813. There were also other women, including an actress, to whom he refers in his correspondence with Virieu. Like many of his contemporaries, he apparently considered lower class women and married women of his own class fair game for his sexual adventures.

In August 1812 Lamartine made what seems to have been his first visit to Paris, the traditional goal of ambitious young Frenchmen. Between April and September 1813 he made a second visit to Paris as the secretary of the comte de Pierreclau, the unsuspecting husband of his mistress. Unfortunately, Lamartine had few friends and little money, and in May became ill. Finally his anxious mother brought him home. The countryside in autumn was, he claimed, his element. Like other Romantic writers he believed that he could achieve his fullest communion with nature during autumn, when the swirling mists and falling leaves reflected his own self-doubt and melancholy. Thus inspired, while staying at Milly in October 1813 he began writing verse tragedies. He even considered having one of his poems printed (anonymously).[23] At the same time he also suffered from the deepest despair. Frequently ill, always short of money, lacking any real occupation, he found his family critical and restrictive, and their attitude towards him particularly irksome after his months of independence in Italy and Paris. He was also alarmed at the moral and spiritual consequences of his own dissipated existence and rejection of the teachings of the Catholic Church.[24]

The fall of Napoleon's Empire interrupted this life of indolence, depression and irresponsibility. Following the retreat from Moscow in 1812 and the unsuccessful German campaign of 1813, Napoleon, unable to halt the Allied armies invading France and deserted by his own élite, finally abdicated on 6 April 1814. During January 1814

Austrian troops occupied Mâcon and the surrounding area, an operation accompanied by a considerable amount of fighting, some of which Lamartine personally witnessed. As mayor of Milly, Lamartine also became the *commune*'s representative in dealings with the Austrians. After Louis XVIII's restoration, Pierre de Lamartine left Mâcon for Paris to obtain a reward for his years of loyalty to the Crown, thus joining in the rush for places, preferments and honours provoked by the change of régime. Eventually he secured for himself the Cross of Saint-Louis (19 July 1814), and for his son a commission in the Noailles Company of the royal bodyguard (15 July 1814). However, Lamartine was unenthusiastic about joining the cavalry, fearing he would waste time and money,[25] and the bodyguard itself became increasingly unpopular, composed as it was of *émigrés*, royalists and young aristocrats. Towards the end of July Lamartine reported to his regiment, on garrison duty at Beauvais, There, as usual, he was bored and ill, and spent his spare time writing poetry and reading. Altogether he disliked Beauvais. and at the end of August managed to be transferred to Paris.

Seeing little future for himself in the army, Lamartine began to consider applying for a sub-prefecture. For a young aristocrat like Lamartine, the prefectoral administration was an obvious alternative to the army as a career choice. Lamartine hoped that a sub-prefecture would give him an occupation, make him financially independent of his family, and improve his marriage prospects. He asked the comte Germain, prefect of Saône-et-Loire, to recommend him to his friend and brother-in-law, the baron de Barante, then prefect of Loire-Inférieure and related to the abbé de Montesquiou, Minister of the Interior. Shortly afterwards he made a similar request of Clériade Vacher, who in August had been appointed sub-prefect of Roanne in the department of the Loire and who Lamartine believed was on friendly terms with Barante. Their recommendations to Barante, and his own approaches to the abbé de Montesquiou and François Guizot (*secrétaire général* at the Ministry of the Interior), were, Lamartine reported, well received, but no sub-prefecture was forthcoming.[26] Therefore in November he successfully applied for leave and returned home, allowing himself to be delayed by 'enchantresses . . .'[27] During the winter of 1814-1815 he seems to have had another affair, with a married woman; and he joined in the series of balls, suppers and entertainments with which royalist society in Mâcon celebrated the return of the Bourbons.

By January 1815 Lamartine was complaining of his boredom with these festivities and of his 'sad state of apathy and moral malaise'.[28] As was so often to be the case, he turned to poetry and politics. On 7 January 1815 he read to the Academy of Mâcon a verse elegy to Parny, who had died the previous month and whose love poems had served as one of his models; and at approximately the same time he was corresponding with a friend about the role, responsibilities and accountability of a government minister in a parliamentary system, obviously with France's new constitution in mind.[29] Soon Lamartine had more pressing political problems to consider. On 1 March 1815 Napoleon landed in France after his escape from Elba, and twelve days later spent the night at Mâcon. Perhaps after some hesitation, Lamartine decided to rally to the Bourbons. He left Mâcon for Paris on 11 March to rejoin his regiment; and with his regiment he followed Louis XVIII's hasty flight through northern France. While Louis XVIII crossed the French frontier and sought refuge at Ghent in Belgium, the royal bodyguard was disbanded at Béthune (north of Arras in the Pas de Calais), after being pressed but not attacked by soldiers loyal to Napoleon. From Béthune Lamartine fled to Mâcon in borrowed civilian clothes. To avoid arrest or conscription he went to stay with a family friend who lived in the Jura, and then left France for Switzerland. An individual's behaviour during the Hundred Days often came to serve as a political test. By escorting Louis XVIII out of France and by subsequently going into exile, Lamartine (for whatever reasons) actively and publicly identified himself with the Bourbons.

Lamartine's self-imposed exile ended with Napoleon's second abdication (22 June 1815). He rejoined his regiment in Paris at the beginning of August, only to resign his commission three months later on the grounds of ill-health. The resignation of his commission left him without an income or occupation at a time when, certainly in his mother's opinion, he needed both. His mother wrote to him on 21 August that she wanted him to become a sub-prefect, arguing a sub-prefecture would give him more 'considération' than anything else and would promote his marriage prospects. The sub-prefecture of Louhans (Saône-et-Loire), among others, was shortly due to become vacant, and she urged him to enlist the support of the comte Germain, one of the principal landowners in the *arrondissement*.[30] Lamartine took this advice and applied to Pasquier (acting Minister of the Interior) for the Louhans sub-prefecture, encouraged by the support of Barante (*secrétaire général* at the Ministry of the Interior) and Rigny (Saône-et-Loire's new prefect). But his hopes were dashed on 26 September 1815, when a new government was formed.

In despair Lamartine asked Clériade Vacher to approach Barante on his behalf, before Barante was dismissed.[31] This appeal came to nothing, but Lamartine was far from daunted. Indeed, judging by the number of his requests for support, by now he really wanted the job. Eventually he achieved a minor success in late November, when Rigny sent Vaublanc a list of six candidates for the Louhans sub-prefecture; Lamartine's name was there, but only in fifth place. However, Rigny gave him an appreciative report: his conduct during the Hundred Days, membership of one of the most distinguished Mâconnais families, and father's possession of the Cross of Saint-Louis, were all favourably noted. Vaublanc, in consultation with the deputies for Saône-et-Loire, drew up a short-list headed by Lamartine and a candidate from Louhans called Grillet. A final effort was made by Mme de Lamartine, who on 4 December wrote Vaublanc a long letter stressing her son's suitability, and pointing out that although he was not a Louhannais, he did have a married sister (Cécile de Cessiat) residing and owning property in the district.[32] Nevertheless, just when he seemed to be on the verge of being appointed, a royal ordinance of 20 December suppressed the sub-prefectures in the *chef-lieu* of each department. The government, anxious to avoid Louis XVI's financial difficulties, and short of money because of the Hundred Days, the Second Treaty of Paris and the indemnities imposed on France, felt obliged to make this economy. Consequently Lamartine suddenly had a new rival in the former sub-prefect of Mâcon, Chastelain de Belleroche, who had abandoned his eighty-year-old father, his wife and his seven children to follow Louis XVIII into exile during the Hundred Days. Belleroche was in fact appointed sub-prefect of Louhans in January 1816.

Lamartine's hopes had thus been gradually raised over a period of nearly five months, during which he had constantly pressed his candidature and incurred many expenses through living in Paris. Then suddenly and unexpectedly a rival had appeared and secured the appointment. Temporarily Lamartine succumbed to despair. He needed a government post to solve his financial problems, provide his mind and energies with a serious occupation, satisfy his family, and give him, at the age of twenty-five, a sense of security for the present and the future. But now he did not know what to do or how to succeed.[33] A more philosophical attitude soon replaced this despair. On 8 February 1816 he wrote to a friend that there were only two real possessions in life, health and independence, and that both would inevitably be lost in any career. Instead of wearing oneself out for twenty years over tables and columns of figures, one should marry and raise a family.

He acknowledged, however, that circumstances compelled him to look for a job. Therefore he had decided to stay in Paris and try to enter the diplomatic corps or the Ministry of the Interior rather than apply for another sub-prefecture.

Meanwhile, to dispel boredom, Lamartine had begun to write political articles for a Paris newspaper.[34] If written, the articles do not seem to have survived or to have been published, but evidence of his thoughts on politics at this time can be found in his private correspondence. He considered that the royalists, with whom he identified, were given to self-purging, and that this, as in the case of the Jacobins, would lead to their downfall. If the process of division were to be constantly pursued, eventually there would be nothing left to divide. Such would be the achievement of those royalists 'sans tache et sans tolérance', who spurned all those whom they regarded as less royalist than themselves. He compared himself to Cassandra, who for ten years had predicted the fall of Troy, but who refused to leave her comrades and finally shared their fate.[35] Presumably he was reacting against the White Terror and the purges which followed the Second Bourbon Restoration, and against the reactionary majority of the Chamber of Deputies known as the 'Chambre introuvable'. Nevertheless he remained a self-declared royalist.

From his gloomy speculations Lamartine was roused by the news that with Belleroche's transfer (8 April) to the sub-prefecture of Chalon-sur-Saône, the Louhans sub-prefecture was once more vacant. The marquis de Vaulchier (who had succeeded Rigny as prefect of Saône-et-Loire in January 1816), although he had never met Lamartine, included him in his list of three candidates for the Louhans sub-prefecture sent to Vaublanc on 15 April. He also provided a report on Lamartine similar to Rigny's. However, there was another candidate for the post, Milon de Villiers. His credentials were formidable: a former *auditeur* at the Conseil d'Etat, he had served as a sub-prefect for over four years; and his supporters included the prince de Condé, the Archbishop of Rheims, Marshal Macdonald and Talleyrand. Not surprisingly, on 25 April Milon de Villiers obtained the post.[36] It is clear, therefore, that Lamartine's talents, support, and social and political background ensured he was short-listed for appointments. But his comparative youth, and lack of a law degree, previous administrative experience, or patrons at Court or ministerial level, handicapped him. Moreover, after Napoleon's fall a severe contraction of official posts occurred, resulting in a surplus of experienced administrators. At the same time the Restoration Monarchy had numerous devoted royalists to reward, and a limited budget to balance. Consequently the failure of Lamartine's persistent efforts to secure a subprefecture was a typical experience for many of his contemporaries; and, again typically, it doubtless contributed to his growing disillusionment with the Restoration Monarchy, and to his sense of pessimism, frustration and dissatisfaction.

During the summer of 1816 Lamartine was clearly very depressed: he had failed three times to become a sub-prefect; an obscure marriage project had foundered on his family's opposition, and the refusals of his uncles to give him any money; and his great friend Virieu had left France as a *secrétaire d'ambassade* on a diplomatic mission to Brazil, causing a separation which Lamartine compared to that between a lover and his mistress.[37] Once more Lamartine began writing poetry, and he thought of having some of his poems published privately. But even the consolation of the Muse was denied to him, since by the end of June he was so ill that he could scarcely write a letter.[38] After his return to Mâcon his doctor advised him to take a cure at Aix-les-Bains in newly independent Savoy. Accepting this advice, at the beginning of October 1816 he arrived at Aix, where he met Julie Charles. In contrast to the long succession of transient affairs he had previously experienced, he was to have with her (at least according to his writings) the romance of his life.[39]

Julie Charles was the wife of Jacques Alexandre César Charles, the inventor of the hydrogen balloon, who had become permanent secretary of the Academy of Sciences and librarian of the French Academy. They had married in 1804 when she was only twenty and he fifty-seven. With no children, Julie's principal occupation was running a distinguished literary and political *salon*, and she had almost certainly had affairs before meeting Lamartine. On account of her failing health, during July 1816 without her husband she had come to Aix, where she and Lamartine very quickly fell passionately in love and, according to a letter by Lamartine to Virieu, became lovers.[40] There followed a period of just over three weeks which later inspired Lamartine's most famous poem, 'Le Lac'. Both Lamartine and Julie Charles had come to Aix in poor health and in a melancholy frame of mind; from the relevant letters that have survived, both seem to have been very emotionally involved with each other, though Julie perhaps more so than Lamartine; but both knew their affair could not last — Julie was married, six years older than Lamartine, and so ill that Lamartine already believed she was dying.[41] Their romantic idyll ended on 26 October, when Lamartine and Julie had to leave Aix, Lamartine for

Mâcon and Julie for Paris.

Lamartine had two main preoccupations during November and December 1816, his relationship with Julie Charles and his continued desire to become a sub-prefect. Unfortunately, none of Lamartine's letters to Julie has survived, but he did write about her to Virieu, who had returned to Paris by December. He claimed his love for her was the most violent ever contained in a man's heart, and he described her as 'une femme d'un esprit supérieur et d'une âme ardente'. However, he also claimed that whereas previously they had been lovers, now their relationship was more like that between a mother and her son.[42] As regards some form of state employment, Lamartine's patron, Germain, recommended him to the Minister of the Interior when the sub-prefect of Meaux died on 9 November. Germain had not had time to consult Lamartine in advance, but had certainly acted in accordance with his wishes, though Lamartine was the third of three candidates for the vacancy, which was quickly filled by Germain's first choice, Amédée Bouteleau, Lamartine's senior and a former sub-prefect.[43] Nothing daunted, Lamartine continued to supplicate his friends and acquaintances for a sub-prefecture. Partly to further this objective he once again left Mâcon for Paris in January 1817, though he was also very anxious to see Julie, visiting her in her husband's flat at the French Academy immediately on arrival in Paris on 8 January. Six days previously he had written to Nina de Pierreclau, his former mistress, breaking off relations with her.[44]

Lamartine's friend Virieu accommodated him in a room in the Hôtel Richelieu, rue Neuve-Saint-Augustin. There Lamartine lived for four months, seeing Julie Charles regularly. From her five surviving letters to Lamartine it is clear Julie loved him with an almost desperate intensity. Her desperation stemmed from the knowledge that she was probably dying, the fact that Lamartine now regarded her like a mother, and the discovery through his poems that he had apparently loved an Italian servant girl.[45] However, she resigned herself to the situation, and devotedly helped Lamartine by introducing him to her husband and their influential friends — Bonald (the monarchist and Catholic writer, and a deputy in the Chamber since 1815),[46] Lainé (Minister of the Interior in the first Richelieu Government, May 1816 — December 1818), Mounier (a member of the Conseil d'Etat since 1815), and Rayneval (*directeur des chancelleries* in the Ministry of Foreign Affairs, 1815-1820). Similarly, Virieu introduced Lamartine to his cousins, the comtesse de Sainte-Aulaire, wife of a Breton aristocrat, and the marquise de Raigecourt, a former lady-in-waiting to

Mme Elizabeth (Louis XVI's sister), whose husband had served as an *aide-de-camp* to the comte d'Artois (the future Charles X) in 1792, and who maintained a royalist and Catholic *salon* in the rue de Bourbon.[47] Through the comtesse de Sainte-Aulaire Lamartine met Albertine duchesse de Broglie (Mme de Staël's fourth child) and her husband, a politically independent peer.[48] In this way he made his entrée into the *salons* of Paris society, where his charming manner, handsome and elegant appearance, and considerable poetic gifts won him ready acceptance.[49] According to his *Mémoires politiques*, he presented Mounier with a study of the possible role of the old French nobility under a parliamentary constitution, which was well received.[50] Certainly he established social contacts which were later of immense importance. They prepared the way for the success of the first published collection of his poetry; they were an indispensable asset when he came to apply for diplomatic appointments and membership of the French Academy; and they helped to identify him with a milieu that was Catholic, royalist and aristocratic.

For financial reasons Lamartine left Paris on 4 May 1817. The day before his departure he finished a poem on the death of the duc d'Enghien, for whom a memorial had recently been constructed in the chapel of the *château* of Vincennes.[51] The poem's subject and sentiments were presumably designed to establish his political sympathies and win him favour in royalist circles. During the summer he considered in a desultory way marrying a Mlle du Vivier. In poor health, in June he took a cure at Vichy, and on 21 August returned to Aix-les-Bains, where he had arranged to meet Julie Charles. But, too ill to go to Aix, she spent the summer at Viroflay near Versailles. In her absence Lamartine sought consolation by writing a poem dedicated to Bonald, 'Le Génie', and by associating with yet another woman whom he had met at Aix, Eléonore de Canonge.[52] Having returned to Mâcon in early October, on Christmas Day 1817 he learnt that Julie Charles had died in Paris on 18 December.[53]

The death of Julie Charles was probably not quite the traumatic shock Lamartine subsequently suggested. His initial passion had cooled considerably, and her death had long been expected. Certainly Lamartine quickly resumed his former preoccupations: in January 1818 he asked the marquise de Raigecourt if she knew of any ambassador or minister in need of a secretary;[54] and by the beginning of February he was daily composing large numbers of verses for a tragedy called 'Saül'. Julie's death, however, obviously contributed to the melancholy that led him during March to make a will leaving Virieu all his manuscripts.[55] 'Saül' was finished by the middle of April. Lamartine, seeking instant fame, decided he wanted to have it performed at the Comédie Française by the celebrated actor François-Joseph Talma, and asked Virieu to see Talma about this presumptuous proposal. In July Virieu took up an appointment as *secrétaire d'ambassade* at Munich, so Lamartine himself came to Paris on 5 September to see Talma, who first asked for changes to be made and then rejected the play as too old-fashioned (10 October). Lamartine also failed in his attempts to be appointed *secrétaire d'ambassade* with Virieu at Munich. His domestic situation remained similarly unresolved. He failed to summon up enough enthusiasm to marry either Mlle du Vivier or a Mlle Elisa Boscary. Nor did he realise his vague ideas of travelling to Naples, Greece, Jerusalem, Turkey, and Persia.[56] Nevertheless, he was warmly received by the marquise de Raigecourt. Through her he again met the comte and comtesse de Sainte-Aulaire (the former had recently been elected to the Chamber), and he was introduced to the comte, later duc, Decazes. Having served as Minister of Police from September 1815 to December 1818, Decazes became Minister of the Interior and Louis XVIII's chief minister until February 1820, and in August 1819 he married a daughter of the comte de Sainte-Aulaire. Thus when Lamartine left Paris in October 1818 he had acquired new influential friends and patrons.

After spending the winter of 1818-1819 despondently in Milly and Mâcon, in February Lamartine returned to Paris to stay once more at the Hôtel Richelieu. In Paris he was again invited to the *salons* of the duchesse de Broglie, the marquise de Raigecourt and the comtesse de Sainte-Aulaire. He also met Joseph Michaud (a member of the French Academy and editor of an ultra-royalist Paris newspaper, *La Quotidienne*), Eugène Genoude (a devout Catholic, contributor to conservative newspapers, and author of a translation of the Bible used by Lamartine in his poetry), and the marquise de Montcalm (sister of the duc de Richelieu and hostess of an important Paris *salon*). He dined with Bonald and vicomte Mathieu de Montmorency (another devout Catholic and former *émigré*, who was to become Minister of Foreign Affairs, December 1821 – December 1822); and he was invited to give private readings of his poems by, among others, the duc d'Orléans. In addition, ten to twenty copies of a collection of his poems are said to have been privately printed and circulated. His admirers included the duc de Rohan, who invited Lamartine to spend Easter week with him at his *château* of La Roche-Guyon. There, in this sumptuous setting and in the company of the Duke, Montmorency and Genoude,

Lamartine wrote a poem called 'La Semaine Sainte'.[57] In it he suggests the profound peace and religious devotion that characterised his stay at La Roche-Guyon. After their return to Paris the Duke introduced Lamartine to the abbé de Lamennais. It was hoped that Lamennais would recommend him to his friend the duc de Narbonne, the French ambassador in Naples and a nephew of the duc de Rohan.[58]

In presenting himself to his influential friends as a sincere royalist, devout Catholic and sentimental lover, Lamartine was hypocritically playing roles so as to further his personal advancement. He was already a sceptic in politics and religion, and he continued to have sexual relations with women, many of whom, like the Italian princess Léna de Larche with whom he had an affair during the spring of 1819,[59] seemed to develop a passionate devotion to him even though (or because?) he usually treated them very badly. In July 1819 Lamartine travelled to Chambéry to see his sister Césarine, who in February had married the comte Xavier de Vignet, brother of his old friend Louis de Vignet. Coincidentally, a rich English widow, Mrs Birch, and her only daughter, Marianne, were also staying in Chambéry at the time.[60] Lamartine had already met Marianne at Césarine's wedding, and he met her again in Chambéry at the beginning of August. Almost immediately he decided he wanted to marry her — to the delight of Marianne, who admired his poetry and had fallen deeply in love with him. For Lamartine, Marianne's attractions were neither physical nor romantic. She was not beautiful, and he did not fall passionately in love with her. However, he clearly wanted to marry; and he saw in Marianne a capable, accomplished and devoted woman with whom he seemed to have much in common and who would make him an excellent wife. Above all he knew that Marianne was due to inherit a considerable fortune. Class prejudice and Romantic temperament probably encouraged him to despise the bourgeoisie, and in his poetry he idealised romantic love. However, his social background probably also encouraged him to seek a *rentier* existence; he regularly overspent the allowance provided by his family; and he appreciated that official salaries for sub-prefects and junior diplomats were considered inadequate. His previous potential marriage partners and his choice of Marianne certainly suggest that he aimed to secure through marriage a substantial private income.

Lamartine formally proposed to Marianne in a letter sent from Aix-les-Bains on 14 August.[61] After being accepted, he returned to Mâcon at the end of August to confront his family. His mother recorded that the prospect of a 'rather romantic' marriage with a foreigner and a Protestant could scarcely have been 'more uncongenial to his uncles and aunts, with their severe and coldly rational attitudes'.[62] However, she herself was sympathetic. After receiving confirmation that Marianne was rich and well-connected, Lamartine's father wrote on 21 September to Mrs Birch requesting Marianne's hand for his son. Mrs Birch replied that such an alliance would not be part of her plans and prospects for her daughter. She told Lamartine, who had also written to her, that she wanted her daughter to marry a man of her country and religion.[63] In addition, although probably ignorant of the extent of Lamartine's debts at this time, she was well aware that he had no position and no earned income; and she and Marianne seem to have learnt something of his past love affairs.

Between September and December 1819 three obstacles in the way of the marriage were removed. Lamartine promised, and convinced Marianne, that he would always remain faithful to her; Marianne decided to become a convert to Roman Catholicism;[64] and Lamartine's family agreed to pay off all his debts, though he remained so short of ready cash that he could buy Marianne a wedding present only by borrowing from a friend.[65] The problem of a position, however, remained, although he was sufficiently confident to turn down a posting in Munich because it carried neither official rank nor government salary.[66] It seemed that Lamartine had set his heart on something more important and remunerative, and his hopes were raised when on 19 November his friend and patron Pasquier became Minister of Foreign Affairs. In diligent pursuit of his career, in December Lamartine once more travelled to Paris and threw himself into *salon* life where, increasingly, he was able to claim attention by reading his own poems.[67] Two months later his efforts had apparently reached fruition: a confidential letter from the duchesse de Broglie at the beginning of February 1820 assured Lamartine that Pasquier would post him to Naples; and the prince de Polignac, in a letter to Genoude on 6 February, was also optimistic.[68]

At this critical moment Lamartine's career seemed threatened. Firstly, he fell seriously ill. Fearing he might die, he confessed to a priest and appointed Virieu his literary executor. Secondly, the assassination on 13 February of the duc de Berry, younger son of the heir to the throne, produced a major political crisis. Theatres were closed, *salon* receptions were cancelled, governmental activity was suspended, while the assassination's causes and consequences became the overriding political preoccupation. However, towards the end of February Lamartine's health improved; on 21 February Richelieu, brother of Lamartine's patron the marquise de Montcalm, formed his second government; and in the move to the Right in French politics after the assassination, some of Lamartine's other patrons, such as Montmorency, Polignac and Rohan, became particularly influential. On 2 March Lamartine could finally inform Mrs Birch that he had been appointed attaché at the French embassy in Naples. (The appointment was not to be officially announced until 27 March.) This news persuaded Mrs Birch to relent and on 10 March she consented to Lamartine marrying her daughter.[69] The next day, with the help of Genoude and Rohan, a collection of twenty-four of Lamartine's poems was published anonymously under the title of *Méditations Poétiques*.[70]

The religious and sentimental character of *Méditations* had an enormous appeal, particularly in Catholic, royalist and aristocratic circles of Paris society. This had already been demonstrated at *salon* readings,[71] which had also provided excellent publicity. More favourable publicity came from conservative newspapers, beginning with review articles by Genoude in *Le Conservateur* (March 1820) and by Victor Hugo in *Le Conservateur littéraire* (15 April 1820).[72] Louis XVIII himself frequently praised *Méditations*,[73] while the Court and government ministers were enthusiastic[74] — the only unfavourable response coming from the comtesse de Genlis and a small group of politicians known as the doctrinaires.[75] The first edition of five hundred copies was almost immediately sold out. A second edition was published in April, a third in May, a fourth in June, and by the end of 1825 fourteen editions had appeared. Lamartine's instant and triumphant literary success helped to confirm his diplomatic appointment. The Government seems to have been concerned to reward a gifted and popular literary figure, who, unlike many contemporary writers, apparently supported the Bourbon monarchy and the Catholic Church. Pasquier, in informing Narbonne of the appointment, stressed that Lamartine had already achieved literary distinction through his very remarkable talents.[76] The official paper, *Le Moniteur*, published a flattering report on *Méditations* and a letter advising Lamartine that the Government was sending him collections of French and Latin classics in recognition of his literary achievements.[77] Thus it is no coincidence Lamartine suddenly achieved in one month all that for years he had been seeking — literary success, a government position, and an immediate and definite prospect of marriage.

Lamartine left Paris at the end of March 1820 and on 12 April arrived at Chambéry, where he met Marianne after a separation of more than seven months. Their marriage contract was signed on 25 May. Mrs Birch gave her daughter a dowry invested in British public funds of £10,000, a very considerable sum. The interest on this capital was to go to herself during her lifetime, apart from 3,500 francs to Lamartine and 1,500 francs to Marianne. Pierre de Lamartine presented his son with Saint-Point, valued at 100,000 francs, on condition he paid annually 2,400 francs to each of his two married sisters, Eugénie de Coppens and Césarine de Vignet. Lamartine's uncles and aunts gave him the family house in Mâcon and a capital sum of 125,000 francs, payable to him, apart from 10,000 francs, after their deaths.[78] On 6 June Lamartine and Marianne were married in the Governor of Savoy's chapel, the ceremony being held at the early hour of seven in the morning to avoid public attention and (in deference to the Protestant Mrs Birch) the need to celebrate mass. Two days later Lamartine and Marianne went through a Protestant marriage ceremony in the hospital chapel at Geneva, to secure Lamartine's rights to his wife's property in England. They left Chambéry on 15 June for Naples where Lamartine was to take up his long awaited diplomatic post. Accompanied by Mrs Birch, the couple passed through Turin, where they saw Virieu, and Florence, where the vicomte de Fontenay, Lamartine's future superior at Naples, entertained them. Lamartine finally arrived safely in Naples, ahead of Marianne and Mrs Birch, in mid-July, thus scotching press rumours that his delayed arrival was due to death from consumption or murder by brigands.

By becoming a diplomat Lamartine joined a very select group of the Bourbon monarchy's servants. The *Almanach Royal* for 1820 lists just sixty people representing France abroad as ambassadors, ministers, *chargés d'affaires* or secretaries. Seemingly, therefore, Lamartine's royalism was again confirmed. As a diplomat he gained first-hand experience of political events, and of a revolutionary situation, in the Kingdom of the Two Sicilies. At the beginning of July 1820 a Carbonari revolt and army mutinies had shaken the autocratic and irresponsible rule of Ferdinand I. Panicked by the spread of the revolt and fearing a rising in Naples, the King had appointed a liberal government and had promised to grant a constitution. These developments strengthened Lamartine's fear of anarchy, his abhorrence of despotism, and his increasing attachment to liberty (though in September 1820 he cynically commented that liberty, like true love, belongs to another world).[79] In addition, Lamartine's posting to Naples introduced him to some of the problems surrounding French diplomacy. After the humiliations of 1815 the French could scarcely ignore an opportunity of playing an important international role, especially in Italy, where Napoleon had dramatically renewed France's traditional involvement.

Having come to power in the anti-liberal reaction following the duc de Berry's murder, the Richelieu Government had to show concern for Ferdinand's authority and safety, since Ferdinand was a Bourbon and a legitimate monarch. Yet any French support of Ferdinand had to take into account France's diplomatic isolation, and the desirability of opposing Austrian influence in Italy and of not alienating French liberals and constitutional monarchists. Besides studying these important matters, Lamartine did not neglect his literary career. Presumably in return for Genoude's help and services, he favourably reviewed Genoude's translation of the Bible for *Le Défenseur* (August 1820), a royalist Paris newspaper recently founded by Bonald and Lamennais.

The news of the birth on 29 September of a posthumous son to the duc de Berry turned Lamartine once more to poetry. French royalists were delighted, hoping the so-called *enfant du miracle* would ensure the Bourbon dynasty's survival; and the Sicilian Court specially welcomed the news, since the duchesse de Berry was a granddaughter of Ferdinand I. Doubtless out of a sense of duty and with an eye to his own advancement, Lamartine celebrated the event by composing an 'Ode sur la Naissance du duc de Bordeaux'.[80] This poem is not, however, an expression of undiluted royalism, since it suggests that in the modern age a king, in order to conserve his throne, should demonstrate his virtues as well as exercise his rights. Meanwhile, despite the interest of a civil war breaking out in Naples and of the Great Power congresses at Troppau and Laibach, Lamartine was growing discontented with his job – particularly his low status and salary. Also Marianne was now about seven months pregnant, and Lamartine must have been concerned about the welfare of his wife and child with the situation in Naples so uncertain. For these personal reasons, and presumably because Lamartine saw no career opportunities for himself in Naples, on 20 January 1821 with official permission the Lamartines and Mrs Birch left the city.

Before a large Austrian army invaded the Kingdom of the Two Sicilies from the Papal States in March, the Lamartines had settled in Rome, where on 15 February Marianne gave birth to a son, named Alphonse. The family left Rome at the end of April for Florence, which they rapidly decided was much more congenial than Naples. Therefore Lamartine set about cultivating the French minister at Florence, an ultra-royalist and amateur poet called the marquis de La Maisonfort with whom he began to exchange poems. After spending the summer at Aix-les-Bains and the autumn at Saint-Point, Lamartine visited Paris in December to try to obtain a new diplomatic post. On

3 January 1822 he dined with Montomorency, who had been appointed Minister of Foreign Affairs the preceding month. He was offered the position of *secrétaire de légation* at Florence, an appointment he reluctantly declined since it would have involved the incumbent's dismissal.[81] On 14 May 1822 the Lamartines had another child, a daughter who was christened Julie in memory of Julie Charles. The choice of name, persumably Lamartine's, showed little concern for Marianne's feelings, though Julie was later modified to Julia. During the summer of 1822 Lamartine, with his wife, son and mother-in-law, made a three-month visit to London. There he met friends and relations of Marianne's, was generally impressed by England, and, like many other Romantics, developed a passion for neo-Gothic architecture. Lamartine also seized the opportunity of introducing himself to Chateaubriand, who was then French ambassador in London. Chateaubriand knew of Lamartine's *Méditations*, but he was apparently not at all welcoming when Lamartine called on him.[82] This London visit ended in tragedy: the Lamartines' son became very ill, and eventually died in Paris (probably of tuberculosis) on 4 November 1822.

For Lamartine and his wife the death of their only son was a terrible loss. They remained in Paris until the beginning of April 1823, obviously reluctant to return to Mâcon and its associations with Alphonse. In Paris Lamartine renewed his usual preoccupations of cultivating his patrons and writing poetry, while the ninth edition of *Méditations Poétiques*, including four new poems, was published on 28 December 1822. Four days later Chateaubriand, now Minister of Foreign Affairs, placed on half pay all diplomats on leave. Spurred on by financial necessity as well as by grief, in February and March Lamartine wrote a long poem, 'La Mort de Socrate'. During the summer of 1823 he worked on other poems, which appeared on 27 September as *Nouvelles Méditations Poétiques*, 'La Mort de Socrate' having been published seven days previously. While on his usual summer holiday at Aix-les-Bains he learnt of Chateaubriand's decision to appoint the comte de Boissy to the much coveted and now vacant post of *secrétaire d'ambassade* at Florence. Initially he reacted to this new career disappointment with great annoyance, but in September he sent Chateaubriand a presentation copy of 'La Mort de Socrate', clearly in order to cultivate him.[83]

Late in 1824 Lamartine stood unsuccessfully for election to the French Academy, the famous State-supported learned society founded through Cardinal Richelieu's initiative in 1635. On 5 November a vacancy had occurred with the death of Pierre-Louis de Lacretelle. His brother, Charles, lived at Cormatin (Saône-et-Loire) and also belonged to the Academy. Hoping Charles de Lacretelle would support a compatriot, Lamartine's family persuaded Lamartine to stand for election. In agreeing, he claimed that he was prompted not by personal ambition but solely by a desire to please his family. Nevertheless, he acted quickly: arriving in Paris on 8 November, he energetically made visits, attended dinners, wrote letters, and followed the election campaign in the press. Among members of the Academy, his supporters included Bonald, Chateaubriand, Daru, Lainé, Michaud and Villemain. Among non-members, his long-standing patrons, the marquise de Montcalm and the comtesse de Sainte-Aulaire, exerted their influence, while the young Victor Hugo wrote to various academicians to enlist support for Lamartine.[84] However, on 4 December, with just three votes more than Lamartine, the literary essayist and historian Joseph-François Droz was elected. Lamartine blamed his failure on 'a cabal consisting of five or six animals', 'a fork supper coterie', and felt that he had let down his family — particularly his father — who apparently attached great importance to his success.[85] The defeat was not unexpected: his candidature had been a list-minute affair; he was seventeen years younger than Droz; and his ultra-royalist reputation put off liberals, including Charles de Lacretelle. Lamartine had been pessimistic and, almost certainly foreseeing defeat, had left Paris for Mâcon the day before the election. Altogether his behaviour was quite characteristic — agreeing to his candidature with avowed reluctance, working hard to secure his election, carefully following newspaper editorials, and blaming his failure on the secret plotting of his opponents.[86]

Throughout the first months of 1825 Lamartine suffered from his habitual ill-health; he once more complained that he was embarrassingly short of money; and he continued to write poetry. On 14 May 1825 he published 'Le Dernier Chant du Pèlerinage d'Harold', a poem commemorating Byron's death the previous year. This was followed by the 'Chant du Sacre', published on 28 May to celebrate Charles X's coronation the next day. 'Chant du Sacre' suggests that kings should concern themselves with the sufferings of the oppressed and the misfortunes of the innocent, and the poem ends with an ode to liberty. Copies of the poem sold very well, but a reference to the crîmes allegedly committed by Philippe-Egalitè during the Revolution greatly displeased his son, the duc d'Orléans.[87] Lamartine claimed to have written the poem to demonstrate that, although not without some liberal sentiments, he was a sincere royalist.[88] Also he doubtless wanted to flatter Charles X, whose favour he had seemingly already won. In September

1824 and again in February 1825 the prefect of Saône-et-Loire had recommended him for the Legion of Honour because of his celebrity as a poet. The recommendation had been accepted; and the knighthood had been given a special distinction since, together with a similar award to Victor Hugo, it had been announced on 29 April separately from other coronation honours.[89] As with 'La Mort de Socrate', Lamartine took care to send Chateaubriand a copy of the 'Chant du Sacre', which contained a short eulogy of him.[90]

Another mark of royal favour came on 3 July 1825, when Lamartine was finally appointed second secretary at the French legation in Florence. He had coveted this post since 1821; and it had been promised to him in November 1824 by Prévôt, head of the chancellery division in the Ministry of Foreign Affairs.[91] When actually appointed, however, Lamartine was unenthusiastic − claiming he had accepted only because Italy would suit his wife's health.[92] Before leaving for Italy in mid-September the Lamartines had Charles Nodier, Victor Hugo and the comte Alfred de Vigny to stay at Saint-Point.[93] While anxious to remain independent of any literary group, Lamartine wanted to cultivate these distinguished and influential young writers, particularly since Victor Hugo had supported his candidature in the Academy election and Charles Nodier had favourably reviewed his poetry in the important Paris royalist newspaper, *La Quotidienne*. When the Lamartines arrived in Florence at the beginning of October, the head of the French legation, the marquis de La Maisonfort, was in Lucca. La Maisonfort represented France in the Duchies of Lucca, Modena and Parma as well as in the Grand Duchy of Tuscany, and the Tuscan Court was then in temporary residence at Lucca, which since 1815 had in effect been a satellite of Tuscany. Consequently, Lamartine at once left Florence for Lucca, where his arrival, according to La Maisonfort, excited great interest on account of his fame and reputation as a poet. As a special honour on 18 October Lamartine was presented to the Grand Duke Leopold II and his wife, before attending a state dinner given for the diplomatic corps. After this privileged reception he quickly became immersed in the social round of the Tuscan Court and subsequently of Florence, one of Europe's most fashionable cities.[94]

No doubt the social round was made easier for Lamartine by the fact that there seems to have been little actual work for him at the legation. However, in August 1825 he entered an important competition set for junior French diplomats by the Minister of Foreign Affairs to guide him in making appointments and promotions. Each candidate was invited to submit a *mémoire* in answer to one of eight questions. Lamartine's choice was: 'What should be understood in politics by the terms "natural friend" or "natural enemy"? And what European states can or should be regarded by France in these categories?'[95] He chose this question, he explained, because it was the most practical and consequently the most useful. His *mémoire* began by asserting that politics was a science dependent on facts, not theories. A state did not have permanent friends or enemies. Instead, its foreign relations should be determined by its own interests and the general situation. To clarify these factors for the formulation of French foreign policy, Lamartine proceeded to survey the major powers: Russia — the country determining the world's future; Austria — conservative, but vulnerable to revolutionary movements in Germany and Italy; Prussia — weak and of little significance; Britain — the pivot of the world, though lacking firm foundations for its pre-eminence; Spain — lethargic and backward; Italy — an abstraction that could never become a single nation; Turkey — an affront to civilisation; the United States — unjustifiably neglected by Europe. Like many of his contemporaries, Lamartine underestimated the potential of Prussia and the pressure for Italian unity. He was also over-critical of Britain, claiming that its élite fled from their native country like exiles to parade throughout Europe the Orient's luxury and indolence, and that its patriotism was merely haughty intolerance, its religion merely oppressive fanaticism, its public wealth merely paper, its liberty merely licence, and its monarchy merely a façade. Indeed, according to Lamartine, Britain's decline was imminent. Lamartine's marriage to Marianne, recorded impressions of his visit to England in 1822, and relations with representatives of the British élite in Florence, strongly contradict these views. With his customary hypocrisy, he was evidently hoping to create a favourable impression by pandering to the religious, political and anglophobic prejudices common in the Ministry of Foreign Affairs and among many ultra-royalists.

From his survey of the major powers Lamartine concluded that Russia was France's most natural ally, Austria her most constant enemy. Consequently, France should establish the best possible relations with Russia and be on her guard against Austria. Since Britain was a major rival, French interests should be particularly defended against those of Britain, above all in Spain and the Mediterranean. In Italy, France should attempt to form a federation of states under her protection. American republicanism prohibited close relations between monarchical France and the United States. Other powers were of minor significance. Altogether, Lamartine's *mémoire* was rather short and did not contain much detailed information or analysis, but it was well written and full of opinions and recommendations, even if many of those were quite conventional. The comtes de La Forest, de La Garde and d'Hauterive judged the twenty-three anonymous *mémoires* entered for the competition. La Garde detected irritating Romantic tendencies in Lamartine's *mémoire*, and complained it was both 'slight and profound, penetrating and superficial, trenchant and judicious'.[96] The other examiners, however, were very impressed; and in August 1826 it was placed fourth in the first class. Since the candidate placed second had submitted two *mémoires*, Lamartine was third in a field of twenty-two, clearly a considerable achievement. Certainly he believed he had improved his standing in the Ministry of Foreign Affairs and his promotion prospects.[97]

Earlier in the year, one of Lamartine's poems had jeopardised his position as a diplomat. At the beginning of January 1826 a Neapolitan political exile living in Tuscany published a pamphlet attacking Lamartine for uncomplimentary references to Italy in 'Le Dernier Chant du Pèlerinage d'Harold'. Lamartine quickly replied in another pamphlet, arguing that the references to Italy reflected Byron's views, not his own, and that he had already praised Italy in his *Méditations Poétiques*.[98] However, his critic refused to be mollified and the outcome was a duel (19 February 1826), in which neither participant was seriously injured. Extremely concerned about the potential impact on his career, the day before the duel Lamartine misleadingly wrote to the marquise de Montcalm that La Maisonfort had suggested his resignation, obviously hoping that she would defend him in influential Paris circles.[99] He later sent his old patron, Montmorency, a long letter explaining the incident and expressing his anxiety about the possible press coverage. In fact, the Minister of Foreign Affairs reported to La Maisonfort that the King and the Government were quite satisfied with Lamartine's conduct, while Montmorency wrote a friendly and understanding note to Lamartine, and Montmorency's cousin, the duc de Montmorency-Laval (French ambassador at Rome), fulsomely praised Lamartine in his letters to La Maisonfort.[100] Subsequently, in another poem Lamartine took care to publicise his love of Italy. Inspired by a destructive landslide at Tivoli, he composed 'La Perte de l'Anio', which was published in the important Italian review, *Antologia* (March 1827).

Meanwhile, from 15 October 1826 Lamartine acted as *chargé d'affaires* at Florence while La Maisonfort went on extended leave. This temporary promotion meant an increase in status and salary, the opportunity to correspond directly and regularly with the Minister of Foreign Affairs, and the responsibility for running the French legation and conducting France's relations with the Grand Duke. In the context of French diplomacy, Tuscany was far from being a state of the first rank; and, as La Maisonfort had warned Lamartine, Italy at this time was experiencing 'a desolating tranquillity for diplomats of some zeal'.[101] Florence, nevertheless, had some diplomatic importance. For much of the year it was visited by large numbers of distinguished Europeans, while its liberal atmosphere encouraged the free exchange of ideas and information. Lamartine energetically embarked on his new duties, which were principally social. In October 1826 he entertained the novelist Sophie Gay and developed a close and lasting friendship with her daughter, Delphine.[102] At the end of the month he was host to the ducs de Blacas and Montmorency-Laval, the former being French ambassador at Naples. On 4 November he celebrated Charles X's birthday by organising a special mass in the legation chapel and a dinner the following day — an innovation which was so successful that he similarly commemorated the anniversary on 21 January of Louis XVI's execution. Also, once a week he usually arranged a dinner for members of the diplomatic corps and prominent French visitors to Florence, while less formally he welcomed a number of personal friends. The flow of guests and visitors continued in 1827 — Sophie and Delphine Gay during May and June, the duc de Richelieu in July, the wife of the Minister of War in September, Talleyrand and Sophie and Delphine Gay again in October, and the novelist Stendhal in November. At the beginning of December Lamartine went on a visit to Modena and Parma, where he dined with their respective dukes and duchesses; and towards the end of the year he mentions in his letters and dispatches meeting important French visitors such as Marshal Soult and the comte de Boislecomte (deputy director of the political section in the Ministry of Foreign Affairs), as well as various foreign aristocrats.

This social activity was important for Lamartine. As the legation's acting head he could entertain and cultivate influential French visitors to Florence, even if they were his social and professional superiors. Also, he could befriend prominent Italians,[103] as well as diplomats and other foreigners in Florence, and he had access to the Grand Duke of Tuscany. Lamartine liked the Grand Duke, and admired his liberal rule and commitment to public works such as drainage and irrigation schemes. This sympathy and respect were reciprocated. By January 1827 Leopold was seeing Lamartine alone once or twice a week for hours at a time; and in August he made him a commander of the

Tuscan order of St Joseph, which Lamartine hoped would be an asset in his diplomatic career.[104]

Despite his success with the Grand Duke, Lamartine did not always create a good impression at this time: for Alfred de Vigny (who met him in Charles Nodier's Paris *salon* in June 1826) he was the spoilt favourite of society; and in October 1827 he did not impress the young Henry Edward Fox (later the fourth Lord Holland).[105] On the other hand, Stendhal considered him to be very welcoming, while the comte de Castellane reported that he had simple and agreeable manners, and did not suffer from 'la fatuité poétique'.[106] Similarly the Countess of Blessington, Byron's friend and subsequently mother-in-law of Lamartine's distant cousin, the comte d'Orsay, wrote:[107]

> I have seen M. de Lamartine, and greatly like him. He is very good-looking and distinguished in his appearance, and dresses so perfectly like a gentleman, that one would never suspect him to be a poet ... Altogether he is a delightful companion, as well as a very gifted poet; and is formed to be as much esteemed in society as his works are admired in the study.

Thus, through a cultivated appearance, an ingratiating manner, and a studied underplaying of the poet, Lamartine attempted, with considerable success, to make himself agreeable to Florence's cosmopolitan society. Typically, a desire for self-advancement prompted such behaviour, which, again typically, was partly hypocritical. He privately wrote that his diplomatic career had intensified his dislike of the nobility, which he regarded as 'one of the biggest stupidities which humanity had ever produced!'[108]

Lamartine's official dispatches reported such matters as the pregnancies of the Grand Duchess, and the King of Wurtemberg's arrival at Leghorn 'for the benefit of sea bathing'. Occasionally he had more important subjects to discuss — the evacuation of Austrian troops from Naples, the Greek war of independence, and the disputes between Tuscany and the Turkish rulers of Tripoli and Algiers. He was an early advocate of French intervention in Algeria in support of Tuscany; and he predicted that the port of Algiers, though difficult to capture from the sea, could be taken from the land side by a force of seven or eight thousand men.[109] On several other topics he expressed personal opinions: he criticised Canning's pro-revolutionary sympathies, suggested the establishment of an official newspaper for circulation abroad to explain the French government's policies and objectives, and revealed his liberal inclinations by indicating alarm at the rumour that eighty-two French bishops had been created peers, and by praising Tuscany's enlightened administration. For Italy itself he favoured an informed, moderate and practical liberalism, aiming at constitutional reform in some of the Italian states and a greater degree of Italian independence, but opposed to secret conspiracies and further revolutionary upheavals. Altogether Lamartine's dispatches were carefully composed; and they impressed Charles X and his Foreign Ministers Damas and La Ferron-nays.[110]

Throughout much of his stay in Florence Lamartine evidently enjoyed an unusual degree of happiness and contentment. In February 1827 he wrote that he wanted to remain *chargé d'affaires* in Florence for twenty years;[111] and in December he bought a villa there, partly so as to have a permanent residence in Italy. Yet his life in Florence had its drawbacks. He complained that La Maisonfort resented his friendship with Leopold II, while the work at the legation was not very challenging and he soon grew dissatisfied with the relatively junior rank of *chargé d'affaires*. Also, the endless obligation to provide and attend social functions deprived him of the leisure and solitude he valued so highly. Revealing his growing disenchantment, in his letters he again began to dwell on the ennui and melancholy of his youth, and he increasingly aspired to some form of diplomatic promotion. Almost immediately after his arrival in Florence he had informed the marquise de Montcalm that he wanted the post of first secretary at Turin when it became vacant. Subsequently he expressed interest in becoming first secretary at Constantinople, Lucca, Naples or London. When La Maisonfort died unexpectedly (2 October 1827), Lamartine formally requested to remain *chargé d'affaires* at Florence.[112] He repeated this request on learning that he was under consideration for the post of *secrétaire de légation* at Brussels, which he did not regard as a promotion and would have declined.[113] While realising that he was too junior to be appointed minister at Florence, he was very conscious of his age (nearly forty), of his and Marianne's poor health, of the needs of his daughter Julia and of his increasingly dependent mother-in-law, of the desirability of being reasonably close to Mâcon, and of his new financial independence derived from property inherited from his uncles. Thus he would accept neither a demotion nor a transfer to an unattractive capital, and he informed his superiors that, failing a suitable post in Italy or London, he would apply for a period of leave to be effective on La Maisonfort's replacement. True to his word, when La Maisonfort's successor, the baron de Vitrolles, arrived in Florence at the end of July, Lamartine successfully applied for leave and with his family left Florence for Mâcon on 24 August. During a Paris visit in October he had an audience with Charles X, who expressed satisfaction with his services and told him that he had read his dispatches with great interest, and he was also well received by La Ferronnays, Minister of Foreign Affairs since January, and by senior officials in the Ministry.[114] Best of all, he returned to Mâcon with the promise of the post of first secretary at London.

Despite this promise of diplomatic promotion, during the winter of 1828-1829 Lamartine began to display publicly his political ambitions. His evolution from successful poet to aspiring politician was not a sudden phenomenon. Even before the publication of *Méditations* he had told the comte de Sainte-Aulaire that he hoped to make his name as a diplomat and 'homme d'affaires' rather than as an 'homme de lettres'.[115] When he first met the vicomte de Melun about 1825 he had surprised him by wanting to discuss politics, not poetry.[116] Although ineligible for election to the Chamber of Deputies until his fortieth birthday in October 1830, he had shown an interest in becoming a deputy since 1827, when his mother had told him that only his age prevented his election as deputy for Mâcon. Very taken with this opinion, Lamartine replied that he would never refuse to represent his department in the Chamber.[117] The following year he privately criticised the political weakness and parliamentary performance of the comte de Rambuteau, the successful Mâcon candidate in November 1827.[118] About October 1828, according to his *Mémoires politiques*, Martignac (Minister of the Interior) and Montbel pressed him to stand as a government candidate in Saône-et-Loire. Lamartine explained he was too young, but stressed he had parliamentary ambitions.[119] Although the interview he describes may have been fictitious, the ambitions certainly were not. At the beginning of November 1828, while staying at his property near Dijon called Montculot (which he had recently inherited from one of his uncles), he initiated large-scale restoration and improvement schemes, and he established a school for twenty-five pupils. Altogether he played the improving landlord and public benefactor. A combination of local notables, mayors, priests, young virgins and cannon triumphantly welcomed his return to Saint-Point on 16 November, thereby satisfyingly demonstrating his prestige in the Mâconnais.[120] As at Montculot, he was soon employing large numbers of workmen in restoring and improving Saint-Point, doubtless partly in order to enhance his future electoral prospects. These, he thought, were quite promising. 'A major preoccupation is my future election', he wrote to Virieu on 27 January 1829. 'If this continues I will have strong support.'[121]

In January 1829 Lamartine first became formally involved in local politics. The Restoration Monarchy's policies of indirect taxation and trade protectionism had adversely affected the French wine industry; and from 1826 three abundant harvests had resulted in enormous quantities of low-quality wine and a sharp fall in wine prices. As a result a Comité central des propriétaires de vignes, representing all of France's wine-producing departments, began a campaign to petition parliament in the interests of vineyard owners. Lamartine composed the petition for Saône-et-Loire's vineyard owners, wine merchants and vine growers. His petition complained about an excessive burden of taxation, and recommended a reduction of customs dues, a reduction or suppression of indirect taxes on wine, and the progressive introduction of free trade. To have been chosen to defend Saône-et-Loire's wine interests was a considerable honour for him, due, presumably, to his family's vineyards, his literary reputation and his membership of the Academy of Mâcon. The petition itself, addressed (unlike several petitions in the same campaign) to both Chambers, not just the Chamber of Peers, indicates his early opposition to taxes on essential commodities and his early commitment to free trade, a commitment shared by many large vineyard owners and supported by the important liberal review, *Le Globe*. During April the two Chambers discussed the petitions, of which there were seventy-two, Lamartine's attracting special and favourable comment.[122]

Lamartine's petition also attracted favourable comment from various newspapers, Paris and provincial, liberal and conservative; and it promoted his electoral prospects without alienating the Government. The only Mâcon newspaper at this time, *Le Journal de Saône-et-Loire*, published the petition's full text on its front page (28 January 1829). Saône-et-Loire's prefect mentioned the petition in his regular report to the Minister of the Interior, while asserting it was not an act of political opposition.[123] *L'Echo de Vaucluse* of Avignon referred to the sound judgment, superior character and public generosity which distinguished Lamartine, and extensively quoted the petition. *Le Journal des Débats*, an important conservative Paris newspaper, gave the petition a long and favourable notice, and cited it at length. Lamartine's eloquent prose, sensible arguments and firm grasp of the subject were specifically praised. An abbreviated version of this notice appeared in the royalist *Gazette de France*; and the liberal *Courrier francais*, having noted Lamartine's authorship, described the petition as a 'very remarkable piece of prose', an opinion shared by the young Charles de Montalembert.[124] Victor Hugo, after reading the notice in *Le Journal des Débats*, wrote to congratulate Lamartine. Meanwhile, a diplomatic colleague, the vicomte de Marcellus, had advised him that when eligible he should represent Saône-et-Loire in the Chamber, and that he himself would support him.[125] Such suggestions were clearly welcome. On 6 February 1829 Lamartine wrote to a friend: 'I am beginning to join the ranks of the parliamentary candidates in my province.'[126] To another friend he predicted that he would be a deputy in a few years, judging by the offers of support he was receiving from all parties; and to Virieu he described poetry as a childish activity for someone who, like himself, was thirty-eight, adding, 'My selection as a deputy is universally discussed.'[127]

Just when Lamartine's political prospects began to look promising, his diplomatic career suffered yet another reverse. La Ferronnays fell seriously ill, and was provisionally replaced as Minister of Foreign Affairs in January 1829. This, Lamartine believed, severely reduced his chances of being appointed first secretary at London. He considered resigning from the diplomatic corps, and claims to have offered his resignation in February 1829.[128] However, in the middle of May he revisited Paris to be lionised in the *salons*. At a dinner offered by Genoude at the end of May he recited one of his poems, and favourably impressed Montbel, shortly to be influential in government.[129] A young man at the beginning of June was overcome with emotion on being introduced to him by Victor Hugo: 'I have never seen poetry produce such a profound effect', Lamartine wrote disarmingly to his wife.[130] Later that month he was invited to a reading of one of Chateaubriand's works in Mme Récamier's *salon*,[131] and he also met the important literary critic Sainte-Beuve for the first time.[132] His visit, in fact, was a social and literary triumph: 'He is here, riding on an ever higher wave of popularity', observed his mother, while David d'Angers noted that at some well-attended function 'the eyes of five hundred people were enthusiastically and admiringly directed towards Lamartine'.[133] In addition, Lamartine was offered 40,000 francs for his forthcoming collection of poems; and, although not immediately given a new diplomatic appointment, officially he was strongly dissuaded from resigning.[134] Towards the end of June he returned to Mâcon, where he suffered from boredom and ill-health. On 2 July he wrote to Virieu: 'I am dying of suffering, ennui, headaches, rheumatism, fever, stomachache and gout.'[135]

This despondency was totally unjustified, for Lamartine's standing in official circles had never been higher. On 8 August 1829 Charles X challenged French political opinion by appointing a government in which notoriously unpopular figures held the key posts: La Bourdonnaye (Minister of the Interior) and Bourmont (Minister of War) were widely regarded as betrayers of Napoleon and France, while Polignac (Minister of Foreign Affairs and the Government's head) was considered to personify ultra-royalism. Such a government offered great temptations to Lamartine, particularly since Polignac had earlier supported him, but the temptations were tempered by doubts concerning the Government's durability and Polignac's reactionary reputation. Lamartine received an invitation on 14 August to come to Paris immediately to help Polignac in the reorganisation of the Ministry of Foreign Affairs, in which he was promised a senior position.[136] In his *Mémoires politiques* he adds that Genoude wrote to him on Polignac's behalf, and that he was offered the post of *secrétaire général* and director of the political section.[137] This constituted a remarkable offer for a diplomat who had previously occupied only junior posts and had suffered numerous career disappointments. However, Lamartine had much impressed Charles X by his dispatches from Florence and during their meetings in Paris. Polignac was a friend of Lamartine's devoted collaborator, Genoude, and had taken an interest in Lamartine as early as 1820. Other members of the Polignac Government, such as Montbel (Minister of Ecclesiastical Affairs and Public Instruction), having met Lamartine socially and admired his literary talents, may have backed the offer. Within the Foreign Ministry itself Lamartine had several influential supporters, notably Boislecomte, Bourjot, Hauterive and Rayneval, and his excellent relations with Saône-et-Loire's prefect may also have helped.[138]

Polignac presumably saw in Lamartine a diplomat of proven ability and royalist opinions, whose literary reputation and *salon* popularity would help improve his Government's bad public image. He was clearly unaware of Lamartine's private liberal sympathies and his increasing alarm at the reactionary tendency of government policies since Charles X's accession. Lamartine in fact refused Polignac's offer, while maintaining his claim to the first secretaryship at London. He explained to Virieu in a letter of 16 August that he opposed what the Polignac Government stood for. Since he now believed a revolution might overthrow the dynasty, he evidently did not want to compromise his principles by associating himself with an unpopular and unsuccessful Government.[139] Nor did he wish to harm his future political prospects, which he was carefully cultivating. In private letters he refers to his attending a *réunion municipale*, giving a dinner to parliamentary electors, meeting members of the *conseil général* and local notables, and to his general willingness to stand as a parliamentary candidate.[140] But, given his frustrated ambitions, his refusal of office must have been a difficult decision; and initially he seems to have viewed his act of self-denial with some regret.[141]

In his letter to Virieu of 16 August 1829 Lamartine reported he had the previous day scribbled his electoral manifesto for some future occasion.[142] Although no more than an unfinished draft, it is the fullest outline of his political position he had yet prepared.[143] He began by dissociating himself from all political parties. Their passions and prejudices, the blind obedience they imposed and the factional strife they encouraged, were all distasteful to a man of honour. Such a person could never justify the abandonment of man's three noblest attributes, 'personal integrity, freedom of choice, individual conscience'. Also, a man of honour would always clearly state his political creed to his fellow citizens. Recent events, Lamartine claimed, had formed his own political opinions. The Revolution had led him to abhor the sanguinary excesses of popular democracy and the anarchy accompanying violent upheavals. The Napoleonic period had taught him to oppose military dictatorships and wars of conquest in search of glory. The Bourbons had returned to France with the Charter; and the memory of the past, the horror of anarchy, the hatred of despotism, and the hope of liberty had rallied to them all generous hearts.

In these circumstances Lamartine had become a constitutional royalist. But he was a royalist by reason, not faith, regarding the monarchy as the guarantor of order, the upholder of the law, and the symbol of continuity; he believed in those personal liberties and parliamentary institutions established by the Charter; and he opposed a republic in France on practical, not ideological, grounds. The manifesto is an early indication of Lamartine's desire to remain independent of all political parties, and to base his policies on his own beliefs and principles. It is also another indication that he had developed liberal sympathies and that his royalism was rooted in reason, not emotion. An element of contradiction, however, is already apparent: as a liberal Lamartine wanted to safeguard individual liberty, but as a royalist he wanted to safeguard order, which he described as the first need of any society.

Notwithstanding his refusal to help Polignac, and his evident liberal sympathies, Lamartine still wanted a suitable diplomatic post abroad. On 15 September 1829 he wrote to his friend Marcellus, who had just been appointed under-secretary in the Ministry of Foreign Affairs. Stressing his age, length of service, and the promises made to him by previous ministers, he warned Marcellus that he would resign unless offered a first secretaryship at London, Rome, Constantinople or Vienna.[144] Five days later he received a letter from Polignac himself, stating that he did not understand Lamartine's position and inviting him to Paris.[145] However, at this point Lamartine's literary ambitions took precedence. It seems that he was not prepared to visit Paris because of a new French Academy election. After pressure from friends he agreed to stand, but as in 1824 he privately denied any personal ambition for a seat in the Academy, claiming that he was concerned only to please his father. Although he refused to campaign in person, he had many influential supporters including Barante, Brifaut, Chateaubriand, Cuvier, Lainé, Royer-Collard, and Villemain. Outside the Academy he could count on *Le Journal des Débats* and 'les dames du Faubourg Saint-Germain'. This support, and his outstanding reputation as a poet, resulted in his being elected on 5 November by nineteen votes, against fourteen for the military historian, Philippe de Ségur.[146] At last, five years after his previous narrow defeat, his poetic achievements had been publicly recognised by the highest authority, and he was now one of the forty members of France's most select and prestigious literary institution.

Immediately after the election Lamartine returned to Paris to thank his supporters and receive the congratulations of his friends. Perhaps because of his literary success he dined at least twice with Polignac, who suggested he might serve as French minister to the newly emergent state of Greece.[147] However, the news of his mother's accidental death on 16 November suddenly shattered his good fortune. From his correspondence it is clear that he was overwhelmed by this unexpected and devastating loss; and in his poem, 'Le Tombeau d'une Mère', written between November 1829 and April 1830, he suggests how much he had loved and admired his mother, and how her death had plunged him into despair and shaken his belief in the existence of God. Such sentiments may well have been genuine — his mother had certainly had a very great influence over him, even into adulthood. Yet he may also have exploited his mother's death to cultivate a newspaper and gain favourable publicity. Certainly *L'Echo de Vaucluse* published (29 November 1829) on his mother's death a notice which was apparently both exclusive and inspired, and possibly based on a communication from himself. Subsequently *L'Echo de Vaucluse* published several of his poems, reflecting his increasing awareness of the importance of publicity. During 1829 and 1830 at least twelve of his poems appeared in newspapers, reviews or in pamphlet form, whereas in the previous eight years only half as many had been individually published.

The French Academy formally admitted Lamartine on 1 April 1830. It was a social and literary event, and the first time Lamartine had delivered a public speech in Paris. After paying tribute to his mother and his predecessor, Lamartine used the occasion to outline his political position. The future of the French people, he asserted, was indissolubly linked to that of the French monarchy. He condemned the excesses and extremes of both anarchy and despotism. The human mind, he declared, had been awakened by a new religious spirit, a spirit based on a private and sincere religion inspired by conscience and faith. Politics were no longer the practice of the arts of corruption and deception, for the principles of Christianity had gradually taken seed in political life; and the French monarchy's duty was to protect and encourage the Christian principles of morality, reason and liberty, through upholding the Charter and through appropriate legislation.[148] Subsequently Lamartine claimed that, despite pressure from the duc de Rohan and others, he had identified himself with the liberal opposition, whose so-called Address of the 221, implicitly insisting on the principle of ministerial responsibility to parliament, had been followed by the dissolution of the Chamber on 19 March.[149] In fact his speech was very imprecise, and could be interpreted as a declaration of support for either Charles X and Polignac, or their liberal opponents. This ambiguity did not escape the notice of contemporaries,[150] and was criticised by the leading Paris liberal newspaper, *Le Constitutionnel*. However, as Lamartine noted with delight, newspapers ranging from the ultra-royalist *Gazette de France* to the left-wing *National* praised his speech; and with public opinion so much in his favour, he hoped to secure a new diplomatic post.[151]

Serious difficulties, however, arose about the diplomatic post in Greece. Polignac, Montbel and the King still encouraged Lamartine to believe the appointment imminent, and news of the posting even appeared in the press. Yet for the moment Greece had no head of state to whom he could be accredited. It was this, rather than any 'intrigue de bureau' led by Boislecomte, that prevented Lamartine's appointment.[152] Nevertheless, he was able to take advantage of the delay in his posting by spending time in Paris editing and arranging the publication of a two-volume collection of his poems, *Harmonies Poétiques et Religieuses*, which appeared in mid-June.[153] Most of the poems in *Harmonies* had been written in Florence and several had already appeared in newspapers and journals besides *L'Echo de Vaucluse*. For example, 'Le Premier Amour' had been published in *La Mode*, a fashionable society journal with a large circulation and edited by Emile de Girardin. *La Mode* had earlier welcomed Lamartine's election to the French Academy and enthusiastically described his admission ceremony; and, as he doubtless hoped, *La Mode* favourably reviewed *Harmonies*. Lamartine sent one pre-publication copy of *Harmonies* to Chateaubriand, who thanked him in flattering terms,[154] and another to Adolphe Thiers, who had recently helped found *Le National*, an important Paris left-wing newspaper. *Le National* had published (3 April) a long and complimentary article on Lamartine's reception and speech at the French Academy, and two articles discussing Lamartine and 'the new school of poetry' (11 and 27 April). On 21 June Thiers in *Le National* gave *Harmonies* a generally complimentary review. Lamartine sent him an appreciative letter, and similarly thanked two other favourable critics, Sainte-Beuve and Charles Nodier.[155] In contrast, when *Le Journal des Débats* failed to review *Harmonies* Lamartine complained to its editor, Aimé Martin. This duly resulted in a good review, and the usual letter from Lamartine.[156] Altogether Lamartine carefully exploited his contacts with newspapers, journals and critics to secure favourable publicity. In so doing he was not concerned just with his literary reputation. To the comte de Carné's compliments on *Harmonies* he replied in June 1830 that if his verses possessed any merit, it would be to assist his election as a deputy.[157]

External events were, however, about to impose their own structure on Lamartine's political and diplomatic life. Determined to retain the Polignac Government, Charles X had responded to parliamentary opposition as manifested in the Address of the 221 by dissolving parliament (19 March 1830). The subsequent general parliamentary election of 3 July resulted in an increased liberal majority in the Chamber of Deputies. Lamartine approved of the dissolution of parliament;[158] and in Mâcon he apparently supported the successful royalist candidate in the July election.[159] Yet at the same time he privately revealed that he sided with neither the Polignac Government nor the liberal opposition, that' he believed a revolution was imminent, and that he feared popular anarchy more than governmental despotism.[160] Charles X reacted drastically and unconstitutionally to the liberal electoral victory: he agreed to the publication on 26 July of four ordinances which suspended the liberty of the press, dissolved the new

Chamber, further restricted the franchise, and ordered another general election for September. The publication of the ordinances immediately provoked a popular rising in Paris, and during three days of fighting Charles X lost control of his capital. A group of prominent liberals then seized the political initiative by securing parliamentary approval for a revision of the Charter and for the accession of the duc d'Orléans as Louis-Philippe, King of the French.

Lamartine learnt of the July Days and subsequent change of régime while on his customary summer holiday at Aix-les-Bains.[161] To Virieu he wrote that the revolution had not surprised him, merely its rapidity and success, and that he was very concerned about the danger of anarchy, which he wanted to avoid at all costs. Consequently he argued that the new régime should be accepted, provided the essentials of monarchy, liberty, religion and stability were maintained. Since the situation was so serious, political scruples had to be set aside, and apathy and inaction were inexcusable.[162] By the end of August he had decided to go to Paris to declare his allegiance to the new régime as a demonstration of support against the danger of anarchy, and to resign from the diplomatic corps out of respect for the Bourbon dynasty which he had served.[163] Thus he would join neither the legitimist *émigration à l'intérieur* nor those office-seekers who rallied to Louis-Philippe. Instead he would in future never become a member of any faction and his political creed would be the great principles of the Revolution of 1789, which in October 1830 he defined as liberty and legal equality.[164]

Meanwhile, Lamartine had returned to Mâcon on 4 September. Five days later, by which time his fears of popular disturbances in the Mâconnais had been largely allayed, he set out for Paris. On 13 September he had the message conveyed to Louis-Philippe and Mme Adélaide (the King's sister) that he wanted to resign, but would remain a loyal citizen. The following day he repeated this to Molé, the new Minister of Foreign Affairs. Louis-Philippe and Mme Adélaïde replied, again indirectly, that they would have liked to have retained his services but would accept his resignation, trusting that he would support the Government. Lamartine sent Molé a formal letter of resignation on 16 September: with studied politeness, he stressed his willingness to swear an oath of loyalty to Louis-Philippe, but added that for purely personal reasons he wished to resign from the diplomatic corps.[165] The King accepted the resignation with good grace, and Lamartine remained on friendly terms with Molé and the duc de Broglie (the new President of the Conseil d'Etat and Minister of Ecclesiastical Affairs and Public

Instruction). A letter Lamartine wrote to *La Quotidienne*, denying a report that his life and *château* of Saint-Point had been threatened, further enhanced his standing with the King and his ministers who were understandably anxious to quash rumours of popular violence.[166] Thiers, who as one of *Le National*'s editors had played a very influential role in the July Revolution and was now a member of the Conseil d'Etat, wrote at the end of September that he had recommended him to Molé and others, believing he should occupy a position worthy of his talents and reputation.[167] Another encouraging development was an offer to support his candidature in a by-election at Autun, Saône-et-Loire's third *arrondissement*, if Jules de Montépin (a liberal) decided not to stand. However, Montépin did stand, and the offer was withdrawn.[168]

In October 1830 demands for the execution of Charles X's last ministers led to rioting in Paris. Fearing a new revolution, Lamartine responded with a poem addressed to 'the people', 'Contre la peine de mort', which was individually published on 15 December, the day of the ministers' trial. The poem, while praising 'the people' for their heroic role in the July Days, passionately argued against any vindictive executions. Humanitarian considerations and Lamartine's concept of Christian morality partly explain his intervention. The abolition of capital punishment had become an important issue for many French liberals, and Lamartine was drawing close to liberalism at this time. Personal ties and past loyalties also counted. His correspondence concerning the poem shows that he was in personal contact with associates of the fallen Polignac ministry, such as Guiche and Martignac, and that he did not wish to offend those with legitimist sympathies. The correspondence also shows his concern that the poem should be given press publicity, his conviction that political poetry should be written in a popular style so as to maximise its public impact, and his anxiety that he should not in any way embarrass the Government.[169] Clearly Lamartine was seeking publicity, and attempting to exploit his poetic talents in order to promote his future political prospects. The poem's publication had no perceptible influence on the course of events, but constituted the first occasion that Lamartine entered the field of French national politics.

To the general public Lamartine was still the Romantic poet of *Méditations*, the idol of aristocratic society ladies,[170] noted for his emotional sentimentality and for a pious Catholicism and political conservatism derived from his family. However, by the end of 1830 he clearly wanted to become seriously and actively involved in politics.

The considerable ambitions he had displayed, and the persistence and success with which he had exploited his exceptional literary talents, as well as personal contacts and press publicity, suggested that he would make a formidable political impact. At the same time, on social and political questions he was beginning to formulate liberal ideas based on his own interpretation of Christian morality and the ideals of 1789; his support for Louis-Philippe and the Orleanist régime was conditional on their furthering the ideals of 1789 and keeping anarchy at bay; and many of the conflicts and contradictions discernible in his life and career before 1831 remained. Lamartine's future role in French politics was therefore likely to be important, confusing, unpredictable and uniquely personal.

Notes

1.   *Mémoires politiques* in *Oeuvres complètes de Lamartine publiées et inédites*, 41 vols. (Paris, 1860-66),   XXXVIII, pp. 11-12; *Oeuvres de M. A. de Lamartine*, 14 vols. (Paris, 1849-50), I, p. 22.

2.   A. Testot-Ferry, 'Généalogie de la famille Alamartine puis de Lamartine', *Annales de l'Académie de Mâcon*, third series, XXIV (1924-25), pp. 200-9; P. de Lacretelle, *Les Origines et la jeunesse de Lamartine, 1790-1812* (Paris, 1911).

3.   *Mémoires inédits de Mme la comtesse de Genlis*, 10 vols. (Paris, 1825), III, pp. 283 and 285, IV, p. 29, VI, pp. 177-80.

4.   The journal kept by Lamartine's mother is now in the municipal library of Lyons. Extracts from this journal, selected and altered by Lamartine, were published in *Le Manuscrit de ma mère* (Paris, 1871). See C. Joatton, 'Comment Lamartine composa le *Manuscrit de ma mère*, d'après le *Journal* inédit de Mme de Lamartine', *Revue d'histoire littéraire de la France*, July-September 1935, pp. 375-91. The original journal has been extensively cited in H. Guillemin, *Connaissance de Lamartine* (Fribourg, 1942), pp. 13-84, and in M. Domange, *Le Petit monde des Lamartine* (Evian, 1968). See also C. Joatton, *Lamartine, sa mère, et sa nurse, d'après le journal inédit de Mme de Lamartine* (Mâcon, 1931). On Lamartine's mother in general see C. Fournet (ed.), *Les Confidences de Madame de Lamartine à ses filles* (Paris, 1957); C. Latreille, *La Mère de Lamartine, d'après des documents inédits* (Paris and Brussels, 1925); J. de Mestral-Combremont, *Une Mère: Madame de Prat de Lamartine, née Alix des Roys* (Lausanne, 1935).

5.   See J. Fabri, 'Lamartine, élève en philosophie. Un témoignage inédit', *Les Etudes classiques*, July 1962, pp. 283-310; A. M. P., marquis de Luppé, *Les Travaux et les jours d'Alphonse de Lamartine* (Paris, 1948), p. 18.

6.   See M.-F. Guyard (ed.), *Lamartine. Oeuvres poétiques complètes* (Paris, 1963), pp. 1494-9. The poems were first published in 1857, probably with revisions, in A. de Lamartine, *Le Cours familier de littérature*, 28 vols. (Paris, 1856-69), IV, entretien XXIII, pp. 382-5, 403-7.

7.   Gabriel-Henri-Aymon, comte de Virieu-Pupetières, was born in 1788 into one of the oldest families of the Dauphiné. His father was among the royalists killed in the siege of Lyons in October 1793, and he was brought up by his mother and her two sisters. Following the Restoration of 1814 Virieu, like Lamartine, became a member of the royal *garde-du-corps*. In March 1816 he

went as an *attaché* on a special diplomatic mission to Brazil. He was later *secrétaire de légation* at Munich and *secrétaire d'ambassade* at Turin. After his marriage in 1822 he lived in his two *châteaux*, Caillou, near Fontaines-sur-Saône, and Pupetières, between Grand-Lemps and Virieu-sur-Bourbre (Isère). On 7 June 1826 Virieu's wife had a son, who was called Alphonse and whose godfather was Lamartine. Virieu was *président* of an iron and lead foundry in Lyons, and a contributor to *Le Réparateur, journal du Lyonnais et du Forez*. He died on 10 April 1841. See A. Leflaive, *Stéphanie de Virieu* (Paris, 1947).

8. Aimé-Louis, baron de Vignet (1789-1837), was the son of a member of the Royal Senate of Savoy and a nephew of Joseph and Xavier de Maistre. His family owned the *château* of Bissy, near Chambéry in Savoy. He became a diplomat and was *secrétaire d'ambassade* at London (1821-25) and Paris (1825-32), and minister at Berne (1832-36) and Naples, where he died of cholera on 15 July 1837. His brother, the comte Xavier de Vignet, married Lamartine's sister, Césarine, on 6 February 1819. See L. Séché, *Les Amitiés de Lamartine* (Paris, 1911), pp. 17-98.

9. Nicolas-Prosper Guichard de Bienassis (1789-1855) was the son of a doctor. His mother, after the death of her first husband, married the marquis de Montlevon, who bequeathed to him the *château* of Bienassis, near Crémieu in the Isère. He lived a quiet life on his estate, becoming mayor of Villemoireu and a local *juge de paix*, and dying at Bienassis on 27 May 1857. See M. Levaillant, 'Un Ami de collège de Lamartine: Prosper Guichard de Bienassis', *Revue des Deux Mondes*, 15 November 1924, pp. 329-60, 1 December 1924, pp. 607-38.

10. Luppé, *Lamartine*, pp. 21-2.

11. See E. Magnien, *Dans l'intimité de Lamartine* (Mâcon, 1955), p. 11.

12. A. de Lamartine, *Nouvelles Confidences* (Paris, 1851), p. 105.

13. See C. and M. Armand, 'Un Précurseur malchangeux: Lyon Desroys, poète, oncle de Lamartine', *Annales de l'Académie de Mâcon*, third series, XXX (1935), pp. 233-40; J. Paul-Dubreuil, 'Etudes Lamartiniennes: le suicide d'un poète (Lyon des Roys, oncle de Lamartine)', *Visages de l'Ain*, no. 105, 1969, pp. 18-30.

14. For a list of authors read by Lamartine, based on his correspondence and arranged chronologically, see G. Lanson (ed.), *Lamartine. Méditations Poétiques*, 2 vols. (Paris, 1915), I, pp. xiv-xvii.

15. See J. Richer (ed.), *Alphonse de Lamartine: lettres à Clériade Vacher, 1811-1818* (Paris, 1963), p. 6.

16. Lamartine to Henri Roch-Dupuys, 24 April 1810; Bibliothèque Nationale, nouvelles acquisitions françaises, 16581, f. 6. On Roch-Dupuys (1791-1859) see L. Lex and P. M. Siraud, *Le Conseil général et les conseillers généraux de Saône-et-Loire, 1789-1889* (Mâcon, 1888), p. 197, and M.-R. Morin, 'Lamartine inédit. Lettres de Lamartine à Henry Dupuys (1809-1848)', *Bulletin du bibliophile*, 1972, fasc. I, pp. 26-44, fasc. IV, pp. 404-14.

17. Lamartine to Bienassis and Virieu, 28 March and 14 May 1810; V. de Lamartine (ed.), *Correspondance de Lamartine*, 6 vols. (Paris, 1873-75), I, pp. 220 and 241.

18. See A. Duréault, 'La Première passion de Lamartine', *Annales de l'Académie de Mâcon*, third series, XIV (1909), pp. 220-46; F. Letessier, 'Lamartine, Cellarius et la danse', *Mercure de France*, March 1959, pp. 546-50.

19. See R. Doumic, 'Le Carnet de voyage de Lamartine en Italie', *Le Correspondant*, 25 July 1908, pp. 263-79.

20. See A. Verdier, *Les Amours italiennes de Lamartine. Graziella et Lena* (Paris, 1963), pp. 78-89. On Dareste de La Chavanne see F. Letessier, 'Lamartine et les Dareste de La Chavanne', *Annales de l'Académie de Mâcon*, third series, LIV (1978), pp. 33-55.

21.   Letter dated 27 May 1812; Luppé, *Lamartine*, p. 41.

22.   Anne-Joséphine (1786-1865), known as Nina, was the daughter of General Dézoteux. She had married in 1807 Antoine-Guillaume, later comte de Pierreclau (1784-1830), and lived in the *château* of Cormatin near Milly. See L. Barthou, *En Marge des 'Confidences': lettres inédites de Lamartine* (Abbeville, 1913); Dr R. Favre, 'Souvenirs sur une amie de Lamartine: Nina de Pierreclau', *Annales de l'Académie de Mâcon*, third series, XLVI (1962-63), pp. 111-17; Baron de Nanteuil, 'Lamartine, Nina et Léon de Pierreclau', *Revue bleue*, 7 and 21 August 1937, pp. 506-20, 4 and 18 September 1937, pp. 563-7, 2 and 16 October 1937, pp. 614-18, 650-3. By a curious coincidence, Lamartine's first teacher, a local priest called the abbé Dumont, had in his youth seduced a sister of the comte de Pierreclau. See H. Guillemin, *Le Jocelyn de Lamartine* (Paris, 1936), pp. 333-96, and A. Calvet, *Le Voyage de Madame de Piré* (Paris, 1950), pp. 267-81.

23.   Lamartine to Roch-Dupuys, 25 November 1813; B. N., nouv. acq. fr., 16581, f. 36.

24.   Lamartine to Virieu, 29 October 1813; Bibliothèque Historique de la Ville de Paris, Dumesnil Papers, 5707.

25.   Lamartine to Virieu, 16 May 1814; *Correspondance*, II (1873), pp. 33-5. Cf. G. Varenne, 'Lamartine garde du corps à Beauvais en 1814', *Mémoires de la Société académique de l'Oise*, XVIII (1901-3), pp. 489-562.

26.   See Richer, *Lettres à Clériade Vacher*, pp. 51-4.

27.   Lamartine to Virieu, 30 November 1814; *Correspondance*, II (1873), p. 56.

28.   Lamartine to the comtesse de Pierreclau, 19 January 1815 (Barthou, *En Marge des 'Confidences'*, p. 13), and to Fréminville, 25 January 1815 (F. Reyssié, *La Jeunesse de Lamartine* (Paris, 1892), p. 179). Claude de la Poix de Fréminville, whom Lamartine first met in Leghorn in October 1811, was successively appointed sub-prefect at Leghorn (January 1811), Rome (January 1812), Foligno (April 1813), and Trévoux in the Ain (August 1814). See his file in Archives Nationales, F[1b] I 160[13] and Reyssié, *La Jeunesse de Lamartine*, p. 178, note 2. For connections between the Virieu and Fréminville families see Leflaive, *Stéphanie de Virieu*, pp. 89, 102 and 221-2. Fréminville was a neo-Platonist, and Lamartine once described him as 'mon cher maître en Platon' (Reyssié, *La Jeunesse de Lamartine*, p. 353).

29.   P.-M. Masson, 'Lamartine et les deux Eléonore', *Revue d'histoire littéraire de la France*, April-June 1913, pp. 249-68; Reyssié, *La Jeunesse de Lamartine*, p. 181.

30.   Latreille, *La Mère de Lamartine*, pp. 40-1; *Mémoires politiques* in *Oeuvres complètes de Lamartine*, XXXVII (1863), p. 26.

31.   Lamartine to Vacher, 28 September 1815; *Lettres à Clériade Vacher*, pp. 55-6.

32.   Lamartine to Fontenilles, c. October-November 1815 (A. N., AA 65 482), and to F.-L. de Lamartine, 11 November 1815 (*Correspondance*, II (1873), pp. 72 and 74); Mme de Lamartine to Vaublanc, 4 December 1815 (A. N., AA 65 482). Cf. L. Barthou, *Voyage à travers mes livres. Autour de Lamartine* (Paris, 1925), pp. 75-81; J. Ruinaut, 'Lamartine candidat sous-préfet', *Le Figaro*, 3 September 1927, p. 5; G. Vauthier, 'Lamartine candidat sous-préfet en 1815', *Bulletin de la Société historique d'Auteuil et de Passy*, vol. X, no. 2, 1er trimestre 1921, pp. 39-42.

33.   Lamartine to Vacher, 21 January 1816; Richer, *Lettres à Clériade Vacher*, pp. 57-9.

34.   Lamartine to Vaugelas; *Correspondance*, II (1873), pp. 82-4.

35.   Lamartine to Vaugelas, 1 March 1816; ibid., II, pp. 85-6.

36. Dossier of A. L. J. Milon de Villiers; A. N., F 1b I 167 [24]

37. C. Latreille, 'La Jeunesse de Lamartine (1811-1820)', *Le Correspondant*, 10 May 1922, pp. 426-7; H. Guillemin, 'Lamartine et sa mère', *La Revue de France*, 15 April 1937, p. 639; Lamartine to Virieu, 29 March or May 1816 (*Correspondance*, II (1873), p. 90, and B. H. V. P., Dumesnil Papers, 5707).

38. Lamartine to Vaugelas, 28 June 1816; *Correspondance*, II (1873), pp. 93-4 and 97.

39. Lamartine described this romance in *Raphael* (Paris, 1850). For more accurate accounts see R. Doumic, 'Les Lettres d'Elvire à Lamartine', *Revue des Deux Mondes*, 1 February 1905, pp. 574-602, 'Le Séjour d'Elvire à Aix-les-Bains', *La Revue latine*, 25 July 1906, pp. 411-17, and 'Elvire à Aix-les-Bains d'après son carnet de voyage', *Le Journal des Débats*, 6 April 1907, pp. 1-2; A. Dupouy, *Elvire inspiratrice de Lamartine* (Paris, 1944); L. Séché, 'L'Elvire de Lamartine', *Le Correspondant*, 25 March 1905, pp. 1220-39, and 'Lamartine et Elvire, d'après de nouveaux documents', *Mercure de France*, 1 February 1911, pp. 543-51.

40. Letter dated 16 December 1816; Luppé, *Lamartine*, p. 51.

41. Ibid., p. 50.

42. Ibid., pp. 49-51 and 60.

43. A. N., F1b I 15640; *Le Figaro*, 3 September 1927, p. 6.

44. Barthou, *En Marge des 'Confidences'*, pp. 16-19.

45. *Revue des Deux Mondes*, 1 February 1905, pp. 582-91 and 600.

46. On Lamartine and Bonald see Lamartine's commentary on 'Le Génie', a poem dedicated to Bonald (*Oeuvres de M. A. de Lamartine*, I, pp. 248-9), and *Le Cours familier de littérature*, II (1856), entretien X, pp. 272-3.

47. For Lamartine's relations with the marquise de Raigecourt see his commentary on 'La Foi' (*Oeuvres de M. A. de Lamartine*, I, pp. 238-9), and *Le Cours familier de littérature*, II, entretien X, pp. 266-8, and XXVII, entretien CLX, pp. 249-59.

48. See A. L. V. C., duc de Broglie, *Souvenirs, 1785-1870*, 4 vols. (Paris, 1886), II, p. 14.

49. Comte de Sainte-Aulaire, 'Lamartine et la politique', *La Revue de Paris*, 15 July 1925, p. 242. Cf. *Le Cours familier de littérature*, II, entretien X, pp. 247-83, and IX (1860), entretien XLIX, pp. 42-55; Lamartine's commentary on 'Le Passé' in *Oeuvres de M. A. de Lamartine*, II, p. 23.

50. *Oeuvres complètes*, XXXVII, pp. 62-4.

51. See A. Chesnier du Chesne, 'La Mort du duc d'Enghien, poème inédit de Lamartine', *Mercure de France*, 1 July 1954, pp. 555-60.

52. See Séché, *Les Amitiés de Lamartine*, pp. 114-34.

53. R. Doumic, *Lettres d'Elvire à Lamartine* (Paris, 1905), pp. 86-7.

54. *Correspondance*, II (1873), p. 147.

55. Lamartine to Virieu, 27 March 1818; ibid., II, pp. 155-6.

56. Lamartine to Virieu, July and 24 August 1818; ibid., II, pp. 210 and 226.

57. The poem was published in *Méditations Poétiques* (1820). Lamartine wrote a commentary on the poem in *Oeuvres de M. A. de Lamartine*, I, pp. 309-11.

58. Lamartine to Virieu, 13 April 1819; *Correspondance*, II (1873), p. 330. On Lamartine's relations with Lamennais see C. Maréchal, *Lamennais et Lamartine* (Paris, 1907), and J.-R. Derré, *Lamennais, ses amis et le mouvement des idées à l'époque romantique, 1824-1834* (Paris, 1962), pp. 562-77.

59. Maria-Madalena Carolina del Mazza (1788-1855) came from an aristocratic Florentine family. At sixteen she married an Italian count who died when she was twenty. In 1812 she married Amant-Elisée-Hondagné de Larche, then

an officer in the French garrison at Florence and subsequently a captain in the Legion of Saône-et-Loire. See Guillemin, *Connaissance de Lamartine*, pp. 87-116; L. Hastier, 'Un Amour de Lamartine. La princesse italienne', *Revue des Deux Mondes*, 1 May 1956, pp. 114-21; A. Verdier, *La Vie sentimentale de Lamartine* (Manoir de la Roderie, 1973).

60. See F. Mugnier, *Le Mariage de Lamartine* (Chambéry, 1884), and W. Fortescue, 'Marianne de Lamartine, née Birch, et sa famille anglaise', *Annales de l'Académie de Mâcon*, forthcoming.

61. R. Doumic, 'Le Mariage de Lamartine: lettres inédites à la fiancée', *Revue des Deux Mondes*, 15 August 1905, p. 831. Lamartine must have decided to marry Marianne within one or two days of seeing her at Chambéry, for his mother wrote to him on 6 August 1819 about the projected marriage. See *La Revue de France*, 15 April 1937, p. 642.

62. *Revue des Deux Mondes*, 15 August 1905, p. 841.

63. Mrs Birch to P. de Lamartine, 28 September 1819, and to A. de Lamartine, 12 October 1819; ibid., p. 842.

64. This may have prompted the comte Joseph de Maistre's 'Lettre à une dame protestante sur la question de savoir si le changement de Religion n'est point contraire à l'honneur', *Le Défenseur*, 18 April 1820.

65. See Lamartine to Virieu, 30 May 1820; *Correspondance*, II (1873), p. 476.

66. See Lamartine to the marquise de Raigecourt, 20 September 1819 (ibid., II, pp. 416-17), and to the comtesse de Sainte-Aulaire, 21 September 1819 (Archives Etrangères, Série personnelle, dossier personnel de Lamartine).

67. L. de Ronchaud (ed.), *Le Manuscrit de ma mère* (Paris, 1905), pp. 217-18; *Journal du maréchal de Castellane, 1804-1862*, 5 vols. (Paris, 1895-97), I, p. 388.

68. V. de Lamartine (ed.), *Lettres à Lamartine* (Paris, 1892), p. 17; M. Levaillant, *Lamartine et l'Italie en 1820* (Paris, 1944), p. 56.

69. *Revue des Deux Mondes*, 1 September 1905, p. 162.

70. For critical editions see G. Lanson (ed.), *Méditations Poétiques de Lamartine*, 2 vols. (Paris, 1915); F. Letessier (ed.), *Méditations* (Paris, 1968); M.-F. Guyard, *Méditations Poétiques. Nouvelles Méditations Poétiques* (Paris, 1969). On the publication of the *Méditiations* see L. Lurine, *Histoire poétique et politique de M. de Lamartine* (Paris, 1848), pp. 21-2.

71. See A. F. Villemain, *Souvenirs contemporains d'histoire et de littérature*, 2 vols. (Paris, 1854-55), I, pp. 455-6.

72. Levaillant, *Lamartine et l'Italie en 1820*, pp. 63-4; *Revue des Deux Mondes*, 1 September 1905, p. 165.

73. P. Mansel, *Louis XVIII* (London, 1981), p. 298.

74. See Lamartine to Virieu, 23 March 1820; *Correspondance*, II (1873), p. 456. Cf. Abbé C. M. D. de Féletz, *Mélanges de philosophie, d'histoire et de littérature*, 6 vols. (Paris, 1828-30), II (1828), pp. 236-44; duchesse de Broglie to Lamartine, 23 April 1821 (*Lettres à Lamartine*, p. 19).

75. 'Les *Méditations*', *L'Intrépide*, no. II, April 1820; Genlis, *Mémoires*, VII (1825), pp. 79-80; C. H. Pouthas (ed.), *Charles de Rémusat: mémoires de ma vie*, 5 vols. (Paris, 1958-67), I, pp. 453-4.

76. Letter dated 27 March 1820; A. E., Correspondance politique, Naples, 143, f. 28.

77. *Le Moniteur universel*, 21 April 1820, p. 521.

78. *Revue des Deux Mondes*, 1 September 1905, p. 171.

79. *Histoire de mon temps: mémoires du Chancelier Pasquier*, 6 vols. (Paris, 1893-95), V (1894), p. 27; *La Revue de Paris*, 15 July 1925, p. 245.

80. See Levaillant, *Lamartine et l'Italie en 1820*, pp. 128-53.

81.   See R. Doumic, 'Lamartine intime de 1820 à 1830: lettres inédites', *Revue des Deux Mondes*, 15 September 1907, pp. 333-5; Levaillant, *Lamartine et l'Italie en 1820*, p. 233.

82.   M. L. J. A. C. de Martin du Tyrac, comte de Marcellus, *Chateaubriand et son temps* (Paris, 1859), pp. 113-14 and 161; *Mémoires politiques* in *Oeuvres complètes de Lamartine*, XXXVII (1863), pp. 182-3.

83.   Lamartine to the baron de Mareste, 6 August 1823 (Levaillant, *Lamartine et l'Italie en 1820*, p. 235); F. Letessier, 'Lettres de Chateaubriand à Lamartine avec des fragments inédits', *Bulletin de la Société Chateaubriand*, no. 19, 1976, p. 16.

84.   See C. Daubray, *Victor Hugo et ses correspondants* (Paris, 1947), pp. 109-13.

85.   Lamartine to Virieu, 12 November 1824 (*Correspondance*, III (1874), pp. 317-18), and to the comte Edouard de La Grange, 13 January 1825 (Luppé, *Lamartine*, p. 115). Cf. L. Barthou, 'L'Election de Lamartine à l'Académie Française', *La Revue de Paris*, 15 September 1916, p. 305.

86.   In general see A. Chesnier du Chesne, 'La Candidature de Lamartine à l'Académie en 1824', *Mercure de France*, 1 March 1934, pp. 287-304; P. de Lacretelle, 'La Première Candidature de Lamartine à l'Académie', *La Grande Revue*, 15 May 1905, pp. 308-18; *Revue des Deux Mondes*, 15 September 1907, pp. 336-43.

87.   See président Henrion de Pansey to Lamartine, 21 May 1825 (*Lettres à Lamartine*, p. 38), and Lamartine to Virieu, 6 June 1825 (*Correspondance*, III (1874), p. 345).

88.   Lamartine to Virieu, 10 May 1825; *Correspondance*, III (1874), p. 340.

89.   Comte de Bourblanc to the Minister of the Interior, 28 September 1824 and 16 February 1825 (A. N., F^{1,d} III 1811); A. Dumas, *Mes Mémoires*, 5 vols. (Paris, 1954-68), III (1966), pp. 182-3; *Le Moniteur universel*, 29 April 1825, p. 653.

90.   *Bulletin de la Société Chateaubriand*, no. 19, 1976, pp. 18-19.

91.   See Lamartine to Virieu, 12 November 1824; *Correspondance*, III (1874), p. 318.

92.   See Lamartine to the marquise de Montcalm, 31 August 1825; E. de Lévis Mirepoix, prince de Robech (ed.), *Un Salon politique sous la Restauration. Correspondance de la marquise de Montcalm* (Paris, 1949), p. 264.

93.   See J. Janin, 'Charles Nodier, Victor Hugo et le comte Alfred de Vigny chez M. de Lamartine, au château de Saint-Point', *Bulletin du Bibliophile*, 1865, pp. 361-73; M. A. E. Mennessier, *Charles Nodier. Episodes et souvenirs de sa vie* (Paris, 1867), pp. 269-75. In 1825 Victor Hugo, Charles Nodier and Lamartine considered collaborating on a book to be entitled *Voyage en Suisse* (Mennessier, *Charles Nodier*, p. 266). On Lamartine and Vigny see E. Dupuy, *Alfred de Vigny. Ses amitiés, son rôle littéraire*, 2 vols. (Paris, 1910-12), I, pp. 283-317.

94.   La Maisonfort to the baron de Damas, 20 October 1825 (A. E., Correspondance politique, Toscane, 165); Lamartine to the marquise de Raigecourt, 5 November 1825 (*Correspondance*, III (1874), p. 367), and to the marquise de Montcalm, 7 November 1825 (*Correspondance de la marquise de Montcalm*, p. 266); *Comtesse de Sainte-Aulaire. Souvenirs* (Périgueux, 1875), pp. 261 and 263.

95.   The manuscript of Lamartine's *mémoire* is in A. E., Attachés et surnuméraires, 125, concours de 1825-1826, vol. I, pp. 344-58. The text has been published in L. de Contenson, *Lamartine secrétaire de légation. Son mémoire de concours en 1826* (Paris, 1925), and in H. Deloncle, 'Alphonse de Lamartine. Un mémoire inédit', *La Nouvelle Revue*, XIV, January 1882, pp. 52-79. Cf.

L. Babonneix, *Un Mémoire politique de Lamartine* (Sens, 1925). For a draft of the *mémoire* see B. N., nouv. acq. fr., 25091, ff. 170-80. In general see A. Meininger, 'D'Hauterive et la formation des diplomates', *Revue d'histoire diplomatique*, January-June 1975, pp. 25-69.

96.   A. E., Attachés et surnuméraires, loc. cit., f. 98.

97.   Lamartine to Virieu and Genoude, 1 and 11 August 1826; *Correspondance*, III (1874), pp. 407 and 414.

98.   *Sur l'Interprétation d'un passage du cinquième chant de Childe-Harold* (Lucca: François Baroni, 1826). A copy is in B. H. V. P., Dumesnil Papers, 5712. The pamphlet was dated 5 January 1826 (*La Nouvelle Revue*, January 1882, p. 54), but was probably not published until February 1826 (see La Maisonfort to Damas, 28 February 1826; A. E., Correspondance politique, Toscane, 166, f. 30).

99.   L. Guerrini, 'Lamartine, secrétaire de légation', *La Revue de Paris*, 15 October 1915, pp. 812-28, 15 November 1915, pp. 341-63; *Correspondance de la marquise de Montcalm*, p. 267.

100.   *Correspondance*, III (1874), pp. 383-8; A. E., Correspondance politique, Toscane, 166, ff. 20-3, 24-7 and 34; *Lettres à Lamartine*, pp. 48-9; A. E., France 1770-1843, Nouvelles acquisitions, 1877, ff. 337, 351 and 353.

101.   *Lettres à Lamartine*, p. 40.

102.   See L. Séché, *Delphine Gay, Mme de Girardin, dans ses rapports avec Lamartine* (Paris, 1910), pp. 61-147.

103.   See U. Mengin, 'Lamartine et Manzoni, leurs relations amicales et leurs opinions politiques', *Mélanges de philologie, d'histoire et de littérature offerts à Henri Hauvette* (Paris, 1934), pp. 623-34; baron de Nanteuil, 'Un Ami italien de Lamartine', *Mercure de France*, 15 September 1937, pp. 497-511; M. Foresi, 'Lamartine e l'Italia in alcune sue lettere inedite', *Nuovo Antologia*, July-August 1916, pp. 3-15; A. Carraresi (ed.), *Lettere de Gino Capponi e di altri a lui*, 6 vols. (Florence, 1882-90).

104.   Lamartine to H. Dupuys, 1 August 1827; B. N., nouv. acq. fr., 16581, f. 49.

105.   H. Blaze de Bury, 'Mes Souvenirs sur la *Revue des Deux Mondes*', *Revue internationale* (Florence), 10 February 1888, pp. 321-2; Earl of Ilchester (ed.), *The Journal of the Hon. Henry Edward Fox* (London, 1923), p. 235.

106.   H. Martineau and V. Del Litto (eds), *Correspondance de Stendhal*, II (Paris, 1967), p. 127; *Journal du maréchal de Castellane*, II (1895), p. 92. Cf. V. Jacquemont, *Letters to Achille Chaper; intimate sketches of life among Stendhal's coterie* (Philadelphia, 1960), pp. 101-2.

107.   M. Gardiner, Countess of Blessington, *The Idler in Italy* (Paris, 1839), pp. 368-9.

108.   Lamartine to the marquise de Barol, 26 September 1827; V. P. Ponti, *Lettere inedite di Alphonse de Lamartine alla marchesa di Barolo* (Turin, 1926), p. 49. On the marquise de Barol and Lamartine's relations with her, see: G. A. Dufour, *La Famille des seigneurs de Barol* (Turin, 1884); Lamartine's commentary on 'La Perte de l'Anio', *Oeuvres de M. A. de Lamartine*, III (1850), p. 214; A. M. J., vicomte de Melun, *La Marquise de Barol, sa vie et ses oeuvres* (Paris, 1869).

109.   Lamartine to Damas, 15 May and 6 July 1827, 26 January 1828; A. E., Correspondance politique, 166, ff. 205, 229 and 281.

110.   Damas to Lamartine, 7 December 1826, and La Ferronnays to Lamartine, 14 April 1828; ibid., 166, ff. 142 and 332.

111.   Lamartine to the comte de Sercey, 13 February 1827; *Correspondance*, IV (1874), p. 12.

112. *Correspondance de la marquise de Montcalm*, pp. 265 and 271; A. E., Série personnelle, dossier personnel de Lamartine; Lamartine to Damas, 16 October 1827 (A. E., Correspondance politique, Toscane, 166, f. 254).
113. Lamartine to Damas, 1 November 1827; dossier personnel de Lamartine.
114. Lamartine to his mother, 14 October 1828; *Correspondance*, IV (1874), p. 191.
115. *La Revue de Paris*, 15 July 1925, p. 242.
116. Comte E. Le Camus (ed.), *Mémoires du vicomte Armand de Melun*, 2 vols. (Paris, 1891), II, p. 54.
117. *La Revue de Paris*, 1 May 1937, p. 72; *Correspondance*, IV (1874), pp. 95 and 107-8.
118. Ibid., IV (1874), pp. 113-14 and p. 157.
119. *Oeuvres complètes de Lamartine*, XXXVII, pp. 238-40.
120. Lamartine to the marquise de Barol, 12 November 1828; Ponti, *Lettere inedite*, p. 65.
121. *Correspondance*, IV (1874), pp. 214-15.
122. The petition, with an additional *mémoire* (not by Lamartine), was published in pamphlet form: *Pétition des propriétaires de vignes, négocians en vins et cultivateurs du Département de Saône-et-Loire* (Mâcon: Dejussieu, 1829). A copy is in B. H. V. P., Dumesnil Papers, 5712. The petition has been published in C. Sprietsma, 'Lamartine et Théophile Foisset', *Revue des cours et conférences*, 15 December 1935, pp. 55-60, and *Lamartine et Théophile Foisset* (Paris, 1936), pp. 12-18. See also A. Chesnier du Chesne, 'Une Pétition de Lamartine', *Le Temps*, 22 April 1933, p. 5; Fournet, *Les Confidences de Madame de Lamartine*, p. 164.
123. Comte de Puymaigre's report of 18 April 1829; A. N., F⁷6771, dossier 13.
124. *L'Echo de Vaucluse*, 19 February 1829, pp. 2-3; *Le Journal des Débats*, 3 February 1829, p. 2; *La Gazette de France*, 7 February 1829, p. 3; *Le Courrier français*, 3 February 1829, p. 2; P. de Lallemand, *Montalembert et ses amis dans le romantisme, 1830-1840* (Paris, 1927), p. 68.
125. *Lettres à Lamartine*, pp. 59 and 57.
126. Lamartine to Giuliano Frullani; *Mercure de France*, 15 September 1937, p. 502.
127. Lamartine to Sercey, 1 April 1829 (*Le Figaro* (literary supplement), 22 August 1931, p. 5), and to Virieu, 16 March 1829 (*Correspondance*, IV (1874), p. 228).
128. Lamartine to Virieu, 25 February 1829; ibid., IV, p. 226.
129. *Souvenirs du comte de Montbel, ministre de Charles X* (Paris, 1913), p. 206.
130. Letter dated 3 June 1829 (*Revue des Deux Mondes*, 15 September 1907, pp. 348-9). The young man was almost certainly Victor Pavie (see V. Pavie, *Oeuvres choisies*, 2 vols. (Paris, 1887), II, pp. 74-6).
131. *Revue des Deux Mondes*, 15 September 1907, p. 349; *Souvenirs et correspondance, tirés des papiers de Madame Récamier*, 2 vols. (Paris, 1860), II, p. 379.
132. See J. Bonnerot (ed.), *Correspondance générale de Sainte-Beuve*, 16 vols. (Paris, 1935-70), I, p. 138. On Lamartine's relations with Sainte-Beuve see A. Chesnier du Chesne, 'Lettres de Lamartine à Sainte-Beuve', *Revue des Deux Mondes*, 1 November 1933, pp. 73-101; Sainte-Beuve to Jules de Saint-Amour, 24 November 1856 (*Correspondance générale de Sainte-Beuve*, X (1960), pp. 318-19); *Lettres à Lamartine*, pp. 281-4; R. Fayolle, 'Sainte-Beuve et Lamartine ou l'histoire d'un désillusionnement', in P. Viallaneix (ed.), *Lamartine. Le Livre*

du centenaire (Paris, 1971), pp. 223-62.
133.   J. B. de Crèvecoeur de Perthes, *Sous dix rois. Souvenirs de 1791-1860*, 8 vols. (Paris, 1863-68), IV (1863), p. 444; *Revue des Deux Mondes*, 15 September 1907, p. 349; L. Cerf (ed.), *Souvenirs de David d'Angers sur ses contemporains* (Paris, 1928), p. 27; F. Baldensperger (ed.), *Oeuvres complètes d'Alfred de Vigny*, VII, *Correspondance* (Paris, 1921), p. 187.
134.   *Revue des Deux Mondes*, 15 September 1907, p. 348; Ponti, *Lettere inedite*, p. 72.
135.   *Correspondance*, IV (1874), p. 243.
136.   Lamartine to Virieu, 16 August 1829; ibid., IV, p. 253.
137.   *Oeuvres complètes de Lamartine*, XXXVII, p. 249.
138.   See J. F. A. Boudet, comte de Puymaigre, *Souvenirs sur l'émigration, l'Empire et la Restauration* (Paris, 1884), pp. 325-6.
139.   *Correspondance*, IV (1874), pp. 253-4.
140.   See Lamartine to the comte E. de La Grange, 14 February 1829 (ibid., IV, p. 218), to the marquise de Barol, 25 July 1829 (Ponti, *Lettere inedite*, p. 71), to the marquis G. Capponi, 27 August 1829 (V. de Lamartine (ed.), *Correspondance de Lamartine*, 4 vols. (Paris, 1881-82), III (1882), p. 157), and to the marquise de Montcalm, 29 August 1829 (*Correspondance de la marquise de Montcalm*, p. 278).
141.   See Lamartine to the marquise de Montcalm, 29 August 1829; *Correspondance de la marquise de Montcalm*, p. 278.
142.   *Correspondance*, IV (1874), p. 253.
143.   The manuscript, in the French Academy Library, has been published in A. Chesnier, 'Le Premier Manifeste électoral de Lamartine', *Les Nouvelles littéraires artistiques et scientifiques*, 23 January 1932, p. 4.
144.   C. Latreille, 'Lettres inédites de Lamartine', *Le Correspondant*, 25 June 1926, p. 822.
145.   *Correspondance*, IV (1874), p. 266; *Mémoires politiques* in *Oeuvres complètes de Lamartine*, XXXVII, p. 251.
146.   See, in addition to *Lettres à Lamartine* and Lamartine's published correspondence: Daubray, *Victor Hugo et ses correspondants*, p. 132; J. Loth, 'Lettres inédites adressées à M. Brifaut ou écrites par lui', *Précis analytique des travaux de l'académie des sciences, belles-lettres et arts de Rouen*, 1875-76, pp. 341-8; M. Levaillant and G. Moulinier (eds.), *Chateaubriand. Mémoires d'outre-tombe*, 2 vols. (Paris, 1964), I, p. 384; E. de Perceval, *Le Vicomte Lainé*, 2 vols. (Paris, 1926), II, pp. 483-4; E. Pitou, 'Lamartine candidat à l'Académie française', *L'Intermédiaire des chercheurs et curieux*, LXXXI (1920), p. 326; *Journal de Viennet, pair de France, témoin de trois règnes* (Paris, 1955), pp. 90-1; J. B. M. A. Challamel, *Souvenirs d'un hugolâtre. La génération de 1830* (Paris, 1885), p. 37. On Lamartine and Brifaut see C. Brifaut, *Souvenirs d'un académicien sur la Révolution, le Premier Empire et la Restauration*, 2 vols. (Paris, 1921), I, pp. 275-80, and E. J. Delécluze, *Souvenirs de soixante années* (Paris, 1862), pp. 200-1.
147.   *Revue des Deux Mondes*, 15 September 1907, pp. 350-1.
148.   P. Béraud, *Souvenirs parlementaires* (Moulins, 1841), p. 400; *Souvenirs de Madame Delahante*, 2 vols. (Evreux, 1906-07), I, pp. 241-2; *Journal de Viennet*, p. 98; *Discours prononcés dans la séance publique tenue par l'Académie française, pour la réception de M. de Lamartine* (Paris, 1830), pp. 16-17.
149.   *Mémoires politiques* in *Oeuvres complètes de Lamartine*, XXXVII, pp. 258-9. Cf. C. de Lacombe, *Vie de Berryer, d'après des documents inédits*, 3 vols. (Paris, 1894-95), I, p. 363.
150.   See E. Géraud, *Un Homme de lettres sous l'Empire et la Restauration* (Paris, 1893), p. 259.

151. M. Levaillant (ed.), *Lamartine: correspondance générale de 1830 à 1848*, 2 vols. (Paris, 1943-48), I, pp. 22 and 26.

152. Ibid., pp. 18-19, 22-3, 24 and 30-1.

153. See J. Olivier, *Paris en 1830. Journal* (Lausanne, 1951), p. 113 and note 1.

154. *Bulletin de la Société Chateaubriand*, no. 19, 1976, p. 20.

155. *Correspondance générale*, I, pp. 43-4, 35-7, and 45-7.

156. Ibid., I, pp. 38-9, 44 and 48-9.

157. L. J. M. comte de Carné, *Souvenirs de ma jeunesse au temps de la Restauration* (Paris, 1872), p. 128. Cf. *Le Correspondant*, 10 December 1873, p. 825.

158. *Correspondance générale*, I, p. 18.

159. *Mémoires politiques* in *Oeuvres complètes de Lamartine*, XXXVII, p. 241. Cf. Olivier, *Paris en 1830*, p. 148.

160. *Correspondance générale*, I, pp. 35, 36 and 38.

161. *Souvenirs de Madame Delahante*, I, pp. 242-5; A. F. P. comte de Falloux, *Mémoires d'un royaliste*, 2 vols. (Paris, 1888), I, p. 42; C. Fournet, *Lamartine et ses amis suisses* (Paris, 1928), pp. 70 and 186-92.

162. Letter dated c. 5-6 August 1830; *Correspondance générale*, I, pp. 55-6.

163. Lamartine to Virieu, 29 August 1830; ibid., I, p. 57.

164. Ibid., I, pp. 68-9 and 83.

165. Ibid., I, pp. 374-5, 61 and 62.

166. *La Quotidienne*, 16 September 1830, p. 2; *Correspondance générale*, I, pp. 60-1. Lamartine had the letter republished in *Le Journal de Saône-et-Loire*, 24 September 1830 (*Correspondance générale*, I, pp. 376-7).

167. Letter dated 26 September 1830; *Lettres à Lamartine*, p. 115.

168. *Correspondance générale*, I, p. 376. Although Lamartine did not stand, two electors voted for him (L. Lacomme, *Les Élections et les représentants de Saône-et-Loire depuis 1789* (Paris, 1885), p. 74).

169. *Correspondance générale*, I, pp. 72-98.

170. See duc de Broglie (ed.), *Lettres de la duchesse de Broglie, 1814-1838* (Paris, 1896), pp. 41-2; comtesse Dash, *Mémoires des autres*, 6 vols. (Paris, 1896-7), II, pp. 42 and 198.

2 THE PURSUIT OF PRINCIPLE, 1831-1843

Créer une force, et attendre le jour où les affaires viendront la chercher par une nécessité évidente et invincible sans contestation ni avec soi-même ni avec les autres, voilà mon rôle.
— Lamartine to Virieu, February 1838

In 1831 Lamartine first stood for election to the Chamber of Deputies and first published a comprehensive statement of his political ideas. Although he did not win a seat until January 1833, and although his early political publications did not attract widespread public attention, he soon achieved national stature as a prominent parliamentary deputy and as a successful political publicist. Initially he presented himself as an independent liberal who generally supported the Government and the July Monarchy, but whose abandonment of the Bourbon dynasty was not apparently complete. However, after 1831 his political position slowly changed: he became a champion of a whole range of humanitarian causes; he discovered 'the social question', particularly the problems of urban poverty, and began to urge reforms which would alleviate human suffering and spread property ownership; and he gradually identified himself with political radicalism and with the opposition, as the behaviour of leading politicians and the character of government policies increasingly alienated him from the July Monarchy régime. Finally, in a major parliamentary speech delivered on 27 January 1843 he condemned the July Monarchy's entire political system and announced that he was joining the left-wing opposition.

Lamartine's political and parliamentary career was obviously influenced by the Revolution of July 1830. The Revolution occurred at a critical time for Lamartine: he had recently developed an active interest in politics and a strong attraction to liberalism; and he had shown a new ambition to be a politician rather than a diplomat. Until the July Days, as was so often to be the case, his political position remained somewhat ambiguous while he kept his political and career options open. But the July ordinances and Charles X's overthrow both destroyed his faith in the legitimists, as the supporters of the Bourbons came to be known, and prompted his resignation from the diplomatic corps. The July Revolution seemed to be a triumph for liberalism. The reactionary and unconstitutional Charles X was replaced by the more moderate Louis-Philippe; and a series of liberal measures sustained the liberal promise by relaxing press censorship, by introducing elections for local councils and for the officer ranks of the National Guard, by lowering the tax and age qualifications for parliamentary deputies, and by reducing the tax qualification for electors so as to double the electorate's size. However, notwithstanding his liberal sympathies, Lamartine had informed Louis-Philippe of his inability to serve the new régime because of his residual loyalty to the Bourbons. This did not mean that he intended to join the legitimist *émigration à l'intérieur*. Besides his personal ambitions, popular violence during and after the July Days convinced him of the need to support law and order and to participate in public and political life.

At first Lamartine feared that the July Revolution might have adversely affected his electoral chances, but as early as December 1830 he considered standing in a Dunkirk by-election.[1] While his vague hopes of a peerage, entertained in January 1831, failed to materialise,[2] his mother-in-law's long-awaited death (4 March 1831) and the eventual sale of his property at Montculot (26 March 1831)[3] at last gave him the financial independence then essential for a parliamentary career. To secure the inheritance from Mrs Birch, Lamartine and his wife left Mâcon for London towards the end of April 1831. When passing through Paris Lamartine was reportedly very disappointed at having no opportunity to stand for the Chamber of Deputies.[4] However, an opportunity almost immediately arose. Government-backed candidates usually stood in most constituencies at parliamentary elections, but other candidates were free to stand, provided, like Lamartine, they fulfilled the tax and age qualifications, and, preferably, could attract local influential support. At the beginning of May the Lamartines, *en route* for London, stayed with Lamartine's married sister, Eugénie de Coppens, at Hondschoote in the department of the Nord. Eugénie and her husband suggested to Lamartine that in the forthcoming general election he should stand as an independent candidate for the local town of Bergues in the second *arrondissement* of Dunkirk. By 10 May he had agreed; and from London on 6 June he also agreed to stand in Toulon and Mâcon. Once nominated, though, he characteristically claimed indifference towards the result, since he had doubts regarding his oratorical powers and was planning a journey to the Middle East.[5]

Given the absence of organised political parties, personal contact with members of the local élite was an essential element in any election campaign. In the Bergues constituency the de Coppens were an influential family,[6] and they were able to muster the energetic support of, among others, Jean-Louis Debuyser (a local landowner), Charles Delaroière (mayor of Bergues), Saullay de l'Aistre (sub-prefect of Hazebrouck, near Bergues, 1824-30), and Mme Caroline Angebert (wife of a *commissaire de la marine* at Dunkirk, with considerable influence over a local newspaper, *Le Journal de Dunkerque*).[7] In Toulon two legitimists promoted Lamartine's candidature – Ferdinand-Marius Capmas, a former sub-prefect and Lamartine's agent in the sale of Montculot,[8] and a friend of Capmas, Meisonnier de Valcroissant, who in 1822 had become joint owner of the conservative royalist newspaper, *La Quotidienne*.[9] Lamartine's Mâcon campaign was run by François-Louis Aubel, Pierre-Jean Ronot and Philibert-Marie Febvre. Aubel was a local landowner, member of the Academy of Mâcon, and former *substitut du procureur du roi* at Mâcon;[10] Ronot practised law in Mâcon and wrote poetry;[11] and Febvre had long been active in local administration and had served as a *conseiller* in the Saône-et-Loire prefecture.[12] These individuals decided on their own initiative to back Lamartine's parliamentary candidature, because of personal ties with Lamartine and because they admired his poetry. Lamartine on his part accepted their support, even though their political views did not necessarily coincide with his own.

Having decided to stand at Bergues, Lamartine quickly demonstrated his well-established concern for favourable press publicity: he wrote to Mme Angebert, asking her to discourage the Dunkirk newspapers from attacking him, and to his friend Aimé Martin, requesting the insertion of a flattering notice about his candidature in *Le Journal des Débats*, an important Paris newspaper which was both conservative and pro-government. He also tried to exploit his literary contacts with Adolphe Thiers, urging him to see Casimir Périer (the liberal but authoritarian prime minister since 13 March 1831) so that the Government should neither support nor oppose him and move the polling station from Dunkirk to Bergues. While anxious not to lose his indepedence by becoming a government candidate, Lamartine promised to support the Government provided Casimir Périer remained 'l'homme de l'ordre et du pouvoir social'.[13] After a short visit to London (21 May – 11 June 1831), during which he claimed to have had a cordial interview with Talleyrand at the French embassy,[14] Lamartine returned to fight the election at Bergues, where the Government had decided to hold the election. His correspondence indicates that he energetically issued and distributed manifestoes, and publicised them in local newspapers, though just before the election he fell ill with a fever.

In his electoral manifestoes Lamartine continually stressed the need for liberty — 'l'idée mère de nos destinées futures' — defined as: personal and political liberty, protecting all legitimate rights; freedom of thought, with an educational system independent from the Church; freedom of conscience, with the Church separated from the State; freedom in the department, with authority devolved in local affairs; and freedom in the State, with a system which would represent all those classes of the nation with enlightenment to give and interests to defend. This emphasis on liberty and freedom accorded with the prevailing political climate. For example, the Charter of 1830 had liberalised the political system in France and, in deliberate contrast to Charles X, the July Monarchy distanced itself from the Roman Catholic Church. Also prominent liberals and Orleanists, such as the duc de Broglie, Benjamin Constant and Guizot, shared Lamartine's concern for personal and political liberty and for the separation of Church and State. But as recently as August 1829 Lamartine had described himself as a constitutional royalist and had not discussed the parliamentary franchise or the Roman Catholic Church. Thus between August 1829 and June 1831 Lamartine's liberalism had become much more pronounced, obviously reflecting his response to the July Revolution, his realisation that liberalism had become the dominant political force in France (particularly Saône-et-Loire), and his belief that liberalism was the political creed of the future.

Nevertheless, Lamartine's liberal position was not straightforward. In his letters and manifestoes he claimed that he belonged to no party, but to those who had welcomed the Bourbon Restoration, deplored the July Revolution, and accepted the Orleanist régime. He identified in his letters slightly different potential supporters according to the political sympathies of his correspondents, though he evidently hoped that his appeal would be broad, embracing liberals, conservatives and moderate royalists. On the crucial question of the extent of the franchise he was probably deliberately vague, admittedly like at this time many of his contemporaries, including even republicans. Nor was his abandonment of legitimism complete. Like Lamartine, legitimists generally wanted a devolution of local government, though perhaps favoured by Lamartine as a large landowner. Moreover, several of his most prominent supporters — Mme Angebert and Saullay de l'Aistre at Bergues, Capmas and Meisonnier de Valcroissant at Toulon, Aubel and Febvre at Mâcon — had legitimist loyalties with which he took care to sympathise; and he personally sought out the backing of legitimist and conservative newspapers. While many of Lamartine's friends, acquaintances and admirers were, of course, legitimists and conservatives, clearly he was not averse to exploiting them for his own ends. Altogether Lamartine's political position was idiosyncratic, contradictory and easily misunderstood.[15]

The contradictions in Lamartine's political position doubtless deterred some voters. However, 1831 was a time of political flux for many Frenchmen, and Lamartine could hope to capitalise on his literary reputation. At Bergues, a wealthy rural constituency with a large, conservative and legitimist electorate, his royalist past and status as a rich landowner were obvious advantages. In addition, the de Coppens family and their friends supported him. However, the prefect and sub-prefect opposed him because of his alleged legitimism, since he had refused to swear a declaration of loyalty to the July Monarchy; he was publicly attacked as an ultra and an outsider; a pamphleteer called Auguste Barthélemy lampooned him in verse; and his rival, Paul Lemaire, besides enjoying government support, had already won a parliamentary election in the Nord in October 1830, whereas Lamartine had of course never stood before. On 6 July it was announced that Lemaire had won by 198 votes to 181, a very creditable result for Lamartine. At Toulon the baron de Portalis defeated him by an even narrower margin (78 votes to 72), an equally creditable result, especially since Lamartine had no connections with Toulon and had not visited the port during the campaign. Presumably he attracted legitimist votes, since Portalis belonged to an important Napoleonic family and had been made a senior judge after the July Revolution. In the separate constituencies of the town and *arrondissement* of Mâcon he was less successful, the comte de Rambuteau defeating him in the former by 242 votes to 46, and Charles Brosse in the latter by 205 votes to 9. The Mâcon results almost certainly disappointed him, but his candidature against Brosse (mayor of the local *commune* of Cormatin) was not apparently serious, while Rambuteau constituted a formidable political opponent with a strong basis of liberal support, thus leaving Lamartine only a small number of personal and legitimist votes.

Lamartine blamed his defeats at Bergues and Toulon on the malpractices of his opponents, apparently with justice in the case of Toulon where the election was eventually quashed. Although disappointed, he appreciated that the results augured well for the future, and he took care to thank the electors in Bergues and Toulon and his various supporters. He had certainly almost secured election in two constituencies, and his supporters in Bergues and Mâcon had formed political support groups of considerable future significance. This was no mean achievement, particularly since he had despaired of a parliamentary career in the first months of 1831. The electoral campaigns also further indicated his unusual political position: while so many French aristocrats remained loyal to legitimism, Lamartine had become a pragmatic liberal who accepted the July Monarchy as a political necessity; yet, in his eagerness to gain election as a deputy, he had opposed liberal Orleanists (Lemaire, Portalis and Rambuteau), and had himself exploited legitimists, been backed by legitimists and had attracted legitimist votes. Not surprisingly, therefore, particularly in view of his previous identification with the Bourbons, he was still publicly regarded as a legitimist. This misunderstanding of his political position, for which he himself was largely responsible, cut him off from other liberals and from the Government and adherents to the Orleanist régime (who, in any case, were deterred by his less than total commitment to the July Monarchy and only conditional support for Casimir Périer).

After the elections Lamartine used his well-tried literary skills to develop and publicise his political position. He started by replying to Barthélemy with a poem, 'A Némésis'. In this poem he denied having prostituted his poetry and money for political ends, condemned abstention from politics in time of crisis, and reaffirmed his love of liberty.[16] Much more substantial was the comprehensive development of his social and political ideas in a long article which he wrote during September 1831. The article took the form of a letter addressed to Edmond de Cazalès, editor of the *Revue européenne*, a new journal which had pressed — and failed to persuade — Lamartine to join its editorial board.[17] Doubtless Lamartine believed that his political independence might be compromised by a direct editorial connection, and in any case the *Revue européenne* afforded him all the publicity he wanted. The article, entitled 'De la politique rationnelle', was published in full in the *Revue européenne*'s second issue. Shortly afterwards an enlarged version, with the slightly different title of *Sur la politique rationnelle*, appeared as a separate pamphlet printed by Charles Gosselin.[18]

The article's title indicates Lamartine's aims, the statement of a rational political creed and the development of rational policies to meet France's problems. The Romantic poet and former royalist now wanted to present himself as applying reason to politics, reflecting both his concern to be publicly recognised as a politician rather than a poet and his pragmatic evolution from legitimism towards liberalism. Lamartine begins by arguing that the contemporary age was one of social change and renovation, perhaps comparable to the Early Christian Era. The mission of the Restoration Monarchy had been to lead France at this critical time, a mission ignored by the Bourbons, who had committed political suicide in July 1830. Both the July ordinances and the Orleanist seizure of power are condemned: the former violated 'le droit populaire', the latter 'le droit dynastique'. But Charles X had provoked the July Revolution; his actions explained, if they did not justify, the Orleanist seizure of power; and after July 1830 fidelity to the Bourbons was no longer justifiable. Political behaviour should be determined by considering 'le droit du salut du peuple' and 'le droit de la nécessité sociale'. Neither could be served by legitimism. In the existing circumstances the citizen's duty was to serve 'la patrie, la nation, l'humanité', by supporting the July Monarchy. This support, however, should be conditional on the July Monarchy meeting the challenge of the age, defined as the application of human reason or divine truth to the political organisation of modern society, so as to achieve the progressive and universal establishment of a new social order based on individual freedom and equality of rights.

On a practical level, Lamartine declares his belief in a parliamentary form of government with a single head of state (whether king or president scarcely mattered). Everything which promotes liberty, democracy and equality of rights should be encouraged. Therefore an hereditary Chamber of Peers would be unjustifiable; the press should be independent; education should be secular, as universal as possible, and free; and Church and State should be completely separated. Ideally the political franchise should be universal. But the Revolution's excesses have recently discredited democracy, and giving the vote to classes of the population incapable of using it effectively is pointless. The solution lies in a system of proportional and universal representation based on a property franchise, the precise details of which are not clearly stated. Lamartine also recommends a reform of the criminal code, including capital punishment; and he now supports the preservation of France's administrative centralisation. He thought that this programme could be achieved by an enlightened and capable leader – a 'Bonaparte de la parole', a 'Christophe Colomb de la liberté' – and by a faith in human progress and dignity. The Saint-Simonians, he argues, rightly attack materialism and believe in moral and spiritual perfectibility but fail to recognise the civilising roles of Christianity and private property. France needed rational Christian rule; governments would triumph or perish depending on whether or not they provided this. Individuals should not withdraw from politics, like some legitimists after the July Revolution, but serve France by joining the National Guard, voting in elections, standing for parliament, and by supporting progress and democracy. Throughout, Lamartine's argument is suffused with a vague religiosity. He constantly asserts there is a divine presence in human affairs, variously described as God, Christianity, reason or Providence. Also he outlines his own future political role, that of a constitutional royalist whose conscience will lead him to serve his country and advance with the nation, whose honour will prevent him from soliciting for any government position or royal favour, and whose patriotism will place him at his country's disposal in exceptional circumstances.

The philosophical influences on the content of the article are fairly clear. Lamartine claimed that his conservative and legitimist friend Virieu had read and approved practically the entire text,[19] but such figures as Virieu no longer exercised any significant political influence on him, though Virieu may have encouraged him to give legitimism reasonably sympathetic treatment. A new friend and neighbour called Jean-Marie Dargaud, who stayed with the Lamartines during September 1831, may have exercised some personal influence.[20] But Dargaud, a political radical and religious free-thinker, probably only supported ideas and proposals which Lamartine had already outlined in private letters and electoral manifestos. However, Lamartine did draw on the ideas of Saint-Simonianism and of Catholic liberalism. In particular, he followed the Saint-Simonian belief in a cyclical theory of human progress and in the need for a religious sanction of rational doctrines, though he did not yet share the Saint-Simonian interest in economic questions. Of more immediate importance was probably the group of Catholic intellectuals who in October 1830 had founded the liberal Catholic newspaper, *L'Avenir*. Lamartine had known one of the editors, Lamennais, for twelve years, and he had met another editor, Montalembert, several times in Paris during 1830 and 1831.[21] *L'Avenir* had also published his two recent political poems, 'Contre la peine de mort' and 'A Némésis', as well as two of his electoral manifestoes.[22] Like Lamartine, the group around *L'Avenir* believed that France was in a critical state of profound transformation, that only the principles of Christian morality could solve current social and political problems, and that human reason, purged of all human passions, was identical with God's will. They accepted the July Monarchy, but wanted reforms — a free press, an extension of the parliamentary franchise, a secular educational system, and a complete separation of Church and State. But unlike *L'Avenir*'s editors, Lamartine opposed administrative decentralisation and any form of Roman Catholic theocracy in France. Thus, while influenced by and responding to the two major progressive movements in France at this time, he maintained his ideological independence by developing his own personal synthesis.

Anxious to exploit *Sur la politique rationnelle*, Lamartine had copies distributed in Mâcon and Bergues. But he complained that a pamphlet by Chateaubriand on Charles X's exile, published at the end of October 1831, preoccupied the public, while *Sur la politique rationnelle* had fallen completely flat.[23] This certainly applied to the legitimist *Quotidienne* (which commented on 5 November, 'Tout s'efface devant l'écrit de M. de Chateaubriand') and to the leading liberal newspaper, *Le Constitutionnel*. However, the legitimist *Gazette de France* did note Lamartine's publication; his views on the newspaper press were favourably received by the conservative *Journal des Débats* in an article *Le National* reproduced; and a long review appeared in *Le Globe*, since November 1830 a Saint-Simonian journal.[24] *Le Globe* welcomed his commitment to social reform and belief that society was entering a period of fundamental change, but suggested he lacked a full understanding of Saint-Simonian thought, and illogically wanted to transform society while retaining society's traditional foundations, private property and Christianity. Among Lamartine's friends, Dargaud not surprisingly sent him a complimentary letter.[25]

Though *Sur la politique rationnelle* provoked a generally disappointing response, it is nevertheless important in providing a comprehensive statement of Lamartine's political ideas, in clearly stating his break with legitimism, and in further indicating his faith in the political potential of the printed word. His proposed reforms, while lacking originality and ignoring economic problems, were prophetic, both in the short term (a law of 29 December 1831 abolished the hereditary peerage) and in the more distant future (manhood suffrage, free, secular and compulsory education, separation of Church and State). Moreover, his liberal and progressive proposals anticipated his alignment with the party of Movement, those July Monarchy politicians who, unlike those classified as belonging to the party of Resistance, sought significant change.

After completing *Sur la politique rationnelle* Lamartine devoted himself to his estates and entertained various guests. The latter included during November the writer Eugène Sue and Lamartine's cousin Mme de La Haste. Eugène Sue had earned his stay by favourably reviewing *Harmonies*,[26] while Mme de La Haste was escaping from the Lyons silk-workers' rising which began on 21 November. This rising once more aroused Lamartine's fear of popular anarchy. He wrote of 'le 27 juillet du commerce et de la propriété' (a reference to the first of the July Days); and, unlike most of the local legitimists, he took part in a mobilisation of Mâcon's National Guard. However, his fears quickly subsided with the rising's collapse, and he was soon writing that the victorious workers had behaved like seminarists.[27] While a fear of popular anarchy was common among the *notables*, Lamartine soon concluded that industrial society posed major problems which had to be solved by reforms. Thus he suggested that candidates in a literary competition organised by the Academy of Mâcon should consider why urban workers were less happy and moral than their rural counterparts, and what remedies should be adopted.[28] Meanwhile, at the beginning of November he started what was to become his epic poem *Jocelyn*; and in December he contributed a poem, 'Les Révolutions', to the third volume of *Paris, ou Le Livre des Cent-et-Un*, designed to rescue the publisher Ladvocat from bankruptcy. In 'Les Révolutions' he stresses how political societies were constantly being overthrown and replaced, and that when this happened we should not imitate Assyrian kings by burying ourselves together with our wives and children. Thus, through the medium of a poem, he again tried to dissuade legitimists from joining the *émigration à l'intérieur* following the July Revolution.

In January 1832 the death of his first teacher, the abbé Dumont,[29] prompted Lamartine to write an article entitled 'Des Devoirs civils du curé'. His subject was the country village *curé* who, without a family, belongs to all families, and, neither rich nor poor, belongs to all classes. A description is given of the simple patriarchal life the *curé* ought to lead; and it is suggested that he is the only citizen who should remain neutral in the causes, hatreds and party conflicts dividing men and ideologies. Of particular interest is the connection Lamartine establishes beween politics and Christianity. He argues that every moral and political truth has a Christian origin. Thus philanthropy has developed out of the Christian principle of charity, and political equality out of the principle of man's equality before God. As the ideas of Christianity have spread, so errors have been removed and tyrannies have collapsed. Christianity's task, however, is far from completion; and the laws of progress and improvement, which are in harmony with human reason and God's will, forbid man ever to be satisfied with his achievements or to despair of humanity, but command him always to strive after the new horizons continually revealed to him by the Divinity.

'Des Devoirs civils du curé' first appeared in March 1832 in a monthly periodical founded by Emile de Girardin, the *Journal des connaissances utiles*.[30] Girardin himself wrote to Lamartine that the article had been well received and would improve his political standing. He suggested that electoral success would have been guaranteed if Lamartine had published a similar article before his parliamentary candidature the previous year, and advised him to publish articles more often in future. Mme de Girardin (formerly Delphine Gay, now Emile de Girardin's wife) and the *Journal des connaissances utiles* also suggested that the article had made a considerable impact.[31] Certainly *Le Journal de Saône-et-Loire* (25 February) provided some favourable advance publicity (doubtless at Lamartine's own instigation); and *L'Echo de Vaucluse*, which had published several of Lamartine's poems, also cited the article.[32] However, not surprisingly, the spread of a severe cholera epidemic to France and the duchesse de Berry's abortive royalist rising in the Vendée (May-June 1832) remained the chief concerns of Paris newspapers.

A further disappointment had occurred at the beginning of March 1832 when Lamartine had stood as a candidate for the position of colonel of Mâcon's National Guard. Before the election he had warned his supporters of his unsuitability for the post and of his refusal to campaign actively, and he had also realised that his legitimist reputation and social status might deter some voters.[33] Nevertheless, he had undoubtedly wanted the honour and had been confident of success, yet he collected only enough votes to become lieutenant-colonel. His first reaction was to draw up an angry statement intended for publication, but a day later he sent a much more anodyne letter to *Le Journal de Saône-et-Loire*, thanking those who had voted for him and acknowledging his respect for those who had not. Interestingly, he also rewarded one of his supporters, Ronot, by giving him a poem which Ronot touched up and then published as his own work in *Le Journal de Saône-et-Loire*.[34]

Lamartine had planned to leave for Paris on 10 March to vote in a French Academy election. Thiers, one of the candidates, urged him to support 'our party', defined as 'this poor, much-abused, political and literary *juste milieu*'.[35] But Julia fell seriously ill, so Lamartine decided to remain with her at Mâcon and Milly. Meanwhile, on 8 April Lamartine accepted his appointment by the mayor of Mâcon to a health commission, formed in case the cholera epidemic should reach Mâcon.[36] At the same time he began making preparations for a journey to the Eastern Mediterranean; and he composed a second poem for Ladvocat,

'Réponse aux Adieux de Sir Walter Scott à ses Lecteurs', the manuscript of which is dated 6 May. Eight days previously the duchesse de Berry had landed near Marseilles in an attempt to rally support for her son's claim to the French throne. While acknowledging in his poem that he had celebrated in verse the birth of the *enfant du miracle*, Lamartine stresses that the duc de Bordeaux should accept the July Revolution's verdict, and questions whether royal claims can ever justify the shedding of blood. Writing to Virieu on 7 May he described the landing as an act of crass ineptitude, revealing the true character of militant royalism and threatening the most unfortunate consequences.[37] Thus once again Lamartine distanced himself from his royalist past, and from the Romantic sympathy of Chateaubriand and some other legitimists for the duchesse de Berry.

About the end of the first week of May Lamartine decided that the cholera epidemic was not going to reach Mâcon, and resumed his travelling preparations. He was all set to leave for Marseilles on 28 May when Julia's illness returned. A further cause for delay arose with a by-election at Cluny, occasioned by the death (25 April) of Brosse, deputy for Mâcon-*arrondissement*. Asked by Edouard Dubois if he would stand, Lamartine replied on 21 May in very ambivalent terms. He stated that he did not want to be elected a deputy at this moment, but would always reproach himself if through his inaction an unsatisfactory candidate were returned. He therefore remained entirely neutral, not wanting his nomination, but willing to accept it if imposed on him by 'les honnêtes gens'. Similar replies were sent to other supporters of Lamartine in this by-election, Duluat and Gacon.[38] Undeterred, Dubois, Duluat and Gacon had letters published in *Le Journal de Saône-et-Loire* on 2 and 6 June advertising Lamartine's candidature and soliciting support. The by-election was held on 12 June. Lamartine obtained 52 votes, against 170 for Pierre-Christophe-Marcellin Duréault (elected) and 64 for Paul Tondut.[39] Quinet thought Lamartine might be elected after visiting him in May,[40] but Duréault, a local *avocat*, *juge de paix* and landowner, was the official government candidate and *Le Journal de Saône-et-Loire* supported him. Apparently Lamartine did no electoral campaigning and the result did not disappoint him particularly. However, as after the National Guard election, he thanked those who had voted for him in a letter to *Le Journal de Saône-et-Loire*.[41] The same day (14 June) the Lamartines finally left Mâcon for Marseilles and the Eastern Mediterranean.

For a long time Lamartine had wanted to fulfil a typical Romantic fantasy by visiting the lands of the Eastern Mediterranean.[42] The death of Mrs Birch and the Montculot sale meant that extensive foreign travel was now possible for the Lamartines, while Lamartine's electoral defeats and the death on 16 May 1832 of Casimir Périer, who might have offered him government support, seemed to remove the immediate possibility of a political career. In deciding to visit the Eastern Mediterranean Lamartine's motives were partly political. He hoped to find fresh political inspiration in the foreign countries which he visited; he wanted to reward Ferdinand de Capmas and Dr Jean-Waast Delaroière, political supporters at Toulon and Bergues respectively, by inviting them to join him as travelling companions; and he clearly intended to exploit his travels so as to gain favourable publicity. Right from the start the potential significance of his journey in terms of politics and publicity became apparent. While in Marseilles (18 June – 10 July 1832) Lamartine attended a dinner given in his honour, had honorary membership of the Academy of Marseilles conferred upon him, and was sought out by local poets such as Joseph Autran and Jean Reboul. Lamartine described himself as being intoxicated and overwhelmed by this enthusiastic welcome, which he alleged came from 'notabilités' of all political persuasions. If the opportunity arose, he concluded that he would easily be elected deputy for Marseilles.[43] The triumphal character of the Lamartines' journey continued as they sailed via Sardinia, Malta, Greece, Rhodes and Cyprus to Beirut.[44] In the Lebanon and the Holy Land Lamartine was even treated like a visiting prince. However, during a visit by Lamartine to Jerusalem the health of his daughter Julia rapidly deteriorated, and she eventually died on 7 December 1832 – like her brother, probably of tuberculosis. Lamartine and his wife were prostrated with grief, and remained immobilised in Beirut until the following spring. They then returned home overland via Constantinople, Adrianople, Plovdiv, Sofia, Belgrade, Vienna, Stuttgart and Strasbourg, while Julia's coffin was sent by sea from Constantinople to Marseilles.

This first long Middle East tour had a profound influence on Lamartine. He developed a permanent interest in the peoples, religions and civilisations of the Turkish Empire; and he was greatly impressed by his encounter with a patriarchal society, which paid so much respect to religion, beauty and the social hierarchy. Wherever Lamartine went, he enjoyed official and public attention such as he had never before received. Yet the fascination of the Middle East and the triumphal character of his progress were overshadowed by Julia's tragic death. It was nearly two weeks before he could bring himself to break the news to Virieu. 'We no longer live', he confessed, and to Vignet he wrote: 'we have no future, no appetite for life, no hope, no desire for anything'.[45] Lamartine's poem, 'Gethsémani ou La Mort de Julia', illustrates his terrible grief, and his shock that the fatal illness should have occurred while he was visiting the Holy Places in order to pray there. According to the last verse, everything was dead in his arid household; his wife's tear-filled eyes constantly haunted him; he now lived without purpose or joy; the desire to pray and all feelings of hope had been extinguished within him; and the force that was crushing him was God. Altogether Julia's death had a devastating effect on his belief in Catholic dogma and acceptance of the Church's authority, both of which had already been shaken by the condemnation of *L'Avenir's* Catholic liberalism in the papal encyclical, *Mirari vos* (15 August 1832).[46]

Having returned to Mâcon (18 October 1833) Lamartine's first task was to collect Julia's remains from Marseilles and to inter them at Saint-Point. During November he began writing an account of his travels, the *Voyage en Orient*, helped by his young friend Dargaud; and he also again turned to politics. While still in the Middle East Lamartine had received a letter from his sister Eugénie de Coppens informing him that on 7 January 1833 he had been elected deputy for Bergues. After the resignation of the sitting deputy, Paul Lemaire, his candidature had been put forward unsolicited. The Government had been hostile, considering Lamartine a legitimist (the Minister of the Interior had described him as the candidate of the legitimists to the sub-prefect of Dunkirk on 4 January).[47] But Bernard de Coppens, now Hondschoote's mayor and a local National Guard officer, had organised his campaign effectively; and Lamartine had been elected by 196 out of 349 votes cast, with a comfortable margin of 116 votes over his nearest rival. At the beginning of November Lamartine was so depressed that he informed Eugénie de Coppens of his extreme reluctance to enter politics, and up to the last minute he may have hesitated before taking his seat in the Chamber. However, on 13 November he asked his friend Amié Martin to find him suitable accommodation in Paris.[48]

Lamartine also stood for election to Saône-et-Loire's *conseil général* in the canton of Mâcon Nord. Doubtless anxious for government support, he seems to have publicly stressed the moderation of his political views. Saône-et-Loire's prefect reported on 9 November to the Minister of the Interior that, although he had not seen Lamartine, he knew him to be expressing 'les meilleurs sentiments politiques'. In particular, Lamartine had said that he would sit in the centre of the

Chamber, so as to be equally distant from both Berryer (a prominent legitimist) and Odilon Barrot (leader of the so-called dynastic Left).[49] Léon de Pierreclau, however, considered Lamartine's political position to be much more radical. He wrote to his mother on 24 November that Lamartine did not want to join either the Government or the opposition. By principle and instinct a republican, Lamartine wanted a republic, but he appreciated that a republic would be possible only when the masses were ready for it, which at present they were not.[50] These republican sympathies clearly remained private. The consistently pro-Government *Journal de Saône-et-Loire* supported Lamartine's candidature (13 November); and on 17 November he was elected with 56 out of 101 votes cast. Official support probably contributed to his electoral success. According to Saône-et-Loire's prefect, it was also due to his 'poetic genius'.[51] The latter was again publicly recognised by his election to the presidency of the Academy of Mâcon (2 December).

The new parliamentary session opened on 23 December 1833. Lamartine had left Monceau on 16 December for Paris, where he had moved into part of an *hôtel* at 82 (now 80) rue de l'Université in the Faubourg Saint-Germain, one of the most fashionable districts of Paris, particularly for aristocrats and legitimists. For Lamartine its convenient proximity to the Chamber presumably compensated for its reputation. At any rate, it remained his Paris residence throughout his parliamentary career. In the Chamber he took a seat not in the centre but on the extreme right, which apparently confirmed the widely held view that he was a legitimist — contemporaries had mistakenly considered his election at Bergues to have been a legitimist success.[52] Thus Bonald saluted him on 29 December as 'the worthy representative of the royalist party', while Rémusat rather uncharitably commented that Lamartine, generally regarded as a legitimist and a poet, was 'without credit'.[53] However, Lamartine claims that Thiers, then Minister of the Interior, tried to enrol him as a government supporter. He refused, determined to maintain his 'enigmatic independence'.[54] The decision to remain independent of governments and political parties had been taken by 1830.[55] When asked where he would sit in the Chamber, Lamartine had allegedly replied, 'On the ceiling'.[56] Isolation and independence clearly appealed to him. 'I am solitary by nature' he had written in 1830; and as far back as 1819 he had been concerned that a successful application for a diplomatic post might compromise his freedom as a poet.[57]

Initially, Lamartine claimed that he would not make an immediate or regular contribution to parliamentary debates,[58] but, typically, he changed his mind almost at once when the current war between Egypt and Turkey was discussed in the Chamber. Encouraged by his diplomatic experience and recent travels, he delivered his maiden speech on 4 January 1834, and a second speech four days later. He argued that the Turkish Empire's decline might disturb the European balance of power. The solution lay in a congress of European Powers, to establish the principles of a European protectorate over the Middle East and of no unilateral intervention by any one European Power in the Turkish Empire. More controversial was his speech of 3 February on government policy in the Vendée, where the duchesse de Berry had briefly and unsuccessfully attempted to organise a rising during May 1832. Praising Vendéean resistance to the Revolution in 1793, he declared that a general amnesty would be the only certain way of pacifying the Vendée. Thus yet again he gave the impression of being a legitimist. In fact, he was pursuing political objectives which he outlined in his private correspondence. He wanted to appeal to the country's conscience by adopting on major issues positions based on moral principles and national interests. In so doing he would ignore considerations of party politics or short-term popularity. At the same time he would try to form in the Chamber a 'reserve party' of like-minded deputies. Ultimately, he hoped to win over the conscience of the French people, particularly the young and the masses. Lamartine was confident of eventual success. His own conscience was clear; he wanted no more than 'the triumph of the *honnêtes gens* by reason'; and he possessed 'the instinct of the masses'.[59]

Developing his 'social political ideology', Lamartine for example maintained that France should pay the so-called American Debt, consisting of damages claimed by the United States since the Napoleonic Wars (1 April), and criticised a proposal to reduce substantially the State educational budget (8 May). His most important speeches, however, related to the question of public order and popular unrest. In the middle of February 1834 the Lyons silk-workers organised an eight-day general strike. Panicked by this unprecedented industrial action, the Government introduced a bill against illegal associations. Lamartine did not oppose the bill, declaring that a government's first duty is to survive, and that it represents something more important even than liberty — order, peace and security. The proposed measures against illegal associations should nevertheless be applied with extreme caution, and the Government should attempt to discover, and remedy, the causes of popular unrest, instead of merely resorting to repression (13 March). During April a popular revolt occurred in Lyons. It was 'the largest civil disturbance in France between 1830 and 1848',[60] required a substantial military force for its suppression, and encouraged a small republican rising in Paris. Informed of developments in Lyons by Virieu, Lamartine was not without sympathy for the Lyons silkworkers, though he consigned the Paris conspirators to Dante's Inferno.[61] On 13 May he intervened in the debate on additional credits for the Minister of War after the Lyons and Paris disturbances. Again he revealed himself to be a man of order, proclaiming that a government must defend itself and that any measure against anarchy is legitimate. However, he also recommended a comprehensive programme of reforms: more morality and enlightenment in State education, an extension of the parliamentary franchise, permanent enquiries into France's industrial evils, a fairer distribution of wealth, and State assistance for the unemployed to provide them with work either through cooperatives, or through advancing them land and capital for the formation of new agricultural communities within France or abroad. In conclusion, he stressed the need for 'love of the people', 'concern for the happiness of the masses', and 'charity in our legislation'.[62] While imprecise on detail, these radical proposals contained the fundamentals of Lamartine's social and political programme until the Revolution of 1848. Finally, shortly before parliament was dissolved, he spoke in favour of abolishing the death penalty for political offences (15 May).

Throughout his first parliamentary session Lamartine had thus given several important speeches. While receiving little favourable press attention, he had remarkably quickly made his mark and had developed considerable proficiency as a parliamentary speaker. By modern standards Lamartine's speeches are too long and too rhetorical, and even by the more generous standards of his contemporaries he was frequently verbose and discursive. Furthermore, while exploiting friends as research assistants, he was still often inaccurate on precise details; and he hardly ever enlivened his speeches, at least intentionally, with any hint of wit or humour. But he could discuss almost any subject with ease, fluency and a minimum of preparation; he had the ability to perceive and explain the fundamentals of a problem; his language was both brilliant and convincing, his powers of description exceptionally vivid; and on occasion he could appeal to his audience's emotions with great effect. Even political opponents such as Guizot acknowledged as much.[63] In addition, Lamartine began to speak regularly on major issues, on which he usually presented challenging ideas and arguments, and often adopted unpredictable positions. Finally, he enjoyed the advantages of a pleasant voice and a striking appearance.

As a result, he gradually acquired a reputation for being one of the three or four most important orators in the Chamber of Deputies.

During the 1834 parliamentary session, displaying his customary energy and eagerness to publicise his ideas, Lamartine composed a long essay, *Des Destinées de la Poésie*, and two short articles contributed to the *Journal des connaissances utiles*, 'Sur les Caisses d'Epargnes' and 'Ecoles et méthodes'.[64] *Des Destinées de la Poésie* is a mixture of personal reminiscences and philosophical reflections which later served as the second preface to *Méditations*. The theme is the influence of any society on the character of its poetry. Lamartine argues that the militarism and despotism of Napoleon's Empire, while congenial to mathematics, had discouraged poetry and literature, despite the brave efforts of Mme de Staël and Chateaubriand. However, poetry had returned to France with the re-establishment of the Bourbons and liberty. Similarly, Lamartine illustrates from observations made during his recent Middle East travels, how different kinds of poetry suit different peoples. He argues that poetry in France should become rational, philosophic, religious, political and social, reflecting the needs and concerns of French society; it should develop with French institutions and the press; and, like the press, it should increasingly have a popular appeal, so as to become a powerful influence on public opinion. In future, poets should popularise moral truths and rational principles. As in *Sur la politique rationnelle*, Lamartine suggests that France was entering an important period of social reconstruction and reform. The real issue was not the ruling élite's composition or the constitution's character, but whether Christian principles would replace selfish egoism in politics, whether the practical teachings of Christianity would be translated into legislation, and whether all men would finally agree to regard their fellow human beings as brothers rather than as enemies or slaves. He concludes by hoping such changes could be achieved without violence.

In *Des Destinées de la Poésie* Lamartine was partly justifying his transition from *salon* poet and royalist diplomat to popular writer and progressive politician. Also, eager for popularity and anxious to accommodate new trends, he was responding to several contemporary developments. The Saint-Simonians had revived the ancient concept of the poet as the moral guardian and spiritual leader of his people. After July 1830 liberals, socialists and republicans commonly argued that writers and artists should help political and social progress in France, and that literature and art should have a mass appeal. At the same time, they tended to criticise Lamartine's poetry for its melancholy, preoccupation with personal emotions, backward-looking royalism and Catholicism, and élitist appeal. Lamartine was aware of those ideas and criticisms; like other French Romantics, influenced by the July Revolution and subsequent crises, he had become an apostle of progress and humanitarianism; and he had long been interested in public opinion and the press, both of which he realised were becoming increasingly popularised in France. Yet in publicly maintaining his opposition to Bonapartism he was resisting a current trend, to which Hugo among others had succumbed. Politically, *Des Destinées de la Poésie* was characteristically ambiguous: his suggested future role for poets and poetry, and belief that the July Revolution should inaugurate a period of fundamental change in France, identified him with liberal and left-wing opinion, while legitimists could, and did, welcome his praise of Chateaubriand and the Restoration Monarchy. In fact, his self-appointed political task, privately defined in August 1834 as the introduction of reason, religion and morality into politics,[65] was uniquely personal.

Contrasting with *Des Destinées de la Poésie*, the two articles in the *Journal des connaissances utiles* were practical and specific. In 'Sur les Caisses d'Epargnes' Lamartine asserted that the possession of property or capital was essential to human well-being. Unfortunately, many urban workers remained entirely or virtually destitute of property, thus dependent on whatever work they could secure and highly vulnerable to any misfortune. To encourage workers to acquire some capital, in every *arrondissement* savings banks should be established offering 4 per cent interest inclusive of any service charge, accepting deposits as low as one franc, and permitting the immediate withdrawal of savings and interest. By saving regularly, urban workers would acquire insurance against sickness, accident or unemployment, and a moral guarantee against idleness, vice and debauchery. Numerous savings banks were founded throughout France during the July Monarchy and they were quite successful, though few workers could afford to save regularly. Lamartine had supported this development as early as March 1832, when he had given a talk on savings banks to the Academy of Mâcon.[66] The Lyons strike of February 1834 doubtless renewed his interest in the subject, and in June 1834 he and his wife subscribed two hundred francs to a Dunkirk savings bank.[67] Many *notables* shared his faith in savings banks for the poor, regarding poverty as the consequence of immorality and hoping that saving would moralise the poor. Lamartine, too, believed in the fundamental importance and civilising influence of private property and had a vision of a property-owning democracy which would radically alter the plight of urban workers. 'Ecoles et méthodes' criticises the Government's lack of reforming zeal and discusses a familiar Lamartine theme, the significance of the newspaper press. In recognition of the political importance of newspapers in France, Lamartine suggests that the Government should establish the equivalent of a ministry of information.

Before the parliamentary dissolution on 24 May Lamartine made a pre-election visit to his constituency in the Nord.[68] On 20 May he dined with Laurent de Coppens and local National Guard officers. The following day he gave a speech to sugar-beet growers (who constituted an important local agricultural interest) and dined with Charles Delaroière (brother of his travelling companion and a political supporter). A banquet was held in his honour in Hondschoote's *hôtel de ville* on 25 May, when he defined his political position, rather simplistically, as helping governments to do good and preventing them from doing harm, protecting France from the passions of any party, and summoning all loyal opinions to the work of the common good. He described this as a mandate of impartiality, conciliation and progress. Similarly, he privately wrote to Virieu that his ambition was to reconcile the different political factions in France through appeals to reason and conscience. In his electoral manifesto, dated 8 June, he declared that he had not joined any political party. Instead his guides had been patriotism and common sense, and his party had been the country's conscience.[69]

In the general election of June 1834, as in that of July 1831, Lamartine stood in both Bergues and Mâcon (but not Toulon). The day before he arrived in Mâcon on 8 June, *Le Journal de Saône-et-Loire* had announced his candidature in Mâcon-*ville*. In Mâcon the prefecture, *Le Journal de Saône-et-Loire* and a well-organised group of supporters now backed him. He could count on the legitimists and on many personal friends; and he benefited from a swing to the right among the Saône-et-Loire electorate, due to widespread anti-republicanism following the Lyons and Paris disturbances and to a general improvement in the economy. He presented himself in a public letter to the Mâcon electors as a progressive independent.[70] In the elections, held on 22 June, the Nord returned Lamartine unopposed with 257 out of the 271 votes cast, and Mâcon-*ville* with 170 votes to 121 for a republican, Claude-Louis Mathieu. With no opponent, support from friends and relatives of Bernard de Coppens, and the triumphant character of his constituency visit, the Nord result must have been more or less expected. But the Mâcon success was both much less certain and probably more desired. As Lamartine explained in a public letter of thanks, Mâcon was his 'patrie dans la patrie', where the electors were also his neighbours and friends.[71] Clearly very undecided between his prior commitments and virtually unanimous election in the Nord, and his desire to represent his *pays natal*, he finally opted for Bergues on 3 December.

Meanwhile, from 12 to 20 July 1834 Lamartine for the first time attended in Mâcon the annual session of Saône-et-Loire's *conseil général*, an elected committee with considerable powers in matters of local administration. Its thirty members included Duréault (who had just failed to gain re-election to the Chamber), Jean-Louis de La Charme (the newly-elected deputy for Mâcon-*arrondissement*), Henri Roch-Dupuys (a childhood friend of Lamartine's),[72] and Pierre-François Foillard (mayor of Romanèche in the Mâcon *arrondissment* and one of Lamartine's future political supporters). Among topics discussed were roads, canals, railways, savings banks, abandoned children, primary education, and prison conditions. Through the *conseil général* Lamartine met the prefect and important local notables, became involved in local government, acquired a local forum for his ideas, and increased his influence and *considération* in the department. Measures voted in the *conseil général* could publicly demonstrate his authority and give practical expression to his ideas.[73] After the *conseil général* the Lamartines moved from Monceau to Saint-Point. During September some English friends of Marianne's came to stay, as well as various other visitors.[74] Besides entertaining his guests, Lamartine chaired a session of the Academy of Mâcon, supervised his grape harvest, finished the *Voyage en Orient*, and continued writing his epic poem *Jocelyn*. At the beginning of December the Lamartines returned to Paris for the new parliamentary session.

The year 1834 set the basic pattern of Lamartine's life throughout his parliamentary career, though there were variations.[75] Between December and June he normally lived in Paris at 82 rue de l'Université. As well as attending the Chamber and writing political articles, he saw numerous people, replied to a voluminous correspondence and worked on his literary projects. Also, in the course of 1834 the Lamartines' Paris home became a centre of social activity, those entertained ranging from Marianne's English relations[76] to prominent writers and politicians.[77] The summer and autumn were spent in the Mâconnais, with the *conseil général*, the Academy of Mâcon, the grape harvest and estate business, private correspondence as well as political and literary writings, and yet more visitors and guests, amply filling

Lamartine's days. This annual cycle of six months in Paris followed by six months in the provinces was common for members of the wealthy *notable* class to which Lamartine belonged. At the same time the division of Lamartine's year between Mâcon and Paris, and his alternating roles of landowner and man of letters, deputy and *notable*, reflected a conflict between the poet and the politician, and between the man of thought and the man of action. Initially he showed considerable hesitancy before embarking on a political career, claiming that he would prefer 'a life of philosophy in the East' to 'a life of politics' in France.[78] Always unenthusiastic about parliamentary elections, he usually denied to his friends any real desire for election, and suggested that he had been elected against his own wishes. Once elected, he would claim that he regretted leaving his literary and rural activities for politics, that political life filled him with ennui, and that he went to the Chamber with 'a repugnance of the heart and soul'.[79] Certainly he did not allow politics to exclude literary work. With his energy and ambition, he was unlikely to leave his proven literary genius unused, and he hoped that his literary publications would bring political and financial rewards.

In the new parliamentary session Lamartine maintained the previous year's pattern of maverick-like political independence, and he eloquently championed a variety of humanitarian causes. Having declined an invitation to attend a meeting of legitimist deputies, on the grounds (so he claimed to Virieu) of conscience and political independence,[80] on 30 December and 4 January he spoke in the Chamber in favour of a political amnesty, covering both the royalist rising in the Vendée and the workers' rising in Lyons. He argued that the Government had no right to judge political opponents who had resorted to armed resistance and insurrection, since in such cases the judges were inevitably the victors and the accused the vanquished, and the result could therefore be only a travesty of justice. Returning to the ideas which he had developed in his article, 'Sur les Caisses d'Epargnes', on 3 February he urged the Government to promote savings banks for the poor; and, doubtless influenced by memories of his duel in Florence in 1826, he recommended on 28 February the imposition of severe penalties on duellists. In a parliamentary speech delivered on 22 April, for the first time he supported the abolition of slavery. In June 1833 he had personally witnessed the realities of slavery while on a visit to the Constantinople slave market.[81] The following year the Société française de l'émancipation de l'esclavage had been founded, and, together with several prominent politicians, Lamartine had joined this Society.[82] He opposed slavery for humanitarian reasons, but he also wanted slave-owners to be compensated. In a debate on the State secret funds (27 April) Lamartine summed up his position and programme. The July Monarchy had a dual mission, the fulfilment of the 1830 Revolution and the prevention of further revolutions. This required the realisation of the ideals of 1789 by extending political rights and social benefits to the greatest possible number. The Government should extend the franchise, reduce the tax burden for the poor, abolish slavery, encourage overseas colonisation, provide State assistance for abandoned children, and reform capital punishment. Such measures would promote social peace and harmony, and the Christian principle of charity.

Lamartine himself described the 1834-35 parliamentary session as boring, probably reflecting his belief that he had made little impression on his fellow deputies. However, in July 1835 an attempted assassination of Louis-Philippe provided an opportunity for Lamartine to play a prominent role in the Chamber. Parliament was hastily recalled, and the Government presented it with a series of repressive measures affecting the newspaper press and the courts. Lamartine vigorously defended the press in two major speeches (21 and 29 August), for the first time totally opposing important government bills. Although the bills were eventually passed with substantial majorities, his speeches made a considerable impression, both inside and outside the Chamber.[83] At the end of August he returned to Mâcon for the annual session of Saône-et-Loire's *conseil général*. Again he spoke with great effect. In particular, he dissuaded the *conseil général* from approving the transfer of the department's *chef-lieu* from Mâcon to Chalon-sur-Saône.

Meanwhile, Lamartine continued to publish important and widely-read poetry and prose. The *Voyage en Orient*, Lamartine's four-volume account of his Middle East travels, first appeared between April and May 1835.[84] Characteristically, it is full of inaccuracies, liberally provided with Romantic descriptive passages, and concerned at length with his personal, religious and political preoccupations. On politics he argues that the destiny of an orator, such as Demosthenes or Mirabeau, is more tempting than that of a philosopher or poet, since an orator enjoys both literary glory and power over the masses. The ideal, however, would be to combine both destinies. Elsewhere he again suggests that there was a new spirit in the contemporary age — 'la raison générale' — which wanted to promote Christian morality and the Revolutionary ideals of equality and fraternity so as to create a more humane and enlightened society. He also explains why he believes France to be a revolutionary country. The achievement of legal equality has produced an equality of expectations among all classes. Freedom of thought and discussion, as established in a free press, has encouraged public debate and controversy. The expansion of popular education has led to an explosion of ideas, while industrialisation has deprived people of their rural innocence and simplicity and created a large oppressed class, the proletariat. The proletariat must enjoy social justice. Private property rights must be recognised, but so too must the rights of humanity.[85] The *Voyage en Orient* sold quite well, though it received a mixed critical reception. However, favourable reviews appeared in *Le National* and *La Quotidienne* (earning the reviewer a letter of thanks from Lamartine, despite the latter's abandonment of legitimism).[86]

Lamartine's long epic poem, *Jocelyn*, was finally published in February 1836. The fictional diary of a Savoyard priest during the Revolutionary period, the poem recounts the improbable story of the priest's relationship with a young orphaned girl whom for a time he looked after. As usual, Lamartine sent presentation copies to friendly literary critics, to fellow writers such as Hugo, Lamennais and Michelet, and to political supporters such as Mme Angebert and Ronot. Much to his delight, *Jocelyn* was generally well received and temporarily solved his financial problems.[87]

In the 1836 parliamentary session Lamartine, as usual, made several important speeches on such topics as the encouragement of free trade (14 April), the reform of capital punishment (18 April), the ending of slavery (25 May), and the adoption of more humane policies in Algeria (11 June). In August Saône-et-Loire's *conseil général* elected him its chairman, a flattering tribute from his fellow *notables*, especially since he had been a member of the *conseil général* for just three years. The chairmanship made him the department's elected spokesman, and gave him considerable influence over the *conseil général*'s proceedings. On returning to Paris in December Lamartine contracted a fever, which kept him from the Chamber. But he was optimistic about his future political prospects, confident that he enjoyed the respect of an increasing number of deputies and the good will of his old patron, Molé, who headed successive ministerial combinations between September 1836 and March 1839. During May 1837 Lamartine made another triumphal tour of his constituency in the Nord.[88] The *conseil général* re-elected him its chairman in August; and doubtless largely due to his influence it voted for the abolition of slavery and the reform of capital punishment.

In the general parliamentary election of 4 November 1837 Lamartine again stood in Bergues. The Minister of the Interior, Montalivet, instructed the prefect of the Nord on 11 September to support Lamartine's re-election. Yet to the electors Lamartine did not present himself as a government candidate. He insisted that he was 'not a party man, nor a man of the Ministry, nor a man of systematic opposition', but 'un homme social', concerned not with the passing prejudices, passions and dynastic hatreds or loyalties of the moment, but with justice, truth and the country's permanent interests. Once more, Lamartine could rely on the friends and connections of the de Coppens family. Moreover, no rival candidate stood, Salvandy (Minister of Public Instruction) having declined to oppose Lamartine. Thus, perhaps not surprisingly, he was re-elected at Bergues almost unanimously by 322 out of 328 votes cast.[89]

Approaches were made to Lamartine to stand in several constituencies in this election, and he finally agreed to stand in both Mâcon-*ville* and Mâcon-*arrondissement*, as well as in Bergues, although multiple candidatures were then unusual. In Mâcon-*ville* his campaign seems to have been run by Aubel, Febvre and Ronot, and in Mâcon-*arrondissement* by Charmont, Dubois and Gacon.[90] *Le Journal de Saône-et-Loire* and the prefect backed him, despite another public declaration from Lamartine that he was not a government supporter. In his manifesto he proclaimed his intention of acting independently of governments and parties so as to achieve reforms by constitutional means and without revolutions.[91] Also, he insisted on standing in both Mâcon constituencies, notwithstanding government concern that this would harm the prospects of the government candidate, La Charme, in Mâcon-*arrondissement*. Molé even wrote a personal letter to Lamartine, asking him not to cause any difficulties. The Government's concern was justified. In Mâcon-*ville* by 171 votes to 160 Lamartine narrowly defeated Mathieu, whom he had previously defeated in June 1834 but who had won the seat in a by-election in January 1835 after Lamartine had opted for Bergues. In Mâcon-*arrondissement* Duréault, who had successfully contested the constituency against Lamartine in June 1832, lost to him by 187 votes to 145, while La Charme received a derisory eight votes.[92]

This triple electoral victory meant that Lamartine had to decide which constituency he would represent. As early as 7 November he indicated that he might opt for one of the Mâcon constituencies. However, although he obviously wanted to represent his *pays natal*, he was clearly reluctant to disappoint his loyal supporters in the Nord and exchange a safe seat for a marginal one. Despite prompting from the sub-prefect of Dunkirk, it was not until 20 December that a newspaper, *La Dunkerquoise*, announced that he had opted for Mâcon-*ville*, which he confirmed in the Chamber on 12 January 1838.[93] Lamartine's triple election must also have impressed Molé's Government. On 28 December Lamartine claimed to Virieu that the Government had offered him a ministry or an embassy, which he had refused so as to remain faithful to his principle of independence and to his legitimist past.[94] In the by-elections in Mâcon-*arrondissement* and Bergues, following his option for Mâcon-*ville*, he certainly behaved as though he wanted to oppose the Government and still retained residual legitimist loyalties. In Mâcon-*arrondissement* he refused to help the government candidate, La Charme, whom the republican Mathieu defeated in February 1838, and in Bergues he supported a legitimist, the comte de Staplande, who was elected in March 1838. This behaviour may, of course, have been at least partly prompted by Lamartine's appreciation of the respective strengths of republicanism in Saône-et-Loire and of legitimism in the Nord (where many of his supporters were legitimists).[95]

Lamartine's triple election doubtless encouraged him in December 1837 to stand as a candidate for the Chamber's presidency, but he gained just twenty-nine votes. However, those twenty-nine votes indicated that a small but significant number of deputies was now prepared to back his candidature for an important parliamentary post. Since 1834 Lamartine had been trying to create in the Chamber a new parliamentary party, which would cut across all current loyalties and which he described as a 'parti social'. The concept of the 'parti social' may have been borrowed from a Fourierist, Jules Lechevalier, who in the *Revue du progrès social* (June 1834) had suggested the formation of a 'parti social', initially including Ballanche, Hugo and Lamartine. At any rate, a small number of deputies gradually emerged as political supporters and parliamentary allies of Lamartine. In December 1834 he claimed that twenty deputies supported him, and in March 1837 he accurately predicted that he could count on twenty-nine votes.[96] Those deputies who can be identified with the 'parti social' were, in many cases, personal friends of Lamartine. This was true, for example, of the comte de Carné, Emile de Girardin, the marquis de La Grange and the comte de Sade. Other deputies, while not constituting a political party or acknowledging Lamartine as their leader, might regularly support his campaigns against capital punishment, the slave trade, the September 1835 press laws, and government foreign and colonial policies. Such campaigns could, and did, attract support from right across the political spectrum. Thus deputies identified with the 'parti social' included the comtes de Morangiès and Staplande (Lamartine's successor at Bergues), who were legitimists; the baron Deshermeaux, Eugène Janvier and Pierre-Chaumont Liadières, who were normally government supporters; Corcelles, Théodore Ducos, Tocqueville, Destutt de Tracy and Jean-Pierre Pagès, who were members of the liberal opposition; and finally Amédée Desjobert, who was associated with the left-wing parliamentary group led by Odilon Barrot. Significantly, the 'parti social' did not attract either republicans, who considered Lamartine to be fundamentally a monarchist and a conservative, or liberal Catholics such as Lamennais or Montalembert, who opposed the increasingly critical attitude adopted by Lamartine after 1835 towards the Roman Catholic Church.[97]

Once asked to define the 'parti social', Lamartine replied: 'Gentlemen, it is not yet a party, it is much more, it is an idea.' This definition amused his listeners, but he was being perfectly serious. 'A man has no value', he wrote in 1843, 'apart from the idea which he represents.'[98] His ideal politician or public figure was someone who personified in himself an idea, a movement of opinion or a political or moral cause, which totally absorbed and committed him. In 1836 he defined the ultimate objective of the 'parti social' as the restoration of human dignity and morality by the progressive application of reason, justice and charity in all civil and political institutions, so that society could become the expression of God's will instead of the tyranny of the strong over the weak.[99] Such ideals and objectives, theoretically admirable, were scarcely compatible with political realities.

At first Lamartine was confident that the 'parti social' would achieve a dominant position within five years.[100] The twenty-nine votes he received as a candidate for the Chamber's presidency in December 1837 demonstrated that his optimism so far lacked foundation. Nevertheless, he persevered in his determination to remain outside the Government and the Chamber's political factions, and to take a personal and progressive stand on politically neutral questions of conscience. During 1838 he again advocated slavery's abolition (15 February) and capital punishment's reform (18 March). Similarly, he gave a speech suggesting ways of improving the treatment of unwanted and abandoned children to the Société de la morale chrétienne (30 April). The problem was serious: over three hundred children were annually abandoned in Saône-et-Loire alone, and public hostels for such children were being closed by government authorities dominated by the *notable* class,

which generally believed in Malthusian doctrines and wanted to economise on public expenditure. Fearing infanticides and probably guilt-
stricken over his own illegitimate children, Lamartine had opposed
hostel closures in Saône-et-Loire's *conseil général* since 1835. His
speech, printed in various forms in 1838, maintained his opposition
and urged continued government support for unwanted and abandoned
children. Also in August 1838 he drew up a questionnaire on the provisions for abandoned children, a copy of which was sent to every
department in France.[101]

Meanwhile, Lamartine had outlined his general philosophy in 'Le
Livre Primitif', part of another epic poem, *La Chute d'un Ange*, which
was first published on 9 May 1838. 'Le Livre Primitif' contains a series
of injunctions: Man should avoid shedding blood, obey his father,
maintain a rural existence, help those in need, and live in harmony with
his neighbours. Also on 9 May Lamartine discussed in parliament what
was for him a new subject, railway construction. The inadequacies of
Burgundy's road and water transport systems caused many local *notables*, particularly those involved in the wine industry, to support the
construction of railways. Besides such practical considerations, Lamartine, attracted by the Saint-Simonian enthusiasm for public works,
believed in progress, 'the poetry of railways', and the civilising influence
of improved communications.[102] After 1838 he became an enthusiastic
supporter of railways, and of the construction of main railway lines
under State direction. However, like most Burgundy *notables*, he did
not personally invest in railway companies, which gained their capital
principally from Paris bankers and English sources. Thus his promotion
of railways ironically served capitalist interests he disliked, besides
encouraging urbanisation and industrialisation, phenomena he viewed
with concern.

Lamartine now led the active social life of an important deputy.
On 14 March 1838 he dined with General Hoche's widow together with
Barante, Castellane, Cousin, Dupin, Mignet, Thiers, and Villemain;
with other prominent politicians such as Berryer, Dufaure, Guizot,
Sauzet and Thiers, on 17 April he attended a dinner in honour of Lord
Brougham; and he met his old patrons Barante, Molé, Mounier and
Sainte-Aulaire at a dinner given by Pasquier on 21 May.[103] Of course,
the Sainte-Aulaires resented Lamartine's desertion of legitimism,[104]
as did several of his oldest friends including Vignet and his family,[105]
Xavier de Maistre[106] and even Virieu,[107] so that his relationships with
them became more distant. A number of his former acquaintances
also disliked his politics, such as Charles Nodier, whose *salon* in the

Arsenal Library he had frequented around 1830, and Sainte-Beuve, who scarcely ever visited him after 1839.[108] Two of his former patrons, the marquises de Montcalm and de Raigecourt, had died in the 1832 cholera epidemic. There remained, however, a circle of old friends whom he saw regularly in Paris, including Mme Sophie Gay and her daughter Delphine de Girardin, Lainé, the de La Granges, Aimé Martin, and the comte de Sade. Having effected the transition from client to patron, Lamartine now had his own Paris *salon* — Marianne normally received guests on Wednesdays and Saturdays. Those entertained included a host of politicians, writers and journalists, as well as distinguished foreigners such as Franz Liszt (the composer and pianist) and Henry Reeve (future editor of *The Edinburgh Review*).[109] When Delphine de Girardin once discussed famous Paris *salons*, she mentioned those of Mme de Lamartine, Mme Récamier and Mme Victor Hugo.[110] Paris society during the July Monarchy was still sufficiently small for everybody to know practically everybody else, and nearly all those of importance in the capital's political, intellectual or cultural life entered Lamartine's residence at 82 rue de l'Université. To cite just two examples, Delphine de Girardin described a 'gathering of celebrities at Madame de Lamartine's' on 5 March 1841 attended by Guizot, Victor Hugo, Marshal Soult, Horace Vernet, Balzac, David, and the baron Charles Dupin; and in the spring of 1847 Henri de Lacretelle met Chateaubriand, Béranger and Lamennais at Lamartine's Paris *salon*.[111]

Many of Lamartine's Parisian social contacts were *salon* acquaintances rather than close personal friends. Only those friends whom he particularly liked or specially wished to cultivate were normally invited to Monceau or Saint-Point.[112] Also invited were members of his extended family and various English relations of Marianne. He regularly entertained members of the Academy of Mâcon and his local political supporters; and at the end of every summer he usually received his *conseil général* colleagues at Monceau, where he also welcomed members of the local gentry. Occasionally, too, some passing grandee, such as the baron Stürmer (Austrian ambassador at Constantinople) or the Duchess of Sutherland, visited him.[113] In addition, Lamartine offered his assistance to, and corresponded with, a large number of people, many of whom scarcely emerge from their relative obscurity.[114] Authors often sent him complimentary copies of their publications, for which they invariably received a gracious letter of thanks;[115] and, like George Sand and Eugène Sue, he patronised several worker poets, particularly Jean Reboul[116] and two women, Reine Garde and Antoinette Quarré. Such patronage of working-class writers, who were a phenomenon of July Monarchy France, flatteringly demonstrated his importance and influence, and accorded with his views on popular literature.

After spending the summer of 1838 in his usual manner — entertaining innumerable guests, worrying about money and his parliamentary career — Lamartine returned to Paris to find himself embroiled in a major political crisis. Towards the end of 1838 an opposition coalition against the Molé Government was formed by Thiers, whom Molé had succeeded in August 1836, Guizot, who had resigned from Molé's Government in April 1837, and Odilon Barrot, leader of the so-called dynastic Left in the Chamber of Deputies. This coalition made a determined attempt to overthrow Molé during the debate on the speech from the throne in January 1839. This alarmed Lamartine, who supported Molé's peaceful foreign policy and objected to the coalition's backing of Belgium's retention of the territories of Limbourg and Luxembourg. (The London Treaty of 1831 had ceded these to Holland, and Britain and Holland were now pressing Belgium to comply with the terms of the 1831 Treaty.) Fearing the coalition might involve France in a serious international conflict,[117] Lamartine spoke in the Government's defence on 10 and 19 January. Apart from Molé, he was the only important orator on the Government's side in this debate. Molé acknowledges that Lamartine spontaneously offered his assistance, and exerted himself unreservedly on the Government's behalf, while Guizot admits that the Government had in Lamartine a brilliant ally.[118]

At the end of the debate on 19 January 1839 the speech from the throne was finally carried by 221 votes to 208. Molé considered this majority insufficient and obtained a dissolution. About 23 February Lamartine returned to Mâcon for the elections, though he had warned Ronot that he would not do any campaigning.[119] He did send a manifesto to his former constituents in the Nord, arguing that the opposition coalition threatened parliamentary government in France and European peace.[120] On 3 March he was re-elected in Mâcon-*ville* by 192 votes against 123 for Mathieu, who, however, again defeated La Charme in Mâcon-*arrondissement*. At Bergues the comte Roger defeated Lamartine by 186 votes to 140, but many electors there must have assumed Lamartine's success in, and preference for, Mâcon. A dinner was held in Mâcon for two hundred guests to celebrate Lamartine's re-election (18 March). Meanwhile Molé had resigned on 8 March, because of the electoral success of opposition candidates.

Lamartine regarded himself as the leader of the 221 deputies who had voted for Molé and against the opposition coalition, though he emphasised that he was abandoning his political independence only for a limited period and in order to achieve a definite objective.[121] He was also delighted with his apparent popularity and political importance, believing that he alone had prevented war over Belgium.[122] Certainly he had been one of the principal defenders of Molé's Government, and he undoubtedly enjoyed a brief moment of popularity.[123] But, as Guizot points out,[124] his speeches were scarcely reassuring for government supporters. On 10 January 1839 he asked his famous question, 'Is France a nation which is bored?' He went on to proclaim that the July Monarchy's mission was to achieve in the social sphere what 1789 had achieved in the political.[125] After the Chambers had reassembled he made a similar speech on 23 April. Rejecting what he described as Guizot's 'fundamental theory', namely the preponderance of the middle classes, he referred with compassion to 'these miserable masses of workers, thrown out of the workshop onto the street'.[126] Such ideas and attitudes were totally unacceptable to the vast majority of deputies: they registered their opinion by giving Lamartine just five votes when he again stood for the Chamber's presidency on 14 May 1839.

After the ministerial crisis following Molé's resignation, a new government under Marshal Soult was eventually formed on 12 May 1839. This included Lamartine's old friend, Villemain, but excluded Guizot, Thiers and Odilon Barrot. During May and June Lamartine suffered severely from one of his periodic bouts of ill-health.[127] Nevertheless, he did respond to the unsuccessful Paris rising organised by the Society of the Seasons on 12 May. The day after the rising he gave thanks to God for having protected France from the anarchy threatened by barbaric acts worthy of savages. Despite his strong views about the rising he still maintained his opposition to capital punishment for what might be considered political crimes,[128] and the following month he even wrote a letter to the Keeper of the Seals opposing capital punishment for Barbès and his fellow conspirators in the Society of the Seasons.[129] By 1 July Lamartine had sufficiently recovered to give two speeches in the Chamber on the Middle East situation. As in his 1834 maiden speech, he emphasised the Turkish Empire's decline and the need for a congress of European Powers to divide up the Turkish Empire into spheres of influence. He also urged a more active French role in the Eastern Mediterranean. France should try to contain Russia by supporting Austria, and Britain by supporting the Turkish Sultan rather than the rebellious ruler of Egypt, Mehemet Ali. To Lamartine's delight, the speeches were well received by politicians and the press.[130] Before the end of the session he again spoke on the construction of railways (6 July) and the treatment of orphans and abandoned children (15 July). In August he was re-elected chairman of the *conseil général*, while in September he was offered a peerage, which he declined.[131] Instead he continued his attempt to discredit the principles of Guizot and reform under his own leadership the 221 supporters of Molé, in a series of four articles published in *La Presse* and *Le Journal de Saône-et-Loire* during November and December 1839.[132]

By the beginning of 1840 Lamartine's political importance was clearly considerable. But his determination not to accept a government post handicapped him, as did his poor health and lack of money. In February 1840 Soult was defeated in the Chamber over the size of the government grant to be awarded to Louis-Philippe's son, the duc de Nemours. Soult resigned, and on 1 March Thiers was appointed *président du conseil* and Minister of Foreign Affairs. Lamartine disliked Thiers as one of the organisers of an unprincipled and irresponsible attack on Molé the previous year. He also believed that Thiers did not enjoy majority support in the Chambers, and would resort to demogogic means to stay in power. His first major clash with Thiers was over a government proposal to remove Napoleon's remains from St Helena for reburial in Paris at the Invalides. He severely criticised Napoleon in a parliamentary speech on 26 May, arguing that in France Napoleon had destroyed liberty, established a personal dictatorship and created a new hierarchical élite, while in Europe his wars of aggression and foreign conquests had made the Revolution's ideals thoroughly unpopular. One of Lamartine's great oratorical set pieces on a highly controversial and sensitive subject, it won him congratulatory notes from Molé and Villemain,[133] and praise from the conservative press, which had reservations about the popular enthusiasm for Napoleon the war-hero.

In the summer of 1840 Lamartine had the opportunity to impress the public with his views on French government policy and the Middle East. During the previous summer fighting had broken out in Syria between the forces of Mehemet Ali, the ruler of Egypt, and those of the Turkish Sultan. Thiers decided to support Mehemet Ali in his revolt against Turkey so as to increase French influence in Egypt and Syria, but on 14 July 1840 Russia, Austria, Britain, Prussia and Turkey issued an ultimatum to Mehemet Ali calling on him to cease hostilities or face military intervention. Thiers declared that France would not tolerate the use of force by other European Powers against Mehemet

Ali, and began to make preparations for war. The prospect of Thiers involving France in a European war over the Middle East appalled Lamartine. Although distracted by his father's last illness and death (30 August), he attacked the Government's foreign policy in four articles, published first in *La Presse* and *Le Journal de Saône-et-Loire* and later in pamphlet form.[134] Again he suggested the establishment of spheres of influence in the Turkish Empire for Russia, Austria, France and Britain. French support for Mehemet Ali would, he argued, disrupt Anglo-French relations, encourage the formation of a new coalition of European Powers against France, and lead either to a European war or to national humiliation. The articles were widely reproduced by the provincial press and favourably received, particularly by conservatives who feared war would bring economic dislocation and domestic revolution. The development of a popular war fever in Paris and another attempt to assassinate Louis-Philippe (15 October) confirmed those fears for the King and public opinion generally, while abroad the collapse of Mehemet Ali's power in Egypt and a successful British bombardment of Beirut undermined the policy of Thiers. In this crisis situation the Chambers were summoned to meet on 28 October for an extraordinary session. On 20 October Thiers presented Louis-Philippe with the Government's draft for the King's speech from the throne. Louis-Philippe rejected it and, following a day's discussions, Thiers and his government colleagues resigned. After a week of hectic cabinet-making, a new government was formed on 29 October including Marshal Soult (President), Guizot (Foreign Affairs), Duchâtel (Interior) and Villemain (Public Instruction). The Soult-Guizot Government survived with a changing membership until February 1848.

Having returned to Paris for the extraordinary parliamentary session, Lamartine on 23 October reported to his sister, Mme de Cessiat, that he had been offered various government posts, including the Ministry of Foreign Affairs, and that he had spent the morning with Marshal Soult. No firm decisions about the Government's composition were, however, to be made until after Guizot's return from London, where he had been French ambassador since February. But Lamartine thought that he would not join a government which included members of the coalition against Molé. Instead, through personal inclination and desire to maintain his political standing, he would prefer to remain a backbencher independently supporting the new government. Subsequently he was more ambivalent, claiming that he would accept either the Interior or Foreign Affairs, partly out of a sense of duty and partly to implement his new liberal ideas.[135] During the morning of 28 October Villemain tried to persuade him to accept a junior ministry. Lamartine replied that to occupy a position subordinate to Guizot would undermine his reputation among his own supporters, but he would consider an important ministry, such as the Interior. This was more than either Louis-Philippe or Guizot was prepared to offer. Guizot (who had arrived in Paris on 26 October), and possibly Sainte-Aulaire, then tried to interest him in becoming French ambassador at London or Vienna. Again Lamartine gave a qualified refusal, saying that he would accept an extraordinary diplomatic mission, such as the French representative at some European congress, but not a permanent diplomatic post. The latter would take him out of parliament, destroy his political influence, lay himself open to accusations of ambition, and make him Louis-Philippe's personal representative.[136] Lamartine should not have been surprised at his exclusion from the Soult-Guizot Government: he was no friend of Guizot or Louis-Philippe,[137] nor had he attempted to cultivate them; he could not provide a government with a significant bloc of parliamentary supporters; and, despite his complete ministerial inexperience, he had limited his declared ambition to the two most important ministries. Yet in private letters he blamed his exclusion on Molé's 221 former supporters, who had allegedly opposed his appointment on the grounds of his administrative ineptitude and dangerous liberalism.[138]

For a short period Lamartine supported the Soult-Guizot Government. In the Chamber he defended the Government's Middle East policy (1 December); and he reportedly refused to ally with a group of opposition deputies who had become disenchanted with Thiers.[139] Guizot's offers of an embassy were even renewed.[140] But the Soult-Guizot Government decided to adopt a programme, initiated in November 1830 and revived by Thiers in September 1840, for the construction of defensive fortifications around Paris. Liberals tended to favour the project because it provided employment, but vigorous opposition came from radicals (fearing a threat to Parisian liberties), conservatives (disliking an unnecessary extravagance) and legitimists (unwilling to enhance the power of Paris). On 12 January 1841 Louis-Philippe gave Lamartine a long audience, presumably to dissuade him from opposing the fortifications.[141] He was unsuccessful. Nine days later Lamartine for the first time attacked the fortifications in a parliamentary speech. He argued that France should not defend herself behind ditches, bastions and walls, but in open battlefields as far as possible from population centres; that the French army fought best when it enjoyed mobility of action; that neither the army nor the Government could function satisfactorily if besieged and in the midst of a starving population; that a fortified Paris would be a potential danger to civil liberty, and would make possible the capital's domination of France; that the plan threatened to involve the civilian population of Paris in hostilities; and that the whole scheme was futile, since a city of one and a half million inhabitants could not be supplied with food during a siege. In a second speech on 28 January he suggested that authority in a siege situation would eventually pass to the most extreme and violent political groups. These pragmatic arguments could appeal to virtually all shades of political opinion; and they predicted with remarkable accuracy developments during the Franco-Prussian War and the Paris Commune of 1871.

During the rest of the 1841 parliamentary session Lamartine contributed little, except on the revision of the copyright laws. He was appointed chairman of the committee formed to draft a bill. In *La Presse* and in his report on the committee's findings (13, 23 and 30 March) he recommended that copyright laws should apply to literary works for a fifty-year period after the author's death, which became a provision of the new law.[142] By the beginning of May Lamartine was at Monceau, where he composed 'La Marseillaise de la Paix', a plea for international peace in response to a chauvinistic poem by a German, Nikolaus Becker. Again through a poem (published in the *Revue des Deux Mondes*, 1 June 1841), Lamartine sought to exercise political influence on public opinion. After chairing the *conseil général* he wrote letters to Guizot, Duchâtel and Villemain as part of a campaign, ultimately successful, for the establishment of a royal college (as *lycées* were then called) at Mâcon.[143] He had taken a practical interest in education as early as November 1828, when he had founded a school for twenty-four girls at Montculot;[144] and he remained a supporter of female education, while believing that girls should be prepared for domestic roles as wives and mothers.[145] In general, he wanted an educational system not only free and State controlled, but also wholly independent of the Roman Catholic Church. Similarly, he argued for the gradual severance of Church-State ties, complete freedom of conscience in religious matters, and reliance by religious organisations solely on voluntary contributions. Doubtless partly due to his influence, Saône-et-Loire's *conseil général* progressively abolished its grants to the bishopric of Autun.[146]

On 28 December 1841 another election was held for the Chamber's presidency. To Emile de Girardin Lamartine on 25 November had denied wanting the presidency: it was a neutral position, whereas he liked to be committed; it offered the semblance, not the substance, of political power; and he might compromise his future political prospects by making an ill-received ruling from the chair. However, he was persuaded to stand, principally by Molé.[147] On 11 December *La Presse* suggested that he was a candidate only so as not to let down his political friends. Given this apparent reluctance and government opposition his chances were poor, despite backing from *La Presse* and last-minute support from the Thiers faction.[148] In fact the government candidate, Sauzet, was re-elected with 193 votes, Lamartine gained 64 and Odilon Barrot 45. Lamartine had hoped to divide the centre, but nearly all his votes came from legitimist or opposition deputies. This third defeat he regarded as a personal humiliation and an example of the ingratitude of politicians.[149] It was undoubtedly an important factor in his political development, and increasing association with the parliamentary opposition to the Soult-Guizot Government.[150]

Although unsuccessful for the third time in an election for the presidency of the Chamber, Lamartine had attracted a respectable number of votes and he had improved on his performances of December 1837 (twenty-nine votes) and May 1839 (just five votes). In January 1842 Guizot, anxious to cultivate a deputy as influential as Lamartine, thought it important for him to be seen in Mme de Lamartine's *salon*.[151] But on 12 February Lamartine informed his sister, Mme de Cessiat, that he was about to speak 'en homme de grande opposition'.[152] In the Chamber three days later he fulfilled this promise by attacking Guizot's refusal to extend the parliamentary franchise, and by warning that he would oppose the Government if it persisted in its immobilism. Yet, after what Rémusat describes as one of his most remarkable speeches,[153] Lamartine, as chairman of an important committee, co-operated with the Government over railway legislation. Similarly, he defended the Government's adherence to a treaty authorising the British navy to search French ships suspected of involvement in the slave trade (20 May). Thus, perhaps not surprisingly, Guizot continued to try to win him over by offering an embassy (3 June).[154] In the general parliamentary election of 9 July Lamartine was comfortably re-elected in Mâcon-*ville* with 245 of the 311 votes cast. Two days later he received a government offer of the Chamber's presidency, which he refused.[155]

The duc d'Orléans, Louis-Philippe's eldest son and heir to the throne, died after a riding accident on 13 July 1842. The committee formed by the Chamber of Deputies to draw up an address of condolences to the

King delegated the task to Lamartine. His draft, unanimously accepted, included the telling sentence: 'You have lost a son; France has lost a reign'.[156] Privately Lamartine indicated his real feelings: 'What little remained of the monarchy has fallen with this fine young man. The nation must assume the power to govern itself.'[157] During August the Chamber debated the arrangements for a regency in the event of Louis-Philippe dying before the majority of the duc-d'Orléans's elder son. In a major speech on 18 August Lamartine argued in favour of an elected regent and against the exclusion of the duchesse d'Orléans, whereas the King and the Government wanted on the grounds of primogeniture to have designated as prospective regent the duc de Nemours, a reputed conservative. A large majority of deputies voted for the Government's regency bill on 20 August. On the regency bill Lamartine therefore broke with the Government and the conservative majority to align with the left-wing opposition. The *Revue des Deux Mondes* prophetically commented on 1 September, 'M. de Lamartine is moving towards the Left.'

At the end of August Lamartine returned to Mâcon, where he was soon immersed in local affairs. His political position in Mâcon was now impregnable. Besides representing Mâcon in the Chamber and *conseil général*, he had served as lieutenant-colonel of its National Guard, been a member of its *conseil municipal* since 1840, joined its Paris-based *comité viticole*, and was about to be re-elected president of its Academy. Over the years he had formed in his constituency a group of devoted, energetic and influential supporters – Aubel, Dubois, Febvre, Foillard, Gacon, Ronot, and a new recruit, Guigue de Champvans.[158] They organised his electoral campaigns, publicised his speeches and articles, and supported him in various local forums. In return he looked after their interests by, for example, persuading the Government to make Ronot a *juge de paix* in 1839, Champvans an *attaché* in Soult's private office in 1840, and Febvre a *conseiller de préfecture* in 1841.[159] Nor were Mâcon's interests neglected. In 1835 he helped prevent the department's *chef-lieu* from being transferred to Chalon-sur-Saône. During the severe winter of 1837-38 he paid for the free distribution of fire-wood to indigent Mâcon families. After the Saône's flooding in November 1840 he secured substantial government relief for the town.[160] Following disturbances in Mâcon on 9 September 1841 he sent a petition to the King, which ensured lenient treatment for the offenders and earned him favourable local press comment.[161] For several years he was the driving force behind the establishment at Mâcon of a royal college, finally opened in September 1843. As a member of the relevant parliamentary committee, he was to see in 1844 that the Paris-Lyons railway line passed through Mâcon. Consequently, he was elected to the Chamber and *conseil général* with increasingly more substantial majorities. In September 1842 the *conseil général* overwhelmingly elected him its chairman with seventeen out of nineteen votes.

Lamartine's entrenched position in Mâcon made government support unnecessary and an independent or opposition line quite feasible. Saône-et-Loire, and particularly Chalon-sur-Saône, possessed a strong left-wing tradition. After 1830 significant republican opposition to the July Monarchy developed. In the July 1842 general election, of the six deputies elected in the department besides Lamartine, four belonged, in the contemporary phrase, to the 'Opposition de Gauche prononcée' (Chapuys-Montlaville, Lacroix, Mathieu and Thiard). Lamartine's radical stand on various issues, such as the parliamentary franchise, won him left-wing, republican and anti-government support, as he himself fully appreciated. 'Here the *entire* Left is for me', he wrote from Monceau on 10 October 1841.[162] At the same time his radicalism did not lose him support, thanks to his personal prestige as poet and parliamentarian, his local popularity and influence, and his good relations with local legitimists and conservatives – many of whom remained personal friends, and most of whom respected his status as a large landowner, his defence of local interests, and his pacifism during the crisis of 1840. Thus the political situation in Mâcon both permitted and encouraged his evolution towards the Left.

Lamartine's evolution towards the Left had its parallel in his religious development, for he now rejected the doctrinal and temporal claims of the Roman Catholic Church. His radical and free-thinking friend, Dargaud, probably exercised an important influence on him at this time. The deaths of his royalist father (30 August 1840), and of the conservative Vignet (15 July 1837) and Virieu (7 April 1841), may have removed personal restraints on his thought and action. More important were his own restlessness, ennui, personal ambition and political independence. No doubt these could never have been satisfied if he had remained among the Government's conservative supporters, or even if he had been given a senior ministerial appointment. By the autumn of 1842 all that Guizot was prepared to offer in the way of place and patronage had already been declined, while Lamartine's dislike of the policies and composition of successive governments had greatly intensified. He had little respect for the Government's foreign policies, and on internal affairs wrote that the Government's total neglect of the welfare of the masses was becoming increasingly evident. The institutions of July 1830 had degenerated into rule by an oligarchy, and France was advancing towards the despotism of corruption.[163] As for the leading politicians, Lamartine was thoroughly disillusioned by the unprincipled coalition of Guizot, Thiers and Odilon Barrot against Molé, and by their subsequent efforts to gain political power.[164]

It was not just one government policy, but nearly all government policies, that were at fault. It was not just one minister or former minister who was unsatisfactory, they were nearly all equally so. On 5 October 1842 Lamartine privately described Guizot, Molé, Thiers, Passy and Dufaure, all of whom (despite their political differences) had supported the regency bill designating Nemours, as 'five ways of saying the same word'. The following month he tried to encourage La Grange to join the opposition: 'You do not know what it is to be an aristocrat like yourself, holding out your hand to a powerless democracy lying fallen in the ditch! It is the most beautiful role from the time of Rome to Mirabeau.'[165] An aristocrat acting this role not only generously fought for the interests of others: he was also ensuring that the popular movement avoided any excesses or extremism in the future.[166] Always in search of a role, by the autumn of 1842 Lamartine had at last found one. He would conduct a 'great and generous opposition' for four or five years, after which France would turn to him as a final resource. Thus he would bring about 'the insurrection of boredom'.[167]

In a parliamentary speech on 27 January 1843 Lamartine publicly announced that he was joining the left-wing opposition. He blamed the problems and dangers confronting France not simply on the current Government, but on the nation's entire political system. It was the system which was responsible for the September press laws, the fortifications of Paris, the restricted parliamentary franchise, the diplomatic isolation of France, and the widespread corruption in politics. This final break with the conservative deputies who had supported Molé was 'a parliamentary event'.[168] Lamartine claimed that he was inundated with letters – over three hundred in three days – all fanatically enthusiastic, apart from a few abusive anonymous notes.[169] Representative of *notable* opinion were the marquis de Custine, sarcastically commenting, 'Now M. de Lamartine has become the hope of the revolution', and Cuvillier-Fleury (literary editor of *Le Journal des Débats*), observing that Lamartine had taken leave of his senses.[170] Since the autumn of 1842 Lamartine had been warning colleagues that he intended to join the left-wing opposition.[171] Consequently his declaration was not a surprise, but its timing and totality were. Over one of the main current issues, the right of British warships to search French ships suspected of involvement in the slave trade, Lamartine supported the Government against left-wing opposition (which led Dupin to remark that Lamartine was unafraid of the right of search because in January 1843 he had burnt his boats). Moreover, he had attacked not just the Soult-Guizot Government, but the July Monarchy's entire political system. Such a condemnation came rather strangely from a recent self-styled leader of the parliamentary conservatives, and from someone apparently reconciled to the July Monarchy for over twelve years. The seriousness of Lamartine's action was nevertheless recognised. Because of his idiosyncratic political behaviour, it was thought that in the Chamber little had been lost by the conservatives or gained by the left-wing opposition. Yet outside the Chamber his immense personal prestige would reinforce the Left; anyone dissatisfied, for whatever reason, with the July Monarchy's policies and institutions, could turn to him; and his political ambitions might now be less restricted and take more dangerous forms.[172] Thus conservatives feared that he would undermine France's parliamentary system, while his future political role seemed increasingly unpredictable and potentially ominous. Alexander Humboldt compared him to a comet, the orbit of which has still to be calculated.[173]

As Lamartine's speech of 27 January 1843 indicates, his reasons for joining the left-wing opposition were mainly ideological, but, as usual, his ideological position was complex. The prospect of popular anarchy always alarmed Lamartine. His private correspondence in 1830 reveals that he shared the traditional fears and prejudices of the *notables* and property-owning classes. He described 'la force populaire' as more terrible even than 'la force tyrannique'; and he warned Aimé Martin not to stir up the unenlightened proletarian masses, for there he would find prejudice, stupidity, idleness, cruelty and a brutal jealousy of all social superiority.[174] To the Dunkirk electors in June 1831 he insisted that order was his party's primary objective, arguing that order is to liberty what organisation is to life, 'anarchy is death'.[175] Only the government can guarantee order. For better or worse, Lamartine told his fellow deputies on 13 March 1834, the government represents something more vital even than liberty — public peace and order, security of life and property, safety in the streets and in the home. Hence he maintained in the Chamber on 13 May 1834 that 'everything is legitimate against anarchy'.[176]

However, after July 1830 Lamartine differed from most of his fellow *notables* in his idiosyncratic attitude towards the new régime. Although he always claimed to be attached by sentiment to the Bourbon dynasty, he did not join the legitimist emigration into the interior. Nor did he become an Orleanist. While he maintained that the July Monarchy deserved his loyalty, because it supported order against anarchy and because it seemed to promise a new liberal era for France, he nevertheless resigned from the diplomatic corps and, although clearly tempted, never subsequently served Louis-Philippe. At the same time the popular violence accompanying the July Revolution, the severe mortality rates caused by the 1832 cholera epidemic, and the risings in Paris and Lyons of 1832 and 1834, convinced him that strong government, the maintenance of law and order, and the introduction of a more liberal constitution, were not alone sufficient to cope with the danger of popular violence and with contemporary social and economic problems. To defend the institutions of the family and private property, further reforms were necessary. For these pragmatic reasons, Lamartine warned his fellow deputies in 1835 that 'the question of the working class will make the most terrible explosion in contemporary society, if society and governments fail to understand and resolve it'.[177]

In addition to this fear of popular violence and social upheaval, Lamartine's political ideology was inspired by idealism, derived at first from the liberal Catholicism associated with *L'Avenir*, and then, increasingly, from his own interpretation of the principles of the Revolution of 1789, though he would have denied any fundamental clash between the two. While *Sur la politique rationnelle* (1831) clearly betrays the influence of *L'Avenir*'s liberal Catholicism, as early as October 1830 Lamartine wrote to Virieu that the principles of the Revolution of 1789 were among the great and fruitful ideas which periodically renewed the form of human society.[178] He did, however, condemn the revolutionary violence of 1789, and in March 1834 he carefully distinguished between 'the moral, generous and national revolution of 1789' and 'the brutal, demagogic and sanguinary revolution of 1793'.[179] Thus, while firmly condemning popular violence and Jacobin excesses, he believed in the revolutionary principles of 1789 and in their continuing relevance for the development of France. The July Revolution was not limited to the Bourbon dynasty's overthrow and to Louis-Philippe's enthronement. It was a movement with a mission and an idea. The mission was to take up the work begun in 1789. The idea he defined in January 1839 as 'the idea of the masses, the organisation and moralisation of the people, in the widest sense of the term'.[180] Through legislation the July Monarchy should gradually introduce rights, morality and proper organisation into the lives of the mass of the people. The great principles of democracy, charity and fraternity, as derived from Christianity and reaffirmed during the Revolution of 1789, should become a universal feature of everyday life. In this way the July Monarchy would itself carry out a revolution, and thereby prevent new and threatening revolutions in the future. Thus Lamartine sought to avoid revolutionary violence and fundamental economic and social change with moral, political and humanitarian reforms.

By 1843 Lamartine's reform campaigns had largely failed. Not surprisingly, this influenced his views as to how change and progress could be achieved within the existing political system. A letter written on 12 April 1840 perhaps best sums up his initial position: 'My political motto has always been: extremely liberal policies carried out by extremely strong governments, so as to serve the interests and not the passions of the people'.[181] However, in Lamartine's opinion, Louis-Philippe had abandoned his role as the heir to a great revolutionary tradition so that royal and ministerial resistance to any major reform blocked the constitutional processes for change. Consequently the July Monarchy, rather than being an effective bulwark against anarchy and an agent of liberal reform, had become a promoter of popular violence and social upheaval and an obstacle to any significant progress. Hence he had finally ceased being an independent liberal generally supporting the government and had instead joined the left-wing opposition.

In joining the left-wing opposition Lamartine had not yet quite become, in the marquis de Custine's phrase, 'the hope of the revolution'. Besides basically supporting the social and economic *status quo*, in political terms he was far from being a committed revolutionary. Since Lamartine's revolutionary idealism took the form of a commitment to revolutionary principles rather than to revolutionary action, he hoped that the former could be realised without the latter. 'What is France?' Lamartine asked in December 1839. 'France is a country which has made its revolution and which does not want to make another.'[182] 'I am not, as you know, the partisan of revolutions', he told his parliamentary colleagues on 18 August 1842.[183] For the individual there were two ways of effecting change, Lamartine observed in 1836, by revolutions or by proselytising. No honest man would willingly accept the terrible responsibilities of encouraging a revolution; and revolutions were of little purpose unless the time was ripe. Lamartine wanted to see the government itself in a state of regular and permanent revolution. In this way, change could be achieved without any loss or destruction.[184] Yet the Guizot Government had manifestly no intention of establishing a permanent revolution; and Lamartine always admitted that revolutions were sometimes both necessary and desirable. 'I know', he declared in March 1837, 'that there are popular revolutions which fatal acts of aggression unfortunately make necessary', though he added that France wanted change through legislative reform rather than through revolutionary violence.[185] Thus, although revolutionary idealism partly inspired his political ideology, although he admitted that revolutions might be necessary and desirable, and although he now rejected the entire political system of the July Monarchy, his fear of popular anarchy and his social and economic conservatism held him back. Moreover, he was still isolated from the French Left. However, between 1843 and February 1848 he developed a new relationship with the French Left, a relationship to which he brought his idiosyncratic mixture of fear of popular violence combined with revolutionary idealism, and of social and economic conservatism combined with Christian humanitarianism.

Notes

1. *Correspondance de la marquise de Montcalm*, p. 285; H. Cochin, *Lamartine et la Flandre* (Paris, 1912), pp. 45-9.

2. *Lettres à Lamartine*, p. 127; *Correspondance générale*, I, pp. 105 and 106.

3. See E. Drouot, *Un Chapitre de la vie de Lamartine, Montculot-Urcy* (Paris, 1932).

4. U. Mengin, *Les Manuscrits d'Antoir, l'ami de Lamartine* (Paris, 1925), p. 126. On Lamartine's relations with Joseph Antoir (a colleague at the French legation in Florence) see also U. Mengin, 'Lamartine à Florence (1825-1828), d'après des documents inédits', *Annales de l'université de Grenoble*, Section lettres-droit, II, no. 1, 1er trimestre 1925, pp. 41-84.

5. *Correspondance générale*, I, pp. 144, 147 and 149.

6. See L. Fam, *Lamartine. Voyage en Orient* (Paris, 1960), appendix XII, p. 506.

7. See Cochin, *Lamartine et la Flandre*, pp. 72-9, 84-6 and 392-6; Séché, *Les Amitiés de Lamartine*, pp. 173-395, and 'Lamartine candidat à la députation en 1831', *Le Temps*, 24 July 1911, pp. 4-5.

8. See A. N., F^{1b} I 157 [5]; Drouot, *Un Chapitre de la vie de Lamartine*, pp. 59-67.

9. See F. Caussy, 'Les Débuts politiques de Lamartine', *Mercure de France*, 16 November and 1 December 1908, pp. 252-3, 460-8; L. Séché, 'Plages et villes d'eaux romantiques. Hyères-Lamartine, Michelet', *Revue des français*, 10 May 1914, pp. 208-10; 'Lamartine à Hyères: ses débuts politiques dans le Var', *Bulletin de la société des amis du Vieux Toulon*, no. 62-3, 3-4 trimestre 1939, pp. 134-45.

10. See L. de Contenson, 'Quelques lettres de Lamartine', *Revue d'histoire diplomatique*, October-December 1935, pp. 517-25.

11. See A. N., F^{1b} I 172^{16}. Cf. L. E. Arnault, *Oeuvres dramatiques*, 3 vols. (Paris, 1865-67), III, pp. 299-313; P. Bert, *Lamartine 'homme social': Son Action départementale* (Paris, 1924), pp. 16-42; Guillemin, *Connaissance de Lamartine*, pp. 303-8.

12. See A. N., F^{1b} I 160^4.

13. *Correspondance générale*, I, pp. 139-42.

14. *Mémoires politiques* in *Oeuvres complètes de Lamartine*, XXXVIII, pp. 286-9.

15. *Correspondance générale*, I, pp. 139-68; A. Finot, 'Echecs électoraux de Lamartine', *Le Correspondant*, 25 April-10 May 1936, pp. 183-94; *Mercure de France*, 16 November and 1 December 1908, pp. 249-61, 453-68.

16. *Oeuvres poétiques complètes*, pp. 507-10.

17. Carné, *Souvenirs*, p. 262.

18. *Revue européenne*, 15 October 1831, pp. 125-43. Cf. *Correspondance générale*, I, pp. 200-1, 203-4. In 1848 the pamphlet was reprinted in Brussels by J. B. de Mortier with the title, *De la politique rationnelle*, and in London (in English) by H. G. Clarke with the title, *The Polity of Reason*.

19. *Correspondance générale*, I, p. 201; J. des Cognets, *La Vie intérieure de Lamartine* (Paris, 1913), pp. 182 and 187.

20. See E. Quinet, *Correspondance*, 2 vols. (Paris, 1876), II, pp. 122, 130, 150 and 198; des Cognets, *La Vie intérieure de Lamartine*, pp. 13-32; H.-L. Duclos, *Voyage à travers les malentendus et la plaisanterie de l'existence humaine*, 2 vols. (Paris, 1877), I, pp. 290-335; C. M. Lombard, 'Dargaud and Lamartine', *Modern Language Notes*, March 1958, pp. 192-4.

21. Lallemand, *Montalembert et ses amis*, pp. 69-70, 72 and 76. See also P. M. N. Burtin, *Un Semeur d'idées au temps de la Restauration: le baron d'Eckstein* (Paris, 1931).

22. *L'Avenir*, 14 December 1830, 20 July 1831, 20 and 28 June 1831.

23. *Correspondance générale*, I, pp. 234-5. Cf. A. Fontaney, *Journal intime* (Paris, 1925), pp. 64 and 72.

24. *La Gazette de France*, 1 November 1831, p. 2, 6 November 1831, p. 3; *Le Journal des Débats*, 20 November 1831; *Le National*, 21 November 1831, p. 2; *Le Globe*, 7 November 1831, pp. 1243-4.

25. H. Guillemin, *Le Jocelyn de Lamartine* (Paris, 1936), pp. 190-1, note 5.

26. *La Mode*, I (1829), p. 150, III (1830), pp. 19, 283-7, 315-23; *Correspondance générale*, I, p. 214.

27. Ibid., I, pp. 218 and 229.

28. *Le Journal de Saône-et-Loire*, 14 March 1832; *Oeuvres de Lamartine* (Brussels, 1836), pp. 557-9.

29. On the abbé Dumont see Guillemin, *Le Jocelyn de Lamartine*, pp. 333-96.

30. *Journal des connaissances utiles*, no. 3, 1 March 1832, pp. 65-9. Cf. Guillemin, *Le Jocelyn de Lamartine*, pp. 814-19.

31. *Lettres à Lamartine*, pp. 141-2, 146-7; *Journal des connaissances utiles*, no. 8, August 1832, note on page following p. 236.

32. *L'Echo de Vaucluse*, 15 March 1832, pp. 3-4.

33. *Correspondance générale*, I, pp. 249-50; B. N., nouv. acq. fr., 24328, ff. 254-5.

34. *Correspondance générale*, I, pp. 252-4; Guillemin, *Le Jocelyn de Lamartine*, p. 23; *Le Journal de Saône-et-Loire*, 10 March 1832; Guillemin, *Connaissance de Lamartine*, pp. 179-88 and 305.

35. *Lettres à Lamartine*, p. 137.

36. Lamartine to the mayor of Mâcon, 8 April 1832; Bibliothèque Municipale, Mâcon, Havard Papers. Cf. *Le Journal de Saône-et-Loire*, 11 April 1832.

37. *Correspondance générale*, I, p. 274.

38. J. Caplain, *Edouard Dubois, Lamartine et Mme Valentine de Lamartine* (Paris, 1913), p. 10; *Correspondance générale*, I, pp. 277-8; B. N., nouv. acq. fr., 24328, ff. 256-7. Eleven years younger than Lamartine, Dubois owned a farm at Saint-Laurent near Cluny, and was mayor of the *commune* of Château in the Mâcon *arrondissement* (see Caplain, *Edouard Dubois*, and *M. Edouard Dubois* (Cluny, 1896)). Duluat was probably Jean-Marie-Auguste Duluat, a forty-five-year-old *négociant* at Cluny (see A. N., F[1c] III Saône-et-Loire 5, f. 154). Gacon may have been the son of Charles-Ambroise Gacon, former sub-prefect of Lons-le-Saulnier and Saint-Claude in the Jura, and may have met Lamartine through the de Maisods or the de Cessiats (see A. N., F[1b] I 161[1]).

39. Lacomme, *Les Elections et les représentants de Saône-et-Loire depuis 1789*, p. 77. Tondut had formerly been *secrétaire général* in the Saône-et-Loire prefecture, president of the provisional commission in Saône-et-Loire (August 1830), and prefect of the Ain (August 1830-March 1831).

40. Quinet, *Correspondance*, II, p. 207.

41. *Correspondance générale*, I, pp. 281-2.

42. *Correspondance*, II (1873), p. 210, III (1874), pp. 417-18, IV (1874), p. 29; *Correspondance générale*, I, pp. 4, 14, 103 and 109.

43. *Correspondance générale*, I, pp. 286 and 288.

44. A full account of Lamartine's first visit to the Middle East has not been attempted. For this see Lamartine's *Voyage en Orient*, which should be corrected by the following: F.-M. de Capmas, *Notes de M. de Capmas sur son Voyage en Orient (1832-1833) et sur celui de Lamartine* (B. N., nouv. acq. fr., 15945, ff. 1-98); J.-V. Delaroière, *Voyage en Orient* (Paris, 1836); Fam, *Lamartine. Voyage en Orient*; H. Guillemin, 'Un Témoin du voyage de Lamartine en Orient', *Revue des Deux Mondes*, 1 June 1937, pp. 542-64 (cf. Guillemin, *Connaissance de Lamartine*, pp. 189-232); C. Maréchal, *Le Véritable 'Voyage en Orient' de Lamartine* (Paris, 1905). For secondary accounts see H. C. Bordeaux, *Voyageurs d'Orient*, 2 vols. (Paris, 1926), II, pp. 1-131; R. Mattlé, *Lamartine voyageur* (Paris, 1936), pp. 307-87. See also L. Fam, *Lamartine prosateur, d'après le Voyage en Orient* (Paris, 1971); R. Warnier, 'A propos du *Voyage en Orient*', in Viallaneix, *Le Livre du centenaire*, pp. 135-51.

45. *Correspondance générale*, I, pp. 322 and 326.

46. Maréchal, *Lamennais et Lamartine*, p. 277.

47. Cochin, *Lamartine et la Flandre*, p. 417.

48. A. N., C. 1267 A, dossier 112; Cochin, *Lamartine et la Flandre*, pp. 197-8; des Cognets, *La Vie intérieure de Lamartine*, pp. 215-16; *Correspondance générale*, I, pp. 349-50, 354-5 and 359, II, pp. 2-3. The apartment eventually chosen was in a house owned by the comte Hippolyte de La Rochefoucauld (A. P. R. marquis de Massa, *Souvenirs et impressions, 1840-1871* (Paris, 1897), p. 26).

49. A. N., F[1c] III Saône-et-Loire 5, f. 189.

50. *La Revue de Paris*, 1 November 1936, p. 168.

51. Lex and Siraud, *Le Conseil général et les conseillers généraux de Saône-et-Loire*, p. 47; A. N., F[1c] III Saône-et-Loire 5, f. 194.

52. *Souvenirs de Madame Delahante*, I, p. 340.

53. *Lettres à Lamartine*, p. 153; Rémusat, *Mémoires de ma vie*, III, pp. 61 and 229; H. de Lacretelle, *Lamartine et ses amis* (Paris, 1878), p. 6.

54. *Mémoires politiques* in *Oeuvres complètes de Lamartine*, XXXVII, pp. 309-10.

55. *Correspondance générale*, I, pp. 42 and 83.

56.   *Oeuvres de M. A. de Lamartine*, XIII (1849), p. 12; 'Tribune politique', *La Presse*, 2 June 1849, p. 2; *Le Cours familier de littérature*, XII, entretien LXX, p. 260. The story is repeated, with slight variations, by Louis Ulbach in *Nos Contemporains* (Paris, 1883), p. 69, and in *La France parlementaire (1834-1851)*. *Oeuvres oratoires et écrits politiques par Alphonse de Lamartine*, 6 vols. (Paris, 1864-65), I, p. xlii, and by Ernest Legouvé in *Lamartine* (Paris, 1876), p. 15, and in *Soixante ans de souvenirs*, 2 vols. (Paris, 1886-87), II, pp. 361-2.

57.   *Correspondance générale*, I, p.3; *Correspondance*, II (1873), pp. 380-1.

58.   *Correspondance générale*, II, pp. 1-2.

59.   Ibid., II, pp. 10, 11-12 and 28.

60.   R. J. Bezucha, *The Lyon Uprising of 1834* (Cambridge, Mass., 1974), p. 150.

61.   *Correspondance générale*, II, pp. 37-9.

62.   *La France parlementaire*, I, pp. 80, 83 and 84.

63.   F. P. G. Guizot, *Mémoires pour servir à l'histoire de mon temps*, 8 vols. (Paris, 1858-67), VII, p. 31.

64.   An abbreviated version of *Des Destinées de la Poésie* first appeared in *Revue des Deux Mondes*, 15 March 1834, pp. 682-93, followed by extracts and favourable comment by Jules Janin in *Le Journal des Débats*, 27 March 1834. The complete text, dated 11 February 1834, was first published in book form by Charles Gosselin in May 1834. 'Sur les Caisses d'Epargnes' was published in the *Journal des connaissances utiles*, no. 3, March 1834, pp. 60-3, and 'Ecoles et méthodes' in ibid., no. 8, August 1834, pp. 193-5.

65.   *Correspondance générale*, II, p. 60.

66.   Guillemin, *Le Jocelyn de Lamartine*, p. 24, note 2.

67.   *Correspondance générale*, II, pp. 50-1.

68.   Cochin, *Lamartine et la Flandre*, pp. 262-71.

69.   Ibid., p. 419; *Correspondance générale*, II, pp. 49 and 51.

70.   Ibid., II, pp. 55-6.

71.   Ibid., II, pp. 56-7.

72.   See Chap. I, note 16.

73.   See A. N., F^{1C} V^3, Saône-et-Loire, dossier 3; Lex and Siraud, *Le Conseil général et les conseillers généraux de Saône-et-Loire*.

74.   B. N., nouv. acq. fr., 13266, ff. 141-2. Cf. *Revue d'histoire littéraire de la France*, April-June 1955, pp. 187-8, *Oeuvres poétiques complètes*, pp. 1135-6 and 1910, and *Lettres de Frédéric Ozanam*, Vol. I, *Lettres de jeunesse, 1819-1840* (Paris, 1960), pp. 146-7. The other visitors included Alix de Cessiat, the abbé Coeur, Dargaud, Félix Guillemardet, Frédéric Ozanam, Léon de Pierreclau, and Quinet.

75.   What follows is based, *inter alia*, on L. Dintzer, *Lamartine à Saint-Point* (Mâcon, 1943), and comte G. de Caraman, *Une Journée chez M. de Lamartine en 1838* (Toulouse, 1842).

76.   *Correspondance générale*, II, p. 6; L. M. Ragg, *The Lamartine Ladies* (London, 1954), pp. 209-10.

77.   They included Béranger, Corcelles, Cousin, Eckstein, Janvier, Lamennais, Mauguin, Michelet, Quinet, Sainte-Beuve, Tocqueville, Vigny, and Villemain; des Cognets, *La Vie intérieure de Lamartine*, pp. 258-9. On Lamartine and Michelet see J.-M. Carré, 'Lamartine et Michelet, d'après leur correspondance inédite', *Revue des Deux Mondes*, 1 September 1926, pp. 182-211.

78.   *Correspondance de la marquise de Montcalm*, p. 289; *Correspondance générale*, I, p. 153.

79.   Ibid., II, p. 168; B. N., nouv. acq. fr., 13266, f. 22, and 13218, f. 7.

80.   Ibid., II, p. 87.

81.   Lamartine, *Souvenirs, impressions, pensées et paysages, pendant un*

voyage en Orient (1832-1833), 4 vols. (Paris, 1835), III, pp. 314-22.

82. See B. N. M. Appert, *Dix ans à la cour du roi Louis-Philippe et souvenirs du temps de l'Empire et de la Restauration*, 3 vols. (Paris, 1846), III, pp. 83-4 and 90-2.

83. *Correspondance générale*, II, pp. 140-1; *Souvenirs historiques et parlementaires du comte de Pontécoulant*, 4 vols. (Paris, 1861-65), IV, p. 258.

84. An extract, 'Souvenirs d'Orient', was published in *La Revue de Paris*, 16 March 1834, pp. 154-63.

85. *Voyage en Orient*, I, pp. 152-3, III, pp. 260-1, IV, pp. 303-12.

86. *Correspondance générale*, II, p. 115.

87. Ibid., II, pp. 204-5; Guillemin, *Le Jocelyn de Lamartine*, pp. 667-87.

88. *Revue des Deux Mondes*, 15 September 1908, pp. 333-4.

89. *La France parlementaire*, II, pp. 1-3; L. Trenard, *Salvandy en son temps, 1795-1856* (Lille, 1968), p. 339; Cochin, *Lamartine et la Flandre*, pp. 305-22.

90. *Correspondance*, V (1875), pp. 239-41, 248-9.

91. *Le Journal de Saône-et-Loire*, 7 November 1837; *La France parlementaire*, II, pp. 4-5.

92. H. C. F. de Barthélemy, *Souvenirs d'un ancien préfet, 1787-1848* (Paris, 1885), p. 207; Lacomme, *Les Elections et les représentants de Saône-et-Loire*, p. 81.

93. *Correspondance*, V (1875), p. 248; Cochin, *Lamartine et la Flandre*, pp. 383-4 and 422-5.

94. *Correspondance*, V (1875), p. 262.

95. See Barthélemy, *Souvenirs d'un ancien préfet*, pp. 206-10.

96. *Correspondance générale*, II, pp. 81 and 86; *Correspondance*, V (1875), p. 190.

97. G. Goyau and P. de Lallemand (eds.), *Lettres de Montalembert à Lamennais* (Paris, 1932), pp. 222 and 278; Lamennais, *Correspondance générale*, VI (1977), p. 385; Derré, *Lamennais*, p. 576.

98. *La France parlementaire*, II, p. 160, III, p. 453.

99. Ibid., III, pp. 148-9, IV, pp. 235-6; *Correspondance générale*, II, pp. 231-2.

100. Ibid., II, pp. 49-50 and 81.

101. A copy of the questionnaire is in *Mélanges*, B. M., Mâcon, 110422, ff. 5-9.

102. *Life, Letters, and Journals of George Ticknor*, 2 vols. (London, 1876), II, p. 117; *La France parlementaire*, IV, p. 66; *Correspondance*, IV (1882), p. 129.

103. *Journal du maréchal de Castellane*, III, p. 167; *Mémoires de M. Dupin*, 4 vols. (Paris, 1855-61), III, p. 429; *Souvenirs intimes et notes du baron Mounier* (Paris, 1896), p. 216.

104. *Correspondance générale*, II, p. 105; *La Revue de Paris*, 15 July 1925, pp. 241-52; M. Thiébaut (ed.), *Comte de Sainte-Aulaire: souvenirs, Vienne, 1832-1841* (Paris, 1927), p. 55.

105. *Correspondance générale*, II, p. 100; *Correspondance*, V (1875), p. 224.

106. E. Réaume (ed.), *Oeuvres inédites de Xavier de Maistre*, 2 vols. (Paris, 1877), II, pp. 82-4.

107. Des Cognets, *La Vie intérieure de Lamartine*, pp. 304-5; Leflaive, *Stéphanie de Virieu*, p. 122.

108. Dumas, *Mes Mémoires*, IV (1967), p. 351; A. Jal, *Souvenirs d'un homme de lettres* (Paris, 1877), pp. 550-1; M. Salomon, 'Le Salon de l'Arsenal', *La Revue de Paris*, 15 September 1906, p. 322; C.-A. Sainte-Beuve, *Portraits contemporains*, 5 vols. (Paris, 1869-71), I, p. 379.

109. See E. Falconnet, *Alphonse de Lamartine. Etudes biographiques*,

littéraires et politiques (Paris, 1840), pp. 112-13; Lacretelle, *Lamartine et ses amis*, pp. 43-6; Luppé, *Lamartine*, p. 256; Lamartine's correspondence; J. K. Laughton (ed.), *Memoirs of the Life and Correspondence of Henry Reeve*, 2 vols. (London, 1898), I, pp. 41, 43, 45, 62 and 177.

110. Mme E. de Girardin, *Le Vicomte de Launay: lettres parisiennes*, 4 vols. (Paris, 1857), IV, p. 82.

111. Ibid., III, pp. 152-3; Lacretelle, *Lamartine et ses amis*, p. 202.

112. They included (1835-48) Ernest Falconnet, Delphine de Girardin, Huber-Saladin, the de La Granges, Liszt, Xavier de Maistre, Aimé Martin, Eugène Pelletan, François Ponsard, Louis de Ronchaud, Pierre Sauzet, and Quinet.

113. *Correspondance*, V (1875), p. 303; B. N., nouv. acq. fr., 13266, f. 24; Lord R. Gower (ed.), *Stafford House Letters* (London, 1891), pp. 234-5.

114. See Fournet, *Lamartine et ses amis suisses*; P. Gaudillière, *Une Admiratrice de Lamartine. Nathalie Blanchet* (Mâcon, 1931); F. Letessier, 'A Landeau, poète manceau, et Lamartine', *Revue historique et archéologique du Maine*, 1966, pp. 90-3, and 'Lamartine et ses amis nantais', *Sainte-Beuve Lamartine: colloques, 8 novembre 1969* (Paris, 1970), pp. 123-39; M. Roustan, *Lamartine et les catholiques lyonnais* (Paris, 1906); Viallaneix, *Le Livre du centenaire*, pp. 337-43.

115. See, for example, A.-M. Bureaud-Riofrey, *Premier mémoire sur les élections républicaines du département de la Haute-Loire en avril 1848* (s.l., n.d.), p. 36; L. de Maricourt, *Heures d'insomnie* (Paris, 1841), p. xiii.

116. Major F. Whittingham, *Personal Recollections of a Ten Months's Residence in Berlin; also extracts from a journal kept in Paris during the crisis of 1839* (London, 1846), pp. 236, 243, 262-4, 267; C. Pitollet, 'Lamartine et Dumas Père, parrains littéraires de Jean Reboul de Nîmes', *Zeitschrift für französischen und englischen Unterricht*, vol. XII, 1913, pp. 403-39, 496-541; F. Letessier in Viallaneix, *Le Livre du centenaire*, pp. 307-33.

117. *Correspondance*, V (1875), p. 351.

118. H. marquis de Noailles (ed.), *Le Comte Molé, 1781-1855. Sa vie – ses mémoires*, 6 vols. (Paris, 1922-30), VI, pp. 182, 210 and 215; Guizot, *Mémoires*, IV, pp. 288-9.

119. Letter dated 12 February 1839; *Correspondance*, IV (1882), p. 5.

120. Cochin, *Lamartine et la Flandre*, pp. 427-9.

121. *Correspondance*, V (1875), pp. 332, 334 and 356; *La Presse*, 16 February 1839; *La France parlementaire*, II, p. 173.

122. *Correspondance*, V (1875), p. 351.

123. See *La Presse*, 23 January 1839.

124. Guizot, *Mémoires*, IV, p. 290.

125. *La France parlementaire*, II, pp. 148-9.

126. Ibid., II, pp. 190 and 193.

127. *Correspondance de Balzac*, III (1964), pp. 617-18.

128. *Le Correspondant*, 25 June 1926, p. 834, 10 July 1926, p. 23.

129. Ibid., 10 July 1926, p. 23.

130. *Correspondance*, IV (1882), pp. 19-21.

131. *Lettres à Lamartine*, p. 172; *Correspondance*, V (1875), p. 387.

132. The articles were dated 16 and 27 November, 4 and 7 December 1839. See *La France parlementaire*, II, pp. 271-93.

133. *Lettres à Lamartine*, pp. 174 and 176. Cf. E. Bertin (ed.), *Journal et correspondances intimes de Cuvillier-Fleury*, 2 vols. (Paris, 1903), II, pp. 215-16.

134. The articles were dated 22 August, 12, 18 and 30 September 1840. See *La France parlementaire*, II, pp. 357-406.

135. *Correspondance*, V (1875), pp. 482, 484 and 486.

136. Ibid., V (1875), pp. 488-90; *Mémoires politiques* in *Oeuvres complètes*

de Lamartine, XXXVII, pp. 348-51; Rémusat, *Mémoires de ma vie*, IV, pp. 5-6; *La Revue de Paris*, 15 July 1925, p. 247.

137. See Barthélemy, *Souvenirs d'un ancien préfet*, pp. 192-3.
138. *Correspondance*, V (1875), pp. 493 and 495-6.
139. Count C. R. von Nesselrode, *Lettres et papiers du chancelier comte de Nesselrode, 1760-1850*, 11 vols. (Paris, 1904-11), VIII (1910), pp. 86-7.
140. *Correspondance*, V (1875), pp. 515 and 520.
141. *La Presse*, 13 January 1841, p. 2. Cf. *Duchesse de Dino. Chronique de 1831 à 1862*, 4 vols. (Paris, 1909-10), III, p. 11.
142. *La Presse*, 14 and 15 February 1841. Cf. B. N., nouv. acq. fr., 25187, ff. 283-9; *La France parlementaire*, III, pp. 62-71; *Correspondance de Balzac*, IV (1966), p. 233.
143. A. N., 42 AP 120, f. 22, and 2 AP 9; *Revue des Deux Mondes*, 15 September 1908, pp. 347-8.
144. Ponti, *Lettere inedite*, p. 65.
145. *La Mère-institutrice*, I (1834), pp. 291-2.
146. See Humblot Conté to the Minister of the Interior, 11 June 1838; A. N., F^{1b}I 156^7.
147. *Correspondance*, V (1875), pp. 581-2; Luppé, *Lamartine*, p. 299; Hon. F. A. Wellesley (ed.), *The Diary and Correspondence of Henry Wellesley, first Lord Cowley, 1790-1846* (London, 1930), p. 216.
148. *La Presse*, 18 and 19 December 1841; Luppé, *Lamartine*, p. 299; Duvergier de Hauranne to Thiers, 30 November 1841 (B. N., nouv. acq. fr., 20616, f. 26).
149. Des Cognets, *La Vie intérieure de Lamartine*, pp. 302-3; *Le Correspondant*, 10 December 1873, p. 832; *Mémoires politiques* in *Oeuvres complètes de Lamartine*, XXXVII, p. 340; Rémusat, *Mémoires de ma vie*, IV, p. 6.
150 Comte E. d'Alton-Shée, *Mes Mémoires, 1826-1848*, 2 parts (Brussels, 1869), part 2, pp. 162-3; *Mémoires posthumes de Odilon Barrot*, 4 vols. (Paris, 1875-76), I, p. 466; T. Zeldin and A. T. de Diaz (eds.), *Emile Ollivier: journal, 1846-1869*, 2 vols. (Paris, 1961), I, p. 338; *La Revue de Paris*, 15 July 1925, p. 250.
151. J. Schlumberger and J. Naville (eds.), *Lettres de François Guizot et de la princesse de Lieven*, 3 vols. (Paris, 1963-64), III, p. 24; Luppé, *Lamartine*, p. 300.
152. *Correspondance*, VI (1875), pp. 3-4.
153. *Mémoires de ma vie*, IV, p. 15.
154. Des Cognets, *La Vie intérieure de Lamartine*, pp. 307-11.
155. *Revue des Deux Mondes*, 15 September 1908, p. 348.
156. *La France parlementaire*, III, p. 241.
157. Lamartine to Aimé Martin, 17 July 1842; B. N., nouv. acq. fr., 13266, f. 50.
158. Guigue de Champvans (1813-1900) was related to family friends of Lamartine, the de Maisods, and was a member of the Academy of Mâcon. He enthusiastically reviewed *Jocelyn* in *Le Journal de Saône-et-Loire* (12 March 1836) and thereafter provided a valuable link with this important local newspaper by becoming one of Lamartine's regular correspondents. See *Correspondance générale*, II, p. 255; R. D. Genoud, 'Deux amis de Lamartine', *Franche-Comté et Monts Jura*, August 1926, pp. 147-8; C.-E. Thuriet, *Anecdotes inédites ou peu connues sur Lamartine* (Besançon, 1893), pp. 3-4 and 6-7.
159. B. M., Mâcon, Ms. 107, ff. 39-48; A. N., F^{1b} I 157^{15}; *Correspondance*, V (1875), p. 492; A. N., F I 160^4.
160. A. Finot, 'Lamartine et son préfet, 1838-1841', *Le Correspondant*, 25 March 1937, p. 728.

110   *The Pursuit of Principle, 1831-1843*

161.   *Correspondance*, V (1875), pp. 272 and 198; B. M., Mâcon, Ms. 107, ff. 190-1; *Le patriote de Saône-et-Loire*, 12 September 1841, pp. 2-3, and 8 October 1841, p. 2; E. Demaizière, 'L'émeute du port de Mâcon', *Annales de l'Académie de Mâcon*, third series, XXII (1920-21), pp. 193-228.

162.   *Correspondance*, V (1875), p. 562.

163.   H. Guillemin, 'Lamartine: l'entrée dans l'opposition révolutionnaire (1843)', *La Revue de France*, 1 September 1935, p. 75; Carraresi, *Lettere di Gino Capponi e di altrui a lui*, VI, p. 253.

164.   See the remarks of 'un membre', almost certainly Lamartine, in G. de Champvans (ed.), *Le Bien public. Rapport politique, discussion dans la réunion des fondateurs, suivis d'une récapitulation, par M. de Lamartine* (Mâcon, 1844), p. 26.

165.   *Correspondance*, VI (1875), pp. 29 and 38.

166.   On 20 March 1843 Lamartine wrote to Desserteaux: 'You have to draw near to the thunder in order to extract it and control it'; *Correspondance*, IV (1882), p. 156. Cf. H. Guillemin, *Lamartine et la question sociale* (Paris, 1946), p. 203, and *Lamartine: l'homme et l'oeuvre* (Paris, 1940), p. 77.

167.   *Revue des Deux Mondes*, 15 September 1908, p. 348; *Correspondance*, VI (1875), pp. 20-1 and 35.

168.   *La Presse*, 29 January 1843.

169.   B. M., Mâcon, Ms. 107, ff. 70 and 73; *Lamartine et ses nièces: correspondance inédite publiée par le comte de Chastellier* (Paris, 1928), pp. 21 and 23-4.

170.   *Lettres du marquis de Custine à Vernhagen d'Ense* (Brussels, 1870), p. 453; *Journal et correspondances intimes de Cuvillier-Fleury*, II, p. 320.

171.   See A. Jardin (ed.), *Correspondance d'Alexis de Tocqueville et de Gustave de Beaumont*, 3 vols. (Paris, 1967), I, p. 482.

172.   See *Correspondance du duc d'Aumale et de Cuvillier-Fleury*, I, pp. 104-5; *Correspondance générale de Sainte-Beuve*, V, p. 51; *Le Constitutionnel*, 28 January 1843; *Le Journal des Débats*, 28 and 30 January 1843.

173.   Duvergier de Hauranne to Thiers, 13 October 1843 (B. N., nouv. acq. fr., 20616, ff. 163-4); *La France parlementaire*, I, p. lxviii.

174.   *Correspondance générale*, I, pp. 36 and 49.

175.   Ibid., I, p. 156.

176.   *La France parlementaire*, I, p. 80.

177.   Lamartine in the Chamber of Deputies, 3 February 1835; ibid., I, p. 109.

178.   Letter dated 24 October 1830; *Correspondance générale*, I, pp. 68-9.

179.   Ibid., I, p. 68; Lamartine in the Chamber of Deputies, 13 March 1834 (*La France parlementaire*, I, p. 35).

180.   Ibid., I, p. 249, II, pp. 416-17.

181.   Lamartine in the Chamber of Deputies, 5 May 1837; ibid., I, p. 355.

182.   'De la reconstitution des 221', *Le Journal de Saône-et-Loire*, 7 December 1839; *La France parlementaire*, II, p. 290.

183.   Ibid., III, p. 258.

184.   Lamartine to Pierre-Hyacinthe Azaïs, 4 August 1836 (B. N., nouv. acq. fr., 13266, ff. 156-7, and *Revue d'histoire littéraire de la France*, April-June 1955, p. 180); Lamartine to Saône-et-Loire's *conseil général*, 26 August 1843 (*Le Bien public*, 3 September 1843, and *La France parlementaire*, III, p. 409). On Azaïs and Lamartine see M. Baude, *P.-H. Azaïs, témoin de son temps d'après son journal inédit, 1811-1844*, 2 vols. (Lille, 1980), I, pp. 337-449.

185.   *La France parlementaire*, II, p. 148.

186.   Ibid., I, pp. 296 and 308.

3 EMBRACING THE LEFT, 1843-1848

Je m'ennuie et la France aussi. – Lamartine to Mme de Girardin,
22 September 1847

Historians often take for granted Lamartine's inclusion on 24 February
1848 as one of the leading members of the Provisional Government
which proclaimed the Second Republic. Romantic poet, historian of
the Girondins, eloquent opponent of Guizot, Lamartine, it is suggested,
suitably matched the euphoria of the French people, especially in Paris,
during 'the springtime of revolutions'. In fact the almost unanimous
enthusiasm with which he was carried to power by those left-wing and
popular elements responsible for the Provisional Government's formation and membership requires a good deal of explanation.

The February Revolution was directed not just against Guizot and
Louis-Philippe, but also against that social group known as the *grands
notables* which had constituted the political and economic élite of July
Monarchy France. Yet as a provincial aristocrat, owner through inheritance of two *châteaux* and their accompanying estates, chairman of
Saône-et-Loire's *conseil général*, parliamentary deputy, and member
of the French Academy, Lamartine clearly belonged to the *grand
notable* class. Moreover, as is well known, the Provisional Government's membership was principally determined by journalists and
politicians closely associated with the two main Paris republican newspapers, *Le National* and *La Réforme*. However, Lamartine had not
publicly and unambiguously identified himself with either of these
newspapers or with the causes which they represented, namely republicanism and radical reforms. At the same time, although not obviously
a member of the French Left, he had acquired a national reputation as
one of the principal parliamentary opponents of Guizot and the July
Monarchy, and as one of the very few major politicians broadly sympathetic towards the French Left.

In his *Histoire de le Révolution de 1848*, written after June 1848
and published in 1849, Lamartine stressed his complete political
independence on the eve of the February Revolution.[1] This reflected
his concern after June 1848 to disclaim responsibility for the February
Revolution, and to distance himself from the French Left, particularly
socialists and left-wing republicans. An examination of his political
position and of his relations with the French Left in the years leading

up to the Revolution of 1848 suggests a very different picture. While anxious to retain his political independence, continue his opposition to socialism and communism, and keep his political options open, he carefully and consistently cultivated the French Left, and ultimately backed the reform banquet campaign and the republican cause.

Among the many groups which constituted the French Left, the most important in the period following the July Revolution of 1830 was the Saint-Simonians. There are indications that the Saint-Simonian Michel Chevalier, presumably attracted by liberal sentiments in Lamartine's poetry, wanted him to stand in the Dunkirk by-election of December 1830. Certainly in February 1835 he had a letter supporting Lamartine's parliamentary candidature published in a local newspaper.[2] As has been noted, the Saint-Simonian newspaper, *Le Globe*, gave Lamartine's *Sur la politique rationnelle* a long and generally favourable review (7 November 1831); and an article in *Le Globe* of 19 April 1832 suggested the idea of a holy alliance of peoples for the regeneration of art headed by, among others, Lamartine. During his brief visit to Smyrna at the end of May 1833 Lamartine was in contact with a Saint-Simonian group led by Emile Barrault. In a letter published in *Le Moniteur* Lamartine informed one of these Saint-Simonians that he shared their desire for social reform.[3] His account of his Middle East travels, *Voyage en Orient* (1835), refers favourably to the Saint-Simonian emphasis on Christianity and fraternity, although he was critical of Saint-Simonian hostility to the family, private property and organised religion. From 1840 he exchanged cordial letters with the Saint-Simonian leader, Enfantin, even inviting Enfantin to Saint-Point in 1843.[4] Lamartine's evolution towards the Left inspired Emile Barrault to compose a political poem, *Epître à M. de Lamartine*, published in Paris in 1842. Altogether the Saint-Simonians respected and even admired Lamartine, who deliberately encouraged this respect and admiration, though he maintained his opposition to socialism and his attachment to private property and traditional morality.

During the July Monarchy the disciples of Charles Fourier became increasingly important in the development of French socialism. Lamartine disliked Fourier's ideas on free love, believing that they would undermine the family, and he was never of course a socialist. The Fourierests, in turn, were deterred by Lamartine's Catholic and royalist past, and by his personal wealth and social status. Nevertheless the Fourierists, like the Saint-Simonians, believed that writers and artists could, and should, have an important popular and social role; and they welcomed Lamartine's abandonment in his poetry of personal preoccupations for a progressive interest in social and political questions. In 1834 Jules Lechevalier, a former Saint-Simonian and convert to Fourierism, founded the *Revue du progrès social*. In this journal, published only in 1834, Lamartine received praise as a politician (February), had his *Harmonies* complimented as 'social and political poetry' (May), and was designated as a potential leader of social reform (June).

Lamartine's epic poem, *Jocelyn* (1836), disappointed the Fourierists, and a long and rather unfavourable review appeared in one of their newspapers. Lamartine's social thought was considered too imprecise and his plot scarcely appropriate for the contemporary age. Though a reader of the paper wrote to the editor defending *Jocelyn*, the criticism probably caused Lamartine some concern.[5] There were several occasions on which he tried to appease and answer criticism from the Left. For instance in the general parliamentary election of November 1837, although virtually assured of re-election at Bergues, out of apparent vanity he stood in both Mâcon constituencies, defeating the left-wing Mathieu in Mâcon-*ville* by eleven votes. This greatly annoyed Mathieu and Mathieu's brother-in-law, the socialist and left-wing deputy François Arago. Significantly, Lamartine wrote to inform Mathieu how much his electoral defeat had distressed him; and he did not oppose Mathieu's successful candidature in the by-election the following February.[6] Similarly, when a worker-poet, Cécile Dufour, criticised Lamartine in a workers' newspaper, *La Ruche populaire* (September 1840), for having subscribed to anti-democratic sentiments in *Jocelyn*, Lamartine replied with a charming letter insisting on his total devotion to the cause of the people and graciously requesting her to accept a copy of *Jocelyn*, which she had been too poor to buy (*La Ruche populaire*, November 1840).

Although the Catholicism and conservatism in *Jocelyn* attracted left-wing criticism, Lamartine's increasing radicalism gradually received left-wing attention and approval. The first important journal to give Lamartine serious, regular and sympathetic coverage was *La Phalange*, a Fourierist newspaper. *La Phalange* supported Lamartine's opposition to the war-like policies of Thiers during the autumn of 1840, praised his parliamentary report on literary copyright (17 and 19 March 1841), welcomed the pacifism of 'La Marseillaise de la Paix' (4 June 1841), and in December 1841 openly supported his candidature for the presidency of the Chamber of Deputies. He was described as 'the parliamentary deputy who is the best disposed towards questions of social organisation, and the most capable by his influence to contribute to their satisfactory solution'.[7] Subsequent editorial articles identified him as a progressive and intelligent conservative who favoured social progress and reform.[8] During the autumn of 1842 *La Phalange* published complimentary poems addressed to Lamartine by Eugène Pelletan and Emile Barrault (3 and 4 September) as well as the texts of, and extracts from, Lamartine's speeches in his home constituency. Meanwhile his exposition of liberal ideas in the *Voyage en Orient*, and gentle dismissal of the communal ownership of property as a beautiful dream, attempted in vain by philanthropy and Christianity, had been well received by the utopian socialist Etienne Cabet. In fact Cabet suggested, both in his newspaper, *Le Populaire*, and in his *Voyage en Icarie*, that Lamartine was a communist without the courage of his convictions.[9]

Lamartine really began to attract the attention of the French Left after his parliamentary speech of 27 January 1843, when he publicly announced he was joining the left-wing parliamentary opposition. For the French Left generally this was welcome news, particularly since so few deputies or established literary figures sympathised with the Left at this time and since Lamartine had a national reputation as a writer and orator. Of course the Left's factionalism meant that, for instance, the Fourierist Considérant in a leading article in *La Phalange* (29 January), while warmly applauding Lamartine's speech and disassociation from the conservatives, regretted his joining the left-wing parliamentary opposition. On the other hand, *Le Commerce*, a Paris opposition newspaper edited by Charles Lesseps, had no reservations about Lamartine's speech (28 January): 'It was in effect an opposition formula such as we had imagined and dreamt of as providing the only salvation for the country, but such also that could have been developed only by a person of outstanding ability.' In a leading article in *Le Populaire* (10 February), Cabet also enthusiastically welcomed Lamartine's recruitment to the left-wing opposition. Cabet suggested that Lamartine's aristocratic background, literary reputation, former leadership of the conservatives, and political sincerity and independence, all made him a great prize. At the same time, Lamartine received letters of congratulation and encouragement from two of France's most prominent left-wing intellectual Frenchwomen, George Sand and the comtesse d'Agoult.[10] Prompted by her letter, he visited George Sand at the beginning of February. Although thinking him vain and lacking in political skill, George Sand was convinced of his political sincerity; and she was later anxious to secure his support for a newspaper she helped to found in 1844.[11]

During March 1843 'the terrible speeches of M. de Lamartine', and his attacks on the Government, were noted with delight by the most important moderate republican Paris newspaper, *Le National*.[12] Also, *Le Commerce* and *La Phalange* (with some reservations) continued to comment favourably on his parliamentary speeches.[13] On a social level, he apparently began cultivating prominent left-wing figures at this time. About March 1843 a guest observed in Lamartine's Paris *salon* 'all the Left together', including Odilon Barrot and Garnier-Pagès; and with François Arago in May 1843 Lamartine was a witness at the wedding of Ledru-Rollin, a left-wing deputy closely associated with *La Réforme*.[14] Always anxious to secure favourable publicity, during March and April 1843 Lamartine almost certainly inspired the publication of Joseph Bécot's *M. de Lamartine, orateur* and Dargaud's *Nouvelle phase parlementaire*.[15] Also published about this time were Chapuys-Montlaville's *Lamartine. Vie publique et privée*, Gustave de Molinari's *Biographie politique de M. A. de Lamartine*, and the anonymous *Guizot et Lamartine, ou la politique du cabinet du 29 octobre, jugée par un observateur impartial*. These pamphlets were mainly biographical studies, explaining Lamartine's political development and, in particular, his speech of 27 January. They seem to have been part of a concerted campaign not just to make his political position understood, but also to publicise his ideas, enlarge his popular following, and establish his potential for national political leadership.

After the end of the parliamentary session, Lamartine was the guest of honour on 4 June 1843 at a Mâcon banquet organised by a local left-wing newspaper, *Le Progrès de Saône-et-Loire*. To a politically mixed audience, estimated at over a thousand by an official and at over five thousand by Lamartine,[16] he argued that the political situation in France, not his views, had changed, since there had developed a new fundamental demand for democracy, which the Government was ignoring. He imprecisely defined democracy as 'the holy and divine ideology of the French Revolution', which in turn was essentially a development of Christian principles applied to politics. At the same time, he emphasised that he did not want mob rule or violence.[17] Shortly afterwards he wrote to Aimé Martin that he sought a greater degree of national unity, to be achieved and expressed through more democracy. Although again very imprecise, he suggested he meant by more democracy the end of France's domination by a small oligarchy, yet at the same time acceptance of the social hierarchy and constitutional monarchy.[18] He almost certainly sent an account of the banquet and the text of his speech to *Le Commerce*, *Le National* and *La Phalange*, all of which fully and favourably reported the occasion. On 12 June Considérant, editor of *La Phalange*, wrote Lamartine a friendly letter, which, however, gently chided him for having joined the left-wing parliamentary opposition.[19] Lamartine in his reply profusely thanked his 'dear and brilliant defender' for *La Phalange*'s coverage of the Mâcon banquet, and argued that they were both members of the left-wing opposition.[20] *Le National*'s editor, Jules Bastide, also wrote to Lamartine (22 June). He stressed their agreement on many political issues, though, unlike Lamartine at this time, he was committed to a republican constitution for France.[21]

During the summer of 1843 Lamartine realised a long cherished ambition — the founding of his own newspaper. His interest in newspapers and journalism dated from at least 1820, when he showed a lively concern for newspaper review articles of his *Méditations* and was briefly associated with founding *Le Défenseur*. However, as early as 1823, when he declined an invitation from Victor Hugo to collaborate on a new journal, *La Muse française*, he indicated his reluctance to compromise his independence because he did not want to associate himself with editorial policies for which he was not responsible.[22] He fully appreciated the very important role newspapers had come to play in French politics. He was probably influenced by Genoude's newspaper activities, Virieu's involvement in a Lyons newspaper, the ideas of Emile de Girardin and his editorship of *La Presse*, and the development of a local newspaper press in Saône-et-Loire. The idea of founding a newspaper or review of his own was mentioned by Lamartine in 1830 and repeated many times in his correspondence: in 1834 he thought of creating a political review with Ballanche, Lamennais and Jean-Pierre Pagès; in 1836 he hoped to collaborate on a newspaper with Tocqueville, Gustave de Beaumont and Carné; and in 1839 he considered editing or acquiring an interest in *La Presse*.[23] The latter negotiation failed, but Lamartine had in *La Presse* a leading Paris daily newspaper which supported his politics and published his articles. Girardin, however, did not approve of Lamartine's decision to join the left-wing opposition, and from 30 January 1843 *La Presse* ceased to support him. Soon afterwards, *Le Journal de Saône-et-Loire* deserted him for the same reason. This may have finally prompted him to establish his own newspaper.

In October 1842 a new radical opposition newspaper, *Le Progrès de Saône-et-Loire*, had been founded in Mâcon by, among others, Jean-Baptiste Chassipollet (a Mâcon printer), Pierre-Casimir Ordinaire (a medical doctor, amateur poet and free-lance writer, known to

Lamartine through his book on Aix and its environs and his study of the Saône floods of 1840),[24] and Charles Rolland (a recently qualified twenty-four-year-old lawyer and future mayor of Mâcon). At the beginning of October 1842 Lamartine was invited to join *Le Progrès*, but declined so as not to break his old connection with *Le Journal de Saône-et-Loire*. However, at the same time he wrote that he would soon have his own newspaper, called *Le Bien public*.[25] By June 1843 he had broken with *Le Journal de Saône-et-Loire* and had given the impression he was going to take over *Le Progrès* and re-name it *La Démocratie nouvelle*.[26] Between June and August he assembled a group of founder-members,[27] who each agreed to contribute 1,000 francs, except Lamartine, who contributed 10,000 francs. Champvans was appointed editor and *Le Bien public* accepted as the newspaper's title. Since contemporaries did not regard Champvans as a sincere radical,[28] and a concern for the common welfare could command general acceptance, Lamartine thus initially gave *Le Bien public* a characteristically ambiguous political complexion. Certainly Ordinaire, upset at the choice of editor and title, refused Lamartine's offers of an important editorial role and founded his own newspaper, *La Mouche littéraire de Saône-et-Loire et de l'Ain* (5 September 1843 – 29 July 1848). Meanwhile, a specimen number of *Le Bien public* was issued on 10 August 1843, and the paper appeared regularly after the following 3 September.

While founding *Le Bien public* Lamartine composed an article, 'Des publications populaires'. Responding to suggestions from Chapuys-Montlaville, a left-wing deputy for Saône-et-Loire, as to how to improve the popular teaching of French history, Lamartine complained that the working classes lacked suitable reading material. A modestly priced daily newspaper should be created with mass appeal, while containing contributions from all the most eminent writers. Such a newspaper could achieve a moral revolution in ten years, and its editors could exercise enormous influence on public opinion.[29] *La Revue indépendante*, a republican-socialist journal edited by Pierre Leroux and George Sand, first published the article on 10 August 1843, the same day as *Le Bien public*'s specimen issue. The latter contained a statement of principles which repeated Lamartine's belief in the importance of the newspaper press, and described the newspaper as 'the daily book of the human mind'. At the same time, he acknowledged the limitations of a provincial newspaper's influence. However, in Mâcon he could rely on an effective team of supporters and collaborators; *Le Bien public* could be expected to strengthen his position in his constituency and in the department; and he doubtless hoped that Paris newspapers would reprint and comment on *Bien public* articles — certainly his statement of principles was reproduced at length in *Le Commerce, Le National* and *La Démocratie pacifique* (recently founded by Considérant in succession to *La Phalange*).

La Bien public's specimen issue mentions an editorial committee consisting of Dr Bouchard (Mâcon's *premier adjoint*, who had proposed the toast to Lamartine at the Mâcon banquet of 4 June 1843), Alphonse Saclier (a Mâcon lawyer), Charles Rolland and Isidore Dubief. The paper's director was Emile Buy and printer Jean-Baptiste Chassi-pollet. Champvans remained chief editor until December 1844, apart from September and October 1844 when temporarily replaced by Rolland and Dubief. His successor, Jean-Jacques Gizorme, had been a journalist on *Le Commerce* and was a friend of its editor, Charles Lesseps, whom Lamartine seems to have cultivated. *Le Bien public* was issued twice a week, on Thursdays and Sundays, except between December 1846 and October 1847, when it appeared on Tuesdays as well. It ceased publication shortly before 8 August 1848.[30] A letter written by Lamartine in February 1844 suggests that the paper's circulation was about a thousand.[31] The paper was heavily subsidised, and allegedly cost him more than 15,000 francs annually.[32] His role is difficult to determine precisely. His articles were usually published anonymously (though asterisks often indicated his authorship), and often he would just suggest ideas and phrases, leaving the task of composition to others.[33] However, between September 1843 and January 1848 he probably wrote or largely inspired some thirty-eight articles for *Le Bien public*. Other contributors besides the chief editors included Boussin, Dargaud, Dubois, Lacretelle, Rolland, and Charles Lesseps. Annual meetings of the founder-members were held with Lamartine at Monceau (November 1844), Rolland and Garnier-Lacombe in Mâcon (November 1845 and November 1846), and Lacre-telle at Cormatin (October 1847). The chief editor then presented his report, decisions were taken about such matters as the editorship, and Lamartine usually gave a major speech.

Although Lamartine sometimes complained that *Le Bien public* needed livening up, and at least once considered transferring it to Paris,[34] it served him well in Mâcon. It faithfully followed his political direction, published his articles, and fully reported many of his speeches. While its circulation of about a thousand was small (though respectable for a French provincial newspaper at this time), it could achieve a wider readership through availability in cafés and *cabarets*.

More importantly, its controversial character and connection with Lamartine ensured national press attention. At Lamartine's personal request, Girardin republished in *La Presse* several of Lamartine's *Bien public* articles. Occasionally, Lamartine also asked Aimé Martin for publicity in *Le Journal des Débats*, besides having several of his *Bien public* articles published as pamphlets. Thus, through *Le Bien public* he gained a reliable newspaper and considerable publicity. *Le Bien public* also held together a politically significant group, which shared his views and accepted his leadership. In effect, it provided him in Mâcon with the equivalent of a party organisation, a not uncommon role for a journal or newspaper in July Monarchy France, which lacked organised political parties.

From its first appearance, Lamartine successfully exploited *Le Bien public* so as to gain favourable left-wing publicity. *Le Commerce*, *Le National* and *La Démocratie pacifique* fully reproduced a speech by Lamartine to Saône-et-Loire's *conseil général* advocating an extension of the parliamentary franchise, the text of which had appeared in *Le Bien public*'s first regular issue. Lamartine's *Bien public* article of 5 November, 'Application possible des principes de l'opposition au gouvernement', arguing that the opposition embodied the French Revolution's true democratic spirit, which July Monarchy governments had betrayed, was republished in *La Démocratie pacifique* (8 November) and *Le National* (9 November). In *La Démocratie pacifique* the introductory comments on the article concluded, 'we are of the same opposition as M. de Lamartine'. Similarly, two articles by Lamartine in *Le Bien public* for 26 and 30 November, advocating the separation of Church and State, were reproduced by *Le Commerce* (28 and 29 November, 1 December) and extensively quoted by *La Démocratie pacifique* (30 November, 1 December); and another of his *Bien public* articles, on workers and savings banks (10 December), was sympathetically discussed in *Le National* (14 December). Left-wing newspapers almost certainly received from Lamartine the texts of his *Bien public* articles. Similarly, *Le Bien public* serialised George Sand's novel, *Fanchette*, and Lamartine tried to elicit a contribution for *Le Bien public* from Eugène Sue[35] — both George Sand and Eugène Sue being novelists highly regarded by the French Left. In December *Le Bien public* welcomed Considérant's election to the *conseil général* of the Seine in an article which Lamartine took care to bring to Considérant's attention.[36] More explicitly, on 2 February 1844 Lamartine instructed *Le Bien public*'s editor, Champvans: 'Follow the editorial line of the most advanced newspapers, such as *Le Commerce* and *La Réforme*.'[37]

After his return to Paris on 21 January 1844 for the new parliamentary session, Lamartine renewed his attacks in the Chamber on government policy over the fortifications of Paris (2 March), the restricted
franchise (18 March), the stamp tax on newspapers and the September
press laws (4 April), and penal reform (7 May). He also voted against
the speech from the throne. All this must have increased his popularity with the Left, though *Le Commerce* no longer supported him
after 2 April, when Charles Lesseps ceased to be editor. Significantly,
La Démocratie pacifique ran a sympathetic literary and biographical
study of Lamartine by Eugène Pelletan in four separate issues (26
February, 4, 11 and 18 March). Yet, true to his principle of political
independence (recently confirmed in a private letter),[38] and perhaps
mindful of Considérant's advice, Lamartine did not join a specific
opposition group. In 1844, after careful consideration, he abandoned
the idea of forming an opposition alliance with Thiers and Odilon
Barrot.[39] During November, following a three-month Italian holiday,[40]
Lamartine composed an important article re-stating his political position: the Revolution of 1789 was France's political religion, French
governments since 1834 had ignored this, and the entire system in
France should be opposed. First published in *Le Bien public* (21
November), this article was extensively reproduced in *La Démocratie
pacifique* (22 November), and discussed at length in *La Démocratie
pacifique* and in the main Paris left-wing republican newspaper, *La
Réforme* (23 November). Both supported Lamartine's attacks on
government policy, though *La Démocratie pacifique* criticised his
failure to consider the right to work and the organisation of labour,
while *La Réforme* thought him wrong to restrict the Revolution to
1789.

La Démocratie pacifique's criticisms may well have struck home,
particularly in view of the exceptionally favourable editorial on
Lamartine in the paper's issue for 27 November.[41] In any case, he
published in *Le Bien public* (26 and 29 December) two articles on
what he described as the new challenge to the foundation of society,
the socialist doctrines of the right to work and the organisation of
labour, which he maintained threatened the institutions of the family
and private property. The articles proclaimed his belief in the right
to existence rather than in the right to work. A government should
always act to prevent its citizens from starving, and with the privileges
of property-ownership went obligations and responsibilities towards
the welfare of the community as a whole. Thus he opposed the operation of the forces of naked capitalism, considering the doctrines of

'laissez-faire' and 'laissez passer' to be the equivalent of 'laissez souf-
frir' and 'laissez mourir'. Instead, the government should assume
responsibility for public education, poor relief and health care, and
should promote a just and equitable distribution of the nation's wealth.
This should be achieved through indirect means, such as by taxing the
rich and by discouraging the creation of huge industrial monopolies.
However, he completely rejected any direct State intervention in the
country's economic affairs, such as the doctrine of the organisation of
labour implied. If the government were to regulate production and consumption, and control the distribution of income and capital, then any
semblance of economic liberty would be totally destroyed.[42] The two
articles were discussed in no less than four separate issues of *La Réforme* and seven issues of *La Démocratie pacifique*.[43] Both newspapers
were quite critical. *La Réforme* accused him of having a narrow
approach to the subject, and of not wanting complete social reform;
La Démocratie pacifique suggested that he lacked a full understanding
of Fourierist ideas, and harboured an irrational attachment to private
property.[44]

Lamartine's embrace of the French Left thus had its limits, in that
he was not prepared to abandon his relatively conservative position on
social and economic matters. In fact, by the mid-1840s he had
developed an ideology that blended, in a characteristically idiosyncratic way, Christian morality and revolutionary idealism.[45] The Earth,
he believed, had been created by God, who was everywhere worshipped
by nature. Like all living creatures, Man was God's creation, and his
function was to find, love and serve his Creator. In creating Man, God
had endowed him with instincts, which Lamartine defined as a synthesis of reason and emotion. Those instincts forced Man to live in a
political society, because only in a political society could the individual perfect himself, by enlarging his sphere of action through the
family, the State and humanity in general. Society was not a human
invention but divinely inspired. To equip Man to live in society, God
had endowed him with reason (which was a reflection of God's will),
and with the instincts of family and property, so that the institutions
of the family and private property were divine in origin. The family's
function was to perpetuate and moralise the human race. Property's
function was to reward labour, increase public wealth, and ensure
the family's material survival. The function of political society or the
State was to protect and preserve the institutions of the family and
private property. Civilisation, consequently, had three foundations –
the family, private property and the State; and anything which tended

to undermine those foundations — such as Saint-Simonianism, communism or the doctrine of the organisation of labour — opposed Man's instincts and God's will.

Since Man's instincts were given to him by God, and since the State should act in accordance with God's will, it followed that the State ought to encourage Man's family and property-owning instincts. The family should be the fundamental concern of all legislation, and the State should help all its citizens to become property-owners. Lamartine's ideal was a rural patriarchal society, in which ties of family and kinship, and bonds of respect and consideration between master and servant, landowner and labourer, resulted in a humane and harmonious community. Confronted by the problems which urbanisation and industrialisation produced, Lamartine, like many of his contemporaries, thus looked nostalgically to idealised concepts of the family and rural pre-industrial society. Religious, sentimental and Romantic factors doubtless reinforced his belief in the supreme importance of family and property. Clearly the family might serve as an effective disciplining influence and instrument of social control for the urban working class. The family was also indispensable for property's transmission. But Lamartine had an unjustified confidence in State and private charity, and in property's civilising role; and, while the increasing trend towards urbanisation and industrialisation was obviously alarming, since so much contemporary evidence suggested it promoted crime, immorality, poor health and popular violence, his ideal evaded rather than tackled the problems.

In political terms, Lamartine's ideology was inspired by the Revolution of 1789. France was a revolutionary country and the principles of 1789 constituted her political religion.[46] Thus, the French Revolution was not just an historical event but also a continuing source of political inspiration; and, as *La Réforme* had complained on 23 November 1844, the radical phases of the Revolution after 1789 were implicitly rejected.[47] Lamartine wanted to revive a common faith in the ideals of 1789, and establish those ideals as a basis for political action. The ideals of 1789 needed to be revived because they had been corrupted, distorted or ignored. Between 1791 and 1795 anarchy, tyranny, confiscations, executions, desperate wars, and internal conflict disfigured the Revolution. Subsequently, Napoleon embodied the counter-revolution as a military dictator. He substituted despotism for liberty, the nobility for equality, and the aristocracy for the people, and he succeeded in making the Revolutionary ideals unpopular in all the countries which his armies devastated and occupied. With the

Restoration, the Bourbon dynasty had a superb role before it; but Louis XVIII and, more particularly, Charles X, tragically failing to realise their opportunities, had brought France to the verge of chaos.

In fact, since 1791 the opposition, not the government, had upheld the Revolution's ideals. Lamartine's letter to *Le Bien public* of 10 August 1843 had surveyed the heroes of this opposition: in the Constituent Assembly Mirabeau, attacking all forms of absolute power and silencing the thirty voices of the factions; in the Legislative Assembly the Girondins, trying to preserve something solid in a collapsing structure; in the Convention a courageous minority, including Lanjuinais and Boissy d'Anglas, whose energy saved the nation, but who refused to resort to extremism and were not intimidated by the guillotine; under the Empire writers and philosophers such as Mme de Staël and Chateaubriand; under the Restoration a small articulate group headed by Foy, Laffitte and Casimir Périer. After 1830 the reader was obviously supposed to see in Lamartine himself the last of a long line of defenders of the true revolutionary cause. What, Lamartine had concluded by asking, had the opposition always wanted from 1789 to the present? 'Always the same thing: the French Revolution's true ideal, popular sovereignty through legislation and common sense through the fair operation of majority rule.'[48] On whether revolutionary idealism should ever lead to revolutionary action he was, as usual, somewhat ambiguous. For example, referring to 1789 and 1830, he told a deputation of Paris workers in May 1845: 'I myself do not wish to be more revolutionary than two revolutions!'[49] However, also in May 1845, he declared during a parliamentary speech on the fortifications of Paris: 'By all means make revolutions difficult, rare, serious and blameworthy; but allow, in exceptional circumstances, for the possibility of resistance against outrages committed by governments.'[50]

Despite his ideological differences with the French Left, by the beginning of 1845 the most important left-wing Paris newspapers were giving Lamartine extensive coverage; they were taking him very seriously as a politician and political theorist; and, though critical, their remarks were generally sympathetic. The circulation of those newspapers was small (less than 2,000 for *La Démocratie pacifique* and *La Réforme*, about 4,000 for *Le National* and *Le Populaire*), and considerably less than that of *La Presse* (about 22,000), *Le Constitutionnel* (about 25,000) and *Le Siècle* (about 32,000). However, French newspapers at this time achieved a wider readership through availability in cafés and *cabinets de lecture*, and through the reprinting of press material in other newspapers. Also, in the absence of left-wing political parties or labour movements, left-wing newspapers provided the French Left with virtually its only leadership and articulation. Lamartine fully appreciated this, though he did not break completely with the more conservative mass-circulation newspapers. Thus his *Bien public* article of 14 September 1845, 'Pourquoi M. de Lamartine est seul', was reproduced in *La Presse* at his personal request, as well as in *La Réforme, La Démocratie pacifique* and *L'Esprit public*.[51] For their part, left-wing newspapers had come to regard Lamartine as one of the very few prominent political and literary figures sympathetic to the Left in France. While they might criticise him for his failure to support republicanism or radical social and economic reforms, they were rarely hostile towards him. As *La Revue indépendante* put it: 'One can find oneself in disagreement with Lamartine; but one likes him while challenging him, one admires him while contradicting him.'[52] Also, left-wing critics tended to stress their similarities as well as differences of opinion with Lamartine. Prudent Forest, a Fourierist and Chalon-sur-Saône lawyer, in a pamphlet published in 1845 even suggested that there were many Fourierist ideas in Lamartine's poetry, despite the latter's attachment to the family and private property.[53] Lamartine may have encouraged Forest's interpretation by allowing four of his own poems to appear in a Fourierist anthology in aid of the 1840 flood victims – *Harmonies sociales et poétiques* (Paris, 1841). In October 1845 he certainly had Eugène Pelletan (author of the sympathetic study of him in *La Démocratie pacifique*) to stay at Monceau, where on 11 October he entertained to dinner, among others, Mathieu (left-wing deputy for Saône-et-Loire) and Dr Ordinaire (editor of the local left-wing newspaper, *La Mouche*).[54] In addition, he continued to supply left-wing newspapers with his speeches and articles, and with news items concerning himself.

Between 26 December 1845 and 2 January 1846 a congress of representatives from fifty-one French reformist newspapers took place in Paris. Its purpose was to discuss electoral reform and, particularly, the extension of the parliamentary franchise. The congress served as one of the precursors of the reform banquet campaign of 1847-1848; and among the newspapers represented was *Le Bien public* of Mâcon.[55] In January 1846 *La Réforme* paid tribute to the generosity of Lamartine's character, and saluted him as 'one of the noblest representatives of those moral ideas which daily seem to be losing ground in parliament'.[56] *La Réforme* proceeded to comment favourably on several of the important speeches he gave during the 1846 parliamentary session. Similarly, *Le Populaire* on 25 April welcomed his criticisms of the salt tax; and on 25 June *La Revue indépendante* admired a speech he had given on Syria. Most effusive of all, *La Démocratie pacifique* praised his speeches in a succession of editorials, one of which began: 'The people of France should bless the name of M. de Lamartine' (23 April). Meanwhile, in March Lamartine, with François Arago, Odilon Barrot, Dupont de l'Eure, Georges Lafayette, Léon de Malleville, and Alexis Vavin, formed a commission on behalf of the Poles, a traditional concern of the French Left.[57] Perhaps not surprisingly, *Le Populaire* (23 August) hailed Lamartine's virtually unanimous re-election in Mâcon-*ville* on 1 August (by 320 out of 331 votes cast) as a great triumph for socialism. However, at the end of August he refused to chair a committee concerned with the Middle East's liberation from Turkish rule. This so annoyed a Dr Barrachin that he composed a devastating political critique of Lamartine, which he threatened to publish on 1 October if Lamartine did not help him with his Middle East liberation committee. Presumably to take the wind out of Barrachin's sails, Lamartine wrote an article, 'De la crise des subsistances', dated 1 October and sent for publication to *La Démocratie pacifique*, *La Presse* and *La Réforme*, where it was published a day before it appeared in *Le Bien public* on 4 October.[58]

'De la crise des subsistances' tackled the worsening economic crisis in France. A disastrous potato crop and mediocre cereal harvest in 1845 had been followed in 1846 by an exceptionally dry and hot summer, causing a sharp fall in cereal production. The consequent rise in prices encouraged hoarding and speculation. Committed to orthodox liberalism, the Government pursued non-interventionist economic policies apart from maintaining some protectionist tariffs. Prefects were therefore reluctant to purchase cereals for public sale or distribution. However, some municipal councils intervened by blocking the movement of cereals, by regulating their sale and purchase, and by buying cereals for resale at a subsidised price. Also, some members of the *notable* class contributed to public subscriptions for the purchase of cereals and sold their own cereals at low prices or distributed them free. Lamartine's humanitarian sentiments, paternalism as a large landowner, and preoccupation with public order, all influenced his reaction to the crisis. His article opposed any violence and urged employers to increase wages and provide more jobs. He argued for agricultural reforms to increase production, which could be only a long-term remedy. The Government, he thought, should establish a uniform price for cereals throughout France. As a liberal he wanted the Government to ensure the free movement of cereals within France, yet he opposed importing them from abroad. Thus, he hoped the crisis could be solved through the goodwill of employers and through government intervention limited to maintaining a uniform price and internal free trade. Such solutions would not have had a very significant impact on the enormous increase in the cost of living faced by poor families after the summer of 1846. However, Lamartine had been quick to appreciate the gravity of the crisis, and in the autumn of 1846 he practised what he preached by giving considerable sums to the Mâcon poor.[59] *La Réforme* and *La Démocratie pacifique* approved of his article, with reservations. *La Réforme* (4 October) thought that he should have attributed some of the responsibility for the crisis to speculation by capitalists, while *La Démocratie pacifique* (4 October) criticised his opposition to France importing cereals from abroad.

Besides occasionally contributing to parliamentary debates, founding and editing *Le Bien public*, and writing political articles for newspapers, Lamartine had been engaged in writing a substantial narrative account of the French Revolution from the death of Mirabeau (2 April 1791) to the overthrow of Robespierre (27 July 1794), the *Histoire des Girondins*. There were many reasons why he should have embarked on such a project. Among his contemporaries there was a general tendency to turn to history in order to understand the past and explain the present; public interest and enthusiasm in historical subjects were considerable; a mass of primary material relating to the French Revolution had recently been published; significant advances were occurring in the improvement of research methods and development of historical techniques; and close connections existed between the writing and teaching of history and the conduct of political debate.[60] In addition, the spread of education and the development of newspapers had greatly enlarged France's reading public; and, imitating Sir Walter Scott, writers such as Balzac, Dumas, Hugo and Vigny had successfully popularised the historical novel in France. Lamartine himself continually made historical allusions, particularly to the French Revolution, in his parliamentary speeches and newspaper editorials; and his whole political philosophy was based on an historical formulation of the idea of progress, on an interpretation of the Revolution, and on a belief that the ideals and principles of 1789 were still the goals of contemporary France. Lamartine probably chose the Girondins as a subject for several reasons. The rise and fall of a talented group of individuals, and the conflict between the Mountain and the Plain, had an obvious dramatic and popular appeal, as well as revealing what happened to the idealism of 1789, and what became of the revolutionary movement in some of its most critical years. Also, the transition from a conservative monarchy to a radical republic might have an obvious relevance to future developments in France.

After February 1848 many of Lamartine's contemporaries believed that he had written the *Histoire des Girondins* with the intention of encouraging a revolution. Although he did not actually begin working on the *Girondins* until June 1843, he had decided to embark on the project by September 1841,[61] when Louis-Philippe's overthrow by revolution could not have seemed a likely possibility. However, Lamartine undoubtedly hoped that the *Girondins* would have a political message and a political role. When the work first appeared he is supposed to have advised Molé:[62]

> Do not read it . . . It is written for the people. The people are going to play the great role, and must be prepared for it and given an aversion to executions, so that the next revolution will not suffer from the excesses of the first revolution. My duty is to prepare the people and myself, for I will be the leader in a new society.

On the question of violence, he similarly argued in a letter to a critical reviewer (5 August 1847): 'The work is simply a protest in eight volumes against the alleged necessity for violence. . . I have shown on every page that revolutionary murder, in executing victims, only kills the Revolution.'[63] This deliberately exaggerated and over-simplified the message which he hoped to convey to the French people, a message outlined more accurately in a document originally intended as advertisement copy, though never used. The first point made is that the Revolution must be restored in 'the soul of the people', by revealing it purified of the political errors and violence which had been mixed up with its soundly democratic principles. The document goes on to state that those who read Lamartine's work would acquire a knowledge of the events of the Revolution and a love of its genuine principles, and would develop a sense of political morality.[64] Assuming, once again, the self-appointed role of public educator, and concerned, as always, with inculcating morality through literature and politics, Lamartine clearly wanted to rehabilitate the Revolution, by separating its ideals from its crimes and mistakes, and to revive public awareness of the principles of 1789, which he believed should be France's political creed.[65]

Lamartine himself undoubtedly intended to benefit from this exercise in popular political education. He once revealed that his secret ambition was to gain the French people's moral leadership through the widespread acceptance of his ideas and convictions.[66] Privately he expressed the hope of becoming 'the minister of an opinion', so that in the hour of crisis he would emerge as the nation's inevitable and indispensable leader.[67] Before this occurred he was determined to remain 'a man of reserve'.[68] He told a friend in July 1843 that his political objective was impersonal and uniquely divine, and would be revealed in the future.[69] Meanwhile, he had to prepare public opinion, for, as he informed Ronot in 1846, 'future popularity, that is the reality'.[70] The *Histoire des Girondins* could serve these political aims and ambitions by helping him to establish himself as someone who publicly upheld and popularised the principles of 1789, influenced public opinion and enjoyed widespread popularity, and consequently was an obvious leader in a crisis situation.[71]

Lamartine had originally intended that the *Histoire des Girondins* would consist of four volumes, but he ended up writing eight. He had finished the first volume by October 1843, the fourth by the middle of April 1845, and the eighth by the end of December 1846. Concerned, as usual, with the work's critical reception and with the publicity surrounding its publication, he had the influential critic, Jules Janin, read the manuscript before publication to secure his approval.[72] In addition, he arranged that between 15 and 19 March 1847 the main Paris newspapers would publish long extracts from, and large advertisements for, his *Girondins*, which was finally released onto the market two volumes at a time between 18 March and 19 June. Significantly, the extracts he sent to *Le National* and *Le Populaire* concerned Robespierre, but to the conservative *Journal des Débats* he sent extracts giving his assessment of Mirabeau and his description of the flight of the Royal Family to Varennes. The Left's immediate reception of the extracts on Robespierre must have delighted Lamartine. *Le National* observed that he had largely cured himself of the hysteria towards the Revolution so common among those sharing his family and educational background, while *Le Populaire* believed that the passages quoted on Robespierre would give great pleasure to its readers. In later reviews *La Démocratie pacifique* was unreservedly enthusiastic; and *La Revue indépendante* saluted Lamartine, together with Jules Michelet and Louis Blanc (who had also begun publishing histories of the French Revolution), as 'a soldier of the revolution', adding, 'it is always the hymn of revolution which they sing'.[73]

The French Left's favourable, even enthusiastic, reception of the *Histoire des Girondins* is understandable. In the *Girondins*, more publicly and obviously than ever before, Lamartine justified revolutionary violence, accepted republicanism, defended republican heroes, notably Robespierre, and abandoned his previous blanket condemnation of the Jacobin phase of the Revolution, though his radicalism still had its limits. The fall of the Bastille (14 July 1789), the storming of the Tuileries Palace (10 August 1792) and even the expulsion of the Girondins from the Convention (31 May − 2 June 1793), are all described as great revolutionary days. On the other hand, the Paris prison massacres of September 1792 are judged to have been a crime. Lamartine criticises the Constitution of 1791 for its retention of the monarchy and welcomes the proclamation of the Republic (21 September 1792), but at the same time he treats Louis XVI with respect and argues that he should have been deposed and exiled rather than executed. Robespierre and Robespierre's ideals receive strikingly sympathetic treatment, though Marat is depicted as a bloodthirsty monster. The social and economic policies of the Jacobin dictatorship are praised for their idealism, albeit utopian, while the Terror is set in context as well as condemned for its excesses.

The *Histoire des Girondins* came to be widely regarded as one of the causes of the February 1848 Revolution. One communard is even reported to have explained why so many of his generation had become revolutionaries by describing them as 'victims of books', and in particular of Lamartine's *Girondins*.[74] Certainly the work immediately sold exceptionally well and became a subject of great interest and considerable controversy. The publication of the *Girondins*, and the extracts in newspapers, reviews in journals and accompanying public debate, must have helped to publicise France's revolutionary past at a time of deepening crisis. The impact of the *Girondins* was increased by the successful performance in Paris of a play by Alexandre Dumas, *Le Chevalier de Maison-Rouge*, about an episode of the time of the Girondins. The play's chorus, 'Mourir pour la patrie', became one of the most popular revolutionary songs in 1848, indicating how far the French Revolution had caught the popular imagination. In addition, the *Girondins* focused public attention on Lamartine and helped to project him as a major political and literary figure, who was prepared to justify revolutionary violence and defend the ideals, heroes and goals of French republicanism.

In Mâcon it was decided to erect a bust of the celebrated author. Declining this honour, Lamartine agreed to attend a banquet on 18 July 1847 to commemorate the publication of the *Histoire des Girondins*. The banquet, ostensibly a literary occasion, quickly assumed a political character. In 1845 a central committee had been established in Paris to secure the election of reformist candidates to the Chamber of Deputies. Odilon Barrot had persuaded this committee to form a common front to press for an extension of the parliamentary franchise, and a reform meeting, in the form of a public banquet to avoid government restrictions on political meetings, had been held in Château Rouge in Paris on 9 July 1847. There followed a series of reform banquets in provincial towns. The Mâcon banquet of 18 July, however, did not formally belong to this reform banquet campaign. Independently and locally organised, its purpose was to honour Lamartine and celebrate the publication of the *Histoire des Girondins*; and it can be compared to the previous Mâcon banquets honouring him of 18 March 1839 and 4 June 1843. Lamartine had agreed to the banquet proposal in April, before the reform banquet campaign had started, and apparently he did not want his banquet to be openly partisan.[75] Also, he insisted that the banquet should be held in a private yard, not a public square (as originally proposed). However, his well-known opposition to the Government and recent rehabilitation of republicanism in the *Histoire des Girondins*, as well as the banquet's timing, meant that from the start contemporaries identified it with the reform banquet campaign. Moreover, Lamartine himself, with characteristic ambivalence, had indicated in *Le Bien public* that he did not want the politician to give way to the man of letters. The banquet's organisation fell almost entirely on Lamartine's political supporters and on local opponents of the Guizot Government. The prefect and other local officials were invited to attend, but refused, so as not to participate in what would clearly be an anti-government demonstration.[76]

During the morning of 18 July a large crowd assembled in Mâcon, drawn mainly from the region but also from as far as Paris and Switzerland. According to conservative estimates, there were between 1,600 and 1,700 diners and more than 2,000 spectators,[77] whereas the Château Rouge banquet had attracted just 1,200 diners. Scarcely had the banquet's chairman, Charles Rolland (since January 1847 mayor of Mâcon), finished his speech than a thunderstorm broke out, causing some panic. After the storm had ended Lamartine delivered a rousing and emotional speech. 'My book needed a conclusion, and you will make it!', he told his enthusiastic audience. The conclusion was that France should study its revolutionary tradition, separate the Revolution's ideals from its excesses, and learn the lessons of the Revolution for the present and the future. The Revolution was essentially an ideology of peace, individual liberty, popular sovereignty, traditional liberal freedoms, and of succour to the oppressed throughout the world. The July Monarchy would be overthrown if its failure to implement this ideology continued, though Lamartine also declared: 'Revolutions of free governments can be made within the framework of the constitution!' He went on to proclaim his faith in political sovereignty being exercised by all citizens and in 'the republic of intelligence', and to prophesy 'a revolution of public conscience and contempt', while expressing hopes for a peaceful and rational resolution of the crisis.[78]

Possibly upset by the banquet's rather chaotic character, Lamartine seems to have prepared a press release stressing his enthusiastic reception.[79] Two issues of *La Presse* (22 and 23 July) prominently reported the banquet and his speech, which received extensive coverage from the French press generally. Predictably, conservative newspapers feared that he had taken a further step towards the Left, thereby betraying his class and his status as one of France's major literary figures, while left-wing newspapers were delighted. The banquet's development into an anti-government demonstration, the singing of the Marseillaise and other revolutionary songs by some members of the audience during the thunderstorm, and demands by Lamartine and another speaker for electoral reform,[80] firmly identified Lamartine and the Mâcon banquet with the reform campaign. At the same time his widely reproduced speech of 18 July greatly encouraged the organisers of the reform banquets.[81] The enthusiasm of the crowd and the subsequent fan mail impressed Lamartine: he believed that his speech had answered the prevailing mood of public opinion in France; and his conviction was strengthened that he would soon play a decisive role in French politics.[82]

On 5 August Lamartine left Mâcon with Marianne for a holiday near Marseilles. On arrival at Marseilles he was greeted by a workers' demonstration and a local choir's serenading, indications of his popularity. This delighted him and was noted by the press.[83] After renting a small house by the sea for two weeks, the Lamartines moved to the Hôtel des Empereurs in Marseilles. The Marseilles visit again became a public demonstration of Lamartine's popularity, with requests for him to give speeches, banquets held in his honour by the Free Trade Association of Marseilles (24 August) and the Academy of Marseilles (26 August), and an invitation from the Commission of Algerian Colonists to visit Algiers.[84]

Returning to Monceau (16 September), Lamartine found awaiting him an invitation to attend a reform banquet on 19 September at Saint-Quentin. He refused, claiming that he had to stay in the Mâconnais during the grape harvest. However, his refusal was extremely polite, and he stated that he would attend the banquet 'in heart and spirit', adding: 'It is a consolation for me to think that you and your friends have thought fit to inscribe my name among the names of those of whom France never despairs.' This letter, published in *Le National*,[85] was clearly regarded as a public commitment of support to the banquet campaign. The opposition deputies for Saône-et-Loire, including Lamartine, were invited to speak at a reform banquet held at Autun on 27 October. Lamartine sent the banquet organisers a subscription, and *Le National* announced that he would preside,[86] but subsequently he withdrew. Over half the subscribers followed his example, allowing radicals to dominate the banquet.[87] The timing and motivation of his decision are unclear. He privately admitted on 5 October the receipt of 'a multitude of pressing and passionate requests to preside over banquets all over France'. Unenthusiastic, he feared having to attend reform banquets in towns within the department of Saône-et-Loire, such as Autun and Chalon-sur-Saône.[88] Nevertheless, he remained in the Mâconnais — supervising his grape harvest, attending the annual meeting of *Le Bien public*'s founder-members, and writing editorial articles for *Le Bien public*.

The annual meeting of *Le Bien public*'s founder-members (15 October) accepted the resignation of Jean-Jacques Gizorme, the newspaper's editor since December 1844, and appointed his successor, Auguste Guyard. There were almost certainly political reasons for this change of editor. Lamartine's letter accepting Gizorme's resignation denies any personal or political disagreements.[89] However, a contemporary claimed that there had been a personal dispute, presumably over the political direction of *Le Bien public*.[90] Certainly, Gizorme went on to edit a legitimist newspaper, *L'Océan* of Brest, and to clash during the autumn of 1848 with the editor of a local republican newspaper, *Le Finistère*.[91] In contrast, Guyard, while editor of *Le Progrès de la Loire*, had been prosecuted in February 1845 for infringement of the press laws. Found guilty of having discussed a political subject (the organisation of labour) in a newspaper for which caution money had not been paid, and of having encouraged readers to sign a workers' petition circulated by Ledru-Rollin, he had been sentenced to two months' imprisonment and fined 400 francs.[92] Since Guyard was also an ardent Fourierist, his appointment constituted a remarkably left-wing choice.[93]

Le Bien public published on 21 October an article by Lamartine declaring his political principles. He began by proclaiming that his pre-eminent concern was the people, and that he would accept the July Monarchy if it served the interests of the people. The latter would occur only if the July Monarchy pursued a series of objectives, which he proceeded to outline. There should be major constitutional reforms so as to achieve the sovereignty of the people. Those reforms would result in the replacement of the existing Chamber of Peers and Chamber of Deputies by a single National Assembly elected indirectly by all citizens and composed of representatives who would receive salaries and who could not be government employees. Government ministers would be appointed and dismissed not by the King but by majority vote in the National Assembly. In addition, traditional liberal freedoms would be restored in France: freedom of religion, through the complete separation of Church and State; freedom of the press, through the repeal of the September 1835 press laws; and freedom of education and association, through the relaxation of State restrictions. Two major reforms were demanded − the provision of free education on as extensive a scale as possible, and the abolition of slavery in all French territories. On social and economic matters Lamartine remained relatively conservative: he wanted a reduction of taxes on foodstuffs, the introduction of a new tax to provide funds for the poor, the adoption by the State of abandoned children, and a much more comprehensive system of State and private charity.[94]

In demanding a single chamber legislature elected on the basis of manhood suffrage, and a monarch who was a constitutional figurehead rather than an executive head of State, Lamartine had adopted a perceptibly more left-wing political position. Otherwise his declaration of principles contained little that was strikingly new or radical. His demands for the restoration of traditional liberal freedoms, for an extension of State education and for the abolition of slavery, had been made by him many times before and were the sorts of demands widely supported not just by republicans and socialists, but also by liberals and even, to some extent, by conservatives. Also, his social and economic programme remained fundamentally moderate, thus maintaining in this area his ideological differences with the Left. This reflected his continued unwillingness to consider any socialist policy which might apparently threaten the institutions of the family and private property. Perhaps, too, the relatively good harvest of 1847 and the fall in agricultural prices had encouraged him, like many other *notables*, to believe that the worst of the economic crisis was over, whereas in fact urban unemployment was increasing. The conservatism and inadequacy of his solutions to the economic crisis did attract criticism from Pascal Duprat in *La Revue indépendante*.[95] However, at a time when the banquet campaign was gathering momentum, Lamartine's conversion to manhood suffrage delighted *Le National*, which now believed that he was on the point of joining the moderate republicans.[96]

At the end of October Lamartine contributed three articles on France's position abroad to *Le Bien public*. He deplored the failure of France to assist Italian nationalist movements; and, in a situation of imminent civil war in Switzerland, he severely criticised Guizot's decision to support the Sonderbund, a Catholic defensive alliance, rather than its radical opponents.[97] But at the same time he went to considerable lengths to refute *Le Journal de Saône-et-Loire*'s accusation that *Le Bien public* was 'une feuille de doctrines radicales'. He insisted that he had never advocated violent revolution, had always wanted peace, and had vigorously defended society's three pillars, the State, the family and private property.[98] This article greatly disappointed Cabet, who had almost convinced himself that Lamartine was a communist.[99] Showing a similar ambivalence, Lamartine continued to support, but not participate in, the banquet campaign. Refusing an invitation to attend a reform banquet at Lyons, he wrote on 6 November to the banquet's organisers, associating himself with 'the great demonstration', and declaring his belief in the urgent need to democratise the constitution and in the value of exerting the pressure of public opinion on the government. He claimed that he would have been happy to attend the banquet, but, since circumstances had forced him to decline an invitation to attend a reform banquet in his own department, he could not now honourably accept another invitation.[100] To Dr Ordinaire, one of the organisers of the Lyons banquet, he claimed that although he totally supported the banquet campaign, he could not accept Lyons without causing considerable offence, since he had already refused eighteen invitations. He added that he did not regard the role of 'universal guest' and 'national parasite' as personally opportune.[101] However, *Le Bien public*'s issue for 11 November again set a radical tone, with one article suggesting that the Pope should recall the Jesuits from Switzerland, and another resuming Lamartine's criticisms of Guizot's domestic and foreign policies.[102]

During November Lamartine remained at Monceau and Saint-Point, entertaining large numbers of guests.[103] At the same time he began to clarify his attitude towards the reform banquet campaign. When anti-private property sentiments were expressed at the Autun reform banquet of 27 October, he published an article in *Le Bien public* (14

November) reiterating his belief in private property's inviolability, communism's impracticability, and in the social question's solution through fraternity and mutual assistance.[104] When at a reform banquet in Lille on 7 November Ledru-Rollin referred to Lamartine's giant strides towards adopting a democratic political position,[105] Lamartine declared his opposition to artificial political coalitions, and to the appearance of Odilon Barrot and Ledru-Rollin on the same political platform. He also stated that the Autun banquet's transparent communism had surprised and saddened public opinion. But he strongly regretted that unavoidable circumstances prevented him attending a reform banquet at Lyons; and after praising Ledru-Rollin's speech at Lille, he suggested that they both held very similar social and economic views.[106] Thus, while disassociating himself from the extreme socialist Left and maintaining his distance from Odilon Barrot, Lamartine had again publicly supported the reform banquet campaign, and had singled out Ledru-Rollin for special approval. Significantly, *La Réforme* (23 November) reproduced Lamartine's article on the Lille banquet, though the editorial questioned whether he supported social and political equality.

On 30 November Lamartine wrote to his conservative friend, Circourt, that, despite invitations to chair thirty-nine banquets, he 'had only an ear to politics'. His current concern, he suggested, was composing *Raphaël*, a description of his romance with Julie Charles.[107] More truthfully, he confessed to Emile de Girardin on 5 December:[108]

> The banquets obsess me. I have received forty invitations this morning. Don't you consider that an isolated politician whom all the departments of his country invite to preside over banquets is not so isolated as is suggested? Nobody knows how many thousands might join my isolation if I were to give the rallying call.

Perhaps on the brink of giving the rallying call, Lamartine twice indicated that he would attend the Lyons reform banquet of 23 November.[109] He sent a letter of support to the Chalon-sur-Saône reform banquet of 19 December, and persuaded a friend, Henri de Lacretelle, to go in his place. Guyard also went. In one of the banquet speeches Prudent Forest referred to Lamartine as an exponent of the principle of fraternity; and at the banquet Lacretelle met Ledru-Rollin, who questioned him closely about the Mâcon banquet of 18 July and spoke warmly of the *Histoire des Girondins*: 'The most important service which Lamartine has rendered to the Republic, he told me',

Lacretelle reported, 'is that one can now discuss Robespierre without being taken for a cannibal'.[110] Lamartine also suggested that he would attend the Rouen reform banquet of 25 December, even choosing a toast, 'To the reforming of the constitutional opposition', which displeased Duvergier de Hauranne (one of the banquet's organisers). At the banquet itself he was expected to appear at any moment.[111]

In being invited to these reform banquets Lamartine was now associated with certain types of people. The invitation list to one planned by the Paris Ecoles for 22 December included, besides Lamartine: one editor each from *La Réforme, Le National, Le Courrier français, Le Charivari* and *La Revue indépendante*; seven deputies — François Arago, Hippolyte Carnot, Dupont de l'Eure, Garnier-Pagès, Ledru-Rollin, Marie, and General Thiard; Michelet, Mickiewicz and Quinet, along with several other professors popular with the students; and finally Béranger, Louis Blanc, Lamennais, Pierre Leroux, George Sand and Vaulabelle.[112] The list constitutes a virtual roll-call of the leaders of the French Left at the time; and, in addition to Lamartine, it specifically mentions seven future members of the Provisional Government.

Meanwhile, Lamartine continued to publish articles in *Le Bien public*. His article of 16 December on the Lyons reform banquet began:[113]

> Lyons has just given its signature to the new marriage contract between the opposition and the country by the memorable banquet held within its walls. At the banquet there was not one toast, speech or opinion which the most constitutionally-minded citizen could not accept.

Lamartine proceeded to compare the current political situation in France with that in the autumn of 1829; and he argued that July Monarchy governments had perpetrated a series of *coups d'état* against the Revolution's 'esprit' and the ideas, movements and needs of the age, with the September press laws, the law of associations, the fortifications of Paris, the regency law, the refusal to enlarge the franchise or pay deputies salaries, and the Spanish marriages.[114] In *Le Bien public*'s next issue (19 December) Lamartine replied to an open letter from Cabet protesting about *Le Bien 'public*'s attacks on communism.[115] Lamartine's reply stressed private property's civilising influence and how the institutions of the State, family and private property conformed to natural law and human instinct. But he also stressed his belief in toleration and rational debate; and his admonition of Cabet was very gentle – 'Your dream is too beautiful for this world'.[116]

An article on the Chalon reform banquet appeared in *Le Bien public* on 23 December. After a few complimentary words, the article criticised the substitution of *citoyen* for *monsieur*, and other references to 1793 and 1794.[117] A second article (26 December) repeated this criticism and opposed a suggested radicals' conference on Switzerland. Also, the second article contained slightly double-edged comments on Ledru-Rollin, such as 'M. Ledru-Rollin is very intelligible, perhaps too so'. Similarly, Ledru-Rollin was described as having demonstrated at Chalon 'frankness, intellectual boldness, resolution, determination and talent, which have revealed in him the mental and emotional qualities of a party leader'. It was then suggested, 'The country does not want to be a party, it wants to be France.'[118] Yet Lamartine specifically asked Girardin not to reproduce in *La Presse* at least one of the articles, because it was 'too hard on the Barrot-Thiers opposition'.[119] Neither of the articles on the Chalon banquet in fact appeared in *La Presse*, nor, it seems, in any newspaper besides *Le Bien public* (though on 28 December *La Réforme* briefly referred to them, quoting *Le Patriote de Saône-et-Loire*). Clearly, Lamartine did not want his reservations concerning Ledru-Rollin and the reform banquet campaign known outside *Le Bien public*'s readership, presumably so as to keep his political options open.

The Chambers reassembled on 27 December for the new parliamentary session. Kept by illness at Monceau, Lamartine did not leave for Paris until 10 January 1848. In *Le Bien public* of 2 January he strongly criticised the speech from the throne, particularly for having suggested that 'blind' or 'hostile' passions had produced the banquet campaign. Instead, he argued that the campaign was an example of people exercising their political rights, by holding orderly demonstrations and public discussions on matters of national interest.[120] He first spoke in the new parliament on 29 January, when he scathingly condemned Guizot's foreign policies in a speech lasting almost two hours.[121] In a second speech on 11 February he accused the Government of trying to stifle public opinion, and reaffirmed his support for the banquet campaign. The following day *Le National* admired without reservation 'the genius of M. Lamartine', while *La Réforme*, agreeing with everything he had said, described his speech as excellent.

The banquet campaign was planned to climax with a reform banquet in the twelfth *arrondissement* of Paris. The Guizot Government feared this might provoke demonstrations in one of the poorest and most radical Paris *arrondissements*, and the Prefect of Police banned the banquet on 14 January. In his parliamentary speech of 11 February Lamartine was clearly attacking this ban. On 13 February he attended a meeting of about a hundred deputies at Durand's restaurant in the Place de la Madeleine. Right and left-wing opposition groups were represented, those present including Odilon Barrot, Berryer, Carnot, Chambolle, Crémieux, Drouyn de Lhuys, Duvergier de Hauranne, Falloux, Garnier-Pagès, Lesseps, Marie, Rémusat, and Thiers.[122] At the meeting Marie, Drouyn de Lhuys and Chambolle supported a proposal, previously suggested by Marrast and Girardin, that opposition deputies should resign *en masse*, thus forcing the Government to hold a large number of by-elections. With Crémieux, Lamartine was one of the most vigorous opponents of this proposal. Instead, he supported the formation of a banquet commission to organise a reform banquet in the twelfth *arrondissement* of Paris for 20 February. The meeting agreed to this challenge of the Government's earlier prohibition and formed a banquet commission, which did not, however, include Lamartine.[123] His attitude seems to have been contradictory. On 14 February he declined to attend a reform banquet proposed by the Paris Ecoles, because he did not want to participate in an illegal demonstration.[124] Yet the following day he told the marquise de La Grange he would attend the twelfth *arrondissement* banquet, regarding it as a question of honour.[125]

Because of the difficulties of finding a suitable venue, it was agreed at a meeting of the banquet commission on 18 February to postpone the banquet until 22 February. The same day (18 February) Lamartine among others signed a letter accepting an invitation to the twelfth *arrondissement* banquet.[126] A second meeting of opposition deputies was held in Durand's restaurant on 19 February. About two hundred attended, though both Rémusat and Thiers were absent. A proposal not to hold the banquet was criticised by Duvergier de Hauranne but to a large extent supported by Berryer, who was afraid of violence. Dismissing such fears, Crémieux insisted that the banquet should take place, and welcomed the prospect of a massive public demonstration involving the Paris National Guard. Then Lamartine eloquently and persuasively argued that the right of political assembly had to be asserted.[127] According to Alton-Shée (a liberal peer), he convinced the meeting to hold the banquet on 22 February.[128] In Lamartine's *salon* that evening there was much lively discussion of the twelfth *arrondissement* banquet. Alexis Vavin (left-wing deputy for the eleventh *arrondissement* of Paris) declared that he would shoot at any policeman who attempted to arrest him. Lamartine reportedly 'had a somewhat preoccupied air'.[129]

On the morning of 21 February the Prefect of Police signed a decree prohibiting the banquet or any other political meeting. The same day, after the adjournment of debates in the Chamber at five in the afternoon, opposition deputies assembled at Odilon Barrot's house. There Odilon Barrot advised them to avoid an outbreak of violence by not attending the banquet. Similar views were expressed by Chambolle, Thiers, Bethmont and Rémusat. Lamartine had always feared popular violence; and as recently as the previous day (20 February) he had instructed Guyard, editor of *Le Bien public*: 'Do not compromise the newspaper. Do not make it at any price an organ of anarchy'.[130] On the other hand, he had praised the great days of the Revolution in the *Histoire des Girondins*, and at the meeting of opposition deputies on 19 February he had insisted on asserting the right of political assembly, even at the risk of provoking a confrontation with Government forces. Again on 21 February he maintained that the banquet should be held, notwithstanding the ban from the Prefect of Police and the possibility of violence. Presumably he belived that the Guizot Government's reactionary and intransigent character justified holding the reform banquet, and running the risk of violence which this entailed. Despite the speeches of Lamartine and others, the meeting decided by eighty votes to seventeen that deupties should not attend the banquet. Several peers and deputies, including Alton-Shée, Boissy, Courtais, Dupont de l'Eure, Harcourt, Lamartine, Ledru-Rollin, Marie, Marrast and Thiard, refused to accept this verdict. They agreed to meet at ten that evening in Lamartine's residence (which may have deterred some deputies from attending) to concert their plans. At this meeting Lamartine declared that he would, if necessary, go to the banquet alone, accompanied by his shadow.[131] However, Alexis Vavin and Ferdinand de Lasteyrie arrived at about midnight from Odilon Barrot's house with the news that the banquet commission had finally decided not to hold the banquet.[132]

Although the banquet had been abandoned, in Paris during 22 February popular demonstrations and violent clashes occurred, caused by the popular hatred of the July Monarchy, the very severe urban unemployment resulting from the economic crisis, and the political excitement provoked by the reform banquet campaign. Demonstrations continued the following day, when soldiers fired on a crowd outside the Ministry of Foreign Affairs in the Boulevard des Capucines. On this critical day Michelet wrote to Lamartine, although they were not on particularly friendly terms.[133] He urged him to propose an address in the Chamber of Deputies demanding that the King should entrust the maintenance of law and order to the National Guard alone. Michelet emphasised that only Lamartine could perform this task: 'You alone ought to propose the address. You are the *premier des premiers*'.[134] This indicates Lamartine's unique position and prestige on the eve of the February Revolution. He was a national figure; he had re-established his reputation for devastating attacks on government policies; and as one of the most resolute supporters of the twelfth *arrondissement* banquet, he had identified himself with the French Left more closely than ever before.

Lamartine's defiant attitude towards the Government, and determination to attend the banquet, had not passed unnoticed by the moderate republican group associated with *Le National*. On the evening of 23 February Bastide and Marrast, respectively *Le National*'s editor and former editor, asked a publisher called Hetzel to visit Lamartine. The latter told Hetzel that a republic was inevitable. Hetzel then insisted that the republicans needed Lamartine's support if national unity were to be preserved; and it was arranged that Lamartine should meet Bastide and Marrast the following morning in the Palais Bourbon.[135]

By the morning of 24 February Louis-Philippe could not rely on the army or National Guard to defend him against the hostile crowds gathering around the Tuileries Palace. He therefore abdicated in favour of his nine-year-old grandson, the comte de Paris, and went into exile. The question immediately arose as to whether to establish a regency for the comte de Paris or a provisional government which would probably lead to a republic. During the morning of 24 February at a meeting in *Le National*'s editorial office it was decided to press for a provisional government. Several lists of government members were also drawn up. Arago, Marie, Garnier-Pagès and Marrast seem to have been on all the lists, while among others mentioned were Odilon Barrot, Ledru-Rollin, Dupont de l'Eure and Lamartine. Although contemporary sources are not absolutely clear, it seems that Odilon Barrot was quickly dropped and that later lists included Lamartine.[136]

As previously agreed, Lamartine met Bastide, Hetzel and Marrast, together with a republican actor called Bocage, in a small room in the Palais Bourbon before he entered the Chamber of Deputies on 24 February. He promised them that he would speak against the regency and support a provisional government.[137] Odilon Barrot suggests that a pact existed between Lamartine and Bacage, according to which

Lamartine would speak against the regency in return for his inclusion in *Le National*'s list. As evidence of this pact Odilon Barrot points to Bocage shouting in the Chamber, 'To the Hôtel de Ville, Lamartine at our head!'[138] Odilon Barrot is a hostile source on Lamartine. Yet his suggestion is supported by information received by Duvergier de Hauranne indirectly from Bocage;[139] and it is possible that Lamartine's name was added to *Le National*'s list only after the meeting in the Palais Bourbon had taken place.

At the afternoon session of the Chamber of Deputies on 24 February Odilon Barrot proposed that the duchesse d'Orléans, widowed mother of the comte de Paris, should be declared regent of France. In the debate which followed Lamartine demanded the formation of a provisional government. He was not the only deputy to do so – Marie, Crémieux and Ledru-Rollin had all spoken before him to the same effect. Probably, too, the regency's rejection and the establishment of the Provisional Government were determined as much by the fact that the Chamber was invaded by demonstrators, as by anything opposition deputies said. Lamartine's intervention in the debate was nevertheless important, if for no other reason than that it virtually guaranteed his passage to political power.

The content of Lamartine's intervention may have been determined only at the very last moment.[140] Certainly he surprised many of his listeners;[141] and he apparently refused to read out a list of government members headed by his own name.[142] Perhaps he hesitated when confronted with the choice of two roles, the tribune of the people or the defender of fugitive monarchy.[143] Odilon Barrot's defence of the regency may have finally swayed him, though this must remain conjecture.[144] During the debate he offered the legitimist Berryer a place in the Provisional Government (which Berryer refused);[145] and he is reported to have told a crowd at the Hôtel de Ville on the evening of 24 February, 'you need a rallying point around which the country can consolidate itself and guarantee its interests'. He then allegedly asked, 'Do you want the Regency?'[146] His somewhat ambiguous political position would explain such last-minute hesitations and fence-sitting, but many other factors must have encouraged him to reject a regency and demand a provisional government. Besides his old dislike of the July Monarchy, long-standing willingness to accept a republic in France, and increasing identification with the Left, he must have correctly assessed the outcome of the debate, particularly after the invasion of the Chamber had begun. Inebriated with his own popularity, ambitious to emerge as a national saviour at a time of crisis, and concerned to avoid violence and promote national unity, he therefore ultimately decided to join the Revolution and help found the Second Republic.

A period of uproar and disorder followed Lamartine's speech. Lamartine attempted to read out a list of names, beginning with Arago and Carnot, but his voice was drowned in the tumult and he eventually withdrew from the tribune. Dupont de l'Eure then read out a list, but after naming Arago, Lamartine, Dupont de l'Eure and Crémieux, he was silenced in his turn by the noise and general confusion. At a second attempt he announced the names of Lamartine, Ledru-Rollin, Arago, Dupont de l'Eure and Marie. There followed shouts that the Provisional Government should go to the Hôtel de Ville, whereupon Lamartine left the Chamber accompanied by a large crowd. Only then did Ledru-Rollin read out the list of names of those who finally formed the Provisional Government's nucleus: Arago, Crémieux, Dupont de l'Eure, Garnier-Pagès, Lamartine, Ledru-Rollin and Marie.[147]

When the Provisional Government's members arrived at the Hôtel de Ville during the late afternoon of 24 February they were confronted with another government list, agreed on at the offices of *La Réforme*. This list comprised, besides Arago, Dupont de l'Eure, Garnier-Pagès, Lamartine, Ledru-Rollin, and Marie (but not Crémieux), Albert, Louis Blanc, Flocon, Marrast, and Recurt.[148] The names had been chosen early in the afternoon of 24 February, after Martin de Strasbourg and Louis Blanc had communicated *Le National*'s final list.[149] Lamartine's inclusion is interesting, especially since there is no hint of any agreement between Lamartine and members of the *Réforme* group, and since the list was voted in ignorance of his intervention in the Chamber. Apparently his acceptance was due to his popularity in the departments, which would ensure provincial and middle-class support for the new government.[150] Thus by 24 February Lamartine had become indispensable to the two main republican groups. As Alton-Shée puts it: 'There was one man whose eloquence, firmness and courage singled him out for popular admiration, one man whose support was sufficient to tip the balance, and that man was Lamartine'.[151]

Lamartine's inclusion in the February 1848 Provisional Government was thus not surprising, despite his *grand notable* status. By at least 1845 he had emerged as one of the few deputies sympathetic to the Left, and as someone who might give the Left national leadership and popular support. Consequently the left-wing press took him seriously and, while often critical, extensively covered his speeches and articles. Lamartine, for his part, courted this left-wing publicity and approval, and increasingly adopted a more radical political position. Of course, individual members of the French Left were sceptical of him, such as Flora Tristan, who met him and the editor of *Le Bien public* in 1844.[152] Also, Lamartine remained publicly hostile to socialism and communism, and even to radical social and economic policies; he was only gradually converted to manhood suffrage, and did not advocate direct manhood suffrage until after the February Revolution; and he maintained an ambivalent attitude towards the reform banquet campaign. However, with his speeches, articles and the *Histoire des Girondins* he acquired enormous popularity and influence; he became one of the most resolute supporters of the twelfth *arrondissement* banquet; and in the crucial parliamentary debate of 24 February he finally committed himself (for whatever reasons) to the regency's rejection and the Provisional Government's formation. The ambiguities and contradictions in Lamartine's political position nevertheless remained. In opposition this was not of paramount importance, but in government and in revolution his position became much more difficult to sustain.

Notes

1. He claimed to have been 'ni l'homme des Tuileries, ni l'homme des journaux de l'opposition, ni l'homme des banquets réformistes, ni l'homme des conspirations contre la royauté' (*Histoire de la Révolution de 1848*, 2 vols. (Paris, 1849), I, p. 114).

2. Cochin, *Lamartine et la Flandre*, pp. 46-7, 345-6.

3. *Le Moniteur universel*, 18 August 1833, p. 1969; *Correspondance générale*, I, pp. 340-1.

4. F. Letessier, 'Lamartine et le "Père Enfantin" ', *Bulletin de l'Association Guillaume Budé*, October 1967, pp. 333-42.

5. *La Phalange*, 20 July 1836, pp. 60-3; Bouteiller to Considérant, 15 August 1836 (Considérant Papers, A. N., 10 AS 36 (8)).

6. Lamennais, *Correspondance générale*, VII (1978), pp. 251 and 255.

7. *La Phalange*, 15 December 1841, p. 746.

8. Ibid., 15 February 1842, pp. 313-16, 15 July 1842, p. 101.

9. Lamartine, *Voyage en Orient*, IV (1835), p. 311; *Le Populaire*, 10 October 1841, p. 6; E. Cabet, *Voyage en Icarie* (Paris, 1842), pp. 523-5.

10. *Correspondance de George Sand*, VI (1969), pp. 20-2; *Lettres à Lamartine*, pp. 195-8.

11. *Correspondance de George Sand*, VI (1969), pp. 32 and 307; *Le Courrier de la Côte-d'Or* (Dijon), 16 December 1843, pp. 1-2. On Lamartine's relations with George Sand see the note in her *Correspondance*, IV (1968), pp. 910-11, and G. Lubin, 'Lamartine et George Sand', in Viallaneix, *Lamartine. Le Livre du centenaire*, pp. 207-20.

12. See *Le National*, 3, 4, 24 and 30 March 1843.

13. See *Le Commerce*, 3 and 24 March 1843; *La Phalange*, 3, 15 and 24 March 1843, pp. 1720, 1805-10, 1871.

14. E. Daudet (ed.), *Journal de Victor de Balabine* (Paris, 1914), p. 115;

Ledru-Rollin Papers, B.H.V.P., 5959, f. 17.

15.   A copy of the latter has apparently not survived, but it is cited in C.-A. Sainte-Beuve, *Chroniques parisiennes, 1843-1845* (Paris, 1876), p. 16.

16.   A. N., B. B.[18] 1412; B. N., nouv. acq. fr., 13266, f. 67.

17.   *La France parlementaire*, III, p. 379.

18.   Letter dated 16 June 1843; B. N., nouv. acq. fr., 13266, ff. 69-70.

19.   *Lettres à Lamartine*, pp. 201-2.

20.   Letter dated 24 June 1843; A. N., 10 AS 39 (7).

21.   *Lettres à Lamartine*, pp. 203-8.

22.   Daubray, *Victor Hugo et ses correspondants*, pp. 98-101.

23.   *Correspondance générale*, I, p. 31, II, pp. 23, 223 and 240; Lallemand, *Montalembert et ses amis*, p. 86; *Correspondance*, V (1875), pp. 379-80; *Le Correspondant*, 10 July 1926, pp. 23-4. Lamartine considered collaborating with Nisard on a political review in 1836 (D. Nisard, *Souvenirs et notes biographiques*, 2 vols. (Paris, 1888), I, pp. 361-4).

24.   E. Faguet, 'Lettres inédites de Lamartine', *La Revue latine*, 25 November 1902, p. 642.

25.   Lamartine to Champvans, 2 and 8 October 1842; *Correspondance*, VI (1875), pp. 24-5 and 31.

26.   Dr P. C. Ordinaire, *Épisodes de la vie intime d'Alphonse de Lamartine* (Mâcon, 1878), p. 25; *Le National*, 16 July 1843, p. 3.

27.   According to Henri de Lacretelle (son of the Academician Charles de Lacretelle) they included, besides himself and Lamartine, Hippolyte Boussin (a neighbour of Henri de Lacretelle), Léon Bruys d'Ouilly (intimate friend of Byron's last mistress and a local amateur poet, who probably first met Lamartine through Quinet in May 1832), Guigue de Champvans (who had rejoined *Le Journal de Saône-et-Loire* after over a year in Soult's private office), Duréault (former opposition deputy for Saône-et-Loire and member of the *conseil général*), Charles Rolland (co-founder of *Le Progrès de Saône-et-Loire*), and Adolphe de Latour, Garnier-Lacombe and Jean Versaut (Lacretelle, *Lamartine et ses amis*, p. 66). They were soon joined by Lacroix (opposition deputy for Saône-et-Loire and member of the *conseil général*), Mathieu (opposition deputy for Saône-et-Loire), Jacques-Edouard Reverchon (member of the *conseil général*), Ochier (member of Mâcon's *conseil d'arrondissement* and Cluny's deputy-mayor), and Berthier; (*Le Bien public*, 16 November 1843, p. 3).

28.   See F. Tristan, *Le Tour de France; journal inédit* (Paris, 1973), p. 60; L. de Tricaud, *Histoire du départment de l'Ain du 24 février au 20 décembre 1848* (Bourg-en-Bresse, 1872), pp. 48-50.

29.   *La France parlementaire*, III, pp. 386-96. The letter was first published in *La Revue indépendante*, 10 August 1843, pp. 357-66, in reply to a letter from Chapuys-Montlaville, 5 May 1843; see *Correspondance entre MM L.-Napoléon Bonaparte, Lamartine et Chapuys-Montlaville* (Mâcon, 1849), pp. 3-8.

30.   *Le Journal de Saône-et-Loire*, 8 August 1848, p. 2.

31.   Lamartine to Champvans, 24 February 1844; *Correspondance*, VI (1875), p. 97.

32.   Lacretelle, *Lamartine et ses amis*, p. 76.

33.   *Le Bien public*, 14 August 1845; Luppé, *Lamartine*, pp. 310-11.

34.   *Correspondance*, VI (1875), p. 97.

35.   Eugène Sue Papers, B.H.V.P., 3935, f. 692.

36.   *Le Bien public*, 7 December 1843, p. 2; Lamartine to Considérant, 9 December 1843 (A. N., 10 AS 39 (7)).

37.   *Correspondance*, VI (1875), p. 94.

38.   Lamartine to Dubois, 3 February 1843: '*Je prends le terrain et non les hommes de la gauche*'. (*Correspondance*, VI (1875), p. 51.)

39. See Lamartine to Champvans and Ronot, 24 February and 8 April 1844 (ibid., VI (1875), pp. 171-2 and 176). Cf. A. Chambolle, *Retours sur la vie. Appréciations et confidences sur les hommes de mon temps* (Paris, 1912), pp. 183-5; des Cognets, *La Vie intérieure de Lamartine*, pp. 316-20.

40. See Mattlé, *Lamartine voyageur*, pp. 124-36.

41. Lamartine refers to *La Démocratie pacifique* in a letter to E. de Girardin, 16 November 1844; B. N., nouv. acq. fr., 16581, f. 168.

42. *La France parlementaire*, IV, pp. 103-21.

43. *La Réforme*, 31 December 1844, 1, 6 and 8 January 1845; *La Démocratie pacifique*, 29 and 31 December 1844, 2, 4, 7, 8 and 11 January 1845.

44. Auguste Blanqui, on the other hand, thought that Lamartine had been too complimentary of Fourierist doctrines, but was otherwise delighted with the two articles and the general direction of his writings (Blanqui to Lamartine, 22 February 1845; *Lettres à Lamartine*, pp. 218-20).

45. For secondary studies on Lamartine's social and political thought see D. Guérin, 'Les idées sociales de Lamartine', *Revue des sciences politiques*, July-September 1924, p. 396-414; Guillemin, *Lamartine et la question sociale*; M.-F. Guyard, 'Les idées politiques de Lamartine', *Revue des travaux de l'Académie des sciences morales et politiques*, 2e semestre, 1966, pp. 1-16; E. Harris, *Lamartine et le peuple* (Paris, 1932); B. J. Jallaguier, *Les Idés politiques et sociales d'Alphonse de Lamartine* (Montpellier, 1954); M. Maurice, 'Lamartine et la paysannerie', *Europe*, July-August 1969, pp. 62-86; E. Sachs, *Les Idées sociales de Lamartine jusqu'à 1840* (Paris, 1915).

46. *Le Bien public*, 21 November 1844; *La France parlementaire*, IV, p. 88.

47. 'M. de Lamartine dans l'opposition'; *La Réforme*, 23 November 1844.

48. *Le Bien public*, 10 August 1843, pp. 1-2; *La France parlementaire*, III, pp. 399-400.

49. Ibid., IV, p. 204.

50. Ibid., IV, p. 197.

51. Lamartine to Girardin, 10 September 1845; B. N., nouv. acq. fr., 16581, f. 173. *L'Esprit public* was a recently founded Paris left-wing newspaper edited by Charles Lesseps, who, until he resigned his editorship in January 1847, again faithfully supported Lamartine and published his articles.

52. *La Revue indépendante*, 25 November 1845, p. 299.

53. P. Forest, *Défense du fouriérisme* (Paris, 1845), pp. 64-85.

54. *Le Bien public*, 9 October 1845, p. 2, 16 October 1845, pp. 1-2; *La Mouche littéraire de Saône-et-Loire et de l'Ain*, 14 October 1845, p. 2.

55. See *Le National*, 27 December 1845 – 3 January 1846; *La Revue indépendante*, 25 January 1846, pp. 239-45.

56. *La Réforme*, 5 January 1846, p. 2.

57. E. Regnault, *Révolution française. Histoire de huit ans, 1840-1848*, 3 vols. (Paris, 1851-52), III, p. 66.

58. See Dr L.-G. Barrachin, *M. de Lamartine apprécié comme homme politique* (Paris, 1846).

59. *La Mouche littéraire de Saône-et-Loire et de l'Ain*, 23 December 1846.

60. See J. Barzun, 'Romantic Historiography as a Political Force in France', *Journal of the History of Ideas*, June 1941, pp. 318-29; P. Farmer, *France Reviews its Revolutionary Origins. Social politics and historical opinion in the Third Republic* (New York, 1944); G. P. Gooch, *History and Historians in the Nineteenth Century* (London, 1952); S. Mellon, *The Political Uses of History: a study of historians in the French Revolution* (Stanford, California, 1958).

61. See Lamartine to Dargaud, 5 June 1843 (*Le Correspondant*, 10 July 1926, p. 34); Luppé, *Lamartine*, pp. 230 and 312.

62. Comte J. d'Estourmel, *Derniers souvenirs* (Paris, 1860), p. 109. Cf. Lurine, *Histoire poétique et politique de M. de Lamartine*, p. 215; R. Pierrot, 'Lettres inédites sur la Révolution de 1848', *L'Année balzacienne*, I (1960), p. 52.

63. Lamartine to Jules Pautet (municipal librarian of Beaune and editor of the *Revue de la Côte-d'Or*); *Revue de la Côte-d'Or*, 1847, p. 100. Cf. H. Guillemin, 'Lamartine et son *Histoire des Girondins*', *La Revue de France*, 15 March 1939, p. 181; G. Robert, 'Lamartine et le mythe de la Révolution dans l'*Histoire des Girondins*', *Revue des sciences humaines* (Lille), July – September 1947, p. 256, note 71. See also Lamartine to Chamborre, 10 June 1847; *Correspondance*, VI (1875), p. 251.

64. *La Revue de France*, 15 February 1939, pp. 524-5.

65. See Lamartine's undelivered speech, c. June 1840; J. L. Barthou, *Lamartine orateur* (Paris, 1918), p. 126.

66. Legouvé, *Soixante ans de souvenirs*, II, p. 361.

67. Lamartine to Virieu, 6 February 1841 (A. de Chamborant de Périssat, *Lamartine inconnu: notes, lettres et documents inédits* (Paris, 1891), p. 2) and February 1838 (*Correspondance*, V (1875), p. 278).

68. Lamartine to Aimé Martin, 4 October 1843; *La Revue de Paris*, 1 November 1925, p. 45.

69. Lamartine to the père Enfantin, 21 July 1843; *Bulletin de l'Association Guillaume Budé*, 1967, p. 335.

70. Lamartine to Ronot, 7 March 1846; B. M., Mâcon, ms. 107, f. 96, and *Le Correspondant*, 10 July 1926, p. 40.

71. See R. Molho (ed.), *Sainte-Beauve. Cahiers*, I (1973), p. 355.

72. Mergier-Bourdeix (ed.), *Jules Janin. 735 lettres à sa femme*, 2 vols. (Paris, 1973-75), I, p. 233.

73. *Le National*, 15 March 1847, p. 3; *Le Populaire*, March 1847, pp. 3-4; *La Démocratie pacifique*, 2 May 1847, pp. 2-3; *La Revue indépendante*, 10 July 1847, p. 84.

74. P. Thureau-Dangin, *Histoire de la Monarchie de Juillet*, 7 vols. (Paris, 1884-92), VII, p. 51.

75. *La Mouche littéraire de Saône-et-Loire et de l'Ain*, 5 May 1847; Lamartine to Chamborre, 10 June 1847 (*Correspondance*, VI (1875), pp. 250-1).

76. Desserteaux *substitut du procureur du roi* at Mâcon) to the *procureur général*, 22 July 1847 (A. N., BB[18] 1454, dossier A 4183); *Le Patriote de Saône-et-Loire*, 11 July 1847.

77. Report of Desserteaux (loc. cit.); *Le Journal de Saône-et-Loire*, 22 July 1847; Lacretelle, *Lamartine et ses amis*, pp. 98-9.

78. *La France parlementaire*, V, pp. 28-46. Cf. Ponsard to the comtesse d'Agoult, 25 July 1847; J. Vier (ed.), *La comtesse d'Agoult et François Ponsard d'après une correspondance inédite, 1843-1867* (Paris, 1960), p. 40.

79. *Revue d'histoire diplomatique*, October-December 1935, pp. 527-8; Séché, *Delphine Gay*, pp. 130-5.

80. *La France parlementaire*, V, p. 36; *Banquet offert à M. de Lamartine, le 18 juillet 1847. Discours prononcé par J.-M. Gerbaud* (Lyons: de Boursy fils, 1847), p. 11.

81. Comte E. d'Alton-Shée, *Souvenirs de 1847 et de 1848* (Paris, 1879), p. 61; J. E. V. Arago, *Histoire de Paris. Ses révolutions, ses gouvernements et ses événements de 1841 à 1852*, 2 vols. (Paris, 1855), I, pp. 209-10.

82. Lamartine to Dargaud, 20 July and 17 August 1847 (*Correspondance*, VI (1875), pp. 255-6, 264-6); Lamartine at Monceau, 26 July 1847 (*Le Bien public*, 27 July 1847 (Dumesnil Papers, B.H.V.P., 5712), and *La Presse*, 31 July 1847, pp. 2-3); Lamartine to Circourt, 2 August 1847 (B. N., nouv. acq. fr.,

24328, f. 260).

83. *Le Sémaphore de Marseille*, 13 August 1847, p. 2; Lamartine to V. de Cessiat, 16 August 1847 (*Lamartine et ses nièces*, p. 109), and Dargaud, 17 August 1847 (*Correspondance*, VI (1875), p. 265); *La Démocratie pacifique*, 20 August 1847, p. 2.

84. J. Autran, *Oeuvres complètes*, 8 vols. (Paris, 1875-81), VII (1878), pp. 61-6; Lamartine to Dargaud, 31 August 1847 (*Correspondance*, VI (1875), p. 268); *Le Sémaphore de Marseille*, 26-30 August 1847; *La Démocratie pacifique*, 2 October 1847, p. 2. For the texts of Lamartine's speeches see *La France parlementaire*, V, pp. 47-60; *La Revue de France*, 15 August 1939, pp. 491-5.

85. Letter dated 17 September 1847; *Le National*, 24 September 1847, p. 3.

86. See Guillemin to Pagnerre, no date (Pagnerre Papers, A. N., 67 AP 2, f. 44); *Le National*, 12 October 1847, p. 2.

87. J. J. Baughman, 'The Political Banquet Campaign in France, 1847-1848', unpublished PhD thesis (Michigan, 1953), pp. 99-100.

88. Lamartine to Guichard de Bienassis; *Correspondance*, VI (1875), pp. 277-8.

89. Letter dated 15 October 1847 and published in *L'Océan* (Brest), 12 April 1848.

90. C. Gigaud, *Explications de Charles Gigaud rédacteur en chef du journal 'Le Finistère', à ses amis et concitoyens du département* (Brest, 1848), p. 8.

91. See *Appel à M. de Lamartine. Discussion entre les journaux 'L'Océan' et 'Le Finistère'* (Brest, 1848).

92. A. N., BB[18] 1429, dossier A 10 9824.

93. Guyard apparently began his newspaper career as editor of *L'Echo de la Loire* (Roanne). He founded *Le Progrès de la Loire* in Roanne about September 1844, and served as editor of *Le Bien public* from October 1847 until March 1848, when he was dismissed allegedly for refusing to publish electoral material sent to him by subscribers to *Le Bien public* (see *Le Journal de Saône-et-Loire*, 24 March 1848, p. 4). Guyard subsequently became head of the Paris Club de la conciliation démocratique. From 1850 he directed a socialist colony inspired by Fourierist ideas at Saint-Just (Haute-Loire). At Frotez-les-Vesoul (Haute-Saône) he had established a similar community by 1863, when Lamartine sent him letters of support (see A. Guyard, *Lettres aux gens de Frotey* (Paris, 1863), pp. 4 and 9).

94. *La France parlementaire*, V, pp. 73-81.

95. *La Revue indépendante*, 25 October 1847, pp. 321-7.

96. *Le National*, 26 October 1847, p. 3.

97. *Le Bien public*, 24, 28 and 31 October 1847; *Le France parlementaire*, V, pp. 82-105.

98. 'Au *Journal de Saône-et-Loire*' (*Le Bien public*, 31 October 1847); Dumesnil Papers, B.H.V.P., 5712, and the pamphlet published by H. Robert, 1847.

99. *Le Populaire*, 7 and 14 November 1847, p. 3.

100. *Banquet Réformiste de Lyon, 23 novembre 1847. Compte-rendu publié par la commission* (Lyons, 1847), pp. 35-6.

101. *La Revue latine*, 25 November 1902, pp. 655-6.

102. 'Affaires de la Suisse' and 'Au *Journal de Saône-et-Loire*'; Dumesnil Papers, B.H.V.P., 5712.

103. See Ponsard to the comtesse d'Agoult, 10 November 1847 (*La Comtesse d'Agoult et François Ponsard d'après une correspondance inédite*, p. 43), and Lamartine to Mme de Girardin, 18 November 1847 (*Correspondance*, VI (1875), p. 281).

104. 'Le Banquet d'Autun'; Dumesnil Papers, B.H.V.P., 5712, and the pamphlet published by H. Robert (Mâcon, 1847). See also *Discours de M. Ulysse Pic au banquet d'Autun. Lettres à plusieurs journaux. Opinion de M. de Lamartine. Lettre à M. de Lamartine, M. Duvergier de Hauranne, à vol d'oiseau* (Autun, 1847).

105. A. A. Ledru-Rollin, *Discours politiques et écrits divers*, 2 vols. (Paris, 1879), I, p. 337.

106. 'Le Banquet de Lille'; Dumesnil Papers, B.H.V.P., 5712, and the pamphlet published by H. Robert (Mâcon, 1847).

107. G. Bourgin (ed.), *Adolphe de Circourt: souvenirs d'une mission à Berlin en 1848*, 2 vols. (Paris, 1908-9), I, p. xxxvii.

108. *Correspondance*, VI (1875), p. 284. Cf. B. N., nouv. acq. fr., 16581, f. 189.

109. See Jean-François Alcock to Odilon Barrot, 11 December 1847; Odilon Barrot Papers, A. N., 271 AP 1, A7a2. Cf. F. Dutacq, *Histoire politique de Lyon pendant la révolution de 1848* (Paris, 1910), p. 45.

110. Alton-Shée, *Souvenirs*, p. 78; J. Gouache, *Lille: Dijon: Chalon. Banquets démocratiques* (Paris, 1848), pp. 54, 55 and 58; Lacretelle, *Lamartine et ses amis*, pp. 108, 114-19 and 116.

111. See Prosper Léon Duvergier de Hauranne to Odilon Barrot, 11 December 1847 (A. N., 271 AP 4, C196); *Journal du maréchal de Castellane*, IV (1896), p. 9; C. Leroy (ed.), *Lettres inédites provenant de la correspondance de Dupont (de l'Eure) et de celle de Mlle Pauline Dupont, sa fille* (Rouen, 1932), p. 27. Cf. Chambolle, *Retours sur la vie*, p. 218; *Le National*, 25 December 1847, p. 3.

112. Commission du banquet des Ecoles to H. Carnot, 8 December 1847; Carnot Papers, A. N., 108 AP 3, dossier 4.

113. *Extrait du 'Bien public' du 16 décembre 1847* (Mâcon: H. Robert, 1847), p. 1.

114. Ibid., pp. 2-7. 'The Spanish marriages' refers to the marriage on 8 October 1846 between Louis-Philippe's son, the duc de Montpensier, and the Spanish Infanta, which was thought to represent a dynastic rather than a national diplomacy.

115. *Le Populaire*, 12 December 1847, pp. 1-2.

116. *Extrait du 'Bien public' du 19 décembre 1847* (Mâcon: H. Robert, no date); *Le Populaire*, 26 December 1847. Cf. *La France parlementaire*, V, pp. 106-7.

117. *Extrait du 'Bien public' du 23 décembre 1847* (Mâcon: H. Robert, no date).

118. Ibid., pp. 3 and 6.

119. Undated letter, December 1847; *Correspondance*, VI (1875), p. 288.

120. *La France parlementaire*, V, pp. 116-19.

121. Ibid., V, pp. 120-50; E. Biré, *Mes Souvenirs, 1846-1870* (Paris, 1908), pp. 36-7.

122. Besides the sources listed in note 132, see 'Souvenirs de M. Vivien', *Le Correspondant*, 25 September 1905, p. 1066.

123. A. Crémieux, *La Révolution de février* (Paris, 1912), pp. 46-56. The banquet commission's membership comprised Odilon Barrot (chairman), Bethmont, Chambolle, Duvergier de Hauranne, Garner-Pagès, Havin, Léon de Malleville, Armand Marrast, Pagnerre, and Recurt (A. Crémieux, 'La Révolution de février 1848: récits contemporains inédits', *La Revue bleue*, II (1910), pp. 663-4).

124. H. Guillemin, *Lamartine. Lettres inédites, 1821-1851* (Porrentruy, 1944), pp. 85-6.

125. *Revue des Deux Mondes*, 15 January 1938, p. 289.

126.   *Le National*, 21 February 1848.
127.   *La France parlementaire*, V, pp. 164-8.
128.   Alton-Shée, *Souvenirs*, pp. 198-9. Cf. Lamartine to Rolland, 21 February 1848 (*Correspondance*, VI (1875), p. 297). For descriptions of the meeting see I. A. Crémieux, *En 1848. Discours et lettres* (Paris, 1883), pp. 165-77, and A. Crémieux to Mme Nathan, 19 February 1848 (Adolphe Crémieux Papers, A. N., 369 AP 2, dossier 2).
129.   P. Guichonnet, *William de La Rive: un témoin genevois de la Révolution de 1848* (Paris, 1953), p. 9.
130.   B. N., nouv. acq. fr., 24839, f. 369.
131.   Alexandre, *Souvenirs sur Lamartine*, p. 75; Arago, *Histoire de Paris*, I, pp. 207-8; P. Breton (ed.), *Mémoires du marquis de Boissy*, 2 vols. (Paris, 1870), II, pp. 40-1; Legouvé, *Lamartine*, p. 18, note 1; E. Pelletan, *Histoire des trois journées de février 1848* (Paris, 1848), pp. 38-9; L. A. Thiers, *Notes et souvenirs de M. Thiers, 1848. Révolution du 24 février* (Paris, 1902), pp. 21-2.
132.   This seems to be the most probable sequence of events, but contemporary accounts differ: see Alton-Shée, *Souvenirs*, pp. 197-227; Barrot, *Mémoires posthumes*, I, pp. 506-16; Chambolle, *Retours dur la vie*, pp. 234-7; A. A. Chérest, *La Vie et les oeuvres de A.-T. Marie* (Paris, 1873), pp. 87-93; L.-A. Garnier-Pagès, *Histoire de la Révolution de 1848*, 10 vols. (Paris, 1861-72), IV, pp. 184-254; Lamartine, *Histoire de la Révolution de 1848*, I, pp. 52-63; B. Sarrans, *Histoire de la Révolution de février 1848*, 2 vols. (Paris, 1851), I, pp. 270-80; D. Stern, *Histoire de la Révolution de 1848*, 3 vols. (Paris, 1850-3), I, pp. 85-100. For a secondary account see Crémieux, *La Révolution de février*, pp. 55-75.
133.   On their relations see the *Revue des Deux Mondes*, 1 September 1926, pp. 182-211.
134.   Michelet to Lamartine, 23 February 1848; Michelet Papers, B.H.V.P., A 4036. Lamartine replied to Michelet's letter (B.H.V.P., A 4788, f. 15), and prepared an address to the King (B. N., nouv. acq. fr., 23768, f. 6), which was never delivered. Cf. P. Viallaneix (ed.), *Jules Michelet. Journal, 1823-1848*, 2 vols. (Paris, 1959-62), I, pp. 683 and 921.
135.   A. Parménie and C. Bonnier de la Chapelle, *Histoire d'un éditeur et de ses auteurs: P.-J. Hetzel (Stahl)* (Paris, 1953), pp. 86-8. On Hetzel's relations with Lamartine before February 1848 see ibid., pp. 83-4.
136.   See Alton-Shée, *Souvenirs*, p. 287; Crémieux, *La Révolution de février*, pp. 369-72; Garnier-Pagès, *Histoire de la Révolution de 1848*, V, pp. 212-16; L. de La Hodde, *La Naissance de la République en février 1848* (Paris, 1850), pp. 86-7; *Le National*, 29 May and 2 June 1848, p. 3; Sarrans, *Histoire de la Révolution de février*, I, p. 413.
137.   Garnier-Pagès, *Histoire de la Révolution de 1848*, V, pp. 219-20; Hugo, *Choses vues*, pp. 268-9; Parménie and Bonnier de la Chapelle, *Hetzel*, p. 88; Sarrans, *Histoire de la Révolution de février*, I, pp. 458-60; Stern, *Histoire de la Révolution de 1848*, I, p. 225; Thureau-Dangin, *Histoire de la Monarchie de Juillet*, VII, p. 505.
138.   Barrot, *Mémoires posthumes*, I, pp. xi and 553; *Le Moniteur universel*, 25 February 1848, p. 502.
139.   Thureau-Dangin, *Histoire de la Monarchie de Juillet*, VII, p. 505.
140.   See C. H. Phipps, Marquis of Normanby, *A Year of Revolution from a Journal kept in Paris in 1848*, 2 vols. (London, 1857), I, p. 117. Cf. J. J. L. Blanc, *Histoire de la Révolution de 1848*, 2 vols. (Paris, 1870), I, p. 70.
141.   Barrot, *Mémoires posthumes*, I, p. 551; Rémusat, *Mémoires de ma view*, IV (1962), p. 237; P. J. P. Sauzet, *La Chambre des Députés et la Révolution de février* (Paris, 1851), pp. 320-1; Stern, *Histoire de la Révolution de 1848*, I,

p.223; L. Monnier (ed.), *Souvenirs d'Alexis de Tocqueville* (Paris, 1944), pp. 60-1. For Lamartine's rejection of criticism by Sauzet see *L'Union*, 9 May 1851, and B. N., Autographes Rothschild, vol. XIX, f. 1561.

142.   Chérest, *Marie*, p. 115; Ollivier, *Journal*, I, p. 348; Parménie and Bonnier de la Chapelle, *Hetzel*, p. 89; E. Regnault, *Histoire du Governement provisoire* (Paris, 1850), p. 63; L. Monnier (ed.), *Souvenirs d'Alexis de Tocqueville* (Paris, 1944), p. 65.

143.   Lamartine, *Histoire de la Révolution de 1848*, I, pp. 201-5.

144.   Normanby, *A Year of Revolution*, I, pp. 120-1. Cf. Barrot, *Mémoires posthumes*, II, p. 34.

145.   Falloux, *Mémoires d'un royaliste*, I, pp. 267-8; Lacombe, *Vie de Berryer*, II, p. 535.

146.   C. de Lavarenne, *Le Gouvernement provisoire et l'hôtel de ville dévoilés* (Paris, 1850), p. 24.

147.   For a record of the debate see *Le Moniteur universel*, 25 February 1848, pp. 500-2.

148.   Garnier-Pagès, *Histoire de la Révolution de 1848*, V, pp. 268-90. As with *Le National*'s list, there are different versions. See Crémieux, *La Révolution de février*, pp. 422-3.

149.   J. J. L. Blanc, *1848. Historical Revelations: Inscribed to Lord Normanby* (London, 1858), pp. 5, 9-10, and *Histoire de la Révolution de 1848*, I, pp. 64-6; *La Réforme*, 30 May 1848; Sarrans, *Histoire de la Révolution de février*, I, pp. 422-3.

150.   Chérest, *Marie*, p. 116; Garnier-Pagès, *Histoire de la Révolution de 1848*, V, p. 288; La Hodde, *La Naissance de la République*, p. 90.

151.   Alton-Shée, *Souvenirs*, p. 287.

152.   Tristan, *Le Tour de France*, pp. 60-3.

4 GOVERNMENT AND REVOLUTION, FEBRUARY-JUNE 1848

Eh! que faisons-nous donc, Messieurs, que fait aujourd'hui notre pays, si ce n'est pas la plus sublime de toutes les poésies! – Lamartine to a deputation of students, 4 March 1848

La République doit être nationale. – Lamartine to Rolland, March 1848

Contemporaries and historians are agreed that in the French Revolution of February 1848 the division within the French Left between moderate republicans and left-wing republicans became immediately and clearly apparent. There is similar agreement that this division can be seen in the Provisional Government formed on 24 February 1848: Lamartine, together with François Arago, Crémieux, Dupont de l'Eure, Garnier-Pagès, Marie and Marrast represented the moderate republicans associated with *Le National*, while Albert, Louis Blanc, Flocon and Ledru-Rollin represented the left-wing republicans associated with *La Réforme*. The majority position of Lamartine and the moderate republicans in the Provisional Government was reinforced by the distribution of ministerial posts. With the exception of Ledru-Rollin, who became Minister of the Interior, moderate republicans in the Provisional Government gained the main posts, Lamartine as Minister of Foreign Affairs, Crémieux as Minister of Justice, Garnier-Pagès as Minister of Finance, François Arago as Minister of the Navy, Marie as Minister of Public Works, and Marrast as Mayor of Paris. Similarly, those from outside the Provisional Government appointed to important posts were moderate republicans (Etienne Arago, brother of François Arago, as Minister of Posts, Bethmont as Minister of Commerce, General Bedeau as Minister of War, Carnot as Minister of Public Instruction), again with just one exception, Marc Caussidière, the new Prefect of Police.

To a considerable extent, the history of the Second Republic between February and June 1848 can be summarised as the triumph of the moderate republicans over their left-wing opponents, with the Provisional Government's rejection of radical policies, with the failure of a succession of left-wing demonstrations in Paris, with the conservative successes in the April 1848 parliamentary elections, and with the suppression of the Paris workers' rising of June 1848. Probably the most prominent and influential moderate republican within the Provisional Government, Lamartine played a major role in this process: he eloquently and effectively opposed radicalism, he helped to prevent the Government from succumbing to attempted revolutionary *journées*, and, as the principal moderate republican within the Provisional Government, he attracted a remarkable number of votes in the April elections. However, as usual, Lamartine's position was not without complexities and ambiguities: he wanted a Republic which was not just moderate republican but truly national, representing nearly all shades of political opinion; he tried to win over left-wing republicans by persuasion instead of just resisting them by force; he insisted on the inclusion of Ledru-Rollin in the Executive Commission, which succeeded the Provisional Government on 10 May; and, finally, during the June Days he desperately attempted to mediate with the insurgents.

According to Garnier-Pagès, members of the newly formed Provisional Government began to distribute ministerial portfolios at about seven in the evening of 24 February.[1] At this meeting in the Hôtel de Ville, Carnot, Crémieux and Garnier-Pagès agree that Lamartine was unanimously designated Minister of Foreign Affairs.[2] However four eventual members of the Provisional Government were not present. Flocon, Marrast and Louis Blanc joined the Government's first meeting after all the ministerial posts had been allocated, while Albert did not attend at all. Thus they had no part in choosing Lamartine as Minister of Foreign Affairs; and their signatures did not follow the announcement of the new ministerial appointments in *Le Moniteur*.[3] This was significant since they represented the radical republican faction associated with *La Réforme*, which viewed Lamartine with some suspicion and reserve.

Except among radical republicans and the extreme Left, Lamartine's political stature at the time of the formation of the Provisional Government was outstanding, if not preeminent. Only one of the most senior government posts would have suited his qualifications, and indeed his personal ambition. Circourt states that Lamartine wanted to become the Provisional Government's President. This aroused the jealousy of his colleagues, who vested the presidency in the venerable Dupont de l'Eure.[4] Circourt felt that Lamartine had treated him badly when Minister of Foreign Affairs, which coloured what he wrote about him. However on 28 February Lamartine told Normanby, the British ambassador, that he 'had declined the nominal Presidency of the Government, from a fear of exciting jealousy'.[5] If disappointed in his hopes for the presidency, Lamartine was still, as a member of the Provisional Government and Minister of Foreign Affairs, in an extremely powerful position, probably rivalled only by Ledru-Rollin, the Minister of the Interior.

The Provisional Government at once had to decide whether or not to proclaim a republic. Both the *National* and *Réforme* factions represented in the Provisional Government were committed to republicansim, and the crowd of demonstrators surrounding and invading the Hôtel de Ville kept demanding that a republic should be proclaimed. However, the Provisional Government lacked any constitutional mandate, and the proclamation of a republic in Paris might have provoked provincial opposition. After heated discussion the Provisional Government agreed to declare in its first official proclamation that it wanted the republic, provided this were accepted by the people, who would be immediately consulted — a formula inspired by Lamartine.[6] There followed Government decrees dissolving the Chamber of Peers and the Chamber of Deputies, and setting free all political prisoners. The decree dissolving the Chamber of Deputies declared that a National Assembly would be summoned as soon as the Provisional Government could guarantee the public order essential to an election.

The change of régime encountered no significant public opposition in France. Unlike the Revolution of 1830, few officials or office-holders resigned their posts, while many offered to serve the Provisional Government. This reflected an absence of personal loyalty to the July Monarchy, and conservative fears that any opposition might encourage revolutionary violence and undermine the Provisional Government's authority. Nevertheless, from the outset the Provisional Government faced an extremely difficult task. The Second Republic had been proclaimed, but its character had yet to be determined, in very unfavourable circumstances. The Provisional Government lacked any effective military force in Paris, with the demoralisation and disorganisation of the Paris National Guard and of the regular troops in the Paris area, and with the withdrawal of most regular army units from central Paris immediately after 24 February. This military weakness severely handicapped the Provisional Government, since governmental authority had to be re-established after the July Monarchy's overthrow, and since widespread popular unrest existed as a result of the critical situation in the towns, and especially in Paris, due to a collapse of financial confidence and acute unemployment. Moreover in Paris a triumphant and revolutionary crowd virtually besieged the Provisional Government in the Hôtel de Ville, insisting on a radical and socialist republic. On 25 February the revolutionary crowd in particular demanded that the Provisional Government should provide employment, guarantee the right to work, and adopt the red flag as France's national flag.

Within the Provisional Government several members, notably Louis Blanc, wanted to introduce a socialist programme, and the Provisional Government remained defenceless against the revolutionary crowd. The Provisional Government therefore decreed on 25 February that it promised a living wage to every worker and employment to all male citizens, and that it recognised that workers should form associations amongst themselves to secure the legitimate reward of their labour. Also workers were allocated the former royal civil list. The following day the immediate establishment of National Workshops was decreed, to provide government-financed work for the unemployed. These measures did not satisfy many Paris workers, who wanted a government ministry which would intervene in the economy and government direction of the labour force. During the morning of 28 February several thousand Paris workers demonstrated for a 'Ministry of Progress' and the 'Organisation of Labour', demands supported by Louis Blanc but opposed by Lamartine and Garnier-Pagès, who maintained that the future National Assembly should decide such questions and that the Government should confine itself to the role of *commissaire de police*.[7] The Provisional Government compromised by agreeing that a commission of workers' representatives should meet in the Luxembourg Palace under Louis Blanc's chairmanship, to discuss workers' grievances and how to remedy them. Lamartine had little enthusiasm for the National Workshops or the Luxembourg Commission. At the beginning of March he told Normanby that there was a large portion of workers, quietly suffering and really to be pitied, who 'deserved some management', but that he strongly opposed the concept of the 'Organisation of Labour' and regarded the Luxembourg Commission as merely 'a useful safety valve'.[8]

On 25 and 26 February demonstrators at the Hôtel de Ville demanded the Provisional Government's adoption of the red flag as France's national flag. In the Government Louis Blanc proposed the red flag's adoption but gained no support from his colleagues. Eventually Louis Blanc gave in, on condition that a red rosette be worn by government officials and placed on all flagstaffs.[9] Then Lamartine went out and on five separate occasions argued that historically and through international recognition the *tricolore* was France's national flag, whereas the red flag had merely been paraded once on the Champ de Mars (in 1791). Contemporaries agree that this persuaded the crowd to accept the Government's rejection of the red flag.[10] The principle of changing France's national flag when the régime changed had been followed in 1789, 1814, 1815 and 1830. However the Provisional Government's adoption of the red flag — symbol of left-wing republicanism — would have been regarded as a capitulation to popular militancy, and as the precursor of extreme left-wing government policies. Consequently the red flag's rejection greatly relieved the propertied classes, for whom Lamartine became an instant hero. Thus one Parisian wrote in his diary: 'How much I admire Lamartine! He has saved us from the red flag, and this first victory is extremely important!'[11] Opposed to left-wing republicanism, Lamartine also wanted to promote national unity and avoid alienating important sections of the population from the Government. Also as Minister of Foreign Affairs he may have been concerned with the Second Republic's image abroad. Nevertheless about this time he tried to persuade Carnot, son of 'the organiser of victory', to take on the Ministry of War with the argument, 'your name will work wonders there'; and Falloux relates that according to Léon de Malleville (who had been informed by Marrast), Lamartine at first favoured the adoption of the red flag, and succumbed only to his colleagues' arguments.[12] Falloux disliked Lamartine, and apparently no other authority confirms his account, Carnot specifically contradicting it.[13] It is still just possible that Lamartine subsequently claimed credit for an achievement performed under pressure from government colleagues.

The Provisional Government's decision on 26 February to abolish the death penalty for political offences can be attributed unreservedly to Lamartine. He had previously campaigned for this measure, and Louis Blanc, Garnier-Pagès and the comtesse d'Agoult all acknowledge Lamartine first proposed the decree.[14] Apart from long-standing humanitarian convictions, Lamartine wanted to emphasise that the Second Republic would not repeat the Terror of the First at a time when demands might well be made for Guizot's execution. Like the red flag's rejection, the decree had a considerable impact. *La République française* (28 February) welcomed it as 'a wise and intelligent act'; *Le Constitutionnel* (27 February) praised 'the most sublime decree which a nation had ever produced'; and the *Revue des Deux Mondes* (1 March) maintained it had helped to reduce fears and increase public confidence. Yet it is doubtful if the decree actually saved a great many lives. Until June 1848 it was neither necessary nor advisable for the Second Republic's governments to execute their political enemies. During the June Days the decree could not prevent the slaughter in the streets of Paris, though it may subsequently have discouraged the execution of prisoners. Lamartine suggested he and his colleagues were free from any taint of blood, but there is an element of truth in Sainte-Beuve's adaption of Chateaubriand's judgment of Decazes after the duc de Berry's assassination (1820): 'Their feet have slipped in blood.'[15]

In his *Histoire de la Révolution de 1848* Lamartine claims he helped to save the lives of the Royal Family. He states that on the evening of 26 February he went to see the comte de Montalivet, a close friend of Louis-Philippe. He gave the Count some money for the Royal Family, and assured him the Provisional Government had no intention of preventing them from leaving France. He also appointed three *commissaires* to assist the Royal Family, Dargaud, François de Champeaux and Oscar Lafayette (General Lafayette's grandson).[16] On 28 or 29 February Lamartine told Normanby he had threatened to resign unless all members of the Provisional Government signed an order for Louis-Philippe's free conduct out of France. Also Georges Lafayette had been instructed to find Louis-Philippe, provide him with money and escort him out of the country. Similar provisions had been made for the duchesse d'Orléans.[17] Lamartine may obviously have exaggerated. His threatened resignation over an order for Louis-Philippe's safe conduct appears to be unconfirmed. Montalivet in his memoirs admits Lamartine approached him, though not on 26 February but on 1 March, when he refused to disclose the King's whereabouts.[18] Other sources assert the Provisional Government appointed *commissaires* and allocated money to assist the Royal Family's flight.[19] La Hodde states that Caussidière (Prefect of Police) sent him to the Invalides on 26 February to arrest the duchesse d'Orléans, who, however, had left.[20] According to Regnault, on 27 February the Duchess was thought to have been arrested at Mantes. Jules de Lasteyrie immediately went to the Hôtel de Ville to secure an order for her release. The Provisional Government agreed except Lamartine, who declared: 'The people alone have the right to decide.' When Lasteyrie remonstrated, he replied: 'The country's safety depends upon my popularity, which I do not want to risk.' Only Albert's arguments persuaded him to adopt a less uncompromising position, but even then he recommended that the Duchess should be arrested, and detained or released as circumstances indicated.[21] This story is strongly denied by Lamartine and fully supported only by Louis Blanc, who wrote his account ten years after the event and who may have relied on Regnault.[22] Yet during the Revolution of 1848 Lamartine often showed great concern for his popularity, and extreme reluctance to usurp the people's sovereign authority.

Pursuing its declared intention of summoning a National Assembly, the Provisional Government decreed on 2 March the establishment of direct manhood suffrage, and on 5 March chose 9 April as the date for the National Assembly elections. Lamartine claimed responsibility for the decree establishing manhood suffrage,[23] probably with justification. He certainly wanted a National Assembly representing the whole electorate to meet as soon as possible. Left-wing militants, on the other hand, claimed they needed more time to educate public opinion and prepare for a general election, and they wanted to impose a radical programme on the Provisional Government. On 7 March Blanqui, on behalf of the Société républicaine centrale (the first and initially most prestigious of the Paris revolutionary clubs of 1848), presented the Provisional Government with a petition demanding absolute freedom of the press and association, postponement of the National Assembly elections, suppression of the magistrature, and the Government's arming, organising and payment of all unemployed workers. For the Provisional Government Lamartine replied that the September press laws had already been abolished (on 5 March), that the National Assembly elections could not be postponed, and that the right of associaton had to be restricted by considerations of public order. He said nothing about suppressing the magistrature or arming, organising and paying all unemployed workers. However he did say that he and his colleagues considered their first duty, after what they had done to safeguard liberty, was to restore as soon as possible to the nation itself the powers they had seized in the national interest, and not postpone for another minute the quasi-dictatorship circumstances had compelled them to assume.[24] He reacted similarly to Ledru-Rollin's circular, published on 12 March, informing *commissaires* sent to administer the departments that their powers were unlimited, and should be used to secure the election of good republicans to the National Assembly. On 15 March Lamartine publicly denied any Government wish to influence the elections or delegate unlimited powers, and reaffirmed his belief that sovereignty lay in the nation.[25] At a Provisional Government meeting the following day he argued that popular sovereignty would be usurped if the Government imposed itself on France, and even threatened resignation when Louis Blanc suggested postponing elections for a month.[26]

Lamartine was always concerned that the Provisional Government should not be dominated or overthrown by what he regarded as the forces of popular anarchy. As early as 25 February the Government had decreed the immediate formation in Paris of a twenty-four battalion *garde nationale mobile*, a mobilised and paid section of the part-time voluntary National Guard. It was hoped to recruit a government militia from unemployed young men, who might otherwise have supported further revolutionary violence. The original idea was probably not Lamartine's, but he seems to have been the main Government advocate for the formation of this militia, which became the most important military force in Paris until 16 May and which remained consistently loyal to the Government.[27] On 26 and 27 February the Provisional Government also formed a Paris Garde Républicaine, eventually about six hundred strong. As part of a reorganisation of the Paris National Guard, on 14 March the Provisional Government ordered the dissolution of the Guard's élite companies. This order, following Ledru-Rollin's public instructions to his *commissaires*, suggested that the Provisional Government was moving towards the Left, which provoked a protest demonstration at the Hôtel de Ville by several thousand Paris National Guardsmen on 16 March. The following day Paris radicals organised a massive counter-demonstration.

Aware of the likelihood of a popular demonstration in Paris, during the evenings of 15 and 16 March Lamartine saw delegates from the Paris clubs. He became convinced that most of them supported him and that the Provisional Government would not be overthrown.[28] However on 17 March the demonstration's enormous size (possibly over one hundred thousand participated) caught the Provisional Government unprepared and effectively unprotected, so that it had to meet in the Hôtel de Ville about forty delegates representing the various clubs and organisations taking part in the demonstration. A petition was read out demanding the withdrawal of troops from Paris, and the postponement of elections to 5 April for the National Guard and to 31 May for the National Assembly. In reply Lamartine insisted that the Government's authority rested on its complete independence from external pressures, and that it could not allow a group of citizens in Paris to prejudice this independence.[29] Yet the Provisional Government felt compelled to give the impression of withdrawing troops from Paris; and the elections were postponed, from 25 March to 5 April for the National Guard and from 9 to 23 April for the National Assembly.

The 17 March demonstration profoundly impressed Lamartine. Although most of the demonstrators were probably not anti-government, a minority certainly were, some of whom may have shouted anti-

Lamartine slogans.[30] In addition the Government's defencelessness against popular pressure had been clearly revealed. Therefore after 17 March Lamartine pursued a dual policy of trying to win over alienated left-wing elements in Paris and organising military forces for the Government's defence. He at once began cultivating Ledru-Rollin (Minister of the Interior and possibly the Government's most important radical), whom he may have dissuaded from resigning from the Provisional Government;[31] he had interviews with prominent left-wing figures such as Barbès, Blanqui, Cabet, Raspail and Sobrier; and he helped and protected left-wing political clubs and societies, including Sobrier's subversive Club des Clubs.[32] At the same time the Provisional Government decided (20 March) to reduce the Algerian garrison and recall reservists, which eventually produced 27,000 veterans.[33] On 29 March Lamartine persuaded the Provisional Government to recall a further 12,000 troops from Algeria.[34] Ostensibly the troop concentrations reinforced France's frontier armies, but the troops also became available for use in Paris. This dual policy is understandable. The Provisional Government needed to placate the Left and be in a position to defend itself; and François Arago at the Ministry of War, and Marie and Emile Thomas at the National Workshops, pursued policies similar to Lamartine's. Yet Lamartine had an unjustified faith in his personal influence. Also his desire for national unity and harmony, and belief in strong government, encouraged apparent contradictions. He may have persuaded Sobrier not to have joined the Paris demonstration of 16 April,[35] and his left-wing contacts probably provided some useful information. However, his dual policy was open to sinister interpretations; his left-wing contacts aroused the suspicion of moderates and conservatives; and he may have been partly responsible for Sobrier's followers receiving from the Ministry of War on the eve of 16 April 500 muskets and ammunition, which, as critics soon pointed out, could have been used against the Provisional Government.[36]

Although mainly preoccupied with foreign affairs and the Provisional Government's survival, Lamartine did become involved with Hippolyte Carnot's plan for an Ecole d'administration. The new Minister of Public Instruction wanted to establish a training school for future state administrators along the lines of the Ecole polytechnique. His idea, endorsed by a government commission, was accepted by the Provisional Government. Lacking the money to found a new institution, the Government decided to establish the Ecole d'administration in the Collège de France. When professorial appointments were discussed, first Garnier-Pagès and then Marrast suggested they should give lectures to inaugurate the teaching of political science. This prompted Carnot to place the Ecole d'administration directly under the Provisional Government's patronage by inviting Government members to become the first holders of the new chairs. Lamartine enthusiastically welcomed this proposal, and Ledru-Rollin appeared to be personally flattered. Consequently on 9 April twelve new professorial appointments at the Collège de France were announced, including those of Lamartine (to the chair of international law and diplomatic history), Marrast, Garnier-Pagès, and Ledru-Rollin. Apparently none of them actually gave any lectures, and first the chairs and then the Ecole d'administration were suppressed in 1849. Nevertheless it was an interesting experiment and a precedent for later developments, though at the time the professorial appointments of Provisional Government members were the object of a satirical article in *Le Charivari* (11 April) and mocking disbelief in *Le Journal des Débats* (12 April).[37]

After 17 March the Provisional Government's next serious test occurred a month later on 16 April, when demonstrating workers marched from the Champ de Mars to the Hôtel de Ville again to press a more radical programme on the Government, including perhaps a purge of government moderates. Louis Blanc and Albert gave their colleagues several days warning that a peaceful workers' demonstration would take place on 16 April, but by the evening of 15 April Lamartine was seriously alarmed. He had an inconclusive interview with Blanqui, and sent agents to workers' clubs and organisations to try to moderate the forthcoming demonstration.[38] The very survival of the Provisional Government was at risk on 16 April, since it could have been overwhelmed by Paris demonstrators. What actually happened on that day immediately became a matter of dispute, particularly as to who was responsible for calling out the National Guard and thereby saving the Government. According to Lamartine's own account Ledru-Rollin came to see him in the Ministry of Foreign Affairs at about eleven in the morning of 16 April, when he told Ledru-Rollin to order immediately the beating of the *rappel* to mobilise the National Guard. Having said that he would call out the *garde mobile*, Lamartine left the Ministry to see General Duvivier at the *garde mobile* headquarters. In the General's absence, he gave orders for the immediate despatch of four *garde mobile* battalions to the Hôtel de Ville. On leaving he met General Duvivier, who made a few minor alterations to Lamartine's orders and explained he lacked any ammunition, so Lamartine himself went to the National Guard headquarters for ammunition. At first he was unable to convince the authorities of the seriousness of the situation, but General Courtais (commander of the Paris National Guard) arrived and stated that Ledru-Rollin had ordered the *rappel* to be beaten, and that this was about to be effected. Then Lamartine left for the Hôtel de Ville, having arranged that a supply of ammunition should follow him there. Meanwhile General Changarnier, appointed by Lamartine minister at Berlin, had gone to the Ministry of Foreign Affairs to discuss his instructions. Learning of the Government's danger from Marianne, he rushed off to the Hôtel de Ville, arriving at the same time as Lamartine. Preparations for the Hôtel de Ville's defence were at once made by Lamartine, Marrast and Changarnier. To their alarm, although the *garde mobile* battalions began to arrive, the National Guard did not appear. Lamartine, Marrast and Changarnier therefore agreed that Marrast, as Mayor of Paris, should issue fresh orders for the beating of the *rappel*. At long last, thirty to forty thousand National Guards surrounded the Hôtel de Ville just as demonstrators from the Champ de Mars were arriving. Thus was the Government saved.[39]

Hence Lamartine suggested that he had initially proposed the beating of the *rappel*, that Ledru-Rollin had agreed to this proposal but then failed to carry it out, and that his own personal efforts had largely ensured the Hôtel de Ville's defence. Other authorities do not support Lamartine.[40] They suggest Ledru-Rollin saw Lamartine at ten, not eleven, on the morning of 16 April, when Ledru-Rollin had already decided to have the *rappel* beaten. Ledru-Rollin, on his part, claims he did give orders for the *rappel* to be beaten, acting on his own initiative and not as a result of Lamartine's promptings. Caussidière confirms Ledru-Rollin's claims, although two National Guard officers later testified that Ledru-Rollin never gave any such orders.[41] Garnier-Pagès agrees that Lamartine passed on the order to General Courtais, but states that the *rappel* was beaten at different times in different parts of Paris, and first on the orders of Hingray (colonel of the Paris National Guard's tenth legion).[42]

Of particular interest is the report of conversations which the marquise de La Grange had with Lamartine and Changarnier after 16 April. Lamartine confessed to her on 21 April that he had failed to persuade Courtais to order the beating of the *rappel*; and Changarnier informed her on 17 April that on arriving at the Hôtel de Ville the previous day, he had exchanged the following remarks with Lamartine: 'What are you going to do? – Nothing. Die, if necessary! – But what precautions have you taken? – None – And the *rappel*? – Courtais does not want to give the order for the *rappel*.' Changarnier claimed he then told Marrast to sign the order for the *rappel* to be beaten.[43] There was no reason why Lamartine should have admitted his failure with Courtais to the marquise de La Grange, and he made the same admission to Normanby.[44] Also Changarnier's conversations with Normanby and the comte d'Estourmel, and testimony in July to the Commission of Enquiry into the events of May and June 1848, confirm the marquise de La Grange's account.[45] Further, Regnault states that on arriving at the Hôtel de Ville on 16 April Lamartine told Marrast he was prepared for the worst and had made his will.[46] It can therefore be fairly assumed that on the morning of 16 April both Lamartine and Ledru-Rollin wanted to call out the National Guard to protect the Hôtel de Ville, but failed to ensure the necessary orders were issued or effectively obeyed. If this were the case, then only Changarnier's fortuitous intervention and the decisions of a few individuals, such as Colonel Hingray, acting entirely on their own initiative, secured the Hôtel de Ville's defence.

Lamartine responded to the 16 April demonstration as he had responded to that of 17 March. He continued to cultivate Ledru-Rollin and organisations such as Longepied's Comité révolutionnaire, but he also prepared the Armée du Nord's commander, General Négrier, either to use his troops to suppress a Paris uprising or to receive the Government at Lille, if the Government were forced to leave the capital.[47] Similarly, he supported both the issuing of a conciliatory government proclamation about 16 April and the instituting of a criminal investigation into the *journée*.[48]

After the Provisional Government's formation with Lamartine as Foreign Minister, the French newspaper and periodical press paid him numerous personal tributes. On 25 February *Le Correspondant* claimed of Lamartine: 'His splendid conduct, his generous ideas and his inspired language have profoundly touched our heart.' *Le National* wrote on 26 February that the purest and most disinterested sentiments inspired his eloquence. Lamartine had raised his character to the height of his genius, declared Girardin in *La Presse* the next day. The left-wing *L'Ami du Peuple en 1848* admitted (17 February) it greatly esteemed citizen Lamartine. Among provincial newspapers, *L'Impartial de Rouen* (legitimist) commented (28 February): 'Nobody knows better than M. de Lamartine how to strike a sympathetic chord among the masses; nobody understands better than he all the glories of France.' *Le Journal de Saône-et-Loire* (conservative) stated (3 March) that at Mâcon, like everywhere else, there was no one who had not been moved by Lamartine's heroic courage; and *L'Echo du Nord* (moderate republican) observed (14 April) that Lamartine, formerly France's greatest poet, had become her greatest citizen.

In Paris Lamartine's prestige and popularity were enormous immediately after the February Revolution. On 28 February the Baroness Bonde wrote: 'Lamartine's energy and courage are beyond all praise.'[49] 'I forgive Lamartine everything', Sainte-Beuve confessed on 29 February: 'He has been great during these *journées*, and he has brought honour to "la nature poètique." '[50] Even Marshal Bugeaud, the Paris garrison's unsuccessful commander on 24 February, maintained on 3 April: 'Lamartine's generous sentiments are, and still remain, a guarantee.'[51] The erection of a column in Lamartine's honour was suggested for the Place de la Concorde, and the rue Coquenard in the eleventh *arrondissement* was renamed rue Lamartine.[52] A 'cortège sympathique' accompanied Lamartine home on the evening of 25 February, and did not disperse until after he had indicated he was too exhausted to make another speech.[53] The following day he was mobbed on leaving the Hôtel de Ville; and on 27 February he escaped from his admirers and avoided an embarrassing 'triomphe populaire' only by entering the house of Victor Hugo.[54] Shouts of 'Vive Lamartine!' greeted his appearance at the opera on 28 April.[55] Even the socialist newspaper, *La Commune de Paris* (30 April), welcomed his success in the April elections, while as late as 4 May he was publicly acclaimed during the National Assembly's opening ceremonies.[56]

The extreme Left excepted, Lamartine's presence in the Provisional Government provided much needed reassurance. Guizot's resignation, Louis-Philippe's flight, the Second Republic's proclamation, and the outbreaks of popular violence in the Paris region, all in a few days, had a profound impact. The effects were sustained by provincial disturbances and the Paris demonstrations of 17 March and 16 April. There were widespread fears that revolutionary extremism would follow the February Revolution. Lamartine's *grand notable* status afforded a guarantee of personal and political respectability, especially for the wealthier classes. His appeal, however, was wider than this. He had been one of the July Monarchy's best known and most determined opponents before the February Revolution, had played a leading role in the Provisional Government's formation, and had quickly emerged as one of the Government's most prominent members. As such he had rapidly acquired a reputation for moderation. He had rejected the red flag; he had insisted on the abolition of the death penalty for political offences; he had resisted revolutionary wars of liberation; he had publicly opposed Ledru-Rollin's circular giving government *commissaires* unlimited powers; and he had made numerous speeches deploring acts of violence and appealing for national unity and fraternity among all French citizens. Contemporaries therefore regarded him as the leader of the Provisional Government's moderate faction and main opponent of the Government's alleged radicals, Albert, Louis Blanc, Flocon and Ledru-Rollin.[57] Thus his popularity was based on the assumption that he possessed considerable influence and authority, and that he supported moderate republicanism and opposed left-wing extremism.

Lamartine's popularity was tested on 23 and 24 April, when for the first time in history all adult Frenchmen had the opportunity to elect a National Assembly. The system of election adopted (*scrutin de liste départemental*) meant that the departments were single constituencies returning a varying number of representatives according to their populations. In the elections Ledru-Rollin through his *commissaires* tried to secure the return of republicans, but the Provisional Government decided on 15 March not to give government backing to any candidates, although government members, as citizens, could make recommendations.[58] It reached no decision regarding multiple candidatures, despite promptings from the Comité central des élections générales (18 March), and a warning from the *commissaire* of the Nord to Ledru-Rollin (11 April) that multiple candidatures would benefit 'the least extreme and the most wavering members of the Government', notably Lamartine.[59] Typically, Lamartine's attitude towards the elections appears to have been rather ambivalent. He wanted in the National Assembly a group of 'républicains sages', among whom he included himself, while also believing in a Republic embracing all shades of opinion. Similarly, as a government minister he felt he should not campaign for himself, allowing electors the free exercise of their constitutional rights. Yet as a citizen he felt he should publicly indicate those candidatures he supported.[60] Thus he seems to have done nothing to promote his own candidatures, other than accepting his nominations, though he did write letters supporting or encouraging some nineteen actual or potential candidates in various departments.[61] Each candidate thus favoured had some personal connection with Lamartine, but no other pattern of support emerges.

In the April elections there was a massive eighty-four per cent turn-out of those eligible to vote.[62] Ten departments elected Lamartine – Bouches-du-Rhône, Côte-d'Or, Dordogne, Finistère, Gironde, Ille-et-Vilaine, Nord, Saône-et-Loire, Seine and Seine-Inférieure.[63] Within those ten departments were major population centres such as

Paris, Marseilles, Bordeaux, Lille, Rouen, Dijon, Rennes and Le Havre; and the departments were geographically representative with the Nord in the north, Bouches-du-Rhône in the south, Finistère in the west, and Saône-et-Loire in the centre. Lamartine headed the list of candidates in five departments (Gironde, Nord, Saône-et-Loire, Seine and Seine-Inférieure), and was elected either second or third in four more departments (Bouches-du-Rhône, Dordogne, Finistère and Ille-et-Vilaine). In the Côte-d'Or, where he was the tenth and last candidate to be elected, apparently many electors did not vote for him because they assumed he would, if successful, opt for another department, and they did not want to go to the polls a second time.[64] The ten departments returned Lamartine with 1,283,501 votes, a number far greater than that obtained by any other candidate;[65] and in the Seine he came ahead of every other member of the Provisional Government.

How can Lamartine's astonishing electoral triumph in the April elections be explained? The electoral system had encouraged the formation of political clubs and electoral committees to draw up lists of agreed candidates for each department. In Paris a group of moderate republicans formed on 9 March a Comité central pour les élections générales.[66] On 28 March this committee chose by election thirty-four candidates to represent the department of the Seine in the National Assembly. Lamartine was listed second after Dupont de l'Eure (the Provisional Government's President). *Le National* (30 March) published the list, of which in addition a million copies were reputedly printed.[67] The conservative Comité pour les libertés civiles et religieuses also supported Lamartine,[68] as did leading moderate, conservative and legitimist newspapers, such as *L'Assemblée Nationale*, *Le Constitutionnel*, *La Gazette de France*, *Le Siècle* and *L'Union*. Only the extreme Left refused to recommend him to the electorate – Blanqui's Société centrale républicaine, the Comité révolutionnaire (composed of delegates from 150 left-wing Paris clubs), and newspapers such as *La Réforme*, *La Commune de Paris* and *L'Ami du Peuple en 1848*.[69] However, even in Paris left-wing republicans were in a minority: Ledru-Rollin, their main candidate, came twenty-fourth in the Seine election.

This pattern of support for Lamartine from moderate republicans, conservatives and legitimists, and opposition from left-wing republicans, also occurred in the provincial departments which elected him. There were, however, local variations: Saône-et-Loire, for example, was obviously a special case, being Lamartine's personal political fief. Of the twelve members of the Commission départementale which had replaced the prefect in Mâcon on 26 February, the president (Carteron) and eight others were Lamartine's friends,[70] while another friend, Rolland, continued as Mâcon's mayor to head the *conseil municipal*. After the Commission départementale had itself been replaced on 14 March by Charles Mathey (a left-wing deputy for Saône-et-Loire before February 1848 and now the department's *commissaire*), the former members of the commission actively campaigned for Lamartine's candidature.[71] On 10 April Paul St Estienne-Cavaignac (a cousin of General Cavaignac) was appointed *commissaire* for Saône-et-Loire. He toured the department energetically campaigning, though principally for Ledru-Rollin.[72] However, at this time Lamartine enjoyed a unique popularity in Mâcon and in Saône-et-Loire generally: his bust was solemnly paraded through Mâcon's streets on 27 February; St Estienne-Cavaignac reported on 12 April that local opinion regarded him as a 'divinity';[73] and all local clubs, committees and newspapers seem to have backed his candidature. In the elections, of those who voted 99.1 per cent voted for Lamartine, and he received all the votes cast in fifteen cantons. Yet cracks existed in this apparent unanimity. As early as 9 April *Le Bien public* had stressed Lamartine's endorsement of Ledru-Rollin's candidature in Saône-et-Loire. Also St Estienne-Cavaignac had secured the publication of a letter by Lamartine supporting Ledru-Rollin, and he may have prompted *Le Bien public*'s renewed backing of Ledru-Rollin on 20 April. But the conservative *Journal de Saône-et-Loire* (22 April) urged its readers not to vote for Ledru-Rollin, despite the recommendations of Lamartine and *Le Bien public*; and after the elections, in which Ledru-Rollin came thirteenth with 68,462 votes, well behind Lamartine (first with 129,879 votes) and Rolland (seventh with 117,864 votes), St Estienne-Cavaignac complained to Ledru-Rollin on 27 April that Rolland and the Lamartine party had obstructed Ledru-Rollin's candidature.[74] Further, Lamartine attracted votes for different reasons: some believed he represented the party of order and moderation, others hoped he would ally with the radicals to effect a profound transformation of society.[75]

Personal factors helped Lamartine in several provincial departments which elected him besides Saône-et-Loire. In the Bouches-du-Rhône he was known from his visits to Marseilles of June 1832, August 1834 and August 1847, and the department's *commissaire*, Emile Ollivier, was a personal friend.[76] The electoral committee of the canton of Morlaix, Finistère, chose Lamartine to head their list of recommended candidates perhaps through Charles Alexandre's influence.[77] Another influential friend of Lamartine in Finistère was Jean-Jacques

Gizorme, a past editor of *Le Bien public* and now editor of a legitimist newspaper, *L'Océan* of Brest, which on 14 April supported Lamartine's candidature. Lamartine's old friend Théodore Ducos, nephew of the Gironde's *commissaire*, Henri Ducos, president of the Gironde's moderate republican Comité central républicain, and successful candidate himself in the Gironde, invited Lamartine to stand in the department.[78] Influential friends and relatives of Lamartine lived in the Nord, where a constituency had returned him to the Chamber of Deputies in January 1833 and June 1834. According to one report, Seine-Inférieure's moderate republican Comité central républicain initially picked Armand Marrast as their main candidate. Marrast declined and recommended Lamartine, a recommendation the committee accepted, possibly through the influence of Lamartine's friend, Alphonse Karr.[79]

Numerous hastily formed electoral committees backed Lamartine's candidature in the provincial departments which elected him. The political complexion of those committees seems to have been legitimist, conservative or moderate republican, with left-wing republican committees supporting him only in the Nord, Saône-et-Loire and Seine-Inférieure.[80] Outside Saône-et-Loire, the political complexion of provincial newspapers which supported his candidature was either legitimist or conservative,[81] a rare exception being the moderate republican *L'Echo du Nord* of Lille,[82] though provincial newspapers did not openly criticise or oppose him at this time. Provincial newspapers favourable to Lamartine generally emphasised his candidature's partisan character, by representing him as a member of the Provisional Government's moderate group, as an opponent of left-wing republicanism, and as Ledru-Rollin's direct antithesis. *Le Journal de Rouen* (23 April) thought Lamartine, together with Dupont de l'Eure, Marrast and Garnier-Pagès, practised the kind of republicanism France needed. For *Le Périgord* (16 April) Lamartine personified order and moderation, and that part of the Provisional Government which Ledru-Rollin called the bourgeois dictatorship, but which it called society's safeguard. *Le Courrier de la Gironde* (15 April) argued he represented a principle: 'in the Provisional Government he is the symbol of order and of respect for property and true liberty, as M. Ledru-Rollin is the symbol of violence, communism and the oppression of all honourable citizens. It is a duty to elect M. de Lamartine to protest energetically against M. Ledru-Rollin.' The argument that it was necessary to vote for Lamartine in order to vote against Ledru-Rollin occurs several times. Electors in the Côte-d'Or were exhorted to reject Ledru-Rollin's circulars and Louis Blanc's revolutionary utopias, and to vote for

Lamartine.[83] More bluntly, *L'Impartial de Rouen* declared (23 April) it was supporting Lamartine's candidature solely to counter-balance that of Ledru-Rollin.

Roman Catholic bishops and clergy, who were an important conservative influence in the April elections, also tended to identify Lamartine as a conservative and as an effective counter to Ledru-Rollin. In the Côte-d'Or the Comité électoral catholique chose Lamartine as their first candidate, while a conservative Catholic newspaper, *Le Spectateur de Dijon*, advised its readers (18 April): 'Do you want the Terror? Vote for Ledru-Rollin. Do you want the Republic? Vote for Lamartine.' Combined Catholic, conservative and legitimist influences were particularly strong in Finistère, where again Lamartine was seen as an opponent of Ledru-Rollin. The legitimist *Impartial du Finistère* reported (19 April) that when a government *commissaire* toasted Ledru-Rollin at a public banquet, the entire assembly replied, 'Vive Lamartine!' To combat Ledru-Rollin's candidature in Ille-et-Vilaine, the Bishop of Rennes and his Comité de démocratie chrétienne chose Lamartine to head their list of candidates, for which parish priests actively and effectively campaigned.[84] Thus a republican newspaper, *Le Progrès* of Rennes, complained (3 May) that with one exception those elected in Ille-et-Vilaine would represent only the clergy. Similarly, a Lille republican newspaper, *Le Messager du Nord* commented (29 April) on conservative successes in the National Assembly elections: 'in the countryside, especially, the Church has played an odious role'. Meanwhile, Ledru-Rollin's *commissaires* tried to counteract clerical and conservative propaganda: in the Dordogne and Ille-et-Vilaine the *commissaires* omitted Lamartine from their lists of recommended candidates, because Catholics, conservatives and legitimists supported him.[85] Altogether, in the ten departments which elected him left-wing republicans opposed his candidature except in the Nord, Saône-et-Loire and Seine-Inférieure, and in Saône-et-Loire relations between the *commissaire* and Lamartine's supporters were strained. Moderate republican support for Lamartine was forthcoming, particularly in the Bouches-du-Rhône, Gironde, Nord, Saône-et-Loire, Seine, and Seine-Inférieure. In all ten departments Catholics, conservatives and legitimists backed him, so that his candidature acquired a reactionary character, notably in the Côte-d'Or, Dordogne, Finistère and Ille-et-Vilaine.

The April 1848 elections were a remarkable triumph for the more conservative elements within French society. The *notables*, those who had controlled France's political life during the July Monarchy, began to re-assert the political power and influence they had temporarily lost during the February Days; the newly enfranchised peasants seem to have followed the advice of their *notables* and parish priests; provincial voters reacted against the popular violence, increased taxes and interference from Paris which they associated with left-wing republicanism; and radicals and socialists lacked the time and organisation to campaign effectively, had to combat a long exclusion from participation in parliamantary elections, and in Paris backed too many candidates. Lamartine had become nationally identified as the most prominent and influential moderate republican within the Provisional Government. His main support, however, came not only from moderate republicans, who favoured democratic political changes, but also from conservatives, who wanted to halt the Revolution. Conservatives regarded Lamartine and the moderate republicans in the Provisional Government as the most obvious and effective check on the radicals and socialists, particularly after the failure of the Paris demonstrations of 16 April. Thus it was the combined support of moderate republicans and conservatives that explains the enormous number of votes Lamartine and his moderate republican government colleagues received in the April elections. Yet in terms of winning seats in the Assembly, the April elections were a victory for conservatives rather than moderate republicans. A recent analysis suggests the representatives elected in April included 75 ex-peers or nobles and 439 former monarchists, compared to only 55 radicals and socialists and 231 moderate republicans.[86] It was to this Assembly, and to its conservative majority, that Lamartine and the Government were accountable after 4 May.

Although conservatives won a substantial victory in the April elections, fear continued to dominate the mentality of the wealthier classes. By the beginning of May it had become apparent that the Revolution of 1789 was not about to be re-enacted, and that there was not going to be a new Reign of Terror. However, the economic and financial crisis, already serious in February, had grown worse. The political uncertainties undermined confidence, railway communications were disrupted and revolutionary movements abroad reduced international trade. Sales declined, the volume of manufacturing production fell drastically, and the number of urban unemployed considerably increased. At the same time credit became virtually unobtainable; banks, railway companies and insurance firms collapsed; and prices on the Paris Bourse had fallen sharply when it had re-opened on 7 March. The alarm all this provoked is indicated by *Le Journal des Débats*, which on 22 March had reported that an unparalleled crisis was shaking commercial fortunes.

As the danger of a Terror receded, the demand for a restoration of public confidence and renewal of normal economic activity correspondingly increased. Far from having improved the financial and economic situation, the Government and Lamartine were held responsible for a whole series of allegedly socialist measures – the abolition of all titles of nobility; the provision of State relief for the unemployed in the National Workshops; the creation of a workers' parliament, the Luxembourg Commission, which met in the former Chamber of Peers; the threat to nationalise banks, railways and insurance firms; and the imposition of a sumptuary tax on male servants and of a forty-five per cent surcharge on all direct taxation. A decree abolishing slavery in France's colonies and overseas possessions caused considerable alarm in the commercial circles of Bordeaux, Le Havre and Marseilles. *Le Mémorial bordelais* (7 May and 25 June) even held Lamartine personally responsible for 'the disastrous situation' following slavery's abolition in the colonies. The Government replaced practically all prefects and sub-prefects, and dismissed numerous *procureurs généraux*, mayors, municipal officials, National Guard officers, and magistrates, although the latter's appointments were supposed to be permanent and non-political. Their successors often alienated vested interests, and were frequently recruited from outside the ranks of the wealthy and well known. Lamartine himself, by recalling practically all of France's senior diplomats, must have annoyed a number of powerful and influential families. Further annoyance must have been caused by many of his Foreign Ministry appointments, and by his patronage of such personal friends as Guigue de Champvans *commissaire* in the Ain), Fernand Delahante (allowed to remain *receveur général* for the department of the Rhône after his bank's collapse), Charles Mathey (*commissaire* in Saône-et-Loire, 14 March – 10 April), and Auguste-Edouard Cerfberr (editor of *Le Bien public*, March – August 1848, and prefect of Saône-et-Loire, 14 June 1848 – November 1849).[87]

Of equal importance to the deep anxieties about the worsening economic crisis was the alarm over Lamartine's alliance with Ledru-Rollin. For most conservatives and many moderate republicans, Ledru-Rollin had by the spring of 1848 become one of the most dangerous radicals. He had assisted incursions of French and foreign workers into Belgium, the South German states and Savoy; he had sent out *commissaires* into the departments to take over local administrations and 'republicanise' the provinces; and he had issued bulletins which in tone and content had outraged moderate and right-wing opinion. In the April elections many had voted for Lamartine simply because he was believed to be Ledru-Rollin's major opponent within the Provisional Government, yet he had publicly supported Ledru-Rollin's candidature in Saône-et-Loire and had continued to co-operate with him as a government colleague.

Before the April elections Ledru-Rollin had ended the Provisional Government's initial honeymoon with moderate and conservative French newspapers. His circular declaring government *commissaires* possessed unlimited powers provoked criticism from *L'Assemblée Nationale* (14 March), *Le Siècle* (15 March) and numerous conservative newspapers in the provinces. The first important Paris newspaper to break openly with the Government was *La Presse*: in a leading article on 28 March Girardin announced a complete change of attitude towards the Provisional Government, and subsequently became one of its severest critics. Private criticism of Lamartine himself developed from April onwards. George Sand after the *journée* of 16 April compared Lamartine to Lafayette, describing him as ambitious, ineffective, and attempting to reconcile all men and ideas, while in fact being politically inconsistent and personally isolated; and on 25 April Balzac despairingly wrote, 'If you knew the stupidity of Lamartine's words and actions!'[88] Serious public criticism of Lamartine began with his insistence that Ledru-Rollin should be included in the Executive Commission elected by the National Assembly to succeed the Provisional Government.

The Executive Commission's character and composition were discussed at a series of meetings between 4 and 9 May. Lamartine wanted the Commission's members not to hold ministerial office and to include Ledru-Rollin. Among others, Marie, Marrast and Dupont de l'Eure opposed Ledru-Rollin's inclusion. Executive Commissions consisting of Arago, Lamartine, Garnier-Pagès, Marrast, Marie or Dupont de l'Eure, or of just Arago, Lamartine and Garnier-Pagès, were proposed. Lamartine, however, insisted on Ledru-Rollin.[89] Ledru-Rollin had other supporters, such as Bastide, Boiselcomte and Caussidière,[90] but Lamartine's support was almost certainly crucial. The enormous number of votes he had received in the April elections made him uniquely influential; and in the National Assembly on 9 May he urged unity and conciliation, and the formation of a representative Executive Commission. Consequently, on 10 May the National Assembly elected to the Executive Commission, besides Arago, Garnier-Pagès, Marie and Lamartine himself, the controversial Ledru-Rollin.

Baffled contemporaries explained Lamartine's alliance with Ledru-Rollin in various ways. His action stemmed from a romantic desire to perform a splendid and poetic act of chivalry;[91] he owed Ledru-Rollin a secret obligation because of some personal or financial scandal;[92] he wanted to guarantee his political future in case the Left gained power;[93] he hoped republicans and bourgeoisie would unite to make him president;[94] he calculated that if the Left were a powerful force within the Government, then his services would be indispensable as a moderator and mediator;[95] or he feared that if the Government were to become the organ of a particular party, the direction of political affairs would inevitably pass either to the leading parliamentarians of the previous régime or to the militant radicals of the revolutionary clubs.[96]

Such contemporary explanations tend to be too simple and too cynical. Lamartine repeatedly maintained he wanted a representative and non-partisan republican government. On 26 February 1848 he told the comte de Carné: 'The Republic will be everybody's government: it will seek out all those with ability, wherever they may be found.'[97] To a deputation from the Fraternité Society he declared: 'Previous republics were in effect, partisan republics; we want this republic to be the republic of the entire nation.'[98] In the National Assembly on 9 May he argued that the people had not entrusted its destinies to one party alone, but to all the main parties which then formed the basis of public opinion, and to all those who had inspired the people.[99] Factional and partisan was how he described the revolutionary government which temporarily occupied the Hôtel de Ville on 15 May.[100] After the June Days he emphasised that 'concorde' was the only foundation on which the Republic could be built; and in 1850 he claimed to have won support for the idea of 'this unanimous Republic', in which no party monopolised power.[101]

While in government during 1848 Lamartine wanted to be popular among all classes, satisfy practically every shade of opinion, and win the support of nearly all political groups. With equal enthusiasm he sought the approval of Paris *salons* and revolutionary clubs. He attempted simultaneously to please Joseph Sobrier and Lord Normanby. He was prepared to offer a diplomatic post to August Blanqui and an embassy to the marquis de La Rochejacquelein.[102] On 16 April he welcomed National Guardsmen, who were shouting 'Death to the Comunits! Death to Cabet', but the following day invited Cabet and his wife to stay at 82 rue de l'Université.[103] Similarly he always tried to outmanoeuvre Louis Blanc, yet vigorously opposed his arrest at a Provisional Government meeting on 19 April.[104] Altogether he was continually labouring to achieve a general reconciliation.[105] This desire for a republic which united, and a popularity which transcended, the divisions of social class and political faction was undoubtedly sincere. It accorded with his belief in social *fraternité* and political harmony; it logically followed from his fear of anarchy and dislike of violence; it was consistent with the principle of independence he had rigorously maintained as a parliamentary deputy; and it can be compared to his non-partisan approach in the *Histoire des Girondins* and admiration for Mirabeau, whom he describes as the arbitrator who moderated the different political factions.[106]

Yet clearly Lamartine's personal relations with Ledru-Rollin were an important factor. They must have been quite close by 1843, when Lamartine served as a witness at Ledru-Rollin's wedding. During the eight months or so preceding the February Revolution they adopted increasingly similar political positions, and apparently developed considerable mutual respect. Lamartine very publicly opposed Ledru-Rollin's circular informing *commissaires* their powers were unlimited, which suggested he was Ledru-Rollin's major opponent within the Provisional Government, but their relationship survived this disagreement. According to Edouard Dubois, Lamartine had little fear of Ledru-Rollin, believing he could destroy and manipulate him, and describing him as 'a good lad' and 'a joker'.[107] Although Lamartine may well have deliberately misrepresented his relationship with Ledru-Rollin to the conservative Dubois, his vanity probably led him to underestimate Ledru-Rollin and exaggerate his personal influence over him. In fact Ledru-Rollin may have put considerable pressure on Lamartine. During the night of 7 May Ledru-Rollin reportedly remained with him till two in the morning, talking so loud as to keep Marianne awake.[108] Even if Ledru-Rollin did not gain an ascendancy over Lamartine, their personal ties must have made Lamartine extremely reluctant to exclude him from the Executive Commission. Dubois also reported that Lamartine wanted Ledru-Rollin in the government rather than in the opposition, regarding him as much less dangerous than Louis Blanc.[109] Throughout the Revolution of 1848 Lamartine certainly feared the Second Republic might slide into anarchy, a new Terror, and the dictatorship of a Paris revolutionary movement. He apparently calculated that Ledru-Rollin had considerable influence over the Left and the Paris popular movement, and would support the Government in a crisis, as he had done on 17 March and 16 April, providing he had not been alienated. Ledru-Rollin's inclusion in the Executive Commission was therefore one way of preparing for an extremist Paris uprising.[110]

So far as his own political position was concerned, Lamartine realised his alliance with Ledru-Rollin might cost him his popularity.[111]
However he believed that his almost universal appeal had brought him
to power in February 1848 and won him his votes in the April elections. If he headed a political reaction he calculated he would undermine his own political position and future potential.[112] He did not
appreciate that his popularity was not personal but due to his reputation as the most effective moderate republican and opponent of radicalism within the Provisional Government. Conservatives opposed
conciliating the Left and the Paris revolutionary movement, and, as
the leading advocate of conciliation, Lamartine increasingly attracted
their hostility. Given the strength of the Assembly's conservative
majority, this was politically fatal.

Lamartine's policy of conciliation was based on another miscalculation – that he would remain indispensable as a moderator and mediator,
especially if Ledru-Rollin remained in government. As Goudchaux told
the Commission of Enquiry into the events of May and June 1848:
'He [Lamartine] always wanted to remain a moderator; he believed
that he could dominate everyone by the force of his rhetoric.'[113] The
success of his speeches during and immediately after the February
Days, his substantial influence in the Provisional Government, and
his electoral truimph in April, made such a miscalculation understandable, but there is no doubt that after the February Days his
popularity inebriated him,[114] and that his personal vanity clouded
his political judgment. A number of stories concerning his remarks
and behaviour during 1848 illustrate this vanity. When Marrast informed him of his success in the April elections, Lamartine reportedly
jumped up from his seat and, with his arm extended and eyes raised
to heaven, declared, 'I am now a head above Alexander the Great and
Caesar!', afterwards adding modestly, 'At least so they say!'[115] The
day of the National Assembly's opening Lamartine met Normanby
and asked him if he had seen the procession to the Palais National.
After Normanby had replied in the negative, Lamartine then said:
'Oh! it was most satisfactory! Magnificent! Such universal cries of
"Vive Lamartine!" '[116] Two days later, at an official reception in the
Ministry of Foreign Affairs, Lamartine promised the Belgian ambassador's wife his personal protection for Belgium.[117] During crises he
was extraordinarily concerned about the text of his speeches: on
16 May he sent a secretary to Falloux to ask him for his recollections of what he himself had said on entering the Hôtel de Ville's

courtyard the previous day.[118] Even after the catastrophes of June 1848, Lamartine allegedly responded to praise of a new portrait of himself with the remark: 'Yes, there is something of Lord Byron in this portrait, but the statesman is more in evidence.'[119]

Lamartine's support of Ledru-Rollin had an enormous impact. According to Tocqueville, 'an undescribable disappointment, terror and anger seized the Assembly and the nation.'[120] Representatives in the Assembly indicated their views by voting the transference of power to the Executive Commission by only 411 votes to 385, and by giving Lamartine fewer votes than any other Commission member besides Ledru-Rollin.[121] *Le Constitutionnel* on 13 May expressed the view of a substantial section of French editorial opinion. People had voted for Lamartine because they opposed Ledru-Rollin. Since Lamartine had then used this popular mandate to force the Assembly, against its will, to include Ledru-Rollin in the Executive Commission, he was guilty of a complete betrayal of public confidence. As *Le Courrier de la Gironde* (12 May) succinctly and bitterly complained: 'We are threatened with having Ledru-Rollin; *Lamartine is responsible!*'

Opposition to the Government was not confined to moderates and conservatives. The urban working classes, particularly in Paris, were still hoping for a much more radical government stance, and on 15 May their impact was great enough to threaten another revolution. On that day an enormous crowd of thousands of demonstrators surrounded the National Assembly. The demonstration's pretext was to petition the Assembly for French aid to the beleaguered Poles, but in fact the Assembly's already apparent conservatism at least partly caused the demonstration; and some of the demonstrators clearly attempted to provoke a revolutionary *journée*, and replace the Executive Commission with a radical republican government. To that end, they proceeded to invade the National Assembly and an alternative revolutionary government occupied the Hôtel de Ville. The Executive Commission had received advance warning of the demonstration and had taken various security precautions, but a successful military parade in Paris on 20 April and the results of the National Assembly elections had probably encouraged a dangerous over-confidence. The precautions taken were rendered largely useless by a series of miscalculations and misunderstandings, and by the National Guard's unsatisfactory response.[122] On learning of the Assembly's imminent danger of invasion, Lamartine left the Assembly and attempted unsuccessfully to dissuade the demonstrators from entering. After the Assembly's invasion he tried to make a speech, but demonstrators prevented him from reaching the tribune. A young man called Hirshler allegedly rescued him from this embarrassing and potentially dangerous situation, by insisting he should leave the Assembly because Marianne was seriously ill. Outside the Assembly Hirshler told him he had invented Marianne's illness as an excuse for extricating him from the demonstrators. Overcome with heat, shock and exhaustion, Lamartine then retired to the Assembly's library. Once the National Guard had cleared the Assembly, Falloux and others persuaded Lamartine and Ledru-Rollin to go to the Hôtel de Ville, where the self-styled provisional government formed during the demonstration was dissolved.[123]

In his account of the *journée* of 15 May, Lamartine acknowledges the Executive Commission's inadequate protection of the Palais National, and his personal failure to dissuade the demonstrators from entering the Assembly. Yet he blames the Assembly's invasion on the indecision and lack of foresight of the Paris National Guard's commander, General Courtais; he states he gave orders summoning the *garde mobile* and National Guard; and he claims he suggested the march on the Hôtel de Ville which resulted in the revolutionary leaders being arrested.[124] Lamartine probably correctly blamed Courtais, whom the Executive Commission had ordered on 14 May to protect the Assembly against the Polish demonstration,[125] but in other respects his account can be questioned. During 15 May Lamartine does not seem to have given any effective orders to the *garde mobile* or National Guard. General Foucher, who was appointed commander of the army and National Guard during the afternoon of 15 May, reported he received no orders and acted solely according to his information of developments, as apparently did other National Guard officers.[126] Finally Lamartine was persuaded to go to the Hôtel de Ville, and arrived only after its reoccupation by the National Guard. Altogether the *journée* failed not because of Lamartine, but because the demonstrators were badly organised and almost entirely unarmed, and because the bulk of the National Guard eventually rallied to defend the Assembly and suppress the revolutionary government.

15 May was a critical day for the Second Republic. The Assembly's dignity and sovereignty had been attacked, and its members had suffered a very traumatic experience. On the other hand the Paris revolutionary movement had received yet another check, while as a result of 15 May radical leaders' such as Barbès, Blanqui, Raspail and Sobrier were arrested and imprisoned. Polarisation consequently intensified. Conservatives were more anxious than before to close the National

Workshops (many members of which had participated in the demonstration), and destroy the Paris popular movement by force. Equally the bitterness and frustration of Paris workers and radicals had understandably increased. The Executive Commission was widely condemned for not having prevented the Assembly's invasion, Lamartine being specially blamed. For *Le Courrier de la Gironde* (19 May) ultimate responsibility for what had happened lay with Lamartine. Thiers wrote to his friend Bugeaud on 16 May that Lamartine had been the cause of everything, these last few days.[127] 'Monsieur de Lamartine, above all, has fallen drastically in public opinion', observed the comte de Castellane on 17 May.[128] The Assembly shared those views, giving Lamartine's speech on the events of 15 May a very hostile reception.[129] 15 May also demonstrated that the National Guard, although generally loyal, might not be immediately effective. Consequently the Executive Commission dismissed National Guard commanders and increasingly relied on the regular army for the maintenance of order in Paris.

Developments after 15 May apparently confirmed the view that Lamartine was guilty by association. Caussidière's passive role and doubtful loyalty during the 15 May demonstration had aroused enormous suspicion, and on 17 May he was compelled to resign from being Prefect of Police. The same day Lamartine wrote him a friendly and respectful note, which *L'Assemblée Nationale* published (3 June). The Government's handling of the proceedings against Louis Blanc, also thought to have been implicated in the 15 May demonstration, attracted much hostile editorial comment. In particular it was remarked that no immediate action had been taken against Louis Blanc after 15 May, and that on Louis Blanc's guilt Crémieux and Flocon had voted negatively, while most of the Executive Commission had abstained.[130] Nor did a parliamentary speech criticising the Executive Commission by Jules Favre, just before his resignation as Under-Secretary of State for Foreign Affairs on 6 June, escape press notice.[131] On 12 June Lamartine even felt obliged to defend himself in the Assembly against accusations of having conspired with Blanqui and Sobrier during 15 May, claiming that he had no more conspired than a lightning conductor conspires with lightning. It is doubtful if this imagery convinced his audience.

Assembly by-elections, partly caused by Lamartine's multiple election in April, were held on 4 June. As in April Lamartine publicly supported at least four candidates, Duréault and Foillard in Saône-et-Loire, Alexandre Rey in the Bouches-du-Rhône, and Antony

Thouret in the Nord. Duréault and Foillard were among his Mâconnais friends and political supporters. Thouret, despite a radical past and association with *La Réforme*, had been a very moderate *commissaire* in the Nord, and with Lamartine had tried to prevent the Assembly's invasion on 15 May. Rey was a moderate republican and contributor to *Le National*.[132] Although Thouret and Rey (but not Duréault or Foillard) were elected, in the by-elections generally votes went to conservative and left-wing candidates, with moderate republicans (who might have supported Lamartine and the Executive Commission) faring badly. Possibly of greater importance, a revival of Bonapartism also occurred, with five departments, including Corsica and the Seine, electing Louis Napoleon Bonaparte, Napoleon's nephew and political heir. In the Assembly on 12 June Lamartine recommended applying the 1832 law, which had exiled the Bonapartes, to Louis Napoleon, partly because shots had just been fired at the National Guard in the name of the Emperor. The following day, Clément Thomas (successor of Courtais as the Paris National Guard commander) cast doubts on Lamartine's version of the shooting; Louis Blanc argued that all laws of proscription were anti-republican; and Jules Favre maintained Louis Napoleon's election to the Assembly made the 1832 laws inapplicable. Of the latter's speech *La Presse* (14 June) remarked: 'His words fell like a lash on the back of the Executive Commission.'

Many felt Lamartine had exaggerated the shooting incident, to obtain the Assembly's approval of a financial subsidy and exploit the Bonapartist danger for his own political ends.[133] Also Lamartine was swimming against a rising Bonapartist tide: large crowds in Paris participated in Bonapartist demonstrations on 12 June; and the following day a very large Assembly majority rejected the motion to exile him. This rejection was regarded as such a serious defeat for the Executive Commission that the resignation of its members was widely thought to be imminent.[134] In fact on 14 June at a meeting of the Government and the Executive Commission Lamartine suggested all members of the Executive Commission should resign. Although this proposal was rejected by thirteen votes to four, Lamartine and Ledru-Rollin still wanted to resign, and the same day instructed Pascal Duprat to announce their resignations to the Assembly. The Assembly's president, however, refused to allow Duprat to interrupt proceedings until 15 June, by which time Lamartine and Ledru-Rollin had been persuaded to change their minds.[135]

While the Executive Commission struggled on, it was generally acknowledged that France lacked effective leadership and needed a strong leader. 'France needs a man for a symbol', observed *L'Assemblée Nationale* on 17 May. *L'Union* on 22 May elaborated this point:

> Where is the man who will lead the Second Republic? Where is Cromwell, Washington or even Lafayette? Nowhere. Thus there is no authority, no guidance, no leadership, which makes everyone ask: 'Where are we going?' The necessity for a leader in a revolution is so obvious that at first the whole of France turned towards Lamartine. A leader was needed, and France thought she had found one.

The same day Xavier Marmier noted in his journal: 'We need a leader. M. de Lamartine could have been this leader, but his alliance with Ledru-Rollin and his inexplicable attitude towards recent events have cost him his popularity.'[136] *L'Union* reverted to this theme on 14 June: 'Everywhere it is said that France needs a leader to save her from anarchy and all the dangers which threaten her.' In the provinces Lamartine had been regarded as France's saviour from anarchy and the social peril. Yet by mid-May provincial newspapers were condemning him for his betrayal of the electorate's trust and confidence. He was now widely believed to constitute with Ledru-Rollin the extreme republican faction within the Government, in opposition to Arago, Marie and Garnier-Pagès.[137]

The Executive Commission finally foundered on its handling of the economic situation and, more particularly, on its closure of the Paris National Workshops. Among the poorer classes great hopes of change and improvement had accompanied the February Revolution, hopes that the Government itself helped to encourage. Those hopes signally failed to materialise. After February the economic situation deteriorated, which for the poor meant rising unemployment. The Government, despite its initial promises, did little to ameliorate conditions for the poor, other than decreeing that articles worth ten francs or less should be returned free of charge from the State pawnshops, and reducing the maximum working day by one hour to ten hours in Paris and eleven hours in the provinces. This inactivity was partly due to the preoccupation of the Provisional Government and Executive Commission with their political survival, and partly because the social question was thought to be the responsibility of the Luxembourg Commission and the National Workshops. Starved of funds, the Luxembourg Commission was really never more than a debating chamber, and its short life ended on 16 May after the Assembly had voted its dissolution. The National Workshops offered minimal financial relief and boring manual work to less than a tenth of those enroled, who finally numbered about 120,000.[138] Furthermore, on 10 May the Assembly rejected long-standing demands from Louis Blanc and others for the creation of a Ministry of Progress. Hence the widespread feeling that the Government had done nothing for the workers and that Lamartine, as the Government's chief spokesman, had offered only words and not deeds. Normanby recorded that when Lamartine tried to reason with demonstrators on 15 May, the remark – 'Enough of your poetry' – silenced him.[139] *La Commune de Paris* had written on 10 May: 'Your poetry sounds good, citizen Lamartine: we all like to listen to its harmonious cadences; but that is no longer enough.' Similarly *Le Père Duchêne* (28 May) published an open petition to Lamartine, which complained:

> We have become accustomed, citizen Lamartine, to your rhetoric and studied gestures, and now we realise that your speeches contain more sonorous words than sincere sentiments, more empty poetry than solid ideas, more lies and promises than truths. . .

Such complaints were not entirely fair. On 23 April Lamartine stated that the problem was to reconcile the sanctity of private property with the need to provide work and increase wages. Thus he opposed any wholesale nationalisation of banks and economic enterprises, such as Louis Blanc proposed.[140] Subsequently Louis Blanc suggested Lamartine feared socialism as children fear ghosts, and owed his first allegiance, not to the ideals of liberty, equality and fraternity, but to the institutions of the State, family and private property.[141] Admittedly Lamartine's *Histoire de la Révolution de 1848* describes the organisation of labour as 'a philosophic mirage', and the National Workshops as 'a temporary expedient, terrible but necessary',[142] but at the time he seems to have wanted some State intervention to provide work for the unemployed, and the nationalisation of France's major railway lines. As early as 27 February the Provisional Government decided to organise 'ateliers de terrassement' which, *inter alia*, would work on two Paris railway stations and the extension of the railway line from Sceaux to Orsay.[143] On 4 April a Provisional Government decree placed the Paris-Orleans and Centre railway companies under sequestration. The Provisional Government discussed railway nationalisation on 13 April, and agreed in principle (with compensation for owners) on 22 and 23 April. The following day a large credit was allocated to extending the railway line from Paris to the German frontier; and on 25 April the Provisional Government adopted a decree for railway nationalisation.[144]

Since February railway nationalisation had been linked to the National Workshops. By the time of the Assembly's opening, conservatives claimed that the National Workshops were too expensive, too unproductive and too dangerous. Certainly the National Workshops were badly organised and concentrated many unemployed workers in Paris, though as regards expense the minimal subsistence wage compared unfavourably with the relatively generous wages paid by the Government to the 16,000 members of the *garde mobile*. On 13 May the Executive Commission accepted a proposal from Garnier-Pagès to close enrolment in the National Workshops, and instead invite workers between eighteen and twenty-five to enlist in the army. Those who refused were to be sent back to their place of origin. At the same meeting Lamartine suggested replacing the National Workshops with a scheme for the clearance of uncultivated land in France and Algeria by unemployed workers, who would be paid partly in money and partly in the land they had cleared.[145] The events of 15 May hardened hostility towards the National Workshops. On 17 May the Executive Commission repeated to Paris mayors the order to cease enrolments in the National Workshops, and accepted a proposal from Trélat (Marie's successor as Minister of Public Works) for a committee to examine the Workshops' current situation.[146] However the same day the Finance Minister, on the Executive Commission's behalf, introduced a bill in the Assembly for railway nationalisation. It was proposed to nationalise all railway lines of commercial and strategic national importance, leaving private companies to run minor railway lines. The bill was referred to the Assembly's finance committee, discussed by the Assembly on 22 June, but withdrawn as a result of the June Days.

The committee on the National Workshops presented its report on 19 May. The Executive Commission decided to suppress the report, probably because it emphasised the principle of the right to work (which the conservative Assembly would have found provocative) and recommended public works projects in Paris (which would have continued many of the problems associated with the National Workshops). On 23 May Trélat and the Executive Commission agreed on the following measures concerning the National Workshops: workers with less than six months' residence in Paris to be sent back to their place of origin; employment offices to be opened for employers seeking workers, with immediate dismissal for those workers refusing employment in private industry; workers sent into the departments to be organised into brigades; and workers to be supplied to the Lyons railway company (which had asked for them), the State advancing their wages. The same day the Minister of Agriculture and Trade announced a proposal for the creation of several agricultural colonies for unemployed workers. The orders actually sent to the director of the National Workshops were harsher than those originally agreed on by the Executive Commission. In particular, unmarried workers aged between eighteen and twenty-five were to enlist in the army or be dismissed from the Workshops. However the Executive Commission continued its policy of closing down the National Workshops while simultaneously trying to provide employment for at least some of their members. Thus on 16 June the Executive Commission agreed that within four days workers enrolled in the National Workshops and aged between eighteen and twenty-five would have to enlist for two years in the army, or be dismissed from the Workshops. However, four days previously the Minister of Public Works had been authorised to spend two million francs on railway-related work, so as to employ the largest possible number of workers from the National Workshops. On 21 June the Executive Commission finally decided to enforce its decree compelling young men enrolled in the Workshops to enlist in the army or be dismissed. The same day the Commission agreed to allocate six million francs for the completion of the Paris-Lyons railway line between Chalon-sur-Saône and Collonges; and on 22 June it received the draft of a bill on agricultural colonies from the Minister of Agriculture and Trade.[147]

While the Executive Commission clearly wanted to close the National Workshops, it did try to find alternative work for the unemployed, with schemes of railway construction and agricultural colonies. Mainly because of pressure from the conservative Assembly and individuals such as Falloux and Montalembert,[148] those schemes did not materialise and the National Workshops were suddenly and brutally dissolved. Lamartine doubtless wanted the National Workshops closed, but he certainly proposed a scheme for land clearance by unemployed workers and had been attracted to the idea of agricultural colonies for many years. Similarly the State purchase of major railway lines, and the allocation of State funds to provide railway-related work for the unemployed, developed logically from his previously expressed ideas. He may well have proposed the completion of the railway line between Chalon-sur-Saône and Collonges, in view of his obvious local interest. His general views on railways in 1848 are possibly indicated by an anonymous article on the current financial crisis in the Paris evening edition of *Le Bien public* for 11 July.

The article argued that the State purchase of railways was the most effective solution for the financial crisis, since the compensation paid to owners would provide considerable funds for private investment and economic recovery. Also the completion of France's main railway lines, essential for the nation's administrative and commercial life, would be ensured. Finally the article suggested that all political revolutions are preceded or accompanied by technological revolutions, and that the railway in a sense symbolised the Second Republic, as the necessary agent of democracy in an age of manhood suffrage.[149]

On 22 June *Le Moniteur* announced that men enrolled in the National Workshops and aged between seventeen and twenty-six were expected to enlist in the army, and would in future be debarred from the National Workshops. The *journée* of 15 May and its aftermath (the dissolution of the Luxembourg Commission, arrest and imprisonment of Albert, Blanqui, Huber and Raspail, and occupation of the houses of Sobrier and Cabet) had finally destroyed the myth of national unity. Paris workers were further antagonised by the Assembly's hostility towards the National Workshops, and by the closure of Paris political clubs. The serious economic situation, and the debate on whether or not Louis Napoleon should be allowed to take up his seat in the Assembly, had encouraged popular unrest, demonstrations and outbreaks of violence. With thousands of workers suddenly being confronted with the choice of army enlistment or immediate deprivation of all financial support, it is not surprising that workers demonstrated in Paris on 22 June. These demonstrations rapidly developed into the insurrectionary movement that began the following day. Lamartine attempted personal mediation with the *barricadeurs*, displaying his own courage and confirming that the June Days were not deliberately provoked by the Government to destroy the radical popular movement in Paris. However, he had no success — as one Paris worker declared after the June Days, 'M. Lamartine was considered to have deceived the people'.[150]

In contrast to his published accounts of the *journées* of 16 April and 15 May, Lamartine was curiously reticent when he came to describe the events of 23 June. Contemporaries criticised the absence of a sufficient number of troops in central Paris on 23 June, and the failure to use those troops that were available to prevent the erection of barricades. Military decisions relating to the disposition and deployment of troops were the responsibility, not of Lamartine and the Executive Commission, but of General Cavaignac, who was appointed supreme commander of all forces in Paris on the morning of 23 June.

Yet Lamartine and his colleagues had consistently been concerned with the military situation in Paris, and can claim much of the credit for the strength of the military forces at Cavaignac's disposal. After 15 May the Paris republican guard had been reorganised, the expansion of the Paris National Guard had continued, and Cavaignac, Governor General of Algeria since 25 February, had been appointed on 17 May Minister of War, an appointment Lamartine had urged as early as 29 April.[151] The Executive Commission discussed military matters on 20 May, and agreed to concentrate a large regular army garrison in the Paris area.[152] Further, on 1 June the Executive Commission accepted a proposal from Lamartine to create three hundred battalions of *garde mobile* in the provinces;[153] and between 5 and 7 June the Executive Commission gained the National Assembly's approval for a law drastically restricting the right of public assembly and facilitating the use of force to disperse crowds.

Lamartine's claim that he had constantly urged the concentration of more troops in Paris seems to be justified;[154] and the military forces in the Paris area on 23 June were larger than those originally decided on by the Executive Commission.[155] However, Arago, Garnier-Pagès and Ledru-Rollin stated or implied that Cavaignac did not execute orders, given by the Executive Commission during the night of 22-23 June, for the Place du Panthéon's occupation early the following morning by two infantry battalions and two cavalry squadrons.[156] Over the strategy to be adopted towards the insurrection, a complete difference of opinion apparently developed between Cavaignac and the Executive Commission. Cavaignac wanted the troops to be concentrated under his control and then launched in massive attacks against the insurgents, whilst the Executive Commission believed every barricade should be attacked as soon as it had been erected.[157] According to Victor Hugo, this difference of opinion led to the following exchange between Cavaignac and Lamartine at about five in the afternoon of 23 June: 'That is enough for today.' − 'But we have still four hours of daylight, which the rioters will exploit while we do nothing!' To which Cavaignac merely repeated: 'That is enough for to-day!'[158]

The Executive Commission had earlier approved the strategy used by Cavaignac during the June Days, and the removal of barricades from Paris streets on 23 June might have required more combatants than Cavaignac could immediately mobilise. Yet it can still be argued that Cavaignac should have acted more decisively on 23 June. Troops may have concentrated with remarkable speed, but Cavaignac did not begin major operations against the insurgents during the afternoon or evening of 23 June. Late in the afternoon of 23 June he did march to General Lamoricière's aid, but only 'in response to Lamoricière's pleas' and, possibly, Lamartine's arguments.[159] Cavaignac then directed the assault on one barricade. The fact that serious fighting occurred in Paris on 23 June is hardly surprising. It could scarcely have been avoided unless the troops had been withdrawn from all parts of Paris controlled by the insurgents. Clearly Lamartine had earlier insisted on concentrating more troops in Paris, and urged taking immediate and vigorous action against the insurgents.[160] Cavaignac's strategy was probably militarily correct, and certainly ultimately successful, but an immediate attack might have saved many lives by preventing the insurrection from spreading.

Meanwhile the conservative Paris newspaper press had continued its campaign against Lamartine and for a strong leader. On 20 June *La Patrie* announced the existence of a new Paris club, the Club de la démocratie militante, with Lamartine, Ledru-Rollin and Ledru-Rollin's former *commissaires* as its principal members. At night-time meetings they allegedly prepared '*en famille* all the comedies which the Executive Commission had been playing for some time before the Assembly'. The previous day a petition had appeared in *Le Constitutionnel*. Addressed to the Executive Commission and supposedly drawn up at the Hôtel de Ville on 15 May, the petition acknowledged 'with gratitude the words coming from Citizen Lamartine's heart', and went on to request a credit for six hundred million francs, the money to be spent in various ways so as to benefit agricultural and industrial workers. An editorial article in *Le Constitutionnel* on 22 June suggested Lamartine had promised to spend six hundred million francs on the furtherance of socialist policies. *La Presse* published the same day the following short dialogue:

The situation must deteriorate even further!
Why?
Because we have only one means of keeping the power which is slipping from us. . .
What means?
Making the dictatorship of General Cavaignac necessary.

With the outbreak of the popular insurrection in Paris on 23 June, conservatives were anxious to seize the opportunity to dismiss the Executive Commission, establish a strong government and crush the Paris popular movement. The National Guard had been discredited by its performance on 15 May, so they turned to the army: on 24 June the National Assembly adopted a proposal from the moderate republican, Pascal Duprat, that Paris should be placed in a state of siege and that all executive powers should be invested in General Cavaignac. Memories of the state of siege proclaimed in Paris siren 1832 prompted some republicans to oppose the measures, but most moderate republicans accepted them. While not wanting a military dictatorship, they believed that only these measures, which they hoped would be temporary, could save the Second Republic.[161] The same day members of the Executive Commission communicated their resignations to the National Assembly.

While doubtless unjustly blamed for the insurrection spreading on 23 June, Lamartine was not quite the saviour of French civilisation that many of his supporters hoped for, or that he himself later claimed to have been. Besides the uncertainty frequently surrounding his motives and actions, and the lack of success accompanying his policies, it seems he made a fundamental misjudgment. As he pointed out in his foreign policy manifesto of 2 March, France's situation in 1848 differed enormously from that of 1792. There was no foreign war to fight, no enemy coalition to defeat, never any question of nation-wide civil war, and no economic crisis comparable to that of the years following 1792. This made a repetition of the Terror of the First Revolution extremely unlikely. Nevertheless the avoidance of such a Terror was a major preoccupation for Lamartine while in power in 1848. A fear of '93 was the dominant characteristic of the mentality of the *notables* at the beginning of the February Revolution,[162] which perhaps indicates the extent to which Lamartine remained the intellectual prisoner of his family and social background.

Although many of the fears experienced by Lamartine and the *notables* after the February Revolution were exaggerated, a Paris revolutionary *journée* might have overthrown the Provisional Government. Lamartine played a considerable part in preventing this. When the Provisional Government, surrounded by the armed victors of the February Days, had no effective military force available for its own defence, it was, as Tocqueville admits, chiefly Lamartine's courage and eloquence which prevented a degeneration into anarchy.[163] In the days following the February Revolution, Marie noted: 'The spoken word was the main strength, the main weapon of the Provisional Government. It was by the spoken word that it reigned over the crowd.'[164] The Provisional Government's acknowledged master of the spoken word was Lamartine: Carnot compared him to Neptune calming the tempests, Sainte-Beuve judged him 'the siren of the moment', and

Sarrans described him as exercising 'a kind of poetic sovereignty over the masses'.[165] He repeatedly harangued demonstrators, replied to innumerable addresses from French and foreign deputations, and generally acted as a most effective government spokesman. Even in the Vendée the prefect noticed how Lamartine's speeches helped maintain order in the department.[166]

Largely because his eloquence was initially so effective in securing restraint and moderation, Lamartine enjoyed a brief period of enormous prestige and popularity. This contributed towards the Provisional Government's ability not just to survive politically, but also to introduce two fundamentally important measures, the establishment of direct manhood suffrage for parliamentary elections (2 March) and the abolition of slavery in all of France's colonies and overseas possessions (27 April). The former Lamartine may have proposed, and the latter (although mainly Victor Schoelcher's work) he certainly supported.[167] Ironically, though, the National Assembly's rapid election, to which Lamartine was so committed, soon led to his dismissal. His popularity with the Assembly's conservative majority rested on the belief that he was the leader of a moderate faction within the Government, in opposition to the alleged extremists headed by Ledru-Rollin, and that he could keep Paris militants under control. This popularity vanished with his insistence on Ledru-Rollin's inclusion in the Executive Commission, and failure to prevent the Assembly's invasion on 15 May. Some sort of clash between the Paris revolutionary movement and the conservative Assembly was probably inevitable, but Lamartine's attempts to conciliate the Left and his alliance with Ledru-Rollin totally alienated the Assembly's conservative majority. At the same time his public failure to offer solutions for the social and economic grievances of Paris workers, and his acceptance of the decree restricting admittance to the National Workshops, helped cause the Paris June uprising. The June Days symbolised the collapse of his policies of mediation and reconciliation, increased suspicion of his duplicity and inconsistency, and rendered him politically irrelevant and dispensable. For his most direct contribution to the French Revolution of 1848 it is, however, necessary to turn to foreign affairs.

Notes

1. Garnier-Pagès, *Histoire de la Révolution de 1848*, V, p. 320.
2. A. N., 108 AP 3, dossier 7, f. 20 (cf. L. H. Carnot, *Le Ministère de*

l'Instruction publique et des cultes, depuis le 24 février jusqu'au 5 juillet 1848 (Paris, 1848), p. 4); Crémieux, *En 1848. Discours et lettres*, p. 323; Garnier-Pagès, *Histoire de la Révolution de 1848*, V, p. 312.

3.   Garnier-Pagès, *Histoire de la Révolution de 1848*, V, p. 320; *Le Moniteur universel*, 25 February 1848, p. 499.

4.   Circourt, *Souvenirs*, I, p. 64.

5.   Normanby to Palmerston, 28 February 1848; Public Record Office (London), F. O., 27, 803, f. 258. Cf. ibid., 27 February 1848 (F. O., 27, 803, f. 228); Guichonnet, *William de La Rive*, p. 13.

6.   *Le Moniteur universel*, 25 February 1848, p. 499; A. N., 108 AP 3, dossier 7, ff. 35-7. Cf. Blanc, *Historical Revelations*, p. 29, and *Histoire de la Révolution de 1848*, I, pp. 84-5; Garnier-Pagès, *Histoire de la Révolution de 1848*, V, pp. 323-4, 344-7; Stern, *Histoire de la Révolution de 1848*, I, p. 251.

7.   Blanc, *Historical Revelations*, p. 90; *Mémoires de Caussidière*, 2 vols. (Paris, 1849), I, pp. 277-8.

8.   Normanby to Palmerston, 3 March 1848 (F. O., 27, 804, ff. 53-4); Normanby, *A Year of Revolution*, I, pp. 166-7.

9.   Stern, *Histoire de la Révolution de 1848*, II, p. 20. In general see M. Dommanget, *La Révolution de 1848 et le drapeau rouge* (Paris, 1950).

10.   A. N., 108 AP 3, dossier 5, ff. 5-6; C. L. de S. de Freycinet, *Souvenirs, 1848-1878* (Paris, 1912), p. 24; C. A. G. L. Gallois, *Histoire de la Révolution de 1848*, 4 vols. (Paris, 1849-50), I, pp. 141-3.

11.   H. Boucher, *Souvenirs d'un Parisien pendant la Seconde République, 1848-1852*, (Paris, 1908), entry for 5 March 1848, p. 76. Cf. Guichonnet, *William de La Rive*, pp. 12-3; V. Hugo to Lamartine, 27 February 1848 (*Lettres à Lamartine*, p. 252); X. de Montépin and A. de Calonne, *Les Trois journées de février* (Paris, 1848), pp. 35-6.

12.   A. N., 108 AP 3, dossier 7, f. 23; Falloux, *Mémoires*, I, p. 313 (cf. C. Alexandre, *Madame de Lamartine* (Paris, 1887), pp. 140-1, note 2).

13.   A. N., 108 AP 3, dossier 5, ff. 4-5.

14.   Blanc, *Histoire de la Révolution de 1848*, I, p. 114; Garnier-Pagès, *Histoire de la Révolution de 1848*, VI, p. 113; Stern, *Histoire de la Révolution de 1848*, II, p. 33. Cf. A. N., 108 AP 3, dossier 5, ff. 8-9.

15.   *Les Cahiers de Sainte-Beuve* (Paris, 1876), p. 104.

16.   Lamartine, *Histoire de la Révolution de 1848*, I, pp. 430-2. On François de Champeaux, who for a time served as a secretary for Lamartine, see F. Letessier, 'En Marge d'une *Méditation*: notes sur deux relations de Lamartine', *Bulletin de l'Association Guillaume Budé*, December 1962, pp. 497-508, and 'Note complémentaire sur Lamartine et M. de Champeaux', ibid., June 1963, pp. 231-5.

17.   Normanby to Palmerston, 28/29 February 1848; Broadlands Mss., Historical Manuscripts Commission (London), GC, NO, 125, 4.

18.   M. C. B. comte de Montalivet, *Fragments et souvenirs*, 2 vols (Paris, 1899-1900), II, p. 198-191.

19.   A. N., 108 AP 3, dossier 6, ff. 4-5; Garnier-Pagès, *Histoire de la Révolution de 1848*, VI, p. 122; C. P. Robin, *Histoire de la Révolution française de 1848*, 2 vols. (Paris, 1849-50), I, p. 363; Sarrans, *Histoire de la Révolution de février 1848*, II, p. 129.

20.   La Hodde, *La Naissance de le République*, p. 103.

21.   Regnault, *Histoire du Gouvernement provisoire*, pp. 104-5.

22.   A. de Lamartine, *Le Conseiller du peuple*, 3 vols. (Paris, 1849-51), II (1850), pp. 133-63; Blanc, *Historical Revelations*, pp. 66-7, and *Histoire de la Révolution de 1848*, I, pp. 112-3. Louis Blanc states it was Ferdinand, not Jules, de Lasteyrie. Cf. Arago, *Histoire de Paris*, II, p. 39.

23. Lamartine, *Histoire de la Révolution de 1848*, II, p. 193.
24. *Le Moniteur universel*, 8 March 1848, p. 565; P. H. Amann, *Revolution and Mass Democracy: the Paris club movement in 1848* (Princeton, 1975), pp. 89-91; M. Dommanget, *Auguste Blanqui et la Révolution de 1848* (Paris, 1972), pp. 20-3; S. Wassermann, *Les Clubs de Barbès et de Blanqui en 1848* (Paris, 1913), pp. 56-9.
25. *Le Moniteur universel*, 16 March 1848, pp. 618-19.
26. Garnier-Pagès, *Histoire de la Révolution de 1848*, VI, pp. 421-5.
27. Blanc, *Histoire de la Révolution de 1848*, I, p. 276; *La France parlementaire*, V, p. 360; Lamartine, *Histoire de la Révolution de 1848*, I, pp. 312-6; Lamartine to Rolland, March 1848 (*Correspondance*, VI (1875), pp. 308-9); C. Merruau, *Souvenirs de l'Hôtel de Ville de Paris, 1848-1852* (Paris, 1875), pp. 46-7; Ollivier, *Journal*, I, p. 368; P. Chalmin, 'Une Institution militaire de la Seconde République: la Garde nationale mobile', *Etudes d'histoire moderne et contemporaine*, II (1955), pp. 40-2.
28. Normanby, *A Year of Revolution*, I, pp. 237-8.
29. *Le Moniteur universel*, 18 March 1848, pp. 631-2.
30. Lamartine, *Histoire de la Révolution de 1848*, II, p. 213; Robin, *Histoire de la Révolution française de 1848*, II, p. 154.
31. Deposition of Marrast, 8 July 1848; *Rapport de la Commission d'enquête sur l'insurrection qui a éclaté dans la journée du 23 juin et sur les évènements du 15 mai*, 3 vols. (Paris, 1848), I, p. 322.
32. Garnier-Pagès, *Histoire de la Révolution de 1848*, VII, pp. 227-8; Karr, *Le Livre de bord*, IV, pp. 179-80; *Marc Caussidière. A ses concitoyens* (Paris, 1848), p. 3; A. Ranc, *Souvenirs – Correspondance, 1831-1908* (Paris, 1913), p. 39; *Rapport de la Commission d'enquête*, I, pp. 143 and 255 (deposition of Caussidière, 5 July 1848); Regnault, *Histoire du Gouvernement provisoire*, pp. 248-52; Sarrans, *Histoire de la Révolution de février*, II, pp. 401-3; Stern, *Histoire de la Révolution de 1848*, II, pp. 320-3. Cf. Wassermann, *Les Clubs de Barbès et de Blanqui*, pp. 106-7 and 122-4.
33. J. M. House, 'Public Force in Paris, February 22 to June 26, 1848', unpublished PhD thesis (Michigan, 1975), p. 74.
34. A. N., 67 AP 8, ff. 106-7.
35. Legouvé, *Lamartine*, pp. 25-7, and *Soixante ans de souvenirs*, II, pp. 370-2.
36. House, 'Public Force in Paris', p. 94.
37. A. N., 108 AP 3, dossier 13, f. 16, dossier 20, ff. 20 and 22; A. A. Cournot, *Souvenirs, 1760-1860* (Paris, 1913), pp. 208-11; *Le Moniteur universel*, 8 and 9 April 1848, pp. 785 and 793; C. Tranchant, *De la Préparation aux services publics en France* (Paris, 1878), pp. 24-34; V. Wright, 'L'Ecole nationale d'administration de 1848-1849: un échec révélateur', *Revue historique*, January-March 1976, pp. 21-42.
38. Dommanget, *Blanqui*, pp. 102-10; Garnier-Pagès, *Histoire de la Révolution de 1848*, VII, p. 372; Stern, *Histoire de la Révolution de 1848*, II, p. 335.
39. Lamartine, *Histoire de la Révolution de 1848*, II, pp. 315-32, and *Lettre aux dix départements* (Paris, 1848), pp. 14-5; deposition of Lamartine, 5 July 1848 (*Rapport de la Commission d'enquête*, I, p. 305).
40. Garnier-Pagès, *Histoire de la Révolution de 1848*, VII, pp. 378-80; Regnault, *Histoire du Gouvernement provisoire*, p. 293.
41. Ledru-Rollin in the National Assembly, 3 August 1848 (Ledru-Rollin, *Discours politiques et écrits divers*, II, p. 45); Caussidière, *Mémoires*, II, p. 21; *Rapport de la Commission d'enquête*, I, p. 208.
42. Garnier-Pagès, *Histoire de la Révolution de 1848*, VII, pp. 380-3.
43. *Revue des Deux Mondes*, 15 January 1938, pp. 311 and 308-9.

44.   Normanby to Palmerston, 17 and 19 April 1848 (F. O., 27, 806, f. 154; Broadlands Mss., 12889, GC, NO, 158, 1); Normanby, *A Year of Revolution*, I, pp. 323-4.

45.   Normanby to Palmerston, 19 April 1848 (Broadlands Mss., 12889, GC, NO, 158, 1); *Derniers souvenirs du comte Joseph d'Estourmel* (Paris, 1860), p. 147; deposition of Changarnier, 11 July 1848 (*Rapport de la Commission d'enquête*, I, pp. 18 and 260).

46.   Regnault, *Histoire du Gouvernement provisoire*, p. 295.

47.   Lamartine, *Histoire de la Révolution de 1848*, II, pp. 233-4; Longepied and Laugier, *Comité révolutionnaire, Club des Clubs et la Commission* (Paris, 1850), pp. 104-5 and 107; Regnault, *Histoire du Gouvernement provisoire*, p. 247; Stern, *Histoire de la Révolution de 1848*, II, p. 343.

48.   A. N., 67 AP 9, f. 153; Chérest, *Marie*, pp. 162-5.

49.   Baroness F. Bonde, *Paris in '48. Letters from a Resident Describing the Events of the Revolution* (London, 1903), p. 18.

50.   *Correspondance générale de Sainte-Beuve*, VII (1957), p. 226. Cf. Sainte-Beauve, *Cahiers*, p. 77.

51.   P. Guiral and R. Brunon (eds.), *Aspects de la vie politique et militaire en France au milieu du XIXe siècle à travers la correspondance reçue par le maréchal Pélissier, 1828-1864* (Paris, 1968), p. 92.

52.   P. Cassagne, *Deux lettres* (Paris, 1848), letter dated 12 March 1848, pp. 8-9; *La Patrie*, 28 February 1848, p. 2; Lacretelle, *Lamartine et ses amis*, pp. 195-6.

53.   Massa, *Souvenirs et impressions*, p. 30.

54.   Lamartine, *Histoire de la Révolution de 1848*, I, pp. 429 and 445-6; *Le Constitutionnel*, 27 February 1848; *Le Journal de Saône-et-Loire*, 3 March 1848, p. 3; *Revue des Deux Mondes*, 15 January 1938, p. 297.

55.   Estourmel, *Derniers souvenirs*, p. 188; C. Limet, *Un Vétéran du Barreau parisien. Quatre-vingt ans de souvenirs, 1827-1907* (Paris, 1908), pp. 171-2; *Le Moniteur universel*, 30 April 1848, p. 914; L. D. Véron, *Mémoires d'un bourgeois de Paris*, 6 vols. (Paris, 1853-55), VI, p. 17.

56.   Caussidière, *Mémoires*, II, p. 86; Captain Chamier, *A Review of the French Revolution of 1848*, 2 vols. (London, 1849), I, p. 198; Normanby, *A Year of Revolution*, I, pp. 362-3.

57.   M. Du Camp, *Souvenirs de l'année 1848* (Paris, 1876), p. 134; E. Kaye (ed.), *Xavier Marmier: journal, 1849-1890*, 2 vols. (Geneva, 1968), I, p. 102.

58.   C. H. Pouthas (ed.), *Procès-Verbaux du Gouvernement provisoire et de la Commission du pouvoir exécutif, 24 février – 22 juin 1848* (Paris, 1950), p. 70.

59.   A. N., F1C II 57 and 56.

60.   See Lamartine to Théodore Ducos, 18 March 1848 (Guillemin, *Lamartine. Lettres inédites*, p. 88), to J. Cordier, 23 March 1848 (D. Monnier, *Souvenirs d'un octogénaire de province* (Lons-le-Saunier, 1871), p. 525), and to Bocage, 12 April 1848 (B. N., 8° Lc.64 916).

61.   Recipients of such letters included Charles Alexandre, Ferdinand Bertucat (*A juge de paix* of Paray-le-Monial), Alexandre Bixio, Bocage, the baron de Chamborant de Périssat (whose father had been a political admirer of Lamartine), Victor Considérant, Joseph Cordier (a former left-wing deputy), Alexandre Dumas, Alfred Dumesnil (son-in-law of Michelet and friend of Dargaud), Alphonse Karr, Henri de Lacretelle, General Laidet (a former deputy and president of the Chamber of Deputies), Mathieu (an *avocat* from the Garde-Freinet, Var), Dr Ordinaire, Jean-Baptiste Payer (first head of Lamartine's private secretariat in the Ministry of Foreign Affairs), François Ponsard, Jean Reboul of Nîmes, Henri Roch-Dupuys, and Emile Souvestre (a Breton novelist and dramatist).

Lamartine may also have encouraged Molé to stand for election (Normanby to Palmerston, 15 April 1848; F. O., 27, 806, f. 139).

62. C. Seignobos, *La Révolution de 1848 – Le Second Empire, 1849-1859* (Paris, 1921), p. 79.

63. Lamartine was also an unsuccessful candidate in the Rhône, where he polled 21,498 votes.

64. *Le Spectateur de Dijon*, 29 April 1848, p. 2.

65. The votes were distributed as follows: Bouches-du-Rhône, 58,355; Côte-d'Or, 41,509; Dordogne, 75,858; Finistère, 104,629; Gironde, 137,609; Ille-et-Vilaine, 100,532; Nord, 227,765; Saône-et-Loire, 129,879; Seine, 259,800; Seine-Inférieure, 147,565.

66. The group included Alton-Shée, Alfred and Alexis Dumesnil, Lamennais, Quinet, Recurt, and Vaulabelle; *La Réforme*, 14 March 1848, p. 2, and *Le National*, 15 March 1848.

67. H. Guillemin, *La Première résurrection de la République: 24 février 1848* (Paris, 1967), p. 301.

68. *Le Journal des Débats*, 22 April 1848.

69. *Le National* and *La Réforme*, 23 April 1848.

70. Bouchard, Boussin, Bruys d'Ouilly, Foillard, Lacretelle, Ordinaire, Saclier and Versaut; J. Seurre, *La Dernière République ou Paris et le département de Saône-et-Loire pendant la Révolution de 1848* (Paris, 1860), pp. 93-4; P. M. Siraud, *Les Administrateurs du département et les préfets de Saône-et-Loire de 1789 à 1885* (Mâcon, 1886), p. 280.

71. Lacretelle, *Lamartine et ses amis*, p. 134.

72. See St. Estienne-Cavaignac's file in A. N., F[1b] I 157[11]. For his misuse of government funds in the electoral campaign see *Le Moniteur universel*, 26 April 1849, p. 1556.

73. St. Estienne-Cavaignac to Dupont de l'Eure; A. N., F[1b] I 157[11], f. 187.

74. A. N., F[1c] III, Saône-et-Loire 5, f. 236.

75. In general see P. Lévêque, 'La Bourgogne de la Monarchie de Juillet au Second Empire', unpublished *doctorat d'Etat* (Paris I, 1976), pp. 964-1055.

76. B. N., nouv. acq. fr. 23768, f., 60; M. T. Ollivier, *Valentine de Lamartine* (Paris, 1908), p. 101, note 1.

77. Alexandre, *Souvenirs sur Lamartine*, p. 117.

78. Lamartine to Ducos, 18 March 1848 (Guillemin, *Lamartine. Lettres inédites*, pp. 88-9); *Le Courrier de l'Ain*, 1 April 1848, p. 3; A. Charles, *La Révolution de 1848 et la seconde république à Bordeaux et dans le département de la Gironde* (Bordeaux, 1945), pp. 116 and 131.

79. *L'Echo du Nord*, 9 April 1848, p. 3; *Le Journal du Havre*, 12 April 1848, p. 3.

80. Lamartine's candidature was supported in the Nord by the Comité central de la société républicaine radicale (*Le Messager du Nord*, 2 April 1848), and in Seine-Inférieure by the Société populaire démocratique des travailleurs (*Le Journal du Havre*, 21 April 1848, p. 3).

81. Provincial newspapers which supported Lamartine's candidature included *Le Courrier de Marseille* (conservative) and *La Gazette du Midi* (legitimist) in the Bouches-du-Rhône, *Le Journal de la Côte-d'Or* (conservative) and *Le Spectateur de Dijon* (conservative and Catholic) in the Côte-d'Or, *L'Echo de Vésone* (conservative), *Le Périgord* (legitimist) and *Le Sarladais* (conservative) in the Dordogne, *L'Amoricain* (legitimist) and *L'Océan* (legitimist) in Finistère, *Le Courrier de la Gironde* (conservative) and, to a lesser extent, *La Guienne* (legitimist) in the Gironde, and *L'Impartial de Rouen* (legitimist) in Seine-Inférieure. Two Rennes (Ille-et-Vilaine) newspapers did not support Lamartine, *L'Auxiliaire breton* moderate republican) and *Le Progrès* (republican).

82.   See *L'Echo du Nord*, 29 March – 24 April 1848. Cf. Cochin, *Lamartine et la Flandre*, pp. 359-60.
83.   *Le Spectateur de Dijon*, 20 April 1848, p. 5.
84.   See H. Goallou, *Hamon, Commissaire du Gouvernement puis Préfet d'Ille-et-Vilaine, 3 mars 1848 – 25 janvier 1849* (Paris, 1973), pp. 75-9.
85.   G. Rocal, *1848 en Dordogne*, 2 vols (Paris, 1934), I, pp. 51-9, 64, 95, 212-4; *Le Progrès* (Rennes), 20 April 1848.
86.   F. A. de Luna, *The French Republic under Cavaignac, 1848* (Princeton, 1969), pp. 107-13. Not enough information is available to permit the political classification of all the deputies elected.
87.   Auguste-Edouard Cerfberr had acquired experience in provincial journalism through founding *L'Echo du Cantal* and editing *Le Courrier de l'Isère*. In 1839 he reported on German and Italian prisons for the French Government. Subsequently he became a prison inspector and in 1843 editor of a weekly *Journal des Prisons et des Institutions de bienfaisance*. Local government, Algeria, mutual benefit societies, electoral reform, prisons, and charitable institutions were all discussed in his numerous publications, one of which favourably described Mme de Lamartine's work with young girls in Paris (A.-E. Cerfberr, *Des Condamnés libérés* (Paris, 1844), pp. 349-52). His brother and fellow prison reformer, Alphonse Cerfberr, published in 1844 *La Vérité sur les prisons, lettres à M. de Lamartine*.
88.   *Correspondance de George Sand*, VIII (1971), p. 414; R. Pierrot (ed.), *Balzac. Lettres à Madame Hanska*, 4 vols. (Paris, 1967-71), IV, p. 323.
89.   See. J. Barthélemy Saint-Hiliaire, 'La Commission exécutive de mai 1848', *Revue politique et parlementaire*, LI, 10 February 1907, pp. 318-24.
90.   Caussidière, *Mémoires*, II, pp. 80-1; Garnier-Pagès, *Histoire de la Révolution de 1848*, IX, p. 9.
91.   Regnault, *Histoire du Gouvernement provisoire*, p. 133.
92.   Sir A. Alison, *Some Account of My Life and Writings*, 2 vols. (Edinburgh, 1883), I, pp. 588-9; Normanby to Palmerston, 11 June 1848 (Broadlands Mss., 12889, GC, NO, 177, 1); R. Pierrot, 'Lettres inédites sur la Révolution de 1848', *L'Année balzacienne*, I (1960), pp. 51-2.
93.   Chérest, *Marie*, note on p. 160.
94.   Guizot to Senior, 1 September 1860; N. W. Senior, *Conversations with M. Thiers, M. Guizot and Other Distinguished Persons during the Second Empire*, 2 vols. (London, 1878), II, p. 383.
95.   Blanc, *Historical Revelations*, pp. 380-1; Normanby, *A Year of Revolution*, I, p. 366; Léon Faucher to Senior, 14 May 1848, in N. W. Senior, *Journals kept in France and Italy from 1848 to 1852, with a Sketch of the Revolution of 1848*, 2 vols. (London, 1871), I, p. 95.
96.   Normanby to Senior, 14 May 1848 (Senior, *Journals*, I, p. 93); Tocqueville, *Souvenirs*, p. 114.
97.   *Le Correspondant*, 10 December 1873, p. 850.
98.   *Le Moniteur universel*, 20 March 1848, p. 644.
99.   Ibid., 10 May 1848, p. 997.
100.   Ibid., 16 May 1848, p. 1054.
101.   Lamartine to Mâcon's National Guard, 29 October 1848 (*La France parlementaire*, VI, p. 17), and to Saône-et-Loire's *conseil général*, 26 August 1850 (Lex and Siraud, *Le Conseil général et les conseillers généraux de Saône-et-Loire*, pp. 130-1).
102.   Garnier-Pagès, *Histoire de la Révolution de 1848*, VIII, p. 44.
103.   *Le Populaire*, 9 July 1848, p. 3; *Correspondance de George Sand*, VIII (1971), p. 423.
104.   Caussidière, *Mémoires*, II, pp. 50 and 61; Garnier-Pagès, *Histoire de*

la Révolution de 1848, VIII, pp. 43-5.

105.   Blanc, *Histoire de la Révolution de 1848*, II, p. 63.

106.   *Histoire des Girondins*, I (1847), p. 14.

107.   Guillemin, *Connaissance de Lamartine*, p. 280.

108.   *Revue politique et parlementaire*, LI, 10 February 1907, p. 321.

109.   Guillemin, *Connaissance de Lamartine*, p. 280.

110.   See Melun, *Mémoires*, I, p. 254.

111.   Legouvé, *Lamartine*, p. 28, and *Souvenirs de soixante ans*, II, p. 373; Ollivier, *Journal*, I, p. 368.

112.   See *Lamartine et ses nièces*, p. 128; Luppé, *Lamartine*, pp. 362-3.

113.   *Rapport de la Commission d'enquête*, I, p. 289, Cf. Rémusat, *Mémoires de ma vie*, IV, p. 266.

114.   See *Lamartine et ses nièces*, pp. 116-20, and Guillemin, *Lamartine, lettres inédites*, p. 87.

115.   Regnault, *Histoire du Gouvernement provisoire*, p. 358. Cf. H. d'Estre (ed.), *Campagnes d'Afrique, 1830-1848. Mémoires du général Changarnier* (Paris, 1930), p. 303.

116.   Normanby, *A Year of Revolution*, I, pp. 362-3.

117.   Princesse C. de Ligne (ed.), *Souvenirs de la princesse de Ligne, 1815-1850* (Brussels, 1923), p. 148. The princesse de Ligne replied that fortunately Belgium still had a King, and had no need of Lamartine's protection.

118.   Falloux, *Mémoires*, I, p. 324.

119.   *Journal et correspondance intimes de Cuvillier-Fleury*, II, p. 457.

120.   Tocqueville, *Souvenirs*, p. 115. Cf. Melun, *Mémoires*, I, p. 254.

121.   The voting was Arago 725, Garnier-Pagès 715, Marie 702, Lamartine 643, Ledru-Rollin 458.

122.   See P. Amann, 'A *Journée* in the Making: May 15, 1848', *Journal of Modern History*, XLII, March 1970, pp. 60-9, and *Revolution and Mass Democracy*, pp. 227-33; House, 'Public Force in Paris', chap. VI.

123.   A. Barbier, *Souvenirs personnels et silhouettes contemporaines* (Paris, 1883), p. 277; Chamier, *A Review of the French Revolution of 1848*, I, pp. 246 and 256-7; Falloux, *Mémoires*, I, pp. 322-3; Tocqueville, *Souvenirs*, pp. 118-9, 125-6.

124.   Lamartine, *Histoire de la Révolution de 1848*, II, pp. 421-49.

125.   Callier Papers, B. N., nouv. acq. fr., 23768, f. 27. For a statement of the case against Courtais, see *Rapport de la Commission d'enquête*, I, pp. 62-3. A more favourable interpretation is in Garnier-Pagès, *Histoire de la Révolution de 1848*, IX, pp. 172-3, 298-9.

126.   Foucher's report to the Executive Commission, 19 May 1848 (*Rapport de la Commission d'enquête*, I, p. 207); A. J. F. Mézières, *Au Temps passé* (Paris, 1906), pp. 61-3.

127.   Cited in H. Malo, *Thiers, 1797-1877* (Paris, 1932), p. 385.

128.   *Journal du maréchal de Castellane*, IV (1896), p. 68. Cf. Du Camp, *Souvenirs*, p. 193.

129.   See *Le Moniteur universel*, 31 May 1848, p. 1219.

130.   See *Le Constitutionnel*, 5 June 1848. Cf. J. Janin to his wife, 3 June 1848: 'Hier, on s'occupait de l'accusation de Louis Blanc, . . . ; l'homme qui disparaît le plus, c'est M. de Lamartine, il tombe sous une impopularité effrayante' (Mergier-Bourdeix, *Jules Janin*, I, p. 359).

131.   See *L'Union*, 6 June 1848.

132.   See *Le Bien public*, 1 June 1848, p. 2, *La Gazette du Midi*, 25 May 1848, and the candidates' *professions de foi*.

133.   See Bonde, *Paris in '48*, pp. 187-8; *Le Journal des Débats*, 15 June 1848; *Le Mémorial bordelais*, 19 June 1848.

134. *Souvenirs de la princesse de Ligne*, p. 306; *Le Constitutionnel*, 15 June 1848; *La Patrie*, 17 June 1848; *La Réforme*, 15 June 1848; *L'Union*, 14 and 16 June 1848.

135. See A. N., 108 AP 3, dossier 16, f. 15; Garnier-Pagès, *Histoire de la Révolution de 1848*, X, pp. 294-301.

136. Marmier, *Journal*, I, p. 128. Cf. *Le Siècle*, 20 May 1848, and the petition to the Assembly in *Rapport de la Commission d'enquête*, II, pp. 291-2.

137. See *Le Courrier de Marseille*, 27 May and 14 June 1848; *La Guienne*, 21 May 1848; *Le Journal du Havre*, 24 May 1848; *Le Mémorial bordelais*, 19 and 20 May 1848.

138. D. C. McKay, *The National Workshops. A study in the French Revolution of 1848* (Cambridge, Mass., 1933), pp. 26-8.

139. Normanby, *A Year of Revolution*, I, p. 393. Cf. Du Camp, *Souvenirs*, p. 169, and P. Audebrand, *Souvenirs de la Tribune des Journalistes, 1848-1852* (Paris, 1867), p. 281.

140. Lamartine to the Society of Political Economy (*Le Moniteur universel*, 24 April 1848, p. 884); Garnier-Pagès, *Histoire de la Révolution de 1848*, VI, pp. 421-3.

141. Blanc, *Historical Revelations*, pp. 81-2, and *Pages d'histoire de la Révolution de février* (Paris, 1850), p. 28. Cf. Caussidière, *Mémoires*, II, pp. 68-9.

142. *Histoire de la Révolution de 1848*, I, p. 329, II, p. 123.

143. A. N., 67 AP 8, f. 16. In general see A. Matagrin, 'Le Rachat des chemins de fer en 1848', *Revue socialiste*, 15 October and 15 November 1904, pp. 417-46, 529-71.

144. A. N., 67 AP 8, ff. 122, 143, 165, 166, 168 and 173.

145. A. N., 67 AP 8, no. 3; B. N., nouv. acq. fr., 23768, f. 27; *Procès-Verbaux*, p. 253.

146. A. N., 67 AP 8, no. 7; B. N., nouv. acq. fr., 23768, f. 27.

147. A. N., 67 AP 8, nos. 12, 32, 36, 41 and 43; B. N., nouv. acq. fr., 23768, f. 28; McKay, *The National Workshops*, pp. 84-90.

148. A. N., 108 AP 3, dossier 17, ff. 1-2.

149. A newspaper called *Le Bien public* appeared in Paris between 24 May and 12 December 1848, with an evening edition for at least 10-18 July. Edited by Eugène Pelletan and Arthur de La Gueronnière, the newspaper supported Lamartine and presumably succeeded *Le Bien public* of Mâcon, which ceased publication about 8 August 1848.

150. *Rapport de la Commission d'enquête*, III, p. 131. Cf. Arago's deposition, 5 July 1848, ibid., I, p. 224.

151. *Le Moniteur universel*, 17 May 1848, p. 1059; House, 'Public Force in Paris', p. 100; F. Letessier, 'Autour du général Cavaignac', *Bulletin de la Société d'agriculture, sciences et arts de la Sarthe*, 1972, pp. 352-3; de Luna, *The French Republic under Cavaignac*, p. 125.

152. B. N., nouv. acq. fr., 23768, ff. 27-8. Cf. Lamartine, *Lettre aux dix départements*, pp. 30-1.

153. Lamartine, *Lettre aux dix départements*, p. 31.

154. Lamartine's deposition, 5 July 1848 (*Rapport de la Commission d'enquête*, I, p. 306); Lamartine, *Histoire de la Révolution de 1848*, II, pp. 453-4, 472-4. Cf. Cavaignac in the National Assembly, 25 November 1848 (*Le Moniteur universel*, 26 November 1848, p. 3355).

155. W. Zaniewicki, 'Un Moyen de recherches en histoire militaire: l'étude des mouvements de troupes (Le retour de l'armée à Paris, mai-juin 1848)', *Revue d'histoire moderne et contemporaine*, October-December 1975, pp. 586 and 598-9.

156. Depositions of Arago, Garnier-Pagès and Ledru-Rollin, 5 July 1848;

Rapport de la Commission d'enquête, I, pp. 229, 285 and 312. Cf. Barthélemy Saint-Hilaire in the National Assembly, 25 November 1848 (*Le Moniteur universel*, 26 November 1848, p. 3352); *Rapport de la Commission d'enquête*, III, p. 247.

157. Ledru-Rollin's deposition; *Rapport de la Commission d'enquête*, I, p. 312. Cf. depositions of Garnier-Pagès and Marie, 5 July 1848 (ibid., I, pp. 285 and 250); Barthélemy Saint-Hilaire in the National Assembly, 25 November 1848 (*Le Moniteur universel*, 26 November 1848, pp. 3352-3); C. Beslay, *1830-1848-1870. Mes Souvenirs* (Paris, 1873), pp. 183-4.

158. Hugo, *Choses vues*, p. 306. Cf. H. Guillemin (ed.), *Victor Hugo: souvenirs personnels, 1848-1851* (Paris, 1952), p. 81; Lamartine, *Histoire de la Révolution de 1848*, II, p. 482.

159. De Luna, *The French Republic under Cavaignac*, p. 141; Lamartine, *Histoire de la Révolution de 1848*, II, pp. 483-4.

160. With reference to the strategy to be employed against the insurgents de Luna writes: 'Only Lamartine had originally sided with Cavaignac' (*The French Republic under Cavaignac*, p. 165). Lamartine certainly suggested the contrary to the Commission of Enquiry (*Rapport de la Commission d'enquête*, I, p. 306), and he indicates a complete difference of opinion between himself and Cavaignac in his *Histoire de la Révolution de 1848*, II, pp. 482-3. In his *Mémoires politiques* Lamartine accused Cavaignac of negligence, and of having an excessive confidence in his subordinates (*Oeuvres complètes*, XXXX (1863), p. 7). See also Barthélemy Saint-Hilaire and Ledru-Rollin in the National Assembly, 25 November 1848; *Le Moniteur universel*, 26 November 1848, pp. 3355 and 3363.

161. See A. Crémieux to Mme Nathan, 23 June 1848; A. N., 369 AP 2, dossier 2.

162. See A.-J. Tudesq, *Les Grands notables en France, 1840-1849: étude historique d'une psychologie sociale*, 2 vols. (Paris, 1964), II, pp. 1002-5.

163. Tocqueville to N. W. Senior, 2 January 1852; M. C. M. Simpson (ed.), *Correspondence and Conversations of Alexis de Tocqueville with Nassau William Senior from 1843 to 1859*, 2 vols. (London, 1872), II, p. 13. Cf. Regnault, *Histoire du Gouvernement provisoire*, p. 130.

164. Chérest, *Marie*, p. 144. Cf. Legouvé, *Lamartine*, p. 23.

165. A. N., 108 AP 3, dossier 8, f. 12; Sainte-Beuve, *Cahiers*, p. 96; Sarrans, *Histoire de la Révolution de février*, II, p. 83. Cf. Alexandre, *Souvenirs sur Lamartine*, p. 119.

166. Tudesq, *Les Grands notables*, II, p. 1026.

167. See the note about the dismissal of Guadaloupe's *procureur général*, hostile to emancipation, in B. N., nouv. acq. fr., 23768, f. 51.

5 MINISTER OF FOREIGN AFFAIRS IN 1848

Nous aurons un système français au lieu de l'isolement. – Lamartine
to Rocher, 5 March 1848

In the afternoon of 24 February 1848 Lamartine was appointed
Minister of Foreign Affairs. While the urgent problems facing the
Provisional Government kept him at the Hôtel de Ville until 26
February, apparently on their own initiative a group of moderate
republicans, including Alton-Shée, Jules Bastide, Alexandre Bixio,
Hetzel, and Sain de Boislecomte, took over the Ministry of Foreign
Affairs. Looking pale and exhausted, Lamartine himself arrived during
the afternoon of 26 February. He accepted his self-appointed entourage, eventually giving them all, except Alton-Shée, Foreign Ministry
or diplomatic posts. He also addressed a short speech to them. Un-
surprisingly, he indicated his personal satisfaction at occupying the
former office of his old rival Guizot, though he ensured that Guizot's
private papers were returned to him intact and unread. He went on to
announce that he would now be resuming his old 'métier'. Though
considered a poet, he claimed that poetry had never been more than a
passing distraction for him, that he had never attached any real importance to his poems, and that he had always been preoccupied with the
great and serious matters of politics.[1]

Lamartine certainly possessed obvious qualifications for his new
post, having served as a junior diplomat during the 1820s and having
thereafter frequently discussed French diplomacy and foreign affairs
in his speeches and writings. In addition he had travelled quite extensively abroad, and his writings had won him an international reputation.
Also, his appointment helped to calm widespread contemporary fears
that the February Revolution might lead to French involvement in a
European war. His aristocratic background, appearance and manner
were likely to make him personally acceptable to the European Powers,
while his reputation as an opponent of belligerent chauvinism, military
glory and Bonapartism, suggested that he would pursue peaceful foreign
policies.[2]

There was, however, some ambiguity and contradiction in Lamartine's views on French foreign policy prior to February 1848. He was
always a self-proclaimed man of peace: 'I have always been, and always
will be, a partisan of peace', he told the Chamber of Deputies on 27

January 1843; in the *Histoire des Girondins* he wrote that 'peace was the first of the Revolution's true principles'; and 'peace between nations' was listed in November 1847 as *Le Bien public*'s first political objective.[3] This commitment to peace was based partly on his interpretation of the Revolutionary and Napoleonic periods. The Girondin war policy, he believed, had fatally diverted the Revolution from its true course, while Napoleon's wars of aggression were a terrible perversion of the Revolutionary ideal. Moreover Napoleon had discredited the Revolution's principles in the countries occupied by his armies. In contrast, not to have disrupted European peace was the supreme achievement of the July 1830 Revolution.[4] Humanitarian considerations also made Lamartine an advocate of peace. He was appalled by the human suffering and loss of life wars inevitably entailed, and maintained that peace was always a necessary precondition for the operation of liberty and justice, and for the progressive application of the principles of 1789. Once he even argued that he was a member of the human race before being a French citizen, concerned with the welfare of humanity in general rather than with his own country's national interests.[5]

Yet a peaceful foreign policy did not mean, for Lamartine, a policy of inaction. France could secure peace on satisfactory terms only through intelligent planning and vigorous action by her government. The 1815 settlement potentially threatened European peace, for it had left France diplomatically isolated and deprived of her natural frontiers. Diplomatic isolation was dangerous because 'an isolated nation is necessarily an armed and suspicious nation'.[6] The remedy was to establish alliances with other states. Consequently in 1839 Lamartine acknowledged 'the happy necessity' of the British alliance; and in 1846 he advocated a new alliance between France and Syria.[7] France's natural frontiers could be restored only through a recognition that the Congress of Vienna's decisions were impermanent and in need of revision. In January 1840 Lamartine asked whether the Treaties of 1815 were 'eternal and immovable like those rivers and mountains that serve as nature's unwritten treaties between peoples?' The rhetorical answer was in the negative, and it was the duty of statesmen everywhere to destroy or modify the stifling Treaties of 1815.[8]

The extent to which France should intervene in other countries, in order to revise the 1815 settlement and further the principles of 1789, was never made absolutely clear by Lamartine. In September 1831, while the Russians were suppressing a Polish revolt, Lamartine wrote in *Sur la politique rationnelle* that French sympathy for Polish heroism did not oblige the French government to risk a European war by intervening.[9] Yet in 1843, referring to Spain, he argued that it was sometimes necessary to defend one's own interests in another country; and in October 1847 he bitterly deplored France's failure to assist the nationalist movement in Italy, and Guizot's decision to support the Sonderbund, not the Radicals, in Switzerland.[10] On 29 January 1848 Lamartine reverted to the Italian Question in the Chamber of Deputies. He urged that France should remain strictly neutral. This meant no active encouragement of Italian revolutionary movements, but it did not preclude giving moral support to such movements; and, if a federation of independent Italian states were to be formed, then France should be prepared to defend that federation in the event of foreign aggression.[11]

Thus on his arrival at the Ministry of Foreign Affairs Lamartine already had ideas about an appropriate foreign policy, albeit rather contradictory ones. At first, as Minister, he enjoyed a considerable degree of freedom. He had no parliamentary responsibilities; domestic matters normally preoccupied his government colleagues; and the February Revolution provided him with a unique opportunity to develop his own policies and select his own diplomats. But the February Revolution also imposed on him several important constraints. The Provisional Government was, on its own admission, a temporary caretaker administration, without the sanction of legitimacy, democracy or international recognition; and its lack of adequate military protection in Paris made it extremely vulnerable to radical popular pressure from within France and to hostile reactions by foreign governments. This was particularly dangerous, since many contemporaries believed that after Louis-Philippe's overthrow and the Republic's proclamation foreign intervention or French aggression might provoke a general European war. One or more of the Great Powers might decide a French republic posed such a serious threat to European peace and the 1815 settlement as to warrant hostile action against it. Equally, a French republican government might launch a war in response to domestic popular pressures and to consolidate its own political position. There was some force in these arguments: the Treaties of 1815 were still bitterly resented in France, with radical opinion unanimously demanding their abolition; and it was also asserted that France must re-establish her natural frontiers, while at the same time the concept of emancipating foreign peoples from the tyranny of their rulers formed an integral and fundamental part of the French revolutionary creed.

Contemporary fears of the February Revolution in Paris rapidly leading to French aggression abroad provoked defensive military measures in Belgium, the German States and Piedmont.[12] Those fears were, however, unjustified: the Provisional Government was financially and militarily unprepared for an immediate campaign, and in no neighbouring state did circumstances favour French intervention. The February Revolution's threat to European stability lay rather in the example it gave of a successful urban revolt against a conservative monarchy, an example that soon proved contagious in Vienna, Milan, Berlin, and elsewhere. Yet until the middle of March it seemed that a European war might have resulted from the reaction of one or more of the Great Powers to the re-establishment of a republic in France.

Britain's naval, economic and financial resources made British support probably indispensable for any successful aggressive action against France. British dislike of Guizot and coolness towards the Orléans monarchy were obvious factors in Lamartine's favour. Lamartine's standing with Lord Normanby (the British ambassador in Paris) was helped by their former acquaintance in Florence,[13] and by Normanby's belief following 24 February that Lamartine had saved Paris from anarchy.[14] Normanby's first reports on him were certainly flattering; and his assessment of Lamartine undoubtedly influenced his advice to Palmerston (the British Foreign Secretary) that he should not be recalled, but should indicate the British government's wish to maintain friendly relations with France.[15] This accorded with Palmerston's instructions to Normanby of 26 February. Normanby was to continue at his post and in unofficial contact with the Provisional Government. Britain wanted 'friendship and extended commercial intercourse with France and peace between France and the rest of Europe'. In return for French non-intervention in Europe, Britain would discourage European intervention in France. 'Upon such a basis', Palmerston concluded, 'our relations with France may be placed on a footing more friendly than they have been or were likely to be with Louis-Philippe and Guizot.'[16] Almost at once, however, Palmerston became less sanguine. 'A general war seems to be impending at the moment when we all were flattering ourselves that peace would last thirty years to come', he wrote to Normanby on 27 February. 'We cannot sit quiet and see Belgium overrun and Antwerp become a French port; and even a war in other directions will sooner or later draw us into its vortex.' The following day he repeated his fears: 'Large republics seem to be essentially and inherently aggressive, and the aggressions of the French will be resisted by the rest of Europe, and that is War'.[17]

Like Normanby, the Austrian ambassador in Paris, Count Apponyi, was impressed by Lamartine's efforts to restore law and order. 'It is thanks to him [Lamartine]', he wrote on 27 February, 'that we have escaped pillage.' Nevertheless he was thoroughly despondent about the future.[18] Metternich himself had been extremely surprised by the February Revolution and tended to see all such events in Switzerland, France and Italy, as the product of a radical conspiracy, directed with skill and intelligence, to overthrow the existing established order.[19] To the British ambassador in Vienna he remarked that 'the present state of affairs in France was just what it was in 1793'.[20] By 1 March Metternich was maintaining he had always doubted the July Monarchy's permanence, but had mistakenly calculated that the French would have restrained their impatience until Louis-Philippe's death. He regretted not so much the latter's fall as the triumph of the revolutionary movement, fearing the French Republic's influence on Italian revolutionary movements.[21] On 7 March Metternich sent identical dispatches to London, Berlin and St Petersburg concerning Great Power recognition of the new French Republic. He emphasised that the Great Powers should act in concert, and suggested the text of a joint *communiqué* to be presented by them to the French government. This began with a declaration of non-intervention in domestic French politics. But the breaking of previous treaties, or French aggression against a neighbour, was to be regarded as equivalent to a declaration of war against all the Great Powers. An imperial manifesto published in the *Vienna Official Gazette* on 10 March restated this position.[22] Three days later, however, Vienna itself experienced its revolution, and thereafter domestic problems prevented the Habsburg government from taking any effective action against France.

The reaction of King Frederick William IV of Prussia to the February Revolution in Paris resembled that of Metternich. On 27 February he wrote a personal letter to Queen Victoria acknowledging his serious alarm at the prospect of the spread of revolutionary principles throughout Europe. He recommended that the sovereigns of Britain, Prussia, Austria and Russia should present France with a united front. Peaceful intentions were to be declared towards France. 'But the first breach of the peace, be it with reference to Italy, Belgium or Germany would be, undoubtedly and at the same time, a breach with 'all of us', and we should, with all the power that God had given us, let France feel by *sea* and by *land*, as in the years '13, '14 and '15, what our union may mean.'[23] The Prussian government did recall some troops from leave, but Baron Canitz, the Prussian Foreign Minister, assured the British minister at Berlin that the views of his government were 'in no way to interfere with the internal Government of that country [France]', although he admitted 'a determination to resist any attempt, if such should be made, to overthrow the territorial arrangements sanctioned by the Treaties of Vienna'.[24] This attitude was publicly stated in an officially inspired article in the *Prussian Universal Gazette* of 2 March, and confirmed four days later by Frederick William on closing the session of the United Committee of the Prussian States. While disclaiming any 'idea of an intervention in the internal affairs of foreign countries', and emphasising the necessity for peace, he declared that the breaking of treaties or an invasion of German territory would cause him to 'prefer even the dangers of war to a disgraceful peace'. He also repeated his conviction that, if necessary, 'the heroic courage of 1813, 1814 and 1815' would not be found wanting.[25] However the Berlin rising of 18 March greatly reduced Frederick William's ability to act against republican France.

The news of the February Revolution caused 'the greatest consternation' in St Petersburg. It is related that the Tsar interrupted a ball in the Winter Palace to declare, 'Saddle your horses, gentlemen: the Republic is proclaimed in France.'[26] Certainly the Tsar immediately placed seven million roubles at his Minister of War's disposal;[27] and the *Journal of St Petersburg* published on 12 March an imperial *ukase* announcing the calling up of reservists and the cancellation of all military leave. In addition Kisselev, the Russian minister in Paris, was recalled, though he remained there in an unofficial capacity.[28] But Louis-Philippe had never really been regarded in St Petersburg as a legitimate monarch. Also any effective Russian action against France involved overcoming enormous practical difficulties and required Austrian or Prussian cooperation. The revolutions in Vienna and Berlin removed the immediate possibility of any such cooperation; and those revolutions, the fate of the King of Prussia (a brother-in-law of the Tsar), and the nationalist movement in Poland, were all soon of much greater concern to the Russian government than events in Paris.

Any immediate or effective resurrection of the Holy Alliance against France was thus out of the question, especially following the March 1848 revolutions. Nevertheless the European Powers were agreed that France must observe the Treaties of 1815, and refrain from giving direct or indirect encouragement to revolutionary movements in other countries. This, and the lack of opportunities for French intervention abroad, suggested the Second Republic would have to pursue a peaceful and relatively inactive foreign policy. Such a policy was unlikely to appeal to Lamartine. It would prevent him playing a striking role, winning popular support, or departing significantly from Guizot's alleged objective of peace at any price. In addition, a peaceful and inactive foreign policy would be resisted by radical government colleagues and subordinates, and by foreign and radical elements, particularly in Paris. It has been suggested that there were between fifteen and twenty thousand foreigners in Paris during February and March 1848.[29] After the February Days many of those foreigners rapidly organised clubs, societies and paramilitary legions. March 1848 saw the founding of the Société démocratique allemande, which formed a Légion démocratique; the Société patriotique belge, which later became the Légion belge-parisienne; the Club de l'émancipation des peuples, which aimed to liberate Italians, Germans and Poles by French arms; the Club de l'émigration polonaise, which wanted to send twenty-four battalions of Frenchmen to the Vistula; and the Club des émigrés italiens, which included among its members Mazzini and Garibaldi.[30] Those clubs could exert pressure on the French government through petitions and demonstrations; their causes could rally a considerable number of groups and individuals; and they could not be easily suppressed, because of their radical popular support and the Government's weakness in Paris.

Foreign clubs and Paris radicals were, however, unrepresentative of French opinion. The Paris press, which both expressed and influenced French opinion, was traditionally hostile to Britain and Russia, and sympathetic towards Ireland and Poland. After the February Days the left-wing press tended to identify with revolutionary movements outside France and suggest that France was setting the example the rest of Europe would follow. Yet in the three weeks following the February Revolution war seems to have been unanimously rejected by the Paris press, on the grounds that foreign intervention in France was extremely unlikely and French intervention abroad both unnecessary and undesirable.[31] After 4 May another force for peace was the National Assembly, in which representatives of the *notable* class predominated. Although the *notables* tended to be suspicious of Britain, they nearly all wanted the maintenance of European peace. Peace was a precondition of economic prosperity and prevented the country's domination by the army. Also wars and rumours of wars were associated with the political violence and social upheaval of the Revolution of 1789.[32]

On 27 February Lamartine issued a brief circular to the members of the foreign diplomatic corps in Paris. He informed them of his appointment as Minister of Foreign Affairs, and of the Provisional Government's desire to maintain good relations with all powers that wanted to preserve the independence of other nations and the peace of the world.[33] Presumably Lamartine's aim was to calm foreign governments represented in Paris, and encourage them to establish diplomatic relations with him and formally recognise the Second Republic. The next day (28 February) an article signed by Emile de Girardin appeared in *La Presse*. While emphasising the difference between the Republics of September 1792 and February 1848, and the Provisional Government's determination not to threaten any country, the article stressed France's willingness to help any oppressed nation. It also suggested that the Minister of Foreign Affairs should address a manifesto to the peoples of Europe, and outlined a new 'open' diplomacy conducted by envoys rather than ambassadors. In fact Lamartine's relations with Girardin and *La Presse* at this time suggest Lamartine almost certainly wrote or inspired the article.[34] Lamartine doubtless intended to test domestic and foreign reactions to his ideas, suggest that his foreign policy objectives and conduct of diplomacy would be republican in character, and prepare public opinion for his manifesto of 2 March.

Lamartine's manifesto of 2 March was addressed to all of France's diplomatic representatives abroad, but it was published on 5 March and clearly designed to be a public policy statement. The manifesto declared that the French Republic had been founded in accordance with natural and national law, and that its existence did not depend on international recognition. The Republic's proclamation was not an act of aggression against any form of government in the world, and war was not an instrument of policy for the Republic. In this the Second Republic differed from the First because circumstances in France in 1848 were totally dissimilar from those affecting foreign policy in 1792. The Treaties of 1815 were stated to have no legal validity in the eyes of the French people, although the territorial arrangements established by those Treaties were recognized as a *de facto* point of departure for the conduct of international relations. Lamartine warned that French military intervention would follow any invasion, or foreign interference in the internal affairs, of Switzerland or the independent Italian States, though he promised France would not conduct propaganda campaigns in neighbouring countries.[35]

The Provisional Government discussed the manifesto on 2 March. According to Louis Blanc and Lamartine's comments to Normanby and Circourt, the manifesto's references to the Treaties of 1815 were not in Lamartine's original draft. Louis Blanc protested and a compromise was attempted. The Treaties received *de facto* recognition, to calm the European Powers, but denied a legal justification or permanent character, to satisfy those sharing Louis Blanc's views.[36] This ambivalence and ambiguity, although apparently forced on Lamartine, seem nevertheless to have reflected his own views, at least so far as Italy was concerned. On 11 March Westmorland, the British minister at Berlin, reported a conversation with Circourt, whom Lamartine had sent as special envoy and *chargé d'affaires* to Berlin. Circourt told Westmorland that if the King of Piedmont were to attack the Austrians in Lombardy, or if the King were dethroned and a republic established, then Lamartine thought it would be almost impossible for the Provisional Government to prevent the French army from giving assistance.[37] While the Paris press gave the manifesto generally a favourable reception, foreign governments were understandably concerned about the denunciation of the Treaties of 1815 and the reference to possible French intervention in Switzerland or Italy.[38]

Besides deciding and proclaiming the principles of his foreign policy, another of Lamartine's initial tasks was that of diplomatic and Foreign Ministry appointments. Within the Ministry of Foreign Affairs he retained a number of key figures, including Pierre Cintrat and the baron de Viel-Castel (department heads in the political section), Anatole Brénier de Renaudière (director of the finance department), the historian François Mignet (director of the archives), and Théodore de Lesseps (assistant director of the commercial section). The most important new appointments were those of Jules Bastide (*secrétaire général*) and Sain de Boislecomte (*chef du cabinet*). Lamartine also created a private secretariat headed by first Jean-Baptiste Payer and then Colonel Camille-Antoine Callier, and including François de Champeaux, Charles Hugo and Paul de Saint-Victor.[39] A few of France's representatives abroad retained their posts,[40] and there were also several promotions and transfers.[41] However Lamartine recalled all of France's ambassadors, most of her other diplomats and many of her consuls. While a considerable proportion of those recalled would probably have served the Second Republic, Lamartine and the Provisional Government clearly believed that domestic pressures, and the need for diplomats sympathetic to the new regime and its policies, required this change of personnel. Also Lamartine doubtless enjoyed making so many new appointments. Nevertheless he seems to have personally regretted at least the comte de Boislecomte's dismissal from Berne; and, typically, he invited diplomats he had dismissed to a reception he held in June.[42]

On 16 March Lamartine in *Le Moniteur* announced the suppression of the title of ambassador, except in special cases such as the Republic's signatory of a European treaty or representative at a congress. He also stated that a career in the Republic's diplomatic service should be open to all Frenchmen, and to encourage this the most junior diplomats would be adequately paid. This paralleled the Provisional Government's attempts to make the French army officer corps more socially representative; and Lamartine may have remembered his own financial problems as a junior diplomat. However, in filling important diplomatic posts abroad Lamartine frequently turned to those with whom he had personal and political ties. Circourt (special envoy and *chargé d'affaires* at Berlin) had been a friend of his since 1825, had helped him with his speeches and writings, and had corresponded with him on German affairs during the summer of 1847.[43] Like the marquis de Boissy (minister at Florence) and the duc d'Harcourt (*chargé de mission* to the Holy See), Circourt had also attended the meetings at Durand's restaurant on 19 February and in Lamartine's residence two days later. In the Chamber of Peers Boissy and Harcourt had both expressed political opinions similar to Lamartine's. While on a visit to Florence and Rome during the autumn of 1847, Boissy had sent letters criticising French foreign policy addressed to a 'M. de L.' (possibly Lamartine) in France, and in December 1847 had married an Italian countess, Theresa Guiccioli, whom Lamartine had previously known in Rome.[44] General Thiard (minister at Berne), probably the wealthiest taxpayer in Saône-et-Loire, had been Lamartine's colleague in Saône-et-Loire's *conseil général* and a fellow deputy in the Chamber, where he had supported electoral reform and usually voted for liberal measures.[45] A former Director of the Ecole Polytechnique, General Aupick (minister at Constantinople) seems to have been a social acquaintance of Lamartine.[46] In addition to their personal and political ties with Lamartine, relevant diplomatic experience could be claimed by Circourt (in the Ministry of Foreign Affairs, March-July 1830), Boissy (as a former assistant to Chateaubriand in 1822 and *secrétaire de légation* in Florence, 1823-1825), and Harcourt (as ambassador to Spain, August-November 1830).

Personal ties were obviously a factor in many of Lamartine's other appointments. His nephew Emmanuel de Cessiat was sent as an *aspirant diplomatique* to Rome.[47] Charles de Montherot, another nephew, was appointed an *attaché* at Lisbon. Jussieu de Sénevier (engaged to Lamartine's niece Alphonsine de Cessiat) was made consul general at Leghorn.[48] Fernand Delahante, a member of a family long on friendly terms with the Lamartines, became consul at Jassy in Moldavia.[49] In the case of Emmanuel de Cessiat Lamartine abused his powers of patronage,[50] but Charles de Montherot, Jussieu de Sénevier and Fernand Delahante were retained in the diplomatic service after Lamartine's fall from power, and therefore presumably demonstrated their competence. The first head of his secretariat, Payer, was a botanist and a professor at the Sorbonne. Although apparently completely unknown to him before 24 February, Payer joined his entourage during the February Days and so attracted his attention.[51] Payer's successor, Colonel Callier, had been attached to the Ministry of Foreign Affairs since 1839 and had met Lamartine in the Middle East.[52] Of Lamartine's personal secretaries, Charles Hugo was the son of Victor Hugo (whose support Lamartine was probably anxious to secure),[53] while the father of Paul de Saint-Victor had helped with the publication of *Méditations Poétiques* in 1820 and had been associated with Lamartine in the launching of *Le Défenseur*.[54] Similarly, Lamartine kept his old friend and patron, Fontenay, at Stuttgart, and the comte de Rayneval (whose father had advanced his own diplomatic career) as first secretary at St Petersburg. His contacts with the de Lesseps family[55] may partly explain his patronage of the brothers Théodore (retained in the Ministry of Foreign Affairs), Ferdinand (*chargé d'affaires* at Madrid) and Jules (special envoy at Tunis, where his father had been consul general). The baron d'Eckstein, an old friend of Lamartine, helped him with diplomatic appointments and recruited Edouard Grenier (secretary at Constantinople).[56]

Clearly Lamartine also tried to satisfy the moderate republican faction associated with *Le National*. His *secrétaire général*, Bastide, had impeccable moderate republican credentials, as editor of *Le National* between 1836 and 1846, contributor to the *Histoire parlementaire de la Révolution française* of Buchez and Roux, and founder of the *Revue Nationale* (1847). Sain de Boislecomte, his *chef du cabinet*, had similarly contributed to the *Histoire parlementaire de la Révolution française* and the *Revue Nationale*. Bixio (special envoy and minister at Turin) had worked on *Le National*, while Lamartine himself identifies General Thiard (minister at Berne) with the *National* faction.[57] Other republicans given diplomatic posts were Levraud (secretary at Naples), Benoît-Champy (*chargé d'affaires* at Florence) and Savoye (*chargé d'affaires* at Frankfurt). Of course Lamartine must have felt obliged to appoint at least some republicans, and certain appointments may have been almost forced upon him. Bastide and Hetzel (whom Lamartine seems to have appointed as an additional *chef du cabinet*) were present at the important meeting of moderate republicans with Lamartine on the morning of 24 February; and Bastide, Hetzel, Bixio, Boislecomte and Théodore de Lesseps were all in occupation of the Ministry of Foreign Affairs after 24 February. Direct evidence of pressure on Lamartine over appointments seems to be lacking, though Blanqui did write to him on 28 February, recommending his son and offering his own services.[58]

It was to be expected that Lamartine's appointments would include family connections, personal friends, political allies, and moderate republicans associated with *Le National*. What is surprising is his willingness to conciliate foreign governments. He reportedly attempted to persuade the marquis de Dalmatie to remain at Berlin (without success).[59] However Circourt, an aristocrat, with a Russian artistocratic wife and conservative ideas on revolutionary movements and Polish nationalism, possessed suitable social and political credentials for the Prussian Court. In fact Circourt gained a reputation for being a notorious reactionary so rapidly that on 8 April he was replaced by Changarnier[60] – a republican in so far as he had rallied to the Second Republic after 24 February, but also an army general whom Lamartine may have known personally through their common Saône-et-Loire background. For St Petersburg Lamartine first considered, significantly, another army general, Oudinot (commander in 1849 of the French expedition against the Roman Republic), but finally chose Arigny, whom he assured Kisselev 'was neither revolutionary nor even republican'.[61] Lacour (*chargé d'affaires* at Vienna) and Tallenay (minister at London) were both aristocrats and professional diplomats, important qualifications for gaining acceptance in Austria and Britain. Normanby reported that he had heard Tallenay was 'very worthy' and had 'good intentions', though he added, 'I do not think he [Tallenay] could pass muster as an ambassador even from the most greasy of Republics'. Palmerston, nevertheless, favourably commented on 2 May: 'I am much pleased with Tallenay, who seems a very sensible well disposed man.'[62] Sérurier had served as *attaché* at Brussels from 1836 to 1841, while his father was French ambassador there, and his return as French *secrétaire de légation* was very welcome. The prince de Ligne, the Belgian ambassador in Paris, observed: 'I regard this choice as a veritable triumph of my efforts with M. de Lamartine, and as an act of loyalty on his part towards us.' Hoffschmidt, the Belgian Foreign Minister, agreed.[63] Similarly, Bellocq's later selection as minister at Brussels reportedly gave 'much satisfaction to the Belgian Government'. The British ambassador to Belgium added that Bellocq was

'looked upon as extremely moderate and rather of the tendency called
"Legitimist" '.[64] In Spain Ferdinand de Lesseps had been appointed
to consular posts at Malaga (1839) and Barcelona (1842) before being
promoted *chargé d'affaires* at Madrid, while in Greece Thouvenel was
first recalled, replaced by a certain Guillemot, and then posted back
to Athens – reportedly at the request of King Otho.[65]

There were, however, significant exceptions to Lamartine's apparent
policy of conciliating foreign governments through his diplomatic
appointments. While Bastide and Sain de Boislecomte remained in Paris
(partly, perhaps, so that Lamartine could keep an eye on them, or vice
versa), republicans were posted abroad. Strikingly, though, apart from
Savoye's appointment to Frankfurt (seat of the forthcoming German
national parliament) and Thiard's to Switzerland (a sister republic),
republicans were sent to important posts only in Italy, except the
Holy See (where Harcourt, a Catholic peer, was presumably acceptable). Bixio (Turin), besides being a republican, knew Mazzini and (an
Italian by birth) sympathised with Italian nationalism. Benoît-Champy
(Florence), also a republican, advocated French intervention in Italy.
Levraud (Naples) displayed such uncompromising republicanism, even
failing to express his government's views and quarreling with the local
French naval commander, Admiral Baudin, that eventually he was
recalled (3 June).[66] Lamartine's diplomatic appointments therefore
suggest that he envisaged the open pursuit of republican policies only
in Italy and Switzerland.

Some confusion clearly surrounded Lamartine's diplomatic appointments. On 8 March *Le Constitutionnel*, besides correctly reporting
Thiard's appointment to Berne, announced that Harcourt would be
sent to London, Alton-Shée to Turin, Boissy to Rome, General Fabvier
to Constantinople (an extraordinary choice, since he had fought against
the Turks in the Greek War of Independence), Tracy to the United
States, Beaumont-Vassy to Denmark, and de La Moskowa to Spain.
None of these appointments was in fact made. However, Alton-Shée
was expected at Turin, and Lamartine apparently considered Fabvier
for Constantinople.[67] He certainly told Boissy that he was posting him
to Rome. A delighted Boissy began to make the necessary preparations
for his departure, until reading in a newspaper that the post had been
given to Harcourt. Lamartine then offered him a diplomatic post at
Florence, but, never instructed to leave, Boissy remained in France.[68]
Similarly Circourt relates that Lamartine had previously promised
Savoye's post at Frankfurt to someone else. Circourt himself was
informally promised a post at Washington, a promise not kept.[69] On

a less important level, Lamartine seems to have appointed both Fernand Delahante and the abbé Thions to be French consul at Jassy in Moldavia.[70] Much more surprisingly, Lamartine designated the Biblical King David as French consul at Bremen, in the following manner:[71]

> Shortly after the Revolution of February, he [Lamartine] wrote on the blank leaves of his pocket-book the names of his *protégés*, and sent the list to be provided with places immediately. Previously however, it seems he had scribbled 'David' on the page, and the head of the Cabinet appointed the said David consul at Bremen; the postulant however never came forward, and though the poet does not like being disturbed, Mons. Hetzel was obliged to ask who was the David on his list.
>
> 'He who danced before the Ark', was the answer.
>
> 'Oh dear! I have gazetted him to Bremen!'
>
> 'How very singular! I meant him for a subject for meditation, not for a nomination; but you can cancel it.'

The story, while doubtless embellished, is confirmed by at least two other sources and *Le Moniteur.*[72]

Once appointed, Lamartine's diplomats received a minimum of guidance and information. Between 24 February and 9 May Lamartine sent a total of thirty-seven official dispatches to his individual diplomats abroad. Only seven diplomats received more than one dispatch. The general uncertainty was increased by Lamartine's habit of sending personal agents on secret missions with ill-defined powers – Hetzel and Emile Johannot to Brussels,[73] Eugène Ganneron to Leghorn,[74] Falioni to Venice,[75] Charles Didier to Posen and Cracow,[76] Dr Louis Mandl to Bucharest,[77] and Huber-Saladin to Switzerland.[78] He also offered a secret mission in Germany to the republican Alexandre Weill.[79] While Lamartine invariably instructed his diplomats to co-operate with their respective foreign governments, these agents seem to have been dispatched to 'republicanise' Europe, acting as his equivalent of Ledru-Rollin's *commissaires.* This use of personal agents, like the issuing of public policy statements and the abolition of the title of ambassador, may have been a deliberate attempt to avoid the traditional diplomatic forms and practise a new republican diplomacy. But it is also another example of the confusion and contradiction that characterised Lamartine's conduct of foreign affairs.

Internal recognition of the new régime in France was a matter of great importance and immediate concern for the Provisional Government, particularly Lamartine. The Provisional Government wanted to avoid the diplomatic isolation from which the July Monarchy had suffered, and increase its claims to legitimacy, through securing recognition from foreign governments. Such recognition would also help allay fears arising from the February Revolution, which had transformed France into a republic in an overwhelmingly monarchical Europe and seemingly threatened a European war. In this context France's relations with Britain were exceptionally significant, in view of Britain's economic, financial and maritime supremacy, the enormous diplomatic influence British governments could exert at this time, and Britain's apparent immunity from revolution. Before he had even installed himself at the Ministry of Foreign Affairs, Lamartine sent Alton-Shée on 25 February to inform Normanby that the Provisional Government 'was very anxious indeed to know what line Great Britain was likely to take'.[80] On 28 February Normanby unofficially visited Lamartine. Lamartine told him 'his first desire was the complete development of the English alliance', and hinted that in return for his offers of peace and friendship the British government should formally recognise the Second Republic.[81] Normanby's account of this conversation with Lamartine impressed Palmerston. In a circular of 29 February to the British ambassadors in Vienna, Berlin and St Petersburg, Palmerston instructed them to inform their respective Foreign Ministers that the Provisional Government professed 'the most peaceable intentions', that there was 'no reason whatever to doubt their sincerity', and that European peace would be best served by avoiding any impression of interfering in French affairs. However Palmerston was not prepared to make Normanby officially accredited to the Provisional Government, despite Lamartine's repeated suggestions that he should do so.[82]

The securing of British recognition would have been a great *coup* for Lamartine and the Provisional Government. Foreign diplomats resident in Paris had, of course, been formally accredited to Louis-Philippe. Their diplomatic credentials had lapsed on Louis-Philippe's overthrow, although they all remained at their posts. Lamartine's early overtures to Normanby, and attempts to persuade Palmerston that the British government should recognise the Second Republic, were part of a concerted effort to break out of the diplomatic quarantine in which the Provisional Government had found itself. A willing collaborator in this policy was the United States.

On 24 February Richard Rush, the United States minister in Paris, informed his French friend, Major Poussin, of his ardent desire to be one of the first of the diplomatic corps to recognise the Second Republic and to be presented to the Provisional Government, particularly Lamartine. Poussin relayed this message to Bastide, *secrétaire général* in the Ministry of Foreign Affairs, who responded enthusiastically (25 February); and on 27 February the Provisional Government invited Rush to present himself the following day. Possibly at Lamartine's prompting, *Le Moniteur* on 27 February publicly announced that Rush had already officially visited the Provisional Government at the Hôtel de Ville and had recognised the Second Republic.[83] The same day Rush called on Normanby: he denied *Le Moniteur*'s report while acknowledging his intention to grant recognition, probably the next day, whereupon Normanby counselled caution and delay.[84] After receiving Lamartine's circular to the diplomatic corps of 27 February, the following afternoon Rush at the Hôtel de Ville addressed his 'felicitations' to the Provisional Government.[85] Rush's initiative was a personal decision, prompted by his republican sympathies and the cordial relations which had generally been maintained between France and the United States. Rush acted with the support of his diplomatic staff and of many American citizens resident in Paris and Europe, and, reflecting American public opinion, with the subsequent approval of the United States Congress and government. However it is clear from Bastide's response to the message conveyed by Poussin, from the misleading report in *Le Moniteur*, and from the Provisional Government's enthusiastic reception of Rush on 28 February, that the Provisional Government encouraged, anticipated and welcomed Rush's decision to recognise the Second Republic.[86]

The United States could exert little influence in Europe at this time, and the initiative taken by Rush on behalf of his government was not widely followed. On 27 February the Papal nuncio replied in the most cordial terms to Lamartine's circular announcing the Republic's proclamation.[87] The following day the ministers of Argentina and Uruguay (both republics) made official visits to the Provisional Government.[88] Early in March unfounded press rumours, possibly instigated by Lamartine, suggested that Denmark and Piedmont had recognised the Second Republic, which *Le Moniteur* had to deny.[89] In fact among European states only Switzerland gave the Second Republic's proclamation a popular and official welcome;[90] and Switzerland — small, neutral and recovering from a civil war — was of limited diplomatic and military significance. The problem of the Second Republic's diplomatic isolation therefore remained, and the British position continued to be extremely important for the Provisional Government. On the question of recognising the Second Republic, Normanby

reported to Palmerston (28/29 February): 'Most of the Corps diplomatique has expressed a great desire to know what I was going to do
and a wish to do the same.' Clearly appreciating this, Lamartine (as
Normanby complained) tried to suggest through inspired press leaks
that Anglo-French relations were more cordial than was actually
the case.[91]

At the same time, however, *La Presse* was suggesting that France
should pursue a republican foreign policy, which might obviously
alarm the British government. On 29 February Lamartine dictated a
note for transmission to the Duke of Wellington by Mr J. Wellesley, the
illegitimate son of Wellington's nephew, the Earl of Mornington. He
warned the Duke against 'the accidents of a struggle already begun
between the Provisional Government and the extreme Left' and 'the
shrill complaints of newspapers and their untimely editorials'. These
should not be allowed to interfere with 'the English alliance', which
he claimed he wanted to strengthen.[92] An additional note by Mr
Wellesley makes it clear that Lamartine wanted to prevent the foreign
policy article in *La Presse* from creating an unfavourable impression
in Britain.[93] To do this he was quite prepared to disown and condemn
a newspaper article he had almost certainly written or inspired. Wellington's brief anodyne reply, which Lamartine wanted to make public,
prompted him to write to Wellington confirming the Provisional
Government's pacific intentions, suggesting a Franco-British alliance,
and hoping Wellington — 'the war hero of England' — would become
'the bond of peace' for the two countries.[94] This curious initiative,
which ended here, was unnecessary. By 10 March relations between
Lamartine and Normanby had become so cordial as to attract Queen
Victoria's disapproval, while on 14 March the French *chargé d'affaires*
in London was asked to inform Lamartine how much Palmerston admired his noble and courageous conduct.[95]

Lamartine certainly indicated a desire to cooperate with Britain.
This was particularly noticeable in Spain, doubtless in deliberate contrast with Guizot's arrangement of a marriage between the duc de
Montpensier and the Spanish Infanta (October 1846), which had soured
Anglo-French relations and which Lamartine had criticised as representing a dynastic rather than national foreign policy.[96] Also the
French representative in Naples reportedly prevented a French ship
transporting troops to Lombardy from sailing under a French flag, 'to
avoid giving umbrage to the British government'.[97] Nevertheless,
sources of friction remained between Britain and France. Demonstrations of xenophobia accompanied the February Revolution:

a crowd invaded the British consulate at Bordeaux, broke the window panes and damaged the furniture;[98] and at Rouen popular pressure led to the expulsion of British workers from a number of factories. They were forced to leave so quickly that they left some of their possessions behind and were not paid all the wages owed to them.[99] This led to questions being asked in the House of Commons, formal representations by Normanby, and hostile British newspaper comment.[100] Other sources of friction were the inability of dismissed British workers to withdraw their deposits from French savings banks, the prevention of the export of cattle from the town of Granville, and the nationalisation of the Orléans and Bordeaux Railway Company, which had obtained half its capital from British sources.[101] Lamartine always gave a sympathetic hearing to British complaints arising out of such matters, and with regard to the expulsion of British workers and the prevention of cattle exports, issued what amounted to a public apology.[102]

The Irish Question posed a far more serious threat to Anglo-French relations. In France the Irish nationalist cause was popular, on account of traditional French hostility towards Britain and Catholic and republican sympathies for what was regarded as religious and national oppression. On 13 March Lamartine assured Normanby that he did not regard 'Irish nationality in any other sense except as identical with English nationality'.[103] Yet on 17 March he received a deputation of Irishmen resident in Paris and accepted from them an Irish flag. In his reply to their address he suggested that he hoped Ireland's complete constitutional independence would soon be achieved.[104] On reading this in *Le Moniteur*, Normanby immediately rushed round to the Ministry of Foreign Affairs. Lamartine was attending a meeting, but Normanby insisted that he should see Lamartine at once or obtain an appointment for later in the day. Lamartine then emerged from his meeting and tried to convince Normanby that he had been inaccurately reported. This is most unlikely, although Lamartine had actually argued in 1843 that the goal of Irish independence was a dream.[105] Anyway *Le Moniteur* issued a *démenti* and stated Lamartine had assured Normanby that the Union Jack was the only national flag he recognised in Britain.[106] Sharing Normanby's alarm, Palmerston hinted that the British embassy would be withdrawn from Paris if the French government continued to give direct encouragement to political agitation within the United Kingdom. However Lamartine promised Normanby he would be 'very firm' with any future Irish deputation, and would insist on the Government's adherence to the principle of non-intervention.[107] True to his word, on 3 April he pointed out to a deputation of Irishmen from Dublin, Manchester and Liverpool: 'We are at peace and we wish to remain on good terms not just with one part of Great Britain, but with the whole of Great Britain!: Lamartine added that he had no desire to follow Pitt's example of intervention in the Vendée during the Revolutionary period.[108]

The same day (3 April) Normanby reported to Palmerston that Lamartine had kept his word and had 'given the Irish deputation a good slap in the face'.[109] A delighted Palmerston replied on 4 April: 'Pray tell Lamartine how very much obliged we feel for his handsome and friendly conduct about the Irish Deputation. His answer was most honourable and gentlemanlike, and just what might have been expected from a high-minded man like him.'[110] *The Times* declared, 'We are not ashamed to confess that we felt an unspeakable relief in the perusal of M. Lamartine's reply to the Irish addresses'; and in the House of Commons Sir George Grey (Home Secretary) announced: 'I am persuaded that the disaffected party [in Ireland] have not the slightest chance of assistance from France after the declaration of M. Lamartine'.[111] Clearly any French government involvement in the Irish Question would have had very serious consequences for Anglo-French relations. Assuming *Le Moniteur* correctly reported Lamartine's reply to the first Irish deputation, his remarks require an explanation. In practical terms, Lamartine could not have helped Irish nationalists, and he was apparently extremely concerned to maintain good relations with the British government. Thus on 5 April Normanby informed Palmerston that 'Lamartine was very much pleased this morning when I told him how you had expressed yourself about his answer [to the second Irish deputation]'.[112] Perhaps on 17 March Lamartine was momentarily carried away; perhaps he felt obliged to appear sympathetic to Irish nationalists, particularly with the radical Paris demonstration of the same day against élite National Guard legions; or perhaps, as was so often the case, he was trying to be all things to all people.

Just as the Irish Question complicated Anglo-French relations, so the Polish Question similarly affected relations between France and Prussia, and potentially between France and Russia as well. Again Lamartine, in seeking almost universal approval, pursued somewhat contradictory policies. On 11 March he issued a circular to France's representatives at the Northern Courts stating that, although wishing to remain at peace with Austria, Prussia and Russia, France would not abandon the cause of the re-establishment of a Polish nationality and that the Powers should take steps to emancipate Poland.[113] Yet privately he instructed Circourt on 18 March, 'Make the Berlin cabinet realise that no hostile move will come from the French Government so long as I remain here'.[114] Similarly, to a Polish deputation on 26 March he publicly emphasised that the Provisional Government would not allow its policies to be changed by a foreign nation, however sympathetically regarded in France.[115] On Russia, Circourt was advised on 4 April that if Prussia's initially liberal policy towards the Poles provoked a Russian invasion (as Berlin briefly feared), France would give Prussia military assistance.[116] However, just two days later Lamartine told the Russian minister, Kisselev, not to take seriously his promises to help the Poles, since they were only meant to satisfy public opinion and should not disturb relations with Russia, France's most natural ally.[117]

Initially non-intervention in Poland seemed justifiable. Frederick William on 24 March had promised the Grand Duchy of Posen a separate army and the introduction of reforms. At the same time, however, it had been made known that men under arms would not be permitted to cross German territory on their way to Poland, though small groups of unarmed Poles would be allowed to do so. When Polish *émigrés* in Paris, wanting to return to Poland, demanded that they should be supplied with arms, Lamartine and the Provisional Government refused. Nevertheless, the Provisional Government did agree to give the returning Poles financial support, and to grant assistance to wives and children left behind in France. On 31 March there was a solemn departure ceremony for returning Poles in the Place Saint-Antoine, and the problem was apparently solved.[118]

Unfortunately for Lamartine, this was not the case. The Prussian Landtag ruled on 6 April that Posen would not form part of the German Confederation. The German inhabitants of Posen immediately protested against this exclusion, so on 14 April the Prussian government decided to draw a demarcation line between German and Polish speaking areas. Posen's partition caused enormous ill-feeling amongst the Poles, and by the end of April an armed insurrection had broken out. German public opinion at once became unanimously hostile towards the Poles, and the rising was suppressed with considerable ferocity. The only hope for the Poles lay in foreign intervention. On 26 April Prince Czartoryski wrote Lamartine a personal letter demanding French intervention.[119] *Le Père Duchêne* of 4 May castigated Lamartine's abandonment of Poland in no uncertain terms: 'Citizen Lamartine has said: Cracow is free! The government of Louis-Philippe also said, seventeen years ago: order reigns in Warsaw.' In the National Assembly on 10 May Wolowski made a passionate appeal on behalf of the Poles to the French people. On 13 May a demonstration in favour of Poland was held in Paris, followed by the massive Paris demonstration of 15 May, when the Assembly was invaded and the Government almost overthrown. 15 May associated the cause of Polish independence with forces hostile to the Executive Commission, which consequently abandoned any interest in French mediation or intervention.

Lamartine did instruct Circourt on 7 May to complain to the Prussian government about Prussian obstacles preventing Polish *émigrés* from returning to Poland. However he added that while the French government could not ignore French sympathies for Poland, it would not forget what the interests of peace required. Thus Lamartine wanted Frederick William to be generous to the Poles, but would not allow the Polish Question to disturb Franco-Prussian relations.[120] Circourt suggests that even this protest was dictated by Bastide and Favre, and its dispatch delayed six days. Further, Lamartine authorised Circourt to read the protest to the Prussian Minister of Foreign Affairs, but not to leave him a copy, thereby presumably reducing the protest's force.[121] Champeaux did ask Circourt on 9 May to do all he could to prevent massacres in Posen, possibly at Lamartine's prompting.[122] Otherwise Lamartine apparently did nothing for the Poles. He defended his policy of inaction in the Assembly on 23 May, showing that he had remonstrated with the Prussian government for its policy towards Posen. Any further action, was he argued, impossible: France's frontiers were insufficiently secure; the danger of Prussia joining an enemy coalition was too great; the Government lacked the necessary military force; and the practical difficulties resulting from the distance between France and Poland were insuperable. Lamartine concluded with ill-founded optimism that victory was no longer on the side of the big battalions, but on the side of justice and the inalienable rights of nations.[123] In fact circumstances had dictated the policy thus defended, and Lamartine was less than honest on the consequences for the unfortunate Poles.

Lamartine suggested his abandonment of the Irish and the Poles showed his desire for peace and non-interference in other countries, rather than his willingness to appease Britain and Prussia. This argument would have carried more conviction if he had prevented the armed incursions into Belgium, Southern Germany and Savoy. A Société patriotique belge was ,founded in Paris on 27 February 1848, composed of Belgians wanting to overthrow their monarchy by an internal rebellion supported by France, and by French republicans hoping to launch a revolutionary expedition into a country annexed by the First Republic and ruled by a king married to a daughter of Louis-Philippe. At the beginning of March Caussidière, accompanied by two or three Belgian *émigrés*, had an interview with Ledru-Rollin. He told him that two thousand Belgians were ready to leave for their country, and suggested that the Belgians should be escorted by two thousand municipal guards and given a hundred thousand francs. The idea of encouraging a revolution in Belgium, and perhaps its re-annexation to France, undoubtedly appealed to Ledru-Rollin, but he knew that the Provisional Government as a whole would never approve. At a second meeting with Caussidière, however, Ledru-Rollin agreed to supply the Belgians with free transport.

On the evening of 24 March about eight hundred Belgians presented themselves at the Gare du Nord to take advantage of the Provisional Government's offer of free transport to Belgium. There were two quite separate groups — unemployed Belgian workers, often with wives and children, who simply wanted to return home, and members of the Légion Belge, who thought they were starting a revolution. With difficulty they were all persuaded to travel in the same train. Charles Delescluze, the government *commissaire* in the Nord, had been informed in advance of the train's arrival. Believing that the passengers were just returning workers, and hoping to avoid any incident with the local inhabitants, he arranged with the Belgian authorities that the train should proceed as quickly as possible into Belgium. When the train arrived at Valenciennes at half past four in the morning of 25 March, it was immediately coupled to a Belgian engine and taken without stopping across the frontier. About two hundred Belgians, realising what was happening, succeeded in jumping off the train. The remaining six hundred arrived at Quivévrain in Belgian and were immediately surrounded by Belgian police and soldiers. A few of the Belgians were arrested, and sixty Frenchmen sent back in the train to France.

The main part of the Légion Belge left Paris by train on 25 March in two groups under the leadership of Frédéric Blervacq and Charles Graux. The members of the Légion Belge were granted free transport, given fifteen hundred francs by Ledru-Rollin, and escorted by Ecole polytechnique students. Both parties arrived at Séclin, a small village on the railway line between Douai and Lille, during the morning of 26 March. That evening Delescluze informed General Négrier that one or two convoys of between fifteen and eighteen hundred Belgians would shortly arrive at Lille. He told Négrier the Provisional Government expected him to accommodate the Belgians in the citadel and supply them with arms. Négrier objected that the citadel was full, and that he could not issue arms to foreigners. When Delescluze insisted that he was acting under Ledru-Rollin's orders, Négrier agreed to provide food and an escort. He also sent Gustave Des Essarts to Paris to see Lamartine, who said he had given no instructions. The following day (27 March) he reported the actions he had taken to the Minister of War and asked for further orders.

Blervacq and another Belgian, François-Jules Fosse, who had escaped from the first train at Quiévrain, met Delescluze at Séclin during the morning of 28 March. Delescluze told them to prepare to leave that evening and promised to supply them with arms. Delescluze could promise arms because the previous day he had sent a letter to Négrier, enclosing instructions from the Ministry of War that fifteen hundred muskets should be placed at his disposal for the arming of the National Guard. Négrier received the letter and the accompanying order during 28 March. According to the instructions of Delescluze the arms were duly delivered to an Ecole polytechnique student. The muskets were issued from the armoury at Lille, loaded into five carts, and then taken to the small village of Bondues near the Belgian frontier.

After the departure of the carts, Négrier received a telegraphic message from the Minister of War, approving his earlier measures, particularly his refusal on 26 March to distribute any arms, demanding the immediate recall of the Ecole polytechnique students, and stating unequivocally that the Provisional Government did not want to violate, or assist a violation of, the Belgian frontier.[124] No real attempt seems to have been made to carry out these instructions. Delescluze, under severe criticism for his 'betrayal' of the first train-load of Belgians, had republican sympathies and may have wanted the re-unification of Belgium to France.[125] But on 27 March he expressed to Ledru-Rollin his lack of confidence in the leaders of the Belgian Legion, his reluctance to distribute arms to a force which was clearly no match for the Belgian army, and his scepticism as to the likelihood of a revolution in Belgium. He suggested the Belgians should enter their country unarmed and individually spread propaganda, while the Parisians should return home. However he asked Ledru-Rollin to confirm by telegraph with just one word, 'oui' or 'non', whether or not to arm the Belgian Legion and send it into Belgium. Ledru-Rollin replied 'non'. A short distance from Lille the man in charge of the telegraph, regarding this isolated word as a mistake, did not pass it on.[126]

Receiving no answer, Delescluze late in the evening of 28 March ordered the Belgians to advance. At two the next morning the Belgians reached Bondues, and arms from three of the five carts were distributed to them by Ecole polytechnique students.[127] Almost immediately on entering Belgian territory, the Legion encountered units of the Belgian army. Firing began between the two groups and continued until nine in the morning, when the invaders, knowing they outnumbered their opponents, decided to advance. The Belgian commander then ordered grapeshot to be fired by his two cannon, thereby immediately dispersing the Belgian Legion. Of the Legion seven were killed, twenty-six wounded, and about sixty taken prisoner. The Belgian army lost one man and suffered five or six casualties. So ended the Risquons-tout Affair, as it was called, from the appropriate name of a nearby village.[128]

The Risquons-tout Affair placed Lamartine and the Provisional Government in an embarrassing position. A statement in *Le Moniteur* glossed over the Government's participation in the Affair and suggested that the Belgian Legion had been betrayed by disloyal guides,[129] thus attempting to satisfy both foreign governments and domestic republican opinion. Lamartine, in reply to a protest from Brussels, defended Delescluze and maintained it was not known how the Belgian Legion had acquired its arms. He made the highly improbable suggestion that it had received fifteen hundred muskets from individual French sympathisers or from Belgian sources.[130] These statements and explanations were clearly unsatisfactory. On 5 March Lamartine had stated very categorically to the prince de Ligne that the Provisional Government had no intention of encouraging republican propaganda in Belgium or violating Belgian neutrality.[131] When de Ligne warned him on 11 March of the Belgian Legion's plans, Lamartine promised that no member of the Provisional Government would assist an insurrectionary movement attempting to disturb the peace of Belgium.[132] Yet members of the Belgian Legion had been able to make their preparations quite openly without any opposition from the Provisional Government; they had been supplied with free transport, food and arms by the French authorities; they had been accompanied by Ecole polytechnique students; and they had been helped by Ledru-Rollin and three very important French officials (Caussidière, Delescluze and Marrast). Lamartine may well have wanted to rid Paris of foreign workers, have been powerless to prevent the Belgian Legion's departure, and have been ignorant of the actions of some of his colleagues. However, he must, or should, have been well informed of developments; he could have been more honest and informative with de Ligne; and he may (as Caussidière suggests) have given Fosse moral and financial support.[133] Altogether, particularly after Hetzel and Johannot's mission to Brussels, it is difficult to accept Lamartine's protestations to de Ligne as wholly sincere. The Risquons-tout Affair provoked French press attacks on Lamartine and the Provisional Government, and renewed the suspicions of foreign governments.[134] In Belgium itself the Affair promoted national unity and rallied the country behind its King and government.[135]

Very similar to the Risquons-tout Affair were the expeditions of German refugees from France into Southern Germany. The success of liberal movements in the German States, and the outbreak of peasant revolts in Baden, Bavaria and Wurtemburg, encouraged a belief in the imminence of revolution in Southern Germany. Accordingly the Société démocratique allemande was formed in Paris to organise an expedition which would start a revolutionary movement. On 24 March the Provisional Government, after a long discussion, decided to grant sixty thousand francs to those Germans wishing to return home, but refused the demand for arms.[136] At the same time Lamartine told Normanby he had no objection to the repatriation of foreign workers, providing they were unarmed and did not travel in organised groups. He made similar assurances to the Baden and Bavarian governments while, however, complaining to them that Ledru-Rollin had prevented him using the telegraph to Strasbourg.[137] In fact on 30 March between fifteen and eighteen hundred members of the Société démocratique allemande left Paris by train for Alsace in an organised group, many of them carrying weapons obtained privately. An invasion scare seized the Rhineland States, provoking their governments to order military alerts. Lamartine told Normanby he had arranged with Arago and Ledru-Rollin 'that the columns of Germans on their march towards Strasbourg should be prevented by force, if necessary, from passing the Frontier'.[138] However, on 12 April members of the German Legion entered Baden from France. A larger group of some twelve hundred German legionnaires crossed the Rhine during the night of 23 and 24 April. After wandering in the Black Forest for three days, they were overwhelmed by a detachment of Wurtemburg troops. The usual apologies and explanations had been made by Lamartine and the Provisional Government, and on 26 April a decree was published ordering the dissolution of groups of Germans in France's eastern departments. This decree had been drawn up on 19 April, but its publication was delayed until after the Assembly elections of 23 April, so as not to lose republican support in the elections.[139] By 26 April the damage had already been done, resulting in an intensification of German national feeling and an increased hostility and distrust of France and her government.[140]

The incursion into Savoy involved a region that was particularly sensitive and of enormous international significance. Any serious violation of France's frontier with Savoy immediately concerned the Kingdom of Piedmont (which included Savoy), at least two European Powers — Britain and Austria — and France's policy towards Italian political developments in general. The Vienna revolution encouraged the outbreak of Italian revolts against the Austrians in Milan and Venice on 17 March. Radetzky, the Austrian commander in Lombardy, evacuated Milan after five days of street fighting and withdrew his forces to the fortified towns known as the Quadrilateral, leaving the greater part of Lombardy in the hands of the insurgents. In Venice the Austrian garrison was persuaded to leave without a serious struggle. To appease republican and Italian nationalist opinion within Piedmont, to prevent the establishment of a Lombard republic, and to acquire territory and the leadership of the nationalist movement in Northern Italy, King Charles Albert of Piedmont decided to assist the Lombard revolt. After some hesitation, on 23 March he announced that he was marching with his army to aid the peoples of Lombardy and Venetia. In fact, not only were his motives as much dynastic and anti-republican as nationalist, but also his decision would, he realised, discourage the Lombards and Venetians from calling in the French.

Lamartine's attitude towards developments in Italy was ambivalent. He wanted to avoid any French involvement in a European war, partly for idealistic and humanitarian reasons, partly so as not to provoke the formation of a coalition of European Powers against France. But he could not ignore domestic pressures for France to assist a republican and nationalist movement. Also there was the enticing possibility that France might regain Nice and Savoy (which had been surrendered in 1815), either as a reward for French military aid or as part of a general territorial settlement of Northern Italy. Charles Albert's defeat by Austria would have been embarrassing for Lamartine and would have strengthened arguments for French intervention. Yet Lamartine could scarcely view with favour the territorial aggrandisement of the House of Savoy, or the creation of a powerful unified state south of the Alps.

Against this background the incursion into Savoy occurred. On 14 March a demonstration was held in the town of Chambéry, Savoy, in support of the February Revolution. In Paris on 19 March two thousand Savoyards presented the Provisional Government with a petition, which contained a reminder that Savoy had formerly been part of France and a declaration of adherence to the French Republic. In reply Lamartine expressed his sympathy for the Savoyards, stated that France was not prepared to break the peace of Europe, and gave a qualified promise of assistance. France would assist independent Italy if attacked by a foreign power; and in the event of a new territorial settlement in Italy, France would ensure that Savoy and France benefited.[141] Savoy's detachment from Piedmont and reunion with France were in fact Lamartine's objectives. On 29 March he even told his Provisional Government colleagues, 'Within six weeks, Savoy will ask to be reunited with France.'[142]

A group of Savoyards resident in Lyons met on 27 March and demanded arms and ammunition from Emmanuel Arago, the government *commissaire* for Lyons and the Rhône. Emmanuel Arago refused: he had received no orders from the Provisional Government and did not want to antagonise Charles Albert. However on 30 March the Savoyards held a large demonstration in Lyons and set out for Savoy. A column of about fifteen hundred men, including some two hundred members of a Lyons political society known as the Voraces, crossed the frontier on 2 April and entered Chambéry the following morning. The invaders occupied the barracks and *hôtel de ville*, formed a municipal commission, and disarmed the national guard. These acts antagonised the local inhabitants. Encouraged by the absence of any reinforcements for the invaders and supported by peasants from the surrounding area, they organised an attack early in the morning on 4 April. After fighting in which several people were killed, the Savoyards and Voraces were overwhelmed, forced to flee, or taken prisoner.[143]

Emmanuel Arago had not supplied the Savoyards with arms, but he had given them passports and assistance, and had not prevented them from acquiring arms or crossing the frontier into Savoy as an organised body. His attitude seems to have been rather undecided. He wrote to Lamartine on 4 April suggesting the Savoyards wanted reunion with France, but questioning whether the French should take Savoy while Charles Albert was fighting the Austrians.[144] On 31 March Normanby reported that Lamartine, while not concealing his wish for Savoy's eventual reunion with France by peaceful means, had given positive orders for the expedition's prevention, if necessary by force.[145] French officials had certainly given their Piedmontese counterparts advance warning of a possible attack on Chambéry; and Lamartine later claimed that he had proposed using the French Army of the Alps to restore order at Chambéry and to prevent incursions from

France into Savoy.[146] Lamartine probably never made this proposal to the Piedmontese, who would have rejected it as a violation of their territory and a threat to their sovereignty. If he did send orders to prevent the Chambéry expedition they had no effect, although he may have helped to prevent the launching of a second expedition into Savoy from Lyons. Consequently he again had to explain the provocative conduct of an over-zealous colleague and subordinate to a sceptical foreign government.[147] The Piedmontese, while not seriously threatened by the Chambéry expedition, naturally became more suspicious of the French, believing that Emmanuel Arago in particular might have done more to prevent the incursion.

Piedmontese suspicions of the French were sustained by the formation of the Army of the Alps, a French military force with headquarters at Grenoble.[148] On 7 April the marquis de Brignole, the Piedmontese ambassador in Paris, complained in the strongest possible terms to Lamartine about suggestions that the Army of the Alps might enter Savoy. Lamartine gave the formal assurance of the Provisional Government that Piedmont's sovereignty and independence would be respected. This did not entirely satisfy Turin, and on 9 April Brignole requested Lamartine that the Provisional Government should withdraw the Army of the Alps from the frontier area.[149] Lamartine replied on 12 April assuring Brignole that the Piedmontese government had no cause for concern.[150] However the previous day he had written to Bixio requesting his opinion on the Piedmontese government and army's reaction to the advance of a French observation corps into Piedmont.[151] Bixio replied by telegraph on 15 April that unsolicited French intervention in Italy would be universally regarded as an act of disloyalty unworthy of France.[152] After communicating this dispatch to the Provisional Government, Lamartine is supposed to have exclaimed: 'They are blind and mad!'[153] On 20 April Bixio conveyed his views in greater detail and with increased emphasis. The fundamental characteristic of the movement currently agitating Italy was that it was above all Italian. Consequently the French army's crossing of the Alps uninvited would for a long time end French influence in Italy. Bixio added that the Alpine forts would fire on French troops and that it would be very difficult to keep a French army in Lombardy well provisioned. However he concluded that an Austrian victory, which he seems to have considered quite probable, would force the Piedmontese government to throw themselves into France's arms.[154] He repeated this conclusion on 15 May, arguing that French military intervention would be acceptable in Turin only in the event of an Austrian victory. 'France', he observed, 'is still popular in Italy, but only so long as she does not intervene, and restricts her influence to her ideas, her good example and her perseverance in respecting nationalities and territories'.[155]

The Piedmontese government's concern over the Army of the Alps was well founded. General Oudinot, commander of the Army of the Alps, on 28 April suggested in a published proclamation to his troops that 'the fraternity of arms' shared by French and Italian soldiers might soon be renewed.[156] On 11 May a report was sent to the Under-Secretary of War about the problems of sending troops into Piedmont by the passes of Mont Cenis and Mont Genève. Another report on the same subject was sent on 17 May.[157] Towards the end of May two officers from Oudinot's staff visited Charles Albert's headquarters.[158] Their mission may well have been to offer Charles Albert the assistance of French toops, or to discover what resistance the French might encounter if they invaded Piedmont. Finally, a detailed plan was prepared for the Minister of War on 13 June for the despatch of the Army of the Alps to Turin.[159]

Lamartine's attitude towards such activities was typically ambivalent. On 27 April Emmanuel Arago wrote to Lamartine, suggesting the formation of supply depots within Piedmontese territory so as to facilitate French military intervention. Lamartine replied by emphasising his conviction that in the present state of affairs great care should be taken to avoid any action apparently threatening war.[160] Similarly, in compliance with the wishes of the Piedmontese Foreign Minister, Lamartine had instructed Admiral Baudin not to take his Mediterranean squadron into Genoa, where the presence of French warships might have encouraged republican unrest.[161] Yet Lamartine's friend, Huber-Saladin, told Normanby on 22 April 'that in the event of the slightest check in Italy', he had 'no doubt the French army would enter Piedmont and Savoy';[162] and, perhaps influenced by the pro-Polish demonstration of 15 May, Lamartine argued at a secret Executive Commission meeting on 19 May that the moment had come to order the Army of the Alps to advance. To prevent Italy from falling again under Habsburg control, and to make France secure by offering a patriotic diversion to French radical elements, the Executive Commission should immediately order its generals to cross the Alps. It should then present the National Assembly with a *fait accompli*. The Assembly would either approve of the invasion, in which case the Government's position would be strengthened, or it would pass a vote of censure, in which case the Government would fall honourably.[163] The following day discussion continued on the question,

'Should Italy be saved despite herself?' Lamartine pointed out the danger to France of the formation of a powerful kingdom controlling the Alpine passes, and the need to occupy Piedmontese territory to secure a frontier which could be easily defended. However the Executive Commission maintained its decision not to intervene unless requested to do so by the Italians.[164]

Lamartine thus considered, and even recommended, French military intervention in Northern Italy. No such intervention occurred for a number of reasons. A majority of Lamartine's colleagues did not support him. Charles Albert rigorously maintained his refusal to accept French assistance or allow French troops into his territory, and no clear appeal came from Milan or Venice for direct French intervention. Any French military action in Northern Italy might have led to a conflict with Britain, since Palmerston and the British government were so determined to check French expansionism; and the German States, particularly Prussia, might have reacted to a French attack on Austrian troops. Nor was French military intervention at first clearly essential to the Italian nationalist cause. The forces of Charles Albert, or even of Pope Pius IX or of King Ferdinand II of the Two Sicilies, might have intervened decisively against the Austrians; the early Austrian successes in Northern Italy were mainly in the Veneto, where rapid French intervention would have been difficult; and Radetzky did not really take the offensive against Charles Albert in Lombardy until July. Finally, the French army was in no condition to invade Italy immediately after the February Days, while by the beginning of June the political situation in France required the presence of troops in the capital and precluded military adventures abroad.

Besides direct military intervention, Lamartine also considered supplying arms. On 27 March he received a deputation from the Association nationale italienne led by Joseph Mazzini. In reply to their address, he told them that if Italy were attacked and unable to defend herself, then 'the sword of France' would be offered for her protection.[165] The same day the Provisional Government of Milan sent a letter to the French government requesting its assistance. In addition it despatched an arms purchasing agent to Toulon.[166] On 30 March the Foreign Minister of the newly revived Venetian Republic personally asked Lamartine to supply him with arms and a warship, and a Venetian envoy to Paris presented Lamartine with this request on 9 April.[167] Another request for French arms was made by the government of Tuscany. The French Provisional Government had already decided on 20 March to send a naval squadron from Toulon to Spezzia,

Leghorn and Naples.[168] The aim was presumably to demonstrate French power and give moral support to Italian nationalist and republican movements. However, Lamartine gave the squadron's commander, Admiral Baudin, careful instructions not to damage Anglo-French relations, particularly over Sicily; and he assured Normanby that this was not a hostile or bellicose move, merely a flag-showing exercise.[169] On 7 April the Provisional Government decided to sell a hundred thousand muskets to the Milanese.[170] It also sent a steam frigate to Venice and promised a supply of arms to Tuscany. Towards the end of April Lamartine abandoned this policy, probably because of the conservative successes in the National Assembly elections and the Provisional Government's need to conserve its financial and military resources. A disagreement over the terms of payment delayed indefinitely the arms shipment to Milan. Lamartine blocked the delivery of twenty thousand muskets to Venice, and informed Tuscany that the Provisional Government could not supply the promised arms because of financial difficulties.[171] Nevertheless, Lamartine continued to pursue secret plans for a new territorial settlement of Northern Italy, but through diplomacy and mediation rather than military intervention or arms assistance.

On 1 April the French *chargé d'affaires* in Vienna offered the Provisional Government's good offices as mediator, should the occasion arise in which mediation would be desirable.[172] At the same time he mentioned to the British ambassador 'the project for settling affairs in Lombardy by some pecuniary transaction, as an indemnifcation to the Austrians for giving up the country'.[173] Towards the end of April Lamartine suggested to Normanby 'that the affairs of Italy should be settled at some European Congress or Conference'.[174] He elaborated his ideas to Normanby on 1 May:[175]

[Since] the Treaties of 1815 had left so untenable a position for France on the side of Lyons . . . it could not be thought unreasonable, if when the independence of Italy was assured with the free consent of France, she should expect some addition in that quarter which would not amount in all to half a million of souls. . . . Should the Austrians retake Venice it would be impossible to restrain French feeling on the subject, and an intervention would become inevitable. After the efforts which the Italians had made within the last few weeks no French government could resist the national impulse. He [Lamartine] knew what he could attempt and what he could not, and though no one was a more determined advocate of the status quo, and a more ardent lover of peace, he could not earn the character of the Guizot of the Republic.

Nothing came of Lamartine's suggestions, but his proposals for a new settlement of Italy were known at the time and have since been reconstructed.[176] France was to be awarded Savoy. To make this acceptable to both Charles Albert and Palmerston, Lamartine was to agree to the granting of the Sicilian throne to a son of Charles Albert. Britain and Piedmont supported this candidature, while Lamartine had favoured a Tuscan prince. At the same time Piedmont would annex Lombardy, while Tuscany would annex Parma and Modena, Austrian agreement being secured by recognition of her sovereignty over Venetia. Lamartine also suggested to the Austrian ambassador that France might support Austria's acquisition of the Danubian principalities (then under Ottoman rule) as compensation for the loss of Italian territories.[177] These proposals, which were developed at the beginning of May, were not acceptable to Bastide, who succeeded Lamartine as Minister of Foreign Affairs on 12 May. In particular, Bastide was not prepared to abandon Venice to Austria so that France could annex Savoy; and on 17 May orders were given for the immediate delivery of twenty thousand muskets to Venice.[178]

Lamartine, therefore, was not quite so determined to maintain the peace of Europe as he subsequently claimed. Ultimately he was probably prepared to sacrifice the British alliance, relations with Piedmont and European peace for intervention in Northern Italy. However, circumstances compelled him to act otherwise. His avoidance of war in 1848 was not in any way a surprising achievement. No foreign country was able or willing to embark on a war against France after the February Revolution. No international conflict arose in which French intervention was essential or even desirable. The French government's financial and military resources were very limited. Nor is there evidence that French public opinion in general wanted a war. The wealthier classes certainly hoped that peace would be preserved, a hope expressed by the conservative newspaper press and widely held by members of the National Assembly, in session from 4 May. Also it is clear that the war party in the Provisional Government and the Executive Commission remained a minority.

In his statements and policies Lamartine showed himself to be ambiguous and inconsistent. This can be seen in his manifesto of 2 March, diplomatic and Foreign Ministry appointments, replies to addresses from foreign nationalist leaders, attitude towards incursions into foreign countries, concept of the Army of the Alps, and position with regard to French military intervention in Northern Italy. All this reflected his own contradictory attitudes and desire to please virtually everybody. In so far as his foreign policy had a consistent aim, it was to break out of the system imposed upon France by the Treaties of 1815. He wanted an alliance with Britain, and was prepared to make a number of concessions to the British government and British public opinion. In return he received nothing concrete, not even diplomatic recognition. He vaguely proposed an alliance to the Russian Tsar, for which he was prepared to sacrifice the Poles.[179] He also wanted an alliance, and even political union, with Switzerland.[180] This was rejected by the Swiss. Above all Lamartine wanted to bring about the French acquisition of Nice and Savoy, either as a reward for armed intervention or through a negotiated settlement.

The ambiguity and inconsistency Lamartine displayed as Foreign Minister inevitably meant that foreign governments and diplomats came to regard him as unbusinesslike and untrustworthy. Special exception was taken to his misleading and confidential leaks to the French press, attempts to placate foreign governments through official channels while simultaneously promoting republican policies via secret agents, and failure to prevent the incursions into Belgium, the Rhineland States and Savoy. Within France conservatives were alienated by his seeming radicalism, while radicals considered that he had betrayed the Italian nationalists and the Poles. In trying to change the 1815 settlement in France's favour, Lamartine was pursuing what had become a traditional French foreign policy aim. But his eagerness for a British alliance was an odd priority for the Second Republic's first Foreign Minister, particularly in view of the ideological gulf separating France from Britain after the February Revolution. An even wider ideological gulf existed between republican France and tsarist Russia. The proposal for an alliance with Switzerland was an obvious nonstarter, due to the determination of the Swiss to preserve their political independence. The aim of annexing Nice and Savoy to France could be defended on strategic grounds, but it seems that Lamartine's motive in pursuing this objective, for which he was prepared to make so many sacrifices, was as much personal vanity as his country's national interests.

On the credit side, Lamartine avoided declaring an unnecessary war or committing a disastrous diplomatic blunder. He also contended reasonably successfully with a number of difficulties and disadvantages — the chaos and confusion inevitable at a time of revolutionary upheaval, the physical limits of his personal authority, the existence of powerful and hostile pressure groups, and government ministers and officials such as Ledru-Rollin, Charles Delescluze and Emmanuel Arago, whose public statements and political actions were often in direct contradiction with what he was trying to achieve. Against this it has been argued that the maintenance of European peace was not in France's true interests in 1848.[181] Certainly the movement towards the creation of strong centralised states in Germany, Switzerland and Northern Italy potentially threatened French security.[182] Like many contemporaries, including Napoleon III, Lamartine did not fully appreciate this. Further parallels can be drawn between Lamartine and Napoleon III. Both pursued contradictory aims. On the one hand they sought a British alliance, acceptance by European governments, good relations with the conservative Powers, and the avoidance of an anti-French coalition. On the other hand they wanted to dismantle the 1815 settlement, pose as the protectors of oppressed peoples and nations, establish a federation of independent Italian states, and acquire Nice and Savoy for France. The revolution of February and March 1848 might apparently have favoured Lamartine's pursuit of those contradictory aims, but this was not so. British influence remained of paramount importance; no real opportunities for French intervention emerged; and French domestic constraints severely limited Lamartine's freedom of action. In fact circumstances affecting French foreign policy between February and June 1848 differed significantly from those operating from the beginning of 1849, or, as Lamartine himself had pointed out, from the beginning of 1792.

Notes

1. E. F. vicomte de Beaumont-Vassy, *Les Salons de Paris et la société parisienne sous Louis-Philippe Ier* (Paris, 1866), pp. 360-4, and *Mémoires secrets du XIXe siècle* (Paris, 1874), pp. 341-3; *La Nouvelle revue*, 1 March 1906, p. 67; Regnault, *Histoire du Gouvernement provisoire*, pp. 253-4; *La Revue de Paris*, 1 September 1899, pp. 74-5; Senior, *Journals*, I, p. 60.

2. See Rémusat, *Mémoires de ma vie*, IV, p. 258.

3. *La France parlementaire*, III, p. 296; *Histoire des Girondins*, V (1847), p. 164; *Le Bien public*, 21 November 1847.

4. 'La Question d'Orient, la guerre, le ministère' (*Le Journal de Saône-et-Loire*, 28 August 1840; *La France parlementaire*, II, p. 372); Lamartine in the Chamber of Deputies, 26 May 1840 (*La France parlementaire*, II, pp. 350 and 351).

5. 'Situation de la France à l'extérieur en 1847', 24 October 1847 (ibid., V, pp. 82-3); 'La Question d'Orient, la guerre, le ministère' (ibid., II, p. 382).

6. Ibid., II, p. 390.

7. Lamartine in the Chamber of Deputies, 1 July 1839 and 5 February 1846; ibid., II, p. 224, and IV, pp. 302-4.

8. Lamartine in the Chamber of Deputies, 11 January 1840; ibid., II, pp. 302 and 305.

9. *Sur la politique rationnelle*, p. 85.

10. Lamartine in the Chamber of Deputies, 3 March 1843, and 'Situation de la France à l'extérieur', *Le Bien public*, 28 and 31 October 1847; *La France parlementaire*, III, p. 316, and V, pp. 96 and 99-105.

11. Ibid., V, pp. 127-8.

12. L. C. Jennings, *France and Europe in 1848. A Study of French Foreign Affairs in Time of Crisis* (Oxford, 1973), p. 2.

13. Normanby, *A Year of Revolution*, I, p. xix; Normanby to Palmerston, 28 February 1848 (F. O., 27, 803, f. 250). See also Dr P. Ordinaire, *Episodes de la vie intime d'Alphonse de Lamartine* (Mâcon, 1878), pp. 26-9.

14. Normanby to Palmerston, 28/29 February 1848 (Broadlands Mss., 12889, GC, NO, 125, 1); Normanby, *A Year of Revolution*, I, p. 187.

15. Normanby to Palmerston, 26, 27 and 28/29 February 1848; F. O., 27, 803, ff. 217 and 225-33, and Broadlands Mss., 12889, GC, NO, 125, 1.

16. GC, NO, 461; F. O., 146, 328. Cf. E. Ashley, *The Life of Henry John Temple, Viscount Palmerston: 1846-1865*, 2 vols. (London, 1876), I, pp. 77-8.

17. GC, NO, 462 and 464, 1; Ashley, *Palmerston*, I, pp. 78-9 and 81-2.

18. Comte R. Apponyi, *Vingt-cinq ans à Paris, 1826-1850*, 4 vols. (Paris, 1913-26), IV, pp. 152 and 155.

19. A. de Klinkowstroem (ed.), *Mémoires, documents et écrits divers laissés par le prince de Metternich*, 8 vols. (Paris, 1880-84), VII (1883), pp. 593-5.

20. Ponsonby to Palmerston, 1 March 1848; F. O., 7, 347, f. 2. Cf. *Mémoires de Metternich*, VII, p. 597.

21. Ibid., VII, p. 589.

22. Ibid., VII, pp. 599 and 601-2.

23. A. C. Benson and Viscount Esher (eds.), *The Letters of Queen Victoria, 1837-1861*, 3 vols. (London, 1907), II, p. 178.

24. Westmorland to Palmerston, 29 February 1848; F. O., 64, 285, ff. 129-30. The Earl of Westmorland (formerly Lord Burghersh) and Lamartine had both held diplomatic posts in Florence at the same time.

25. F. O., 64, 285, f. 155.

26. Bloomfield to Palmerston, 6 March 1848 (F. O., 65, 348); E. Bapst, *L'Empereur Nicolas Ier et la deuxiéme république française* (Paris, 1898), p. 2.

27. Bloomfield to Palmerston, 6 March 1848; F. O., 65, 348.

28. M. N. Pokrovskii, *Pages d'histoire. La méthode du matérialisme historique appliquée à quelques problèmes historiques concrets* (Paris, 1929), pp. 58-60.

29. Garnier-Pagès, *Histoire de la Révolution de 1848*, VII, p. 272.

30. See A. Lucas, *Les Clubs et les clubistes* (Paris, 1851).

31. See L. C. Jennings, 'The Parisian Press and French Foreign Affairs in 1848', *Canadian Journal of History*, September 1972, pp. 121-33; *Le National*, 27 February 1848, p. 2; *La Réforme*, 3 and 6 March 1848; *Revue des Deux Mondes*, 1 March 1848, pp. 925-6.

32. Tudesq, *Les Grands notables*, II, pp. 781-4.

33. C. H. Pouthas (ed.), *Documents diplomatiques du Gouvernement provisoire et de la Commission du pouvoir exécutif*, 2 vols. (Paris, 1953-54), I, p. 1.

34. Direct evidence is lacking, but there is a strong presumption that

Lamartine wrote or inspired the article entitled 'Confiance! Confiance!!' and published in *La Presse* (issue nos. 4307 and 4309, 26 and 25-29 February 1848). This is suggested by contemporaries (Bonde, *Paris in '48*, pp. 29-30; G. Claudin, *Mes Souvenirs. Les boulevards de 1840-1870* (Paris, 1884), pp. 54-5), and by the article's content and language. According to Freycinet, *Souvenirs*, p. 22, Lamartine appealed for 'Confiance! Confiance!' in a speech at the Hôtel de Ville on 25 February 1848; and the article's statement, 'La défiance est comme le paratonnerre qui attire la foudre', recalls Lamartine's remark in the National Assembly on 12 June 1848: 'J'ai conspiré comme le paratonnerre conspire avec la foudre'. Interestingly, *Le Mémorial bordelais* commented on 3 March 1848 (p. 3): 'Nous apprenons que M. Emile de Girardin, depuis la Révolution, a servi constamment de secrétaire à M. de Lamartine'. (Cf. *Le Journal de la Côte-d'Or*, 4 March 1848.)

35. *Documents diplomatiques*, I, pp. 7-11.

36. Blanc, *Historical Revelations*, pp. 218-9, and *Histoire de la Révolution de 1848*, I, p. 234; Normanby to Palmerston, 3 March 1848 (F. O., 27, 804, f. 45); Westmorland to Palmerston, 11 March 1848 (F. O., 64, 285, ff. 208-9). Cf. Stern, *Histoire de la Révolution de 1848*, II, p. 82.

37. Westmorland to Palmerston, 11 March 1848; F. O., 64, 285, f. 209.

38. See Jennings, *France and Europe in 1848*, pp. 16-20.

39. See *Documents diplomatiques*, I, pp. vi-xi. Emile Desages (director of the political section under Guizot) resigned on 24 February, but agreed to give Lamartine technical advice.

40. These included Breteuil (*secrétaire de légation* at The Hague), Fontenay (minister at Stuttgart), Lacour (*chargé d'affaires* at Vienna), Théis (consul general at Warsaw), and Thouvenel (*chargé d'affaires* at Athens).

41. These included: Lobstein, *chargé d'affaires* at Stockholm, formerly secretary at Stockholm; de Lurde, *chargé de mission* at The Hague, formerly minister at Buenos Ayres; Forbin-Janson, secretary at Rome, formerly *attaché* at London; Humann, *chargé d'affaires* at Munich, formerly *secrétaire de légation* at Berlin; Bellocq, minister at Brussels, formerly minister at Florence; Tallenay, minister at London, formerly minister at Hamburg; Sérurier, *secrétaire de légation* at Brussels, formerly *secrétaire de légation* at Rio de la Plata; Ferdinand de Lesseps, *chargé d'affaires* at Madrid, formerly consul at Barcelona.

42. *Le Correspondant*, 10 September 1901, p. 858; *Revue des Deux Mondes*, 15 January 1938, p. 316.

43. See Lamartine to Circourt, 2 August 1847; B. N., nouv. acq. fr., 24328, ff. 260-1.

44. Boissy, *Mémoires*, II, pp. 6 and 19; H. Guillemin, 'Lamartine, Byron et Mme Guiccioli', *Revue de littérature comparée*, July-September 1939, pp. 369-89.

45. See the introduction in L. Lex (ed.), *Souvenirs diplomatiques et militaires du général Thiard* (Paris, 1900).

46. See J. Crépet (ed.), *Correspondance générale de Charles Baudelaire*, 6 vols. (Paris, 1947-53), I, pp. 10-11.

47. See *Lamartine et ses nièces*, pp. 124 and 127.

48. See V. de Lamartine, 'Lamartine inconnu', *La Nouvelle revue*, 1 January 1905, p. 6; comte M. de Germiny, *Souvenirs du Chevalier de Cussy, garde du corps, diplomate et consul général, 1795-1866*, 2 vols. (Paris, 1909), II, pp. 329-33; F. Letessier, 'Lamartine et la famille de Jussieu de Sénevier', *Annales de l'Académie de Mâcon*, third series, LIII (1976), pp. 36-55. Charles-Bernard de Jussieu de Sénevier married Alphonsine de Cessiat on 10 May 1848. On the former see Senza (V. de Jussieu de Sénevier), *En marge de la vie de Lamartine. Souvenirs et correspondance de Ch.-B. de Jussieu de Sénevier, 1845-1867* (Paris, 1925).

49. *Souvenirs de Mme Delahante*, II, p. 521.

50. See B. H. M. comte d'Harcourt, *Lamartine, Barbey d'Aurevilly et Paul de Saint-Victor en 1848. Documents inédits* (Paris, 1948), p. 12; *L'Assemblée Nationale*, 9 June 1848, p. 2.

51. Lamartine, *Histoire de la Révolution de 1848*, I, pp. 277 and 320. See F. Letessier, 'Un collaborateur de Lamartine en 1848: Jean-Baptiste Payer (1818-1860)', *Quatrième journées Européennes d'études Lamartiniennes* (Mâcon, 1980), pp. 121-32.

52. A. Delzant, *Paul de Saint-Victor* (Paris, 1886), p. 32; *Documents diplomatiques*, I, p. vii. Lamartine refers to him as 'M. Caillet' in the preface to his *Voyage en Orient*.

53. Hugo, *Choses vues*, p. 275. Cf. E. M. Grant, *Victor Hugo during the Second Republic* (Northampton, Mass., 1935), p. 4.

54. Claudin, *Mes Souvenirs*, p. 283; Delzant, *Paul de Saint-Victor*, pp. 28-30; Harcourt, *Lamartine, Barbey d'Aurevilly et Paul de Saint-Victor*, p. 13; Maréchal, *Lamennais et Lamartine*, pp. 128 and 133.

55. He had corresponded with the baron de Lesseps on 6 January 1833 (letter now in the Academy of Mâcon); he knew Charles Lesseps, the newspaper editor (see *Correspondance de George Sand*, VII (1970), pp. 273-4); and he also knew the comte de Cabarrus, who was brought up with Emile de Girardin and who married in 1821 Adèle de Lesseps (see Claudin, *Mes Souvenirs*, p. 9).

56. E. Grenier, *Souvenirs littéraires* (Paris, 1894), pp. 12 and 18.

57. Lamartine, *Histoire de la Révolution de 1848*, II, p. 166.

58. *Bulletin de l'Institut français d'histoire sociale*, June 1953, p. 32.

59. Westmorland to Palmerston, 6 March 1848; F. O., 64, 285, f. 159.

60. *Procès-Verbaux*, p. 136.

61. Pokrovskii, *Pages d'histoire*, p. 65.

62. Broadlands Mss., 12889, GC, NO, 161, 1 (Normanby to Palmerston, 24 April 1848), and GC, NO, 477.

63. A. de Ridder, *La Crise de la neutralité belge en 1848: le dossier diplomatique*, 2 vols. (Brussels, 1928), I, pp. 187 (de Ligne to Hoffschmidt, 11 March 1848) and 194 (Hoffschmidt to the Belgian diplomatic corps, 12 March 1848).

64. Howard de Walden to Palmerston, 15 April 1848; F. O., 10, 138.

65. J. E. Driault and M. Lhéritier, *Histoire diplomatique de la Grèce de 1821 à nos jours*, 5 vols. (Paris, 1925-26), II, pp. 322-3; Lyons to Palmerston, 1 April 1848 (F. O., 32, 162, f. 86).

66. Levraud to Bastide, 31 May 1848 (*Documents diplomatiques*, II, p. 599); Napier to Palmerston, 13 June 1848 (F. O., 70, 224); Cussy, *Souvenirs*, II, p. 324; Lamartine, *Histoire de la Révolution de 1848*, II, p. 173; G. Montanelli, *Mémoires sur l'Italie*, 2 vols. (Paris, 1857), II, p. 270.

67. C. T. Azéglio, *Souvenirs historiques de la marquise Constance d'Azéglio* (Turin, 1884), p. 211; A. A. H. marquis de Bonneval, *Mémoires anecdotiques du général marquis de Bonneval, 1786-1873* (Paris, 1900), p. 292.

68. Apponyi, *Vingt-cinq ans à Paris*, IV, p. 191; Boissy, *Mémoires*, II, pp. 75-6, 81-2; Boissy to Bastide, 10 June 1848 (*La Guienne*, 24 June 1848, pp. 1-2). Presumably Lamartine eventually concluded that Boissy – a wealthy Catholic peer who had served as *secrétaire de légation* at Florence between 1823 and 1825 – was too conservative, particularly after the spread of revolutionary and nationalist movements to Tuscany.

69. Circourt, *Souvenirs*, I, pp. 385-6, II, pp. 63 (note 2) and 64. Cf. *Le Bien public* (Paris) and *Le Journal des Débats*, 28 May 1848.

70. H. Guillemin, 'Le rôle de Lamartine dans l'affaire de l'abbé Thions', *Le Figaro* (literary supplement), 7 April 1942, p. 2, and *La Bataille de Dieu* (Geneva, 1944), p. 114.

71. Bonde, *Paris in '48*, p. 191.
72. Estourmel, *Derniers souvenirs*, p. 264; Senior, *Conversations*, II, p. 383; *Le Moniteur universel*, 15 April 1848, p. 836, and 7 May 1848, p. 963.
73. Lamartine to Hetzel, 7 March 1848 (B. N., nouv. acq. fr., 16966, ff. 345-6); Lamartine, *Histoire de la Révolution de 1848*, II, pp. 164-5; Ridder, *La Crise de la neutralité belge en 1848*, I, pp. xi-xii and p. 236, II, pp. 130-1.
74. Cussy, *Souvenirs*, II, p. 322.
75. *Documents diplomatiques*, II, p. 1187.
76. Circourt, *Souvenirs*, I, pp. 363-9; J. Sellards, *Dans le sillage du romantisme. Charles Didier, 1805-1864* (Paris, 1933), pp. 135-54.
77. M. Bucur, 'Lamartine et la Révolution de 1848 dans les Principautés danubiennes', in Viallaneix, *Lamartine. Le Livre du centenaire*, pp. 185-9.
78. H. Bessler, *La France et la Suisse de 1848 à 1852* (Paris, 1930), pp. 35-6; C. Fournet, *Huber-Saladin, 1798-1881* (Paris, 1932), pp. 130-42, and 'Lamartine et son confident Genevois Huber-Saladin', in Viallaneix, *Troisième journées Européennes d'études Lamartiniennes*, pp. 107-16.
79. A. Weill, *Introduction à mes mémoires* (Paris, 1890), p. 184, and *Dix mois de révolution*, pp. 124-5. Instead of Weill, Charles Bernays was sent to Germany; see J. G. Chastain, 'France's proposed Danubian federation in 1848', in R. Holtman (ed.), *The Consortium on Revolutionary Europe Proceedings 1978* (Athens, Georgia, 1980), pp. 104-5.
80. Normanby, *A Year of Revolution*, I, pp. 105-7; Normanby to Palmerston, 27 February 1848 (F. O., 27, 803, f. 241).
81. Normanby, *A Year of Revolution*, I, pp. 132-7; Normanby to Palmerston, 28 February 1848 (F. O., 27, 803, ff. 250-7).
82. See Palmerston to Normanby, 29 February 1848 (F. O., 146, 328), and Normanby to Palmerston, 2 March 1848 (F. O., 27, 804, f. 26).
83. *Le Moniteur universel*, 27 February 1848, p. 508; R. Rush, *Residence at the Court of London. Recollections of the Court of Louis Philippe and the French Revolution of 1848* (London, 1872), p. 454. The United States officially recognised the French Second Republic on 26 April 1848.
84. Normanby, *A Year of Revolution*, I, pp. 130-2.
85. *Procès-Verbaux*, p. 23; *Le Moniteur universel*, 29 February 1848, p. 516; Rush, *Recollections*, pp. 452-3.
86. G. T. Poussin, *Les Etats-Unis d'Amérique, étude historique et d'économie politique, 1815-1873* (Paris, 1874), pp. 169-71; A. M. Brescia, 'Richard Rush and the French Revolution of 1848', unpublished PhD thesis (St John's University, New York, 1968), pp. 97-123.
87. *Le Moniteur universel*, 29 February 1848, p. 516.
88. Ibid.
89. Ibid., 11 and 13 March 1848, pp. 595 and 601.
90. Bessler, *La France et la Suisse*, pp. 28, 29 and 332-8.
91. Broadlands Mss., 12889, GC, NO, 125, 3; *Le Girondin*, 29 February 1848, p. 2; Normanby to Palmerston, 29 February 1848 (F. O., 27, 803, f. 281).
92. P. R. O., Lord John Russell Papers, 30, 22, 7B, ff. 17-8; Sir S. Walpole, *The Life of Lord John Russell*, 2 vols. (London, 1889), II, pp. 32-3.
93. P. R. O., 30, 22, 7B, f. 15; ibid., II, pp. 33-4.
94. P. R. O., 30, 22, 7B, ff. 18, 63 and 91; ibid., II, pp. 34-5.
95. B. Connell (ed.), *Regina v. Palmerston* (London, 1962), p. 69; Cottu to Lamartine, 14 March 1848 (*Documents diplomatiques*, I, p. 197).
96. See Normanby to Palmerston, 17 April 1848 (Broadlands Mss., 12889, GC, NO, 157, 1); 'Voulons-nous être nation? Voulons-nous être dynastie?', *Le Bien public*, 6 October 1846.
97. Minto to Palmerston, 6 April 1848; F. O., 44, 5, f. 233.

98. Charles, *La Révolution de 1848 et la seconde république à Bordeaux*, p. 96.

99. Normanby to Palmerston, 20 March 1848; F. O., 27, 805, f. 63.

100. *Parliamentary Debates*, third series, XCVII, pp. 336 and 458, and XCIX, p. 879; Normanby to Palmerston, 25 March 1848 (F. O., 27, 805, f. 177); *The Times*, 17 March 1848, p. 5.

101. Normanby to Palmerston, 25 March, 6 and 10 May 1848 (F. O., 27, 805, f. 177, and 807, ff. 184-5, 196-8); Normanby, *A Year of Revolution*, I, pp. 262-3.

102. *Le Moniteur universel*, 7 March 1848, p. 555.

103. Normanby, *A Year of Revolution*, I, p. 226.

104. *Le Moniteur universel*, 18 March 1848, p. 633.

105. Normanby, *A Year of Revolution*, I, pp. 244-6; 'O'Connell', *Le Bien public*, 22 October 1843 (*La France parlementaire*, III, pp. 438-41).

106. *Le Moniteur universel*, 19 March 1848, p. 638.

107. Palmerston to Normanby, 21 March 1848 (Broadlands Mss., 12889, GC, NO, 467); Normanby to Palmerston, 24 March 1848 (F. O., 27, 805, f. 152).

108. *Le Moniteur universel*, 4 April 1848, pp. 758-9.

109. Broadlands, Mss., 12889, GC, NO, 150, f. 1.

110. Ibid., GC, NO, 473.

111. *The Times*, 5 April 1858, p. 4; debate of 7 April 1848 (*Parliamentary Debates*, XCVIII, p. 27).

112. Broadlands, Mss., 12889, GC, NO, 151, f. 2.

113. *Documents diplomatiques*, I, p. 145.

114. B. N., nouv. acq. fr., 21684, f. 26, and Circourt, *Souvenirs*, I, pp. 154-5.

115. *Le Moniteur universel*, 27 March 1848, p. 695.

116. B. N., nouv. acq. fr., 21684, f. 30. Cf. Circourt to Lamartine, 31 March 1848; ibid., ff. 356-7.

117. W. J. Orr, 'La France et la Révolution allemande de 1848-1849', *Revue d'histoire diplomatique*, July-December 1979, p. 307.

118. Circourt, *Souvenirs*, I, p. 252; Garnier-Pagès, *Histoire de la Révolution de 1848*, VII, p. 282.

119. P. Henry, 'Le Gouvernement provisoire et la question polonaise en 1848', *Revue historique*, CLXXVIII (1936), p. 221.

120. B. N., nouv. acq. fr., 21684, ff. 16-8; *Documents diplomatiques*, II, pp. 94-5.

121. Circourt, *Souvenirs*, II, pp. 159 and 162; Cintrat to Circourt, 7 May 1848 (B. N., nouv. acq. fr., 21684, f. 19).

122. B. N., nouv. acq. fr., 21684, f. 45.

123. *Le Moniteur universel*, 24 May 1848, pp. 1142-3.

124. *Rapport de la Commission d'enquête*, II, p. 8.

125. Garnier-Pagès, *Histoire de la Révolution de 1848*, VII, p. 291.

126. B. H. V. P., 5961, ff. 247-8; Regnault, *Histoire du Gouvernement provisoire*, pp. 274-5.

127. *Rapport de la Commission d'enquête*, II, pp. 12 and 15.

128. On the Affair see A. R. Calman, 'Delescluze, Ledru-Rollin et l'échauffourée de Risquons-tout', *La Révolution de 1848*, vol. XVII, March-May 1920, pp. 44-50; Caussidière, *Mémoires*, I, pp. 200-08; M. Dessal, 'Les Incidents franco-belges en 1848', *Actes du congrès historique du centenaire de la Révolution de 1848* (Paris, 1948), pp. 107-31; Garnier-Pagès, *Histoire de la Révolution de 1848*, VII, pp. 287-94; L. Maes, *L'Affaire de Risquons-tout* (Mouscron, 1935); P. Quentin-Bauchart, *Lamartine et la politique étrangère de la Révolution de février* (Paris, 1913), pp. 183-206; *Rapport de la Commission d'enquête*, II, pp. 5-15;

Regnault, *Histoire du Gouvernement provisoire*, pp. 270-6.
129.   *Le Moniteur universel*, 2 April 1848, p. 744.
130.   Lamartine to Sérurier, 1 April 1848 (*Documents diplomatiques*, I, pp. 565-7); Normanby, *A Year of Revolution*, I, p. 285.
131.   De Ligne to Hoffschmidt and Lamartine to de Ligne, 5 March 1848; Ridder, *La Crise de la neutralité belge en 1848*, I, pp. 109-10, 138-9.
132.   De Ligne to Hoffschmidt, 11 March 1848; ibid., I, pp. 187-8.
133.   Caussidière, *Mémoires*, I, p. 204.
134.   *La Presse*, 27 March 1848, and *Le Siècle*, 28 March 1848; Circourt, *Souvenirs*, I, pp. 378 and 417-9.
135.   Howard de Walden to Palmerston, 1 April 1848; F. O., 10, 138.
136.   Garnier-Pagès, *Histoire de la Révolution de 1848*, VII, p. 275.
137.   Normanby, *A Year of Revolution*, I, pp. 257-8; Jennings, *France and Europe in 1848*, p. 68; Milbanke to Palmerston, 28 March 1848 (F. O., 9, 100, and 146, 330).
138.   Normanby to Palmerston, 5 April 1848; F. O., 27, 806, f. 37.
139.   Normanby to Palmerston, 22 April 1848; F. O., 27, 806, f. 207.
140.   See in general L. M. Blaison, *Un Passage de vive force du Rhin français en 1848* (Paris, 1933).
141.   *Le Moniteur universel*, 20 March 1848, p. 644.
142.   Garnier-Pagès, *Histoire de la Révolution de 1848*, VII, p. 299.
143.   See F. Dutacq, *Histoire politique de Lyon pendant la Révolution de 1848* (Paris, 1910), pp. 225-48; J. Lovie, 'Une annexion manquée. L'expédition lyonnaise d'avril 1848 en Savoie (Chambéry et l'affaire des 'Voraces')', *Annales du centre d'enseignement supérieur de Chambéry*, Section lettres, 1969, no. 7, pp. 17-80.
144.   *Documents diplomatiques*, I, p. 615.
145.   Normanby to Palmerston, 31 March 1848; F. O., 27, 805, ff. 265-6.
146.   Jennings, *France and Europe in 1848*, pp. 52-3; Lamartine, *Histoire de la Révolution de 1848*, II, pp. 255-6, and *Mémoires politiques* in *Oeuvres complètes*, XXXIX, p. 224.
147.   Normanby to Palmerston, 8 and 10 April 1848 (F. O., 27, 806, ff. 75-9 and 93); Lamartine to Bixio, 8 April 1848 (*Documents diplomatiques*, I, p. 702).
148.   See F. Boyer, 'L'Armée des Alpes en 1848', *Revue historique*, CCXXXIII (1965), pp. 71-100.
149.   Lamartine quoted from these two letters in the National Assembly on 23 May 1848; *Le Moniteur universel*, 24 May 1848, p. 1141.
150.   *Documents diplomatiques*, I, pp. 790-1.
151.   B. N., nouv. acq. fr., 22738, f. 21. Cf. F. Boyer, *La Seconde République et Charles-Albert en 1848* (Paris, 1967), p. 77; Garnier-Pagès, *Histoire de la Révolution de 1848*, I, pp. 239-40.
152.   Boyer, *La Seconde République et Charles-Albert*, p. 79; Garnier-Pagès, *Histoire de la Révolution de 1848*, I, p. 240.
153.   Garnier-Pagès, *Histoire de la Révolution de 1848*, I, p. 241.
154.   *Documents diplomatiques*, I, pp. 931-2; P. Henry, 'La France et les nationalités en 1848', *Revue historique*, CLXXXVI (1939), p. 56.
155.   *Documents diplomatiques*, II, p. 251.
156.   *Le Moniteur universel*, 2 May 1848, p. 925.
157.   *Revue historique*, CCXXXIII (1965), pp. 80-1.
158.   Abercromby to Palmerston, 23 May 1848; F. O., 67, 152. G. A. H. comte de Reiset, *Mes Souvenirs*, 3 vols. (Paris, 1901-03), I, pp. 127-8, implies the officers visited Charles Albert about 19 June. Boyer follows this (*Revue historique*, CCXXXIII (1965), pp. 83-4), but Abercromby's dispatch is more likely to

be accurate.

159.   *Revue historique*, CCXXXIII (1965), p. 82.

160.   Lamartine to E. Arago, 28 April 1848; ibid., pp. 76-7. Cf. Boyer, *La Seconde République et Charles-Albert*, pp. 80-1.

161.   Bixio to Lamartine, 29 March 1848; *Documents diplomatiques*, I, p. 491.

162.   Normanby to Palmerston, 22 April 1848; Broadlands Mss., 12889, GC, NO, 159, f. 1.

163.   Garnier-Pagès, *Histoire de la Révolution de 1848*, X, p. 6. Cf. Lacretelle, *Lamartine et ses amis*, p. 138.

164.   Garnier-Pagès, *Histoire de la Révolution de 1848*, I, pp. 7-10. Another, less detailed, account of these discussions is in ibid., I, pp. 439-43. See also Sarrans, *Histoire de la République en février*, II, p. 304. According to Ledru-Rollin, *Discours politiques et écrits divers*, II, pp. 226-7, a similar discussion was held by the Executive Commission shortly before 24 June 1848.

165.   *Le Moniteur universel*, 28 March 1848, pp. 702-3.

166.   Ibid., 9 April 1848, pp. 794-5; *Le Journal des Débats*, 9 April 1848.

167.   P. Ginsborg, *Daniele Manin and the Venetian Revolution of 1848-49* (Cambridge, 1979), p. 148; Quentin-Bauchart, *Lamartine et la politique étrangère*, p. 238.

168.   *Procès-Verbaux*, p. 81.

169.   Lamartine to Baudin, 21 March 1848 (Circourt, *Souvenirs*, I, note on pp. liv-lvi), and to Normanby, 21 March 1848 (Broadlands Mss., 12889, GC, LA, 36, A).

170.   *Procès-Verbaux*, p. 81.

171.   Quentin-Bauchart, *Lamartine et la politique étrangère*, pp. 278-81; Lamartine to Benoît-Champy, 1 May 1848 (*Documents diplomatiques*, II, p. 8).

172.   Jennings, *France and Europe in 1848*, p. 106.

173.   Ponsonby to Palmerston, 2 April 1848; F. O., 7, 348, f. 8, and 146, 330.

174.   Normanby to Palmerston, 24 April 1848; F. O., 27, 806, f. 232.

175.   Normanby to Palmerston, 1 May 1848; F. O., 27, 807, ff. 11 and 12.

176.   Quentin-Bauchart, *Lamartine et la politique étrangère*, pp. 271-4.

177.   Holtman, *The Consortium on Revolutionary Europe Proceedings 1978*, p. 103.

178.   *Procès-Verbaux*, p. 270. Cf. J. Bastide, *La République française et l'Italie en 1848* (Brussels, 1858), pp. 128 and 137.

179.   Pokrovskii, *Pages d'histoire*, pp. 58 and 61-2.

180.   See Lamartine to Thiard, 18 March 1848 (*Documents diplomatiques*, I, pp. 271-5); Bessler, *La France et la Suisse*, p. 35; H. Guillemin, 'Lamartine et Berne en 1848', *Premières journées Européennes d'études Lamartiniennes*, pp. 25-32.

181.   See E. Tersen, *Le Gouvernement provisoire et l'Europe, 25 février – 12 mai 1848* (Paris, 1948), pp. 76-7.

182.   For a contemporary development of this argument see A. de Broglie, 'De la politique étrangère de la France depuis la Révolution de février', *Revue des Deux Mondes*, 1 August 1848, pp. 293-321.

BONAPARTISM AND BANKRUPTCY, 1848-1869

Ces années, comme les fantômes de Macbeth, passant leurs mains par-dessus mon épaule, me montrent du doigt non des couronnes, mais un sépulcre; et plût à Dieu que j'y fusse déjà couché! – Lamartine reported by Edmond Texier; *L'Illustration*, 19 April 1856, p. 253

The June Days of 1848 were a watershed in French history. The suppression of the Paris workers' rising between 24 and 26 June effectively ended the 1848 Revolution in France and inaugurated a period of reaction, a period which climaxed with Louis Napoleon's *coup d'état* of 2 December 1851 and his proclamation of the Second Empire a year later. For Lamartine the political consequences of the June Days were equally drastic. Whereas before 1848 he had been one of the most prominent members of the Chamber of Deputies, and had played a major role in government between February and June 1848, henceforth he was to remain essentially on the margin of French politics. His political career did not, however, end in June 1848: except for a brief gap (May – July 1849), until the *coup d'état* of December 1851 he continued to serve as a representative in the Assembly, where he made a major contribution to the constitutional debates during the autumn of 1848; in the presidential election of December 1848 he was one of the five candidates defeated by Louis Napoleon; and from 1849 until shortly before his death in 1869 he produced a prodigious volume of historical works and periodical literature, in which he again tried to influence political opinion in France.

The June Days also marked yet another phase in Lamartine's political evolution. Not surprisingly, his old fears of popular violence and anarchy were traumatically confirmed. As a result he broke decisively and permanently with Ledru-Rollin and the left-wing republicans, and he developed a more critical interpretation of France's revolutionary tradition. However, he remained a defender of the February Revolution and of his record in government in 1848; and, in so far as a political label can be attached to him, he remained a moderate republican. As such, like many other moderate republicans, he believed that the Second Republic was threatened more from further popular violence and from the extreme Left than from the military repression and newly emergent Bonapartism of the Right. Towards Bonapartism and Louis Napoleon Lamartine's attitudes were complex and changing: prior to 1848, long-standing ideological hostility to Bonapartism but also cordial relations with members of the Bonaparte family; during the presidential election campaign, suspicious rivalry with Louis Napoleon but also a refusal to campaign publicly against his opponent; between December 1848 and 1851, a period of political and social flirtation with the Prince President followed by increasing concern in 1851 that the constitution might be overthrown; in December 1851, outrage at the Bonapartist *coup d'état*, eventually replaced by a resigned acceptance of the Second Empire coupled with a renewed nostalgic sympathy for the Bourbon monarchy.

After the June Days Lamartine's political position was unenviable. The former Provisional Government had become the object of almost universal execration. It was blamed for the whole traumatic and humiliating experience of the February Revolution, for the failure to maintain law and order in Paris, for the imposition of the 45 per cent increase in the property tax, for the dispatch into the provinces of *commissaires* armed with arbitrary powers, and for the continuation of the economic crisis. As the most prominent member of the Provisional Government, Lamartine inevitably suffered a devastating loss of popularity. Moreover, the June Days had finally shattered his concept of a Republic of fraternity and concord, and had polarised political opinion into two main groups, the so-called Party of Order and the left-wing opposition. While the left-wing opposition now suffered from political and military repression, the Party of Order increasingly turned to Bonapartism and to Louis Napoleon. Since Bonapartism had an obvious historic appeal and could promise a new national consensus, and since Louis Napoleon could be presented as the national saviour who would rescue France from crisis, moderate republicanism and Lamartine were further undermined.

Visitors to Lamartine in July 1848 reported that he viewed his loss of popularity with philosophic resignation and that he feared a renewed outbreak of urban violence in about three months' time.[1] He had retired to the outskirts of Paris, to a villa called Castel-Madrid near the Neuilly Gate of the Bois de Boulogne, but, despite the bleak political scene from both a personal and national point of view, he had no intention of retiring from politics. In any case, during July a commission of enquiry established by the National Assembly to investigate the events of May and June 1848 virtually put him on trial, with other members of the former Provisional Government, while in addition he had to defend his conduct of foreign policy before the National

Assembly's foreign affairs committee. To the commission of enquiry he stressed his rejection of the red flag on 25 February and his strenuous efforts to ensure the availability of adequate military resources in Paris.[2] To the foreign affairs committee he naturally enough defended his record as Minister of Foreign Affairs, and rather misleadingly presented his policies as demonstrating that the Second Republic was a republic of order, peace and fraternity among nations.[3]

Meanwhile, within the National Assembly loose associations or 'réunions' were being formed of representatives who shared political loyalties and common interests. Conservatives, notably Berryer, Falloux, Odilon Barrot, Rémusat and Thiers, joined the Réunion de la Rue de Poitiers. Moderate republicans divided between the Réunion du Palais National (pro-Cavaignac) and the Réunion de l'Institut (anti-Cavaignac), while the Réunion de la Rue de Castiglione attracted left-wing republicans. With Armand Marrast's presidency of the National Assembly due to expire on 19 August, both the Réunion du Palais National and the Réunion de l'Institut proposed Lamartine's candidature. Probably realising that his chances were slim, Lamartine publicly declined to stand (17 August) and Marrast was re-elected.[4] Until the beginning of September Lamartine did not contribute to parliamentary debates. Instead he attempted to justify his political record during the 1848 Revolution in a pamphlet, completed on 25 August and entitled *Lettre aux dix départements* (the ten departments which had elected him in April). In this pamphlet he rebutted the charges, then frequently being levelled at him, of personal ambition, left-wing sympathies and weakness in the defence of law and order. He claimed that he had not contributed to the overthrow of the July Monarchy, and that the formation of the Provisional Government and the proclamation of the Second Republic had been essential for the maintenance of order. Once in power he argued that he had insisted on the necessity of holding elections for a National Assembly as soon as possible, that he had successfully resisted left-wing policies such as the adoption of the red flag or French intervention in Poland, and that he had consistently and effectively striven to prevent anarchy from reigning in Paris.[5]

By the beginning of September Lamartine felt able to return to public life. He chose the crucial debates on France's future constitution in which to make his first parliamentary speeches since his resignation from government. A commission, formed by the National Assembly in May 1848 to prepare a draft constitution, presented its proposals at the end of August. After an introduction, the proposed constitution listed a number of guaranteed civil rights. These included freedom from arbitrary arrest, freedom of religious worship, freedom of association, freedom of assembly, freedom of the press, and the inviolability of private property. On 6 September Lamartine in the Assembly argued that the constitution should contain a declaration of general principles rather than of specific rights. The latter varied according to different times and circumstances; they were incapable of precise definition; and property was inviolable because it was a divine institution, and not because of any human law. On the other hand, Lamartine maintained on 14 September that the Second Republic's citizens had a right not to starve to death, and that in cases of extreme hardship the government had a moral obligation to provide the basic necessities of life. The National Workshops had therefore been a temporary institution, made necessary by circumstance, to save people from hunger and pauperism. This alleviation of the suffering of the masses had been a moral obligation for the Provisional Government; and it had been in accordance with the February Revolution's fundamental principle, which was 'L'idée du peuple'. Echoing Danton, Lamartine concluded: 'Du coeur, Citoyens! du coeur! et toujours du coeur pour le peuple!'[6] The list of guaranteed civil rights became, with only minor modifications, part of the constitution accepted by the Assembly on 4 November, but Lamartine's arguments did have some effect: when finally adopted, the constitution did recognise that the State should provide public works for the unemployed and help those unable to help themselves.

One of the major constitutional questions raised in the Assembly debates was whether there should be a single or two-chamber legislature. Lamartine on 27 September pointed out a number of practical objections to a bicameral system. No group or class existed in France which could satisfactorily form a second chamber, so that a method of determining a second chamber's membership would be difficult to devise. Also, in a crisis there would be conflict over which chamber possessed sovereignty. Lamartine was not opposed to a second chamber on principle. The previous April he had reportedly favoured both a single and double chamber legislature; and he is supposed to have told his chief adversary in the debate, Odilon Barrot: 'You will be right later, but not at present.'[7] Lamartine's speech was probably not decisive in convincing the representatives that they should reject Barrot's arguments, since a majority in the constitutional committee had recommended a single chamber legislature, agreement would not have been easily reached as to a second chamber's character and composition, and it was thought anyway that the Conseil d'Etat would serve as a counterweight to the Assembly.

At the end of May the constitutional committee had agreed that a president chosen by manhood suffrage should hold executive powers, but by September the opponents of Bonapartism and Louis Napoleon were beginning to doubt the wisdom of this proposal. In by-elections on 17 September five departments elected Louis Napoleon, and it was becoming clear that the French electorate might vote for him to be president. Therefore Jules Grévy introduced an amendment substituting for a president a head of a council of ministers, appointed and dismissed at the Assembly's will. Lamartine vigorously opposed this (6 October). There was, he argued, a need for a strong executive authority. In a republic sovereignty lay with the people, who should consequently elect the president. A president elected by the Assembly would inevitably share the Assembly's unpopularity, which might lead to a paralysis of government. Such a president would also be the choice, not of national opinion, but of political parties. National opinion should decide who was to be the president, since circumstances in France did not favour the establishment of a Napoleonic dictatorship. A presidential election by the electorate would rally the population to the Republic. Votes in the Assembly might be bought with offers of patronage, whereas the entire electorate could never be corrupted. Above all, the people had the right to select their rulers, even if they wanted a Bourbon restoration. Lamartine did, however, admit that the system of popular election had its dangers, and he concluded fatalistically: '*Alea jacta est*! May God and the people pronounce! Something must be left to Providence!'[8]

At least three contemporaries, and several historians, have considered Lamartine's speech mainly responsible for the defeat of the Grévy amendment, and of an amendment introduced by Leblond that there should be a president, though elected by the Assembly.[9] Certainly one of Lamartine's most powerful speeches, its impact probably explains why the Grévy and Leblond amendments were defeated so overwhelmingly (by, respectively, votes of 643 to 158 and 602 to 211). Those votes had extremely important consequences: they allowed the establishment of a system by which Louis Napoleon could legally acquire considerable executive authority. Thus Lamartine, despite his opposition to Bonapartism, helped make possible the election of a Bonaparte who would destroy the Second Republic and many of its achievements. According to Falloux, Lamartine calculated that he had a better chance of being elected president by manhood suffrage than by the Assembly. He believed that with manhood suffrage no candidate could win an absolute majority. The presidential candidates would therefore, in accordance with the constitution, present themselves to the Assembly, which Lamartine would be able to win over by his eloquence. Falloux claims that Lamartine made this prediction to the comte de Marcellus, who reported it to him shortly after the presidential election.[10] Calculations of personal advantage may have influenced Lamartine, yet the whole character of his speech suggests, not a spirit of calculation, but a willingness to take a gamble, and a serious underestimation of the potential strength of Louis Napoleon's candidature. Also, Lamartine's argument is consistent with his faith in public opinion, his conviction that the French people should be allowed to determine their own political future, and his previously expressed support for presidential election by manhood suffrage.[11]

After the debates on the constitution Lamartine returned triumphantly to Mâcon on 17 October. That afternoon a large and enthusiastic crowd, including members of the Mâcon National Guard, escorted him to Monceau, where in a short speech he declared that he was bringing back 'an innocent revolution' and praised his audience for their steadfastness.[12] In the following weeks he received several deputations of citizens and national guardsmen from Mâcon and neighbouring communes, and on 15 November was toasted by representatives of the Army of the Alps.[13] To these various deputations he consistently presented himself as a moderate republican who had saved France from anarchy, socialism, a new Terror, and the dictatorship of Paris clubs and factions. Besides firmly distancing himself from left-wing republicans, he praised the peasants and the National Guard, and suggested that the Republic would progressively bring property ownership within the reach of all, thereby steadily swelling the ranks of property's defenders.[14] Thus he again attempted to establish his conservative political credentials, besides appealing to conservative elements and suggesting that the Second Republic would be a conservative institution. When the Republic's new constitution was officially proclaimed in Mâcon on 19 November, Lamartine gave an enthusiastic speech that almost resembled a religious liturgy.[15] He left Mâcon for Paris on 23 November, reaching the capital in time for a National Assembly debate on the June Days.

These weeks of activity for Lamartine, crowded with processions, dinners, speeches, letters, visits and deputations, coincided with the development of the campaign for the presidential election.[16] Throughout the campaign, Lamartine's attitude and behaviour were typically ambivalent. On 6 August he reported that people were again beginning to speak of him as a future president of the Republic. He claimed that he did not believe the rumour, and denied wanting the presidency, but admitted that anything was possible with such a volatile public opinion.[17] In September he privately described Cavaignac as the man of the moment and the indispensable lictor of the Republic, claiming he would vote for Cavaignac rather than himself to be president.[18] Yet just before he left Paris he stated that, while not wanting the presidency, he would accept it out of a sense of duty.[19] The apparent evidence of his continuing popularity in the Mâconnais encouraged a brief period of optimism. On 27 October he wrote that Louis Napoleon had little support, that most of the votes would go to Cavaignac, Ledru-Rollin or himself, and that he would be in the majority in rural areas.[20] However, by early November he had lost hope of gaining election, expecting Cavaignac to win and himself to receive less than 50,000 votes.[21] In a Mâcon speech on 13 November he repeated what he had been telling his friends, that he did not want the presidency, but that his duty to the Republic required him to remain a candidate and serve as president if elected.[22] He also stated that he was not issuing a manifesto or programme, because his name was a manifesto and his term of government office a programme.[23] To the general public he addressed the following declaration, dated 30 November and published in the press at the beginning of December:[24]

> I am not soliciting for votes. I do not want any. However, the Republic may still be faced by difficulties and dangers. There is as much difference between the boldness of soliciting and the weakness of refusing, as there is between ambition and a sense of duty. This sense of duty obliges me not to withdraw my name from the free choice available to the country.

Le Journal des Débats had already, and *Le Loing* of Montargis subsequently, published similar declarations.[25]

Whether or not Lamartine wanted the presidency, he must have realised he had little chance of gaining election. He claimed that he remained a candidate so as to prevent votes going to Louis Napoleon or 'the red candidates' (Ledru-Rollin and Raspail).[26] His refusal to campaign was not out of character. It may be partly explained by physical exhaustion following his period in power, discouragement over the June Days and their aftermath, and habitual ill-health.[27] He may have relied on his *Lettre aux dix départements* and his various

October and November Mâconnais speeches, which *Le Bien public*, *Le Courrier français* and *La Presse* reproduced. Also, he revealed his usual fatalistic resignation to the dictates of Providence. To Marcellus he wrote on 1 November: 'The Holy Spirit is the only great elector in the conclave of peoples. He will blow where He will between 10 and 11 December 1848.'[28] However, it seems that he really did believe his name and record were alone sufficient to win a substantial number of votes.

Such optimism was ill-founded. Throughout France Lamartine was closely associated with the now discredited Provisional Government and Executive Commission, and with the whole traumatic experience of the February Revolution. Among conservatives and moderate republicans his alliance with Ledru-Rollin and alleged failure to maintain law and order fatally counted against him, while left-wing republicans believed that he had betrayed the radical cause. Instead of Lamartine, the main political components of the French electorate could turn to other candidates, conservatives to Louis Napoleon, moderate republicans to Cavaignac, and left-wing republicans to Ledru-Rollin. Nor could Lamartine hope to counter the complex mystique of Bonapartism. In addition, unlike Louis Napoleon and Cavaignac, Lamartine had behind him no 'réunion' among representatives in the Assembly, no financial backing from wealthy bankers and industrialists, and no means of organising an electoral campaign in Paris or the provinces. His candidature was supported by only two Paris newspapers, *Le Bien public* and *Le Courrier français*,[29] and by a handful of obscure provincial newspapers such as *L'Ami du Peuple* of Hazebrouck,[30] *L'Eclaireur des Pyrénées* of Bayonne,[31] *Le Loing* of Montargis,[32] and *La Tribune lyonnaise* of Lyons.[33] Another provincial newspaper, *Le Conciliateur* of Limoges, at first championed Lamartine but then switched to Louis Napoleon;[34] *Le Patriote jurassien* suggested that if readers did not want to vote for Cavaignac, they should vote for Lamartine;[35] and Victor Hugo's *L'Evénement* was reasonably sympathetic to Lamartine, though firmly behind Louis Napoleon. Most newspapers either ignored Lamartine's candidature or dismissed it as being of no importance. Girardin in *La Presse* promoted Louis Napoleon. In Mâcon the conservative *Journal de Saône-et-Loire* if anything favoured Cavaignac, while the left-wing *Union républicaine* advised its readers to vote for Ledru-Rollin.[36]

Although after *Le Bien public* of Mâcon had ceased publication in August Lamartine no longer had a local newspaper supporting him, his position in Mâcon and the Mâconnais had not been eroded. He was elected to Mâcon's *conseil municipal* in July, to Saône-et-Loire's *conseil général* by both Mâcon cantons in August,[37] and to the *conseil général*'s chairmanship for October and November. Also he had secured the dismissal of Paul St Estienne-Cavaignac as prefect of Saône-et-Loire in May, and his replacement in June by Auguste-Edouard Cerfberr, last editor of *Le Bien public* of Mâcon.[38] The mayor of Mâcon, Carteron, was one of his friends and supporters; and in August Ronot had been appointed a member of Saône-et-Loire's *conseil de préfecture*.[39] However, the Mâconnais demonstrations held in his favour during the autumn were essentially gestures of gratitude by local conservative groups for his moderating role in the Revolution of 1848, rather than an indication of future popular support. More revealing, when he visited Cormatin on 26 October he encountered hostility and Bonapartist slogans, the importance of which he significantly dismissed.[40]

Lamartine's public reluctance to become president, and refusal to issue a manifesto or campaign for votes, must have discouraged many potential supporters. In so far as he stood for anything, it was for concord and conciliation, but this was not enough. As *La Presse* explained to its readers on 13 November, 'Once M. de Lamartine had undermined his serious prospects of success by carrying his moderation to the point of indecision, we could not hesitate any longer in rallying to the candidature of Louis Napoleon Bonaparte, who had the support of the people'. Lamartine struck the final blow at his own candidature by failing to defend himself in the Assembly on 25 November, when Cavaignac accused him of inertia before and during the June Days. Apparently Lamartine thought that at such a critical time he should not attack the government's head and the Republic's president.[41] At the beginning of December, twenty-seven members of Saône-et-Loire's *conseil général* publicly announced their support for Cavaignac. It was suggested that Lamartine's failure to speak in the Assembly on 25 November had prompted this announcement.[42] Even Cerfberr issued a proclamation on 6 December suggesting that the electorate should vote for Cavaignac.[43] Nevertheless, to the end Lamartine allowed himself to be deceived by any indication that he was still popular.[44]

The results of the presidential election held on 10 December were:[45]

Louis Napoleon Bonaparte	5,543,520
General Cavaignac	1,448,302
Ledru-Rollin	371,431
Raspail	36,964

| Lamartine | 17,914 |
| General Changarnier | 4,687 |

Lamartine's total included 3,838 votes polled in Paris and 2,286 in Saône-et-Loire, where, however, Louis Napoleon did particularly well in the canton of Mâcon Nord.[46] This massive rejection by the electorate was a terrible blow. Lamartine bitterly complained that he was the object of the blackest, most spiteful and most universal ingratitude imaginable: he had been rejected by the people, for whom he had achieved so much, and by the nobility and bourgeoisie, whose lives and property he had protected throughout his three months in power.[47] Symbolically, on 12 December *Le Bien public* of Paris ceased publication, its editors, Eugène Pelletan and Arthur de La Guéronnière, joining *La Presse*.[48]

Throughout his political career Lamartine publicly and repeatedly attacked Napoleon and opposed Bonapartism. He maintained that Napoleon had subverted the principles of 1789 by establishing a personal military dictatorship which had undermined parliamentary democracy and civil rights; and he condemned the militarism, wars of aggression and pursuit of imperial glory which he associated with Bonapartism. Such views, expressed in numerous speeches, poems and other writings, even prompted Louis Napoleon in 1843 to publish a reply to Lamartine's strictures on the Napoleonic period.[49] However, while imprisoned in the fortress of Ham (1840-1846) Louis Napoleon developed, like Lamartine, an interest in Saint-Simonianism, and in pamphlets and newspaper articles he outlined ideas similar to those of Lamartine on such topics as democracy, poverty, Algeria and the July Monarchy. This apparent coincidence of political views seems to have improved Louis Napoleon's opinion of Lamartine. Whereas in 1843 Louis Napoleon had privately described Lamartine as 'a man wholly antipathetic to me, a regular political-sentimental Don Quixote', by February 1846 he was writing to Lamartine in flattering terms.[50] Moreover, Lamartine's attitude towards Napoleon I was not always wholly negative: for example in May 1840, during a parliamentary debate on the return of Napeleon's remains from St Helena, he described Napoleon as a great general who had tragically failed to fulfil his true historical role.[51] Also, through his mother Lamartine happened to be distantly related to the Bonaparte family; and because of this connection, cousins of Lous Napoleon, the princesse de Canino and her son the prince Pierre Bonaparte, established cordial relations with Lamartine in 1843.[52]

At the end of February 1848 Louis Napoleon arrived in Paris from London, where he had lived in exile since his escape from Ham in 1846. Embarrassed by his arrival in the capital, the Provisional Government and possibly Lamartine himself told him to leave immediately.[53] Louis Napoleon obeyed and returned to London, but he allowed his candidature to go forward in the National Assembly by-elections of 4 June and was elected in five departments, including Corsica and the Seine. In the National Assembly on 12 June Lamartine recommended that the 1832 law exiling the Bonapartes should be applied to Louis Napoleon, while the same day all prefects were ordered to arrest Louis Napoleon should he return to France. Although this order was countermanded on 14 June, following the Assembly's rejection of the exile proposal, Louis Napoleon decided to remain in London.[54] In further by-elections on 17 September five departments again elected Louis Napoleon, whereupon he ended his exile and took his seat in the Assembly. Lamartine and Louis Napoleon were of course rival candidates in the ensuing presidential election, but Lamartine refrained from making personal attacks on Louis Napoleon and from denouncing Bonapartism.

Immediately after his triumphant election to the presidency, Louis Napoleon had to choose his vice-president and form his new government. According to Normanby, Molé told him that there were plans to exclude former republicans from minsterial posts but 'to propose a list of Vice Presidents from that category. It was thought the President might give the Assembly to choose between Arago, Lamartine and perhaps Cavaignac himself.'[55] Another rumour was that Lamartine would be proposed for the vice presidency with Cavaignac and Dufaure. To the comtesse d'Agoult on 24 December Lamartine denied having received any proposals. He did not want the vice presidency, but would accept it out of patriotism so as to be 'an advanced guard to watch over the Republic'.[56] Meanwhile, the comte d'Orsay had sent a letter on 21 December via Sir Henry Bulwer to Louis Napoleon, advising him to form a government with Lamartine as Foreign Minister.[57] A clause in a contract which Lamartine signed with Michel Lévy frères on 30 December, and a letter to his nieces of 3 January 1849, suggest he thought that he might be offered the vice presidency.[58] In his *Mémoires politiques* Lamartine describes how Louis Napoleon invited him to join his first government during a secret meeting in the Bois de Boulogne. He declined, determined not to accept a ministerial post unless Louis Napoleon could not form a government without him. Lamartine's *Mémoires politiques* are not wholly reliable. However, Emile Ollivier states that Louis Napoleon, wanting to form a republican government, approached Lamartine on Duclerc's advice; and according to Victor Hugo Lamartine was offered, and refused, the vice presidency at a dinner held at the Elysée Palace on 12 January 1849.[59]

At this time Lamartine and Louis Napoleon were certainly in regular social contact. On 23 January Lamartine presented the marquis de La Grange at the Elysée Palace; on 30 January Louis Napoleon was on the point of attending a concert organised by the Lamartines at 82 rue de l'Université, but was dissuaded by his advisers; and on 3 March Lamartine himself attended a concert at the Elysée.[60] These social contacts continued in 1850 and until the beginning of 1851, as did suggestions that Lamartine might receive a government post.[61] In the Odilon Barrot Papers a manuscript government list, probably dating from May 1849, on Louis Napoleon's notepaper and possibly in Louis Napoleon's handwriting, assigns Lamartine to the Foreign Affairs Ministry.[62] During 1850 Lamartine was reportedly 'very much in favour at the Elysée'; Louis Napoleon may again have offered him a ministry about April 1851; and Barante feared as late as October 1851 that Lamartine might receive a ministerial appointment.[63] Thus Lamartine became quite friendly with Louis Napoleon, but consistently refused or discouraged offers of a government post. This characteristically ambivalent behaviour may have reinforced Louis Napoleon's conservatism.

While denying himself a government post, Lamartine sought to maintain his public influence and financial independence through political journalism. In April 1849 *Le Conseiller du peuple*, a monthly periodical edited by Lamartine, first appeared. This venture stemmed from a proposal by two Jewish financiers, Moise Millaud and Jules-Isaac Mirès, that Lamartine should produce a popular periodical costing six francs a year, for which they would pay him 2,000 francs a month.[64] Each number consisted of a political editorial ('the advice to the people') and a summary of recent events ('the political almanac'). Later numbers sometimes also included 'literary conversations', which reproduced short extracts from a new edition of Lamartine's collected works. Dubois helped with financial and administrative matters, and occasionally Eugène Pelletan and Paul de Saint-Victor contributed to the editorial work. As the periodical's title suggests, Lamartine stressed the concept of 'the People', who needed to be 'enlightened, moderated, instructed and advised'.[65] Thus he had once again assumed the role of guide and educator of the popular masses. As before, such a role flattered his vanity and reflected his faith in the potential of the newspaper and periodical press, besides providing him with a much needed monthly salary. Also, he hoped through *Le Conseiller du peuple* to continue to influence French politics, and to discredit in the popular mentality socialism, communism and revolutionary violence. For example, he explained the February Revolution in terms of 'the People', who supported the Provisional Government, and the demagogues and clubs, who organised the Paris *journées* and the June insurrection.[66] A modest success, by October 1850 *Le Conseiller du peuple*'s circulation had risen from 5,000 to 40,000.[67]

Besides engaging in these literary and journalistic activities, Lamartine remained a member of the National Assembly. His first speech after the presidential election was on 6 February 1849; on 8 March he condemned French foreign policy towards Italy, particularly French military action against the Roman Republic; and he opposed on 10 March the idea that government ministers should be prohibited from sitting in the Assembly, on the grounds that this would be undemocratic.[68] A few days later he left Paris for Bourges to make a deposition at the High Court trial of those accused of responsibility for the *journée* of 15 May 1848. Thirteen political prisoners, including Albert, Barbès, Blanqui, Courtais, Raspail and Sobrier, appeared before the Court, which also judged in their absence Louis Blanc and Caussidière, now in exile. Despite his anxiety to distinguish himself from left-wing republicans and the conspiracy accusations in his forthcoming *Histoire de la Révolution de 1848*, Lamartine played down the *journée*, probably out of loyalty to former colleagues and embarrassment over past left-wing contacts. Even while at Bourges (12-15 March) he continued working on his *Histoire de la Révolution de 1848*. He also praised Louis Napoleon to his hosts.[69] From Bourges he proceeded to Mâcon, where he arrived on 16 March.[70] After a short stay he returned to Bourges (31 March), leaving the next day for Paris to spend the early summer at Castel-Madrid.

Elections to determine the Legislative Assembly's membership were held throughout France on 13 May 1849. Lamartine stood as a candidate in Saône-et-Loire, at the same time refusing to stand in Paris.[71] During March and April a Comité électoral de Mâcon was formed. Its members included several of Lamartine's former supporters, such as Hippolyte Boussin, Carteron, Hippolyte Duréault, Foillard, Henri de Lacretelle, and Versaut, and Lamartine headed its list of candidates.[72] The Comité constitutionnel communal de l'arrondissement de Mâcon (membership included Charles de Lacretelle and Léonce Lenormand, editor of *Le Journal de Saône-et-Loire*) and at least five other electoral committees also supported Lamartine's candidature.[73] Those committees also backed Louis-Lucien Bonaparte (nephew of the

Emperor Napoleon and cousin of Louis Napoleon), Changarnier (commander of the Paris National Guard), moderate republicans such as
Charles Dariot and Chapuys-Montlaville, and legitimists and Orleanists
such as Edouard de Loisy and Philibert de La Guiche. Thus Lamartine,
like other Saône-et-Loire moderate republicans, featured with Bona-
partists and monarchists on a ticket of social stability and law and
order. This reflected his complete break with left-wing republicanism
since June 1848, his willingness to put his conservatism before his
republicanism, and his consequent local re-emergence as an important
conservative political figure.

In striking contrast to the December 1848 presidential election,
conservatives were generally ill-prepared for the May 1849 Assembly
elections. Typically, in Saône-et-Loire the united moderate republican − Bonapartist − monarchist front was organised only a few days
before the elections, while Lamartine himself does not seem to have
campaigned personally. In many parts of France, including Saône-et-
Loire, conservatives could not afford such disarray and inaction. During
the spring and early summer of 1849 French peasants suffered from a
combination of increased taxation and low agricultural prices, which
often encouraged radical political sympathies. Also, the conservatism
of Louis Napoleon's first government had disappointed many voters.
In particular, the despatch of a French military force to overthrow
the Roman Republic and restore Papal authority in Rome was widely
opposed by republicans and doubtless resented by many taxpayers.
The Left exploited this situation quite successfully, distributing propaganda and organising an effective and united electoral campaign.
A sharp fall in wine prices had severely affected Saône-et-Loire, and
the department, particularly Chalon-sur-Saône, had a well established
left-wing political tradition. The National Guard of Charolles had to be
dissolved on 8 March, after refusing to escort the sub-prefect and his
cortège during the celebrations of the anniversary of 24 February. The
same fate overtook Chalon-sur-Saône's National Guard on the eve of
the elections.[74] The Comité électoral de la Montagne for Saône-et-Loire
(which included Isidore Dubief, Lamartine's former collaborator on
Le Bien public, and Dr Ordinaire, now editor of *L'Union républicaine*)
produced a list of candidates headed by Ledru-Rollin and excluding
Lamartine.[75] The day of the elections red flags and left-wing slogans
were much in evidence; and in a high poll Ledru-Rollin and the left-
wing republican candidates were all elected.[76]

Just failing to gain re-election, Lamartine for the first time since
January 1833 ceased to be a deputy or representative of the people.

Obviously this was a severe blow to him personally and to his Saône-et-Loire political support group, which was beginning to break up. With the decline in his political fortunes and the polarisation of French politics, the political differences among his local supporters had meant that some, such as Emile Buy, Isidore Dubief, Dr Ordinaire and Dr Pascal, had become left-wing republicans, while others, such as Bruys d'Ouilly and Guigue de Champvans, had moved towards the Right. However, as a *notable* and moderate republican, Lamartine was a victim of local and national trends. He did poll 38,972 votes, a marked improvement on his December performance (2,286 votes in Saône-et-Loire and 17,914 in the whole of France). Also, he did considerably better than other candidates on the same electoral slate, such as Changarnier (27,952 votes), Louis-Lucien Bonaparte (24,162 votes), Mathieu (15,608 votes), and Thiard (13,961 votes). Presumably in response to the election results, Lamartine contributed an article on 'Le Socialisme' to *Le Courrier de Saône-et-Loire*. As before, he argued that socialism undermined civilisation's interdependent foundations, the family and private property.[77] He also again stressed the political differences between himself and Ledru-Rollin, stating in mid-June that they were as great as between liberty and tyranny, the Republic and anarchy.[78]

Despite the narrowness of his defeat and the considerable improvement in his popularity, Lamartine was very unenthusiastic about standing again.[79] An opportunity for doing so nevertheless rapidly presented itself. On 20 May one of the parliamentary representatives for the Loiret, Jacques-François Roger, died of cholera. *Le Journal du Loiret*, a local moderate republican newspaper which had backed Louis Napoleon in the presidential election, at once suggested that Lamartine should be elected in Roger's place, and one of the newspaper's contributors, Louis de Cormenin, personally endorsed Lamartine's candidature.[80] Lamartine accepted his nomination and indicated he would almost certainly opt for the Loiret if simultaneously elected there and in another department.[81] He also sent an electoral manifesto, stressing his conservative hopes for the Second Republic.[82] This manifesto, dated 27 June, was read out on 1 July at a meeting of a local conservative electoral committee, the Comité général des opinions modérées, which decided to adopt his candidature.[83] Local newspaper support came from *Le Journal du Loiret* (moderate republican), *La Presse du Loiret* (Bonapartist), and, less enthusiastic, *L'Union Orléanaise* (legitimist), against opposition from the left-wing *Constitution* and *Loing* (which had favoured him in the presidential election to prevent Cavaignac and Ledru-Rollin from splitting the republican vote). According to *Le*

Journal du Loiret (5 July), Lamartine was a member of the moderate republican party, while his main rival, Madier de Montjau, belonged to the socialist party.

Another vacancy existed in Saône-et-Loire. Ledru-Rollin, having been returned in the May elections by five departments (Allier, Hérault, Saône-et-Loire, Seine and Var), was declared after a ballot to be a representative of the Var. Saône-et-Loire conservatives and moderate republicans, anxious to recover from their electoral defeats of 13 May, re-adopted Lamartine as their candidate — a natural choice since he remained the department's most famous public figure, his *Conseiller du peuple* was constantly attacking the extreme Left, and in the May elections he had attracted more votes in Saône-et-Loire than any other conservative or moderate republican candidate. All the local newspapers, except the left-wing *Patriote de Saône-et-Loire*, welcomed his re-adoption. Very ill during June and July, he seems to have taken no personal part in the election campaigns: he apparently stayed in Paris, declining an invitation to visit Orléans so as not to transform a simple act of civic duty into an attempt to solicit votes.[84] However, circumstances favoured conservative and moderate republican candidates such as Lamartine. On 13 June an unsuccessful left-wing insurrection occurred in Paris, which was followed by left-wing demonstrations in several provincial towns, including Courtenay and Montargis in the Loiret and Mâcon and Louhans in Saône-et-Loire. What *Le Journal de Saône-et-Loire* described as 'the baneful events of 13 June'[85] greatly discredited the Left, which also became the victim of a government-inspired wave of repression. The Loiret and Saône-et-Loire by-elections were held on 8 July. In comparatively low polls (many voters abstained because of a cholera epidemic) both departments elected Lamartine, the Loiret by 23,006 votes to 7,309 for Madier de Montjau, and Saône-et-Loire by 29,093 votes to 20,068 for Henry Joly. On 21 July Lamartine opted for the Loiret, explaining to his Saône-et-Loire electors that this was 'an obligatory act of gratitude towards other citizens'.[86]

As usual, these political concerns did not absorb all of Lamartine's time and energy: his output of publications — historical, literary and journalistic — was as great as ever, and he continued to dovetail his writings with his politics. In July 1849 he published in two volumes his *Histoire de la Révolution de 1848*. This work is a clear and deliberate distortion of events and misrepresentation of Lamartine's political role. His consistent aim is to mislead the reader so as to discredit the French Left and the Paris popular movement, and present himself as fundamentally a conservative who had effectively defended life, liberty and property. Thus, he glosses over his evolution towards the Left before February 1848 and qualified support for the reform banquet campaign; he is critical of his speech in Durand's restaurant on 19 February, when he insisted that the twelfth *arrondissement* banquet should be held; he argues that his rejection of the regency of the duchesse d'Orléans on 24 February saved France from chaos, socialism and civil war; and over the red flag episode and the *journées* of 16 April and 15 May he depicts himself as the representative of the forces of reason, law and order, courageously struggling against the furious onslaught of the extreme anarchists, utopian socialists, and republican terrorists. His sudden loss of popularity is not satisfactorily explained. He blames the resentment of the defeated monarchist party, the ingratitude of the working classes, and the threatening activities of the National Workshops. The Executive Commission's fall is attributed to the conspiracy of a small group within the Assembly, which allegedly exploited the situation arising from the events of 23 June. The popularity of the name of Napoleon is the only explanation given for the subsequent development throughout France of overwhelming support for Louis Napoleon.

At the beginning of 1850 Lamartine resurrected and revised his drama, *Toussaint Louverture*, which idealised and romanticised the black slave revolt in Haiti. The play, first performed in Paris on 6 April under the direction of Frédérick Lemaître, was not very successful.[87] Meanwhile, he continued to attend the Assembly, where he spoke against a measure to curb the freedom of newspaper editors (23 March), against the use of deportation as a political punishment (19 and 22 April), and against the introduction of a three-year residence requirement for parliamentary electors (10 and 23 May). On 9 April, in a debate on the construction of a railway between Paris and Avignon, he argued that the State should provide part of the capital, but that the railway should not be wholly State-owned; and he listed the provision of employment among the advantages of constructing the railway. On these topics his interests and attitudes had not changed, though on railways he may have been influenced by discussions with the railway financier, Isaac Péreire.[88]

In June 1850 Lamartine published a popular novel, *Geneviève, histoire d'une servante*, which *Le Conseiller du peuple* began to serialise in July. He described the book as a 'series of tales and dialogues for town and country folk'.[89] The era of popular literature was approaching. Whereas in the past writers had attempted to please royal courts and aristocracies, now they should direct their efforts towards the masses, whose appreciation of beauty and morality could be improved through reading and instruction. Suitable literature for ordinary working class people was not being produced. There was a need for inexpensive books, written about working class people, with plots that were simple and true to life. Freedom of the press, freedom of discussion, industrial expansion, and the spread of primary education had created in France among a considerable portion of the people a demand for suitable reading material. Lamartine declared that he was going to meet this demand, which, he claimed, had been largely ignored; and he repeated his belief that the creation of a cheap, daily, popular newspaper would in ten years produce a revolution in the ideas, morality and well-being of the masses, while the editor of such a newspaper would become in effect the minister of public opinion.[90] These are all well-worn Lamartine themes, though the novel was for him a new literary form. The work of popular social novelists such as George Sand and Eugène Sue doubtless inspired him, but he failed completely to emulate their success – his workers were too obviously idealised portraits, his preaching of Christian moral virtues was too crude, and his settings were too far removed from the factories and urban squalor which increasingly featured in French working class life.

On 10 June the Lamartines left Paris for Monceau, where on 15 June the baron de Chamborant joined them.[91] Two days later they all left for Marseilles and for a new journey to the Eastern Mediterranean. Lamartine was still desperately short of funds with which to pay his creditors, and *Le Conseiller du peuple* was not proving to be the financial success he had originally predicted.[92] He therefore decided to solve his problems by establishing an agricultural community in Asia Minor – an old idea, which he had first mooted in January 1819 and which he had revived in January 1833.[93] By the spring of 1849 Lamartine was critically in need of a new source of income, bitterly disappointed with the results of the presidential election (to the extent of wanting to leave France for Asia Minor and there vegetate and die in voluntary exile), and full of hope that the Turkish government would be grateful for his friendly attitude while Minister of Foreign Affairs. On 24 April 1849 he wrote to the Sultan of Turkey requesting the grant of a concession of land.[94] After receiving a favourable reply he sent Charles Rolland to Constantinople, where Rolland negotiated the lease of four farms near Smyrna. A shortage of money prevented Lamartine from inspecting his new domain, but private loans eventually removed this obstacle.[95]

The Lamartines arrived in Marseilles on 20 June and (to Lamartine's delight) were given a spontaneous demonstration of welcome outside their hotel window.[96] The next day they left Marseilles, accompanied by the baron de Chamborant and François de Champeaux, and sailed via Malta to Constantinople, which they reached on 1 July. Lamartine thanked the Sultan in person[97] and then proceeded by sea to Smyrna. Having inspected his concession, which filled him with enthusiasm,[98] he left Smyrna on 30 July. The journey home was a sad affair, with Marianne falling seriously ill and Champeaux dying at sea off Malta. The Lamartines reached Marseilles on 6 August and Monceau later in the month, enjoying, according to Lamartine, a favourable reception throughout their journey home through France.[99] On arrival at Monceau the *conseil général* re-elected Lamartine chairman, and he tried without success to raise capital for the development of his concession in Asia Minor. As the *conseil général*'s chairman, on 4 September (much to the prefect's satisfaction) he paid his respects to General Castellane, who was on an official visit to the department. Castellane noted that Lamartine had altered and aged, and had been less hostile to the government in the *conseil général*.[100] The following day Lamartine left for London. Staying with relations of Marianne's, he refused a City banquet at Covent Garden, but gave five separate public speeches. His visit's purpose, however, was not achieved. No advances of capital were forthcoming, which led him to complain that everyone was out fox-hunting. Unable to raise any money, he finally agreed to exchange his concession of land for an annual payment of 80,000 piastres, thereby achieving some gain from this costly adventure.[101]

Lamartine returned to Monceau on 22 September. In October the Lamartines as usual entertained numerous visitors at Monceau and Saint-Point. Mme de Cessiat and two of her daughters, Alix and Valentine, came regularly from Collonges near Mâcon, and there was the customary gathering of faithful friends.[102] During November and December Lamartine, helped by Charles Alexandre, concentrated on his writings. He rose at five and went to bed at nine, saw nobody, and with feverish industry tackled a formidable programme of literary production.[103] Between 30 July and 6 September 1850 *La Presse* had serialised *Les Nouvelles Confidences*, a continuation of his romanticized autobiography till the time of his marriage.[104] During the autumn of 1850 he wrote *Le Tailleur de Pierres de Saint-Point* and began *Le Nouveau Voyage en Orient* (an account of his second journey to the Middle East) and a *Histoire de la Restauration. Le Tailleur de Pierres de Saint-Point* (published on 3 May 1851) was, like *Geneviève*, an attempt to produce a simple educational novel with a popular appeal, much of the book taking the form of a dialogue. The novel preached Christian resignation before the will of Providence, an attitude Lamartine evidently wanted to inculcate among the working classes. As in his other works of this nature, he ignored the increasingly important urban working class, the novel's hero being a country stonemason.

On the same lines, though more ambitious, were *Les Foyers du peuple*. With Millaud and Mirès providing the financial backing,[105] they appeared in twelve monthly issues throughout 1851. Besides a variety of literary and historical material, Lamartine published in *Les Foyers du peuple* three long political articles. In the first, dated 27 January 1851, he suggested that the Republic was in danger from a coalition of royalists and dissatisfied republicans. Whereas after the February Revolution he had proclaimed the word 'Confiance', now he proclaimed the words 'Défiance' and 'Conspiration'.[106] At last he was beginning to consider that not just the extreme Left, but also the Right, threatened the Republic, though he continued to give Louis Napoleon the benefit of the doubt. In his second article he argued that republicans should co-operate with Louis Napoleon, who might become the Washington of France, and he condemned the obstructive opposition associated with *Le National*.[107] The third article discussed the proposed revision of the Constitution so as to permit Louis Napoleon's re-election as President of the Republic. Lamartine did not oppose this, provided the electoral law of 31 May 1850 introducing a three-year residence qualification were repealed and manhood suffrage restored.[108]

At the beginning of 1851 the Lamartines had moved to Paris, where they quickly settled down to a laborious and monotonous routine. Lamartine began working before dawn in order to complete his daily quota of thirty pages. He was joined at eight in the morning by Charles Alexandre, who drafted the replies to his correspondence. Practically every day he went for a walk in the Bois de Boulogne. He occasionally attended the Assembly debates, speaking for the last time on 15 March. The Lamartines left 82 rue de l'Université for Castel-Madrid during May, at both addresses continuing to see a fairly wide circle of old friends and new acquaintances.[109] Back in Mâcon, on 31 August, Lamartine persuaded Saône-et-Loire's *conseil général* (which had for the fourteenth time voted him chairman) to reject a motion in favour of revising the constitution to permit the President's re-election. The small majority (23 to 21) voting with Lamartine made Saône-et-Loire one of only four departments to oppose constitutional revision. During September he retired as usual to Saint-Point, where he received his old friends, Dargaud and Louis de Ronchaud. At the end of October a severe and prolonged illness laid him low until after Louis Napoleon's *coup d'état*.[110]

During 1851, in addition to *Les Foyers du peuple*, Lamartine was offered, and accepted, the editorship of a newspaper called *Le Pays*.[111] As his assistant editor Lamartine chose Arthur de La Guéronnière, who had previously edited *Le Bien public* of Paris and subsequently collaborated with Emile de Girardin on *La Presse*.[112] The first issue of *Le Pays* under Lamartine's direction appeared on 9 April 1851. To Valentine de Cessiat Lamartine wrote on 11 April: 'I am conducting a desperate campaign for a moderate Republic against the insane attacks of the monarchists and the socialists.'[113] In his editorial articles he at first told his readers to observe the law and support the civil authorities. However, as the year advanced he became openly critical of Louis Napoleon's readiness to restrict manhood suffrage; he suggested that the President should not stand for re-election; he opposed any total revision of the Constitution; and he wanted the repeal of the law of 31 May 1850.[114] Clearly he now feared that Louis Napoleon's policies threatened the Republic's survival, though he believed that the Bonapartist threat could be successfully checked without resorting to any unconstitutional action, since he retained his faith in democracy and the Republic.[115] Not sharing Lamartine's increasingly hostile attitude towards the President, Arthur de La Guéronnière wrote a study of Louis Napoleon in four parts which appeared in *Le Pays* during September 1851.[116] Lamartine at once complained from Saint-Point that the articles were much too favourable to Louis Napoleon. The following month he told La Guéronnière not to publish a biographical study of the royalist pretender, the comte de Chambord, and angrily complained to Rolland about his own lack of editorial control, but his instructions were partially ignored.[117] La Guéronnière finally proceeded to have an interview with Louis Napoleon on 5 November, when he agreed to support the President and his government.[118]

Towards the end of October 1851 Lamartine planned to leave Mâcon for Paris, but fell violently ill with rheumatism. From his sickbed he sent an article to *Le Pays* expressing his fears for the future, fears based partly on 'the apparent ambition of the President of the Republic, who threatened to undermine the constitution by imposing arbitrary rule or by organising a *coup d'état*, should the constitution not be revised in his favour'.[119] In a second article Lamartine stated that men of goodwill wanted the immediate re-establishment of manhood

suffrage, though they might approve of the constitution's revision so as
to allow the President to be elected for a second term of office. He did
not suggest how a Bonapartist *coup d'état* might be avoided, and,
contrasting with his opposition to the July Monarchy but consistent
with his conservatism since the June Days, he made no appeals to
France's revolutionary tradition. Instead, his last article in *Le Pays*
simply ended with the words, 'Our instincts will save us!!! Long live
the Republic!'[120]

The news of Louis Napoleon's *coup d'état* of 2 December 1851
provoked a furious outburst from Lamartine; and he at once resigned
from the direction of *Le Pays*, explaining he wished to preserve his
reputation as a man of 24 February.[121] On 6 December he drew up a
declaration to his electors in the Loiret, condemning the *coup d'état*
and advising them to establish around the new government 'a cordon
sanitaire of abstention and passive resistance', but the declaration was
never published.[122] The *coup d'état* provoked widespread resistance,
including a protest march on Mâcon and disturbances in the Saône-
et-Loire communes of Cluny, Saint-Gengoux and Tournus, which
doubtless renewed his fears of popular violence; and within a year he
was to write that, although totally opposed to 2 December and its
consequences, he disliked Louis Napoleon much less than his uncle.
'I look the other way', he confessed, 'and I work to earn my bread
and to pay my creditors'.[123] Lamartine's political career was finished –
he ceased to be a member of parliament or of the *conseil général*.[124]
Significantly, his successor as Saône-et-Loire's most important deputy
and chairman of the *conseil général* was Joseph-Eugène Schneider,
director of the Creusot iron works, an example of how the traditional
local dominance of aristocratic landowners was challenged by a new
wealthy class of bankers, merchants and industrialists during the
Second Empire.

In mid-January 1852 Lamartine came to Paris to reorganise his
literary and financial affairs. He still had six volumes of the *Histoire
de la Restauration* to write, but he had resigned from *Le Pays* and
Les Foyers du peuple had ceased to appear. He therefore decided to
found a new monthly periodical called *Le Civilisateur*, costing a modest
fifty centimes, 'for the instruction of the masses in history and morality'.[125] In format, price and aim *Le Civilisateur* was comparable to *Le
Conseiller du peuple* and *Les Foyers du peuple*, reflecting Lamartine's
almost obsessive preoccupation with popular education and popular
approval. However, *Le Civilisateur* was concerned with history, not
politics or literature. Convinced of history's moral value and of the

attraction of studying history through the lives of famous people, he presented a series of biographical studies designed to be both instructive and interesting. His subjects were quite varied, including Socrates, Joan of Arc, Cromwell and Nelson. Lamartine was always careful to single out personal virtues for praise, and to suggest similarities between himself and his subjects. *Le Civilisateur* first appeared on 20 March 1852, and it continued to be published (with the editorial help of Frédéric-Chrétien Schiffer and Guillaume-Marie Lejean) until the end of 1854. Not a success, the periodical ceased publication on the advice of Lamartine's financial advisers, Millaud and Mirès.

Between 1851 and 1853 Lamartine published an eight-volume *Histoire de la Restauration*. In writing his third major historical work Lamartine's aim was partly to discredit Napoleon's political record and legacy, reflecting how Louis Napoleon's destruction of the Second Republic had confirmed his fears and dislike of Bonapartism. Also, as he approached old age, the Restoration period apparently acquired a nostalgic attraction for him; and, while consistently critical of Charles X's attempts to undermine the Charter, and consistently willing to accept the Revolution of 1830, he had always praised the Bourbon monarchy for having established personal liberty and intellectual freedom after Napoleon's dictatorship.[126]

Since Napoleon never returned to France after 1815, he can hardly provide the main theme or major figure for a history of the Restoration. It almost seems, however, as if that were Lamartine's intention. Three volumes are dominated by the Emperor, and other volumes describe his departure from France, life in exile, and death on St Helena. In Lamartine's other histories, a generous allocation of space indicates his sympathy or admiration, but this does not apply to Napoleon's prominence in the *Histoire de la Restauration*. To Lamartine, Napoleon's rule was a terrible disaster for France, Europe and the revolutionary movement. Napoleon was 'the deceiver of the counter-revolution'.[127] The *coup d'état* of 18 *brumaire* – 'this anti-national and anti-revolutionary crime'[128] – flagrantly disregarded the principle of popular sovereignty. Having gained power, instead of establishing the equality of rights, Napoleon created a military nobility; instead of permitting freedom of expression, he maintained a strict censorship and press monopoly; and instead of allowing free discussions, he stifled all criticism and debate. Napoleon could have played a magnificent role in history – that of the Charlemagne of the early nineteenth century. However, he chose to sacrifice ideas, principles, armies and even France herself to his own egotistical ambitions for political power, military glory and immortal fame. More specifically, Lamartine regards the duc d'Enghien's execution as a violation of civilised behaviour and breach of international law. He is contemptuous of Napoleon's reluctance to risk his life during the battle of Waterloo and decision to abandon his army to its fate, as he had done on so many previous campaigns. The whole Hundred Days episode is viewed as an example of Napoleon's callous indifference to France's real interests. Napoleon performed a further disservice to France by bequeathing to her a disastrous political legacy — 'the fanaticism of absolute power allied to the fanaticism of popular radicalism' — which together undermined any form of democratic republic or constitutional monarchy.[129]

In contrast to Lamartine's harsh judgments of Napoleon, his portrait of Louis XVIII is certainly flattering. He claims that Louis XVIII was so popular with the people of Paris that, if given the opportunity, they would have prevented him from leaving the capital in March 1815, and that they turned out in their thousands to welcome him on his return. It is suggested that throughout his years of exile and difficult reign, Louix XVIII always maintained his personal dignity and acted with wisdom and moderation. Lamartine compares him with Henri IV, and places him among the wisest and most intelligent of France's kings. If he had lived another ten years, he would have given to the Restoration not just one reign, but a series of reigns. The cause of the Bourbon monarchy was lost by Charles X. He was too zealous a Catholic, too inexperienced in his judgments of men, too cut off from the mass of his subjects to make an effective ruler. Above all, Charles X failed to realise that the Charter was 'the true spirit of the Restoration'.[130] By attempting to re-establish an absolute monarchy in France, Charles X and Polignac made the Revolution of 1830 inevitable. The Four Ordinances of 25 July 1830 were 'the proclamation of two authorities, the Church and the monarchy, declaring themselves to be in complete and open revolt against the spirit of the age'.[131] The French people reacted immediately and unanimously. The Revolution of 1830 was not a sedition like that of 10 August 1792, but a spontaneous act on the part of all classes and involving the whole of Paris.

As soon as he had finished the *Histoire de la Restauration* Lamartine started a *Histoire des Constituants*, which *Le Siècle* began to serialise in June 1853 and which was finally published in four volumes in 1855. The *Histoire des Constituants* is a companion work to the *Histoire des Girondins* and narrates the history of the French Revolution from the opening of the Estates General in May 1789 to Mirabeau's death and funeral in April 1791. The political interest of the *Histoire des*

Constituants lies in Lamartine's more conservative interpretation of the Revolution. Whereas the outstanding figure in the *Histoire des Girondins* is the radical Robespierre, in the *Histoire des Constituants* it is Mirabeau. If Mirabeau had not become the paid informer of the Court, he could, according to Lamartine, have been a great leader and a mediator between Louis XVI and the people. In general, Lamartine develops what might be described as a moderate republican interpretation of the Revolution. 14 July 1789 is presented as the great revolutionary day, when the same revolutionary fervour united the entire French nation. However, Lamartine claims that after July 1789 the revolutionary movement ceased to be the unanimous and spontaneous expression of the popular will and became instead the product of conspiracy and sedition, as the movement's direction passed from the *philosophes* to the leaders of the factions. The Constituent Assembly is also held partially responsible for the Revolution's misfortunes. Lamartine praises many of the Assembly's achievements, particularly the transference of sovereignty from the King to the people, the abolition of the aristocracy's special rights and privileges, the restoration of Church property to the State, the reorganisation of the judicial and administrative systems, the establishment of the freedom of the press, speech and opinion, and the opening of careers to the talents. However, he claims that the Assembly made three disastrous mistakes – the drawing up of the Declaration of the Rights of Man, the preservation of the monarchy, and the creation of an established State Church.

Despite the financial return from these publications, Lamartine's debts were now the dominating factor in his daily life, partly because *Le Pays* had made a loss. He still owed money to a number of long-suffering friends, including Guichard de Bienassis, and he was forced to borrow 700,000 francs from the Crédit foncier.[132] In May 1853 Lamartine wrote that his total debts amounted to a million francs,[133] yet his financial habits remained largely unchanged. He bought expensive presents for members of his family;[134] he still maintained nine horses and a seigneurial life-style at Monceau;[135] he helped with the education of various children;[136] he continued to lend money to friends such as Dargaud and Léon Bruys d'Ouilly;[137] and his passion for increasing the size of his estates by making new purchases had not abated.[138] In addition, the vines of Monceau and Saint-Point suffered from attacks of frost and other natural disasters, and many of Lamartine's literary products were not a success. In the middle of March 1853 the Lamartines felt obliged to make one economy. They came to Paris and moved out of their apartment at 82 rue de l'Université, first to temporary lodgings and then at the end of April to a house at 31 (shortly afterwards re-numbered 43) rue de la Ville-l'Evêque, quite near the Madeleine and the Elysée Palace.

This abandonment of their beautiful residence in the Faubourg Saint-Germain for an obscure house in a less fashionable district of Paris dramatically emphasised the sharp decline in the Lamartines' material fortunes. Lamartine's friends attempted to give what support they could by forming in April 1853 a company which bought from Lamartine the sole right to publish his works after 1863 (changed in 1860 to after 1 January 1869, or Lamartine's death, whichever should be the sooner).[139] Alfred Dumesnil became the director of the company and first Emile de Girardin and then Emile Ollivier its president.[140] Meanwhile, Lamartine continued to write and to publish. In November 1853 he brought out *Les Visions*, fragments of a great epic poem mostly written in 1821. In addition, he contributed articles to *Le Civilisateur* and composed an eight-volume *Histoire de la Turquie*, published between September 1854 and August 1855, and followed at the end of 1855 by a shorter *Histoire de la Russie*, neither of which is of significant political interest.

The Lamartines maintained their annual routine of spending the first six months of the year in Paris and the latter six months of the year in the Mâconnais. At Monceau and Saint-Point they regularly entertained a small number of old friends,[141] but for Paris society they had almost become social outcasts. Although they still received many visitors in Paris, and were occasionally sought out by distinguished Englishmen such as Charles Dickens and Nassau William Senior, society figures no longer frequented Marianne's Paris *salon* – their place had been taken by obscure, bearded political refugees.[142] When Mme Dosne, the mother-in-law of Adolphe Thiers, was taking the waters of Vichy at the same time as the Lamartines in July 1855, she carefully avoided 'these Girondins'.[143] Lamartine's French Academy colleagues also avoided him, since he had become a source of embarrassment;[144] and he was treated with humiliating disdain by his creditor, Jules-Isaac Mirès, and by Emile de Girardin's second wife.[145]

At the beginning of 1856 some fresh financial disaster, or series of disasters, overtook Lamartine, losing him a very large sum of money.[146] In desperation he produced his 'last arrow',[147] *Le Cours familier de littérature*. Like *Le Conseiller du peuple*, *Les Foyers du peuple* and *Le Civilisateur*, this was another monthly periodical which was cheap (the annual subscription cost twenty francs), popular in appeal, and produced almost entirely by Lamartine, who also supervised subscriptions and distribution.[148] As before, he was trying to inculcate morality among the masses through presenting a personal and popular interpretation of literature and of the lives of eminent people. The preface to each number, or 'entretien', informed the reader he was embarking on 'a course of taste and discernment', written in a familiar conversational style, which Lamartine hoped would appeal to people's interest, imagination and emotions.[149] Apart from a few autobiographical articles, and discussions of Indian and Chinese literature and philosophy, the subject-matter was invariably a study of the life, thought and writings of a single individual, with a special emphasis on whatever Lamartine considered to be edifying. A catholic mixture of individuals was chosen — mostly prophets, poets, philosophers and writers drawn from the Bible, Classical Greece and Rome, the Italian Renaissance, seventeenth century French literature, and from Lamartine's own acquaintance. The studies were based on hurried and superficial research,[150] and usually include long and frequent quotations. An article on Rousseau illustrates Lamartine's political conservatism since the June Days. Rousseau is criticised for maintaining in *Du Contrat social* that Man is born free, whereas according to Lamartine Man achieves relative freedom only through living in society.[151] Another article reveals Lamartine's prejudice against the United States: he condemns Louis XVI's support for the American colonists in their war of independence, opposes American expansion into Latin America and Mexico, and doubts if a country can have a literature when it allegedly lacks spiritual life, philosophy, history, poetry, and national education. Washington Irving and James Fenimore Cooper are dismissed as being of English and Scottish origin, while credit for Audubon is claimed for France.[152] This prejudice against the United States was probably due to the American government's attitude towards the American debt owed by France, the existence of slavery in the United States, the supposed materialism of American society, and to the American public's reluctance to subscribe to *Le Cours familier de littérature*.

On 9 March 1856 Lamartine's friend, Jean-Baptiste Desplace, left for New York with 20,000 francs on a mission to publicise *Le Cours familier de littérature* in the United States.[153] The trip was a complete failure — Desplace managed to secure only twenty-eight subscriptions and the operation cost Lamartine 40,000 francs.[154] Despite this setback he continued to struggle with his 'forced labours'. Besides *Le Cours familier de littérature*, he produced a two-volume *Vie d'Alexandre le Grand*, of which he wrote five hundred pages in October 1857.[155] He also sent out handwritten letters to all the subscribers of *Le Cours familier de littérature*, his 'family of friends', asking them to renew their subscriptions for the forthcoming year.[156] Despite this expenditure of effort, the proceeds from the subscriptions were insufficient to pay off his debts. In January 1858 he had to raise a million francs in thirteen months.[157] His printer, Ambroise Firmin-Didot, refused on 9 February 1858 to give him any more credit, and the publication of *Le Cours familier de littérature* was suspended for a few months. Again, friends tried to rescue Lamartine. They formed a committee including Chamborre, Dubois, Foillard and Rolland, which suggested a lottery with Monceau and Saint-Point as the prizes.[158] Lotteries were forbidden in France at this time except those benefiting charities, so Lamartine asked the baron de Chamborant if he would approach Morny, President of the Corps législatif, to discover if the Emperor would make an exception. When this was declined, Charles Alexandre proposed instead the holding of a national subscription.[159]

On 19 March 1858 a meeting in Mâcon chaired by Auguste Chamborre endorsed Alexandre's idea of a national subscription for Lamartine and sent a deputation to Paris. Received by the Minister of the Interior on 26 March, the deputation learnt the following day that the government had authorised the subscription and that the Emperor had agreed to make a contribution.[160] A general committee for the Lamartine subscription was constituted in Paris, with Alexis Vavin as chairman, Louis Ulbach as secretary, and an impressive list of friends, literary figures and newspaper editors as members.[161] Donations came from a wide variety of individuals and institutions – Mme Dupont de l'Eure, Franz Liszt, Fialin de Persigny, the comte Jouenne d'Esgrigny, Dargaud, Mlle C. de Parseval, Félix Guillemardet, Pierre de Lacretelle, Dr Ordinaire, Ambroise Firmin-Didot, Alphonse Saclier, Mme Guichard de Bienassis, the Delahantes, Hondschoote's *conseil municipal*, the Imperial Academy of Rheims, and various masonic lodges.[162] A London committee to promote the Lamartine subscription in Britain included such distinguished public and literary figures as Lord John Russell, Sidney Herbert, Edward Ellice, Sir Robert Peel, Sir Edward Bulwer-Lytton, R. Monckton Milnes, Charles Dickens, and W. M. Thackeray. The amount of money raised by this committee remains unclear, though Lord Normanby sent a thousand francs from Florence.[163]

Generally the Lamartine subscription had a very disappointing response. Although the Emperor publicly gave his support, which alienated many republicans, the Ministry of the Interior circulated all prefects reminding them that very strict legislation covered lotteries.[164] Consequently, nearly all the *conseils municipaux* and *conseils généraux* refused to contribute, including (much to Lamartine's disgust) Saône-et-Loire's *conseil général*.[165] In June 1859 a public subscription was opened for the families of soldiers killed or wounded in the Italian campaign. This doubtless adversely affected the Lamartine subscription, and prompted Lamartine to ask at least the Beauvais committee to suspend collecting money for him.[166] Also, the Lamartine subscription encountered much hostility. Victor de Laprade reported from Lyons that people threatened him with violence when he mentioned the name of Lamartine.[167] In Strasbourg Lamartine was not forgiven for his part in proclaiming the Republic in February 1848, or for his alliance with Ledru-Rollin in the Executive Commission.[168] The Bishop of Belley, where Lamartine had been educated, indignantly refused a request for a contribution, declaring that, if the Faith could disappear from 'our dear and Catholic France', Lamartine's responsibility would be greater than that of any other individual.[169] There was a reluctance to subscribe even in the Mâconnais, because Lamartine would not sell his *châteaux* or estates, because he had failed to thank the Emperor for his donation, and because it was thought that any money raised would go to Paris bankers rather than to settling small debts owed to local creditors.[170] Potential British subscribers were discouraged by *The Saturday Review*, which blamed the *Histoire des Girondins* for having caused the Revolution of 1848 and advised its readers to give nothing.[171] 'This subscription will be called the subscription of insult', Lamartine wrote on 25 April 1859; and on 4 May he instructed Alexis Vavin to dissolve the central committee.[172]

Lamartine estimated on 19 February 1859 that his debts amounted to 1,900,000 francs. Since Monceau, Milly and Saint-Point were all heavily mortgaged, and the national subscription had produced only about 160,000 francs, the state of Lamartine's affairs was obviously hopeless.[173] In March 1859 the Emperor offered him, through La Guéronnière, a national donation of 100,000 francs a year or a single payment of two million francs.[174] Determined, as always, to preserve his independence from the government, and especially from a government headed by Napoleon's nephew and heir, Lamartine refused the offer. However, he did not feel any compunction about writing to the *conseil municipal* of Paris on 16 March 1859 with a request for a free concession of land near the Bois de Boulogne on which he could build a house. The *conseil municipal* wisely decided to grant him a house that had already been built called La Petite Muette, at 135 avenue de l'Empereur (now 107-113 avenue Henri-Martin). After the objections of the Conseil d'Etat had been overcome, the Lamartines were duly provided with a rent-free house which served as their Paris retreat from the noise, bustle and literary activity of the rue de la Ville-l'Evêque.[175] The house was a great boon, but did not bring in any money. In December 1859 Lamartine vainly hoped that Napoleon III would buy Monceau for over a million francs as a retirement home for men of letters.[176] Disappointed yet again, he decided to produce a new and complete edition of his collected works (except, presumably for copyright reasons, the *Histoire des Constituants*). This task was undertaken in addition to the composition of monthly articles for *Le Cours familier de littérature*, which continued to be published until after his death. Included in the new edition of his collected works were *Saül* (the tragedy rejected by the Comédie Française in 1818) and the *Mémoires politiques*, both of which had never previously been published. Heralded by much expensive publicity in the Paris press, the first volume appeared on 14 July 1860, and the publication of the forty-one volume edition was completed in 1866. Lamartine also wrote a *Vie de Byron* which *Le Constitutionnel* serialised.[177]

The earnings from these publications were not sufficient to liquidate Lamartine's debts, so with great reluctance he finally parted with some of his properties. On 18 December 1860 he sold Milly to a M. Mazoyer of Cluny for 500,000 francs, and in 1861 the Hôtel Lamartine in Mâcon to his sister Cécile de Cessiat. At the same time drastic domestic economies were introduced. The number of servants was reduced to three, and paintings and rare books disposed of. Only one candle was lit in the candelabra at the rue de la Ville-l'Evêque, while Lamartine's personal appearance became so shabby as to embarrass his friends.[178] Despite all these sacrifices and economies, the extent of his indebtedness and the demands of his creditors tormented Lamartine until he died.

Work remained a great consolation for Lamartine; and, despite his misfortunes, he sustained a remarkable volume of literary production almost to his death. In January 1857 he defended Flaubert's *Madame Bovary* in a letter read out at the novel's trial.[179] Occasionally obscure writers sent him complimentary copies of their books, thereby invariably securing a gracefully written letter of thanks.[180] Otherwise current literary developments did not apparently concern him. In France's politics and foreign policy he maintained a desultory interest. He thought France had fought the Crimean War 'very wisely and very heroically';[181] and, though critical of the French invasion of Italy in 1859, he described Napoleon III's Mexican policies as 'admirable'.[182] On France's political future, he regarded the comte de Chambord's restoration as probable and desirable.[183] However, he does not really seem to have cared. 'As for politics', he wrote to Dubois on 16 March 1863, 'like most of the country, I don't care. I think of myself and of those who depend on me'.[184]

Lamartine's other great consolation in these years of adversity were his family and his old friends. He still received a considerable number of visitors in Paris; and he corresponded with, among others, Boussin, Chamborant, Dargaud, Dubois, Girardin, Texier, and Valette. In the autumn his sisters, accompanied by their children and grandchildren, regularly gathered at Monceau or Saint-Point. Marianne also occasionally entertained her relations, such as her cousin George Birch. Besides Marianne, the most important figure in Lamartine's old age was undoubtedly his niece, Valentine de Cessiat. Ever since she had accompanied him to Italy in 1844, Valentine had enjoyed a particularly close and affectionate relationship with her uncle. In 1855 she joined the Lamartines' household: thereafter she lived with them practically all the year round, acting as nurse and secretary. She became her uncle's tender and devoted guardian, 'the angel of the house',[185] and perhaps the main reason why Lamartine continued the unequal struggle of living.

These social and family relations were a source of sorrow as well as of happiness to Lamartine, since death was always striking down those whom he had known or loved. Delphine de Girardin died in June 1855, Guichard de Bienassis in May 1857, Dr Pascal in November 1860 (while looking after Marianne and Valentine), Dargaud in December 1865, and Léon Bruys d'Ouilly in January 1866. The toll on Lamartine's family was equally heavy, taking his brother-in-law Charles de Montherot (2 January 1862), his married sisters Cécile de Cessiat (7 October 1862) and Sophie de Ligonnès (11 August 1863), and finally his wife Marianne (21 May 1863). She died in the house in the rue de la Ville-l'Evêque, after a painful illness. Lamartine, confined to bed at the time by a violent rheumatic fever, could not comfort his wife during her last moments. Nor could he accompany Louis de Ronchaud and the comte d'Esgrigny, who escorted Marianne's coffin to Saint-Point.[186]

After Marianne's death Lamartine's life continued much as before. He spent half the year at Monceau and Saint-Point and the other half in Paris, though he gave up the lease on the house in the rue de la Ville-l'Evêque in April 1867. Valentine de Cessiat completely replaced Marianne. She became her uncle's constant companion, nursing him when he was ill, writing his letters and copying his articles, and generally looking after his affairs — she even changed her surname to that of Lamartine by an imperial decree of 31 August 1868. Her influence on Lamartine during his last years was considerable. In particular, she gradually persuaded her uncle to return to the fold of the Catholic Church, helped by a priest, Father Hyacinthe.[187] Despite Valentine's devoted ministrations, Lamartine seems to have become increasingly embittered as he grew older. He felt that he had been betrayed by the French bourgeoisie, whose coffers he thought he had saved in 1848, and who had deserted him in his hour of need; by the bankers of Paris, who refused to lend him money and who constituted 'a band of cutthroats for poor men of letters'; by the imperial government, which had first permitted and then forbidden a second lottery on Saint-Point; by the British authorities, who blocked the transfer of his wife's inheritance from London to France; and by the legitimists, for whom he claimed he had sacrificed his diplomatic career in 1830, rejected Louis-Philippe's offers of ministries and embassies, and defended the reigns of Louis XVIII and Charles X in the *Histoire de la Restauration*, but who would not contribute to the Lamartine subscription.[188] Notwithstanding two unexpected legacies, Lamartine now could never hope to repay his debts, which at his death amounted to 2,214,838 francs.[189] The Corps législatif eventually met his immediate financial needs. Mainly as a result of Emile Ollivier's efforts, a 'national compensation' of five per cent annual interest on a capital sum of 500,000 francs was voted to Lamartine on 15 April 1867, the capital being protected from his creditors.[190]

Those who visited Lamartine in his last years noticed that he was looking much older, that his appearance and surroundings had sadly deteriorated, that he made few contributions to the conversation, that a dull and monotonous routine imprisoned him, and that he seemed to be entirely preoccupied with his financial difficulties.[191] His health, never good, was now rapidly becoming worse. Illness regularly tortured him, and with particular severity during May 1867. Towards the end of his life he seems to have been overtaken by despair. To Dargaud he kept repeating, 'I want to die.'[192] One evening in Paris he reached the top of the staircase and refused to move. 'What is the use?' he asked. 'What is the use of going to bed, to begin again in the morning the cruel task? Leave me here!' Only Valentine's tears and supplications could calm him.[193] Another evening at Monceau he disappeared after dinner. Eventually he was discovered wandering across fields like a madman, and his return to the house required much difficult persuasion.[194] In December 1868 he left Monceau for the last time. At the station he refused to leave his carriage, and had to be lifted out by Charles Alexandre and led to his seat on the train.[195] Perhaps he had some premonition that his end was near. After a brief illness, Lamartine died in his Paris house at 135 avenue de l'Empereur during the evening of 28 February 1869, with Arthur de La Guéron-nière and the baron de Chamborant at his bedside.

Napoleon III offered to give Lamartine a state funeral, an offer Valentine declined in accordance with her uncle's wishes. Instead, on 3 March Lamartine's coffin was transported by train from Paris to Mâcon, and from there to Saint-Point, where he was buried beside his mother, his daughter and his wife. Among those present at the funeral were the baron de Chamborant, Charles Alexandre, Victor de Laprade, Alexandre Dumas, Emile Ollivier, Edmond Texier, Louis Ulbach, and representatives of the French Academy and the Republic of Haiti (the latter in recognition of Lamartine's role in the abolition of slavery).[196] In addition, as the parish *curé* noted in his register, 'An extraordinarily large crowd from the Mâconnais and the parishes round Saint-Point took part in the funeral of M. de Lamartine'.[197]

Notes

1. Circourt, *Souvenirs*, II, pp. 413-14; des Cognets, *La Vie intérieure de Lamartine*, p. 425; *Lettres de Madame Swetchine*, 2 vols. (Paris, 1862), I, pp. 392-3; Normanby, *A Year of Revolution*, II, pp. 107-8.
2. *Rapport de la Commission d'enquête*, I, pp. 305-6.
3. *La France parlementaire*, V, pp. 343-53.
4. See *La Presse*, 17 August 1848, p. 3, and *Le Spectateur républicain*, 18 August 1848, p. 2.
5. *Lettre aux dix départements* was first published as a 16-page pamphlet (Paris: Michel Lévy frères, 1848), and reprinted, together with various speeches and Lamartine's foreign policy manifesto of 2 March, in *Trois mois au pouvoir* (Paris: Michel Lévy frères, 1848).
6. *La France parlementaire*, V, pp. 416-27.
7. Normanby to Palmerston, 15 and 29 April 1848 (F. O., 27, 806, ff. 139 and 280); Barrot, *Mémoires posthumes*, II, p. 436.
8. *La France parlementaire*, V, pp. 446-70.
9. Falloux, *Mémoires*, I, pp. 380-1; Melun, *Mémoires*, I, p. 260; O. E. Ollivier, *L'Empire libéral. Etudes, récits, souvenirs*, 18 vols. (Paris, 1895-1918), II (1897), p. 100. The same is implied in Barrot, *Mémoires posthumes*, II, pp. 450-1. Cf. P. Bastid, *Doctrines et institutions politiques de la Seconde République*, 2 vols. (Paris, 1945), II, pp. 111-13; P. de La Gorce, *Histoire de la Seconde République*, 2 vols. (Paris, 1904), I, p. 453; Seignobos, *La Révolution de 1848*, p. 123.
10. Falloux, *Mémoires*, I, pp. 382-3.
11. See Normanby to Palmerston, 15 April 1848; F. O., 27, 806, f. 139.
12. See Alexandre, *Souvenirs sur Lamartine*, pp. 154-5; *Le Bien public*, 2

and 3 November 1848, p. 2; *La France parlementaire*, VI, pp. 1-5; M. Nicolle, 'A propos d'un discours prononcé en 1848 par Lamartine au château de Monceau', *Annales de l'Académie de Mâcon*, third series, XXXIII (1938), pp. 234-45.

13.   Alexandre, *Souvenirs sur Lamartine*, p. 159; Lacretelle, *Lamartine et ses amis*, pp. 144-54; *L'Union républicaine, journal de Mâcon*, 25 October 1848, p. 3; *La France parlementaire*, VI, pp. 27-30.

14.   See *Le Journal de Saône-et-Loire*, 21 November 1848, and *Annales de l'Académie de Mâcon*, third series, XXXIII (1938), pp. 238-42.

15.   *La France parlementaire*, VI, pp. 31-3.

16.   See Lamartine to Dargaud, 4 November 1848; *Correspondance*, VI (1875), p. 334. In general see A.-J. Tudesq, *L'Election présidentielle de Louis-Napoléon Bonaparte, 10 décembre 1848* (Paris, 1965).

17.   Lamartine to V. de Cessiat; *Lamartine et ses nièces*, p. 138.

18.   Lamartine to Circourt; *Correspondance*, VI (1875), p. 324.

19.   Lamartine to H. de Lacretelle, 14 October 1848; ibid., VI (1875), p. 330.

20.   Lamartine to Champvans; ibid., VI (1875), pp. 331-2.

21.   Lamartine to Dargaud, 4 November 1848 (ibid., VI (1875), pp. 334-5); Vier, *La Comtesse d'Agoult et François Ponsard*, p. 45.

22.   *La France parlementaire*, VI, p. 19. Cf. Guillemin, *Lamartine. Lettres inédites*, pp. 94-5, and *Correspondance*, VI (1875), pp. 335, 338 and 345.

23.   *La France parlementaire*, VI, p. 19. Cf. *Le Bien public* (Paris), 4 December 1848.

24.   See *Le Courrier français* and *L'Evénement*, 1 December 1848, and *La Presse*, 2 December 1848, p. 2. Cf. *La France parlementaire*, VI, p. 34, and Lamartine to Champvans, 10 November 1848 (*Correspondance*, VI (1875), p. 340).

25.   *Le Journal des Débats*, 28 October 1848, p. 2, and *Le Loing*, 7 December 1848.

26.   Lamartine to La Grange, 4 November 1848; Luppé, *Lamartine*, p. 377.

27.   See Lamartine to Dubois, 9 November 1848; *Correspondance*, VI (1875), p. 337.

28.   Guillemin, *Lamartine. Lettres inédites*, p. 95.

29.   See *Le Courrier français*, 15 November and 8 December 1848.

30.   See *L'Ami du Peuple* (Hazebrouck, Nord), 9 December 1848. First issued on 22 April 1848, the paper appeared every Saturday under Emile Taverne's editorship.

31.   See *L'Eclaireur des Pyrénées* (Bayonne, Basses Pyrénées), 17 November – 10 December 1848.

32.   See *Le Loing* (Montargis, Loiret), 7 December 1848.

33.   See *La Tribune lyonnaise*, no. 20, December 1848. On this newspaper see C. Bellanger *et al.* (eds.), *Histoire générale de la presse française*, II (1969), p. 194.

34.   See *Le Conciliateur* (Limoges, Haute-Vienne), 22 November 1848, p. 2, and 4 and 7 December 1848. The paper was founded at the beginning of September 1848 as a successor to *L'Avenir national*. The editor was Arthur de La Guéronnière's brother, and one of the contributors was Eugène Pelletan.

35.   *Le Patriote jurassien* (Lons-le-Saunier, Jura), 6 December 1848.

36.   See *L'Union républicaine, journal de Mâcon*, 9 December 1848.

37.   Lamartine was unable to decide for which canton he should opt, but by a ballot it was determined that he should represent Mâcon Sud. See Lamartine to the mayor of Mâcon, 6 September 1848; *L'Union républicaine* (Mâcon), 13 September 1848, p. 3.

38.   See their files in A. N., F^{1b} I 157^{11} and F^{1b} I 157^{12}.

39. See his file in A. N., F¹ᵇ I 1721⁶.

40. Lacretelle, *Lamartine et ses amis*, pp. 148-55; Lamartine to Champvans, 27 October 1848 (*Correspondance*, VI (1875), pp. 331-2).

41. Mme de Lamartine to Mme de La Grange, 29 November 1848; Luppé, *Lamartine*, p. 378.

42. *Le Journal de Saône-et-Loire*, 5 December 1848, pp. 1-2. Cf. *Le Conciliateur*, 30 November 1848.

43. P. Goujon, *Le Vignoble de Saône-et-Loire au XIXᵉ siècle, 1815-1870* (Lyons, 1973), p. 316.

44. See Lamartine to V. de Cessiat, 11 December 1848; *Lamartine et ses nièces*, pp. 149-50.

45. See *Le Moniteur universel*, 22 December 1848, p. 3647. These figures are for metropolitan France. Including votes cast by the army and electors in Algeria, the results were Louis Napoleon Bonaparte 5,572,834, General Cavaignac 1,469,156, Ledru-Rollin, 376,843, Raspail 37,106, Lamartine 20,938 and General Changarnier 4,687.

46. Goujon, *Le Vignoble de Saône-et-Loire au XIXᵉ siècle*, p. 317.

47. See Lamartine to V. de Cessiat, 12 December 1848; *Lamartine et ses nièces*, p. 150. Cf. Lamartine to La Grange, 4 November 1848; Luppé, *Lamartine*, p. 377.

48. See *La Presse*, 23 December 1848.

49. Louis Napoleon to Chapuys-Montlaville, 23 August 1843; *Correspondance entre MM. L.-Napoléon Bonaparte, Lamartine et Chapuys-Montlaville*, pp. 16-21. The letter was first published in *La Patrie*.

50. J. M. Thompson, *Louis Napoleon and the Second Empire* (Oxford, 1965), p. 67; Louis Napoleon Bonaparte to Lamartine, 2 February 1846 (*Lettres à Lamartine*, p. 221).

51. Lamartine in the Chamber of Deputies, 26 May 1840; *La France parlementaire*, II, p. 352.

52. F. Letessier, 'Lamartine et le prince Pierre Bonaparte', *Annales de l'Académie de Mâcon*, third series, LIV (1977), pp. 39-59.

53. J. Hercé, *Un Anglais à Paris*, 2 vols. (Paris, 1893-94), II, p. 3; J. H. Harris, Earl of Malmesbury, *Memoirs of an Ex-Minister*, 2 vols. (London, 1884), I, p. 217. Cf. Lamartine, *Mémoires politiques* in *Oeuvres complètes*, XXXX, pp. 12-14, and A. Lebey, *Louis-Napoléon Bonaparte et la Révolution de 1848*, 2 vols. (Paris, 1907-08), I, pp. 173-6.

54. *Procès-Verbaux*, p. 369.

55. Normanby to Palmerston; Broadlands Mss., 12889, GC, NO, 231, f.1.

56. J. Vier, *La Comtesse d'Agoult et son temps*, 6 vols. (Paris, 1955-62), V (1961), p. 64.

57. W. Connely, *Count d'Orsay* (London, 1952), p. 485.

58. Toesca, *Lamartine*, p. 466; *Lamartine et ses nièces*, p. 155.

59. Lamartine, *Mémoires politiques* in *Oeuvres complètes*, XXXX, pp. 56-60; Ollivier, *L'Empire libéral*, II (1897), pp. 168-70; A Lebey, *Louis-Napoléon Bonaparte et le ministère Odilon Barrot. 1849* (Paris, 1912), pp. 4-9; Hugo, *Choses vues*, p. 376.

60. Luppé, *Lamartine*, p. 380; baron d'Ambes, *Mémoires inédits sur Napoléon III* (Paris, 1909-11), I, p. 272; H. Wikoff, *My Connection with the Foreign Office, and a Glimpse of the French Republic of '48* (London, 1856), pp. 26-8.

61. See. C. G. Bapst (ed.), *Le Maréchal Canrobert: souvenirs d'un siécle*, 6 vols. (Paris 1898-1913), I, pp. 499-500; *Bulletin de l'Association Guillaume Budé*, January-March 1970, p. 149; E. Discailles, *Un Diplomate belge à Paris de 1830 à 1864* (Brussels, 1908), p. 280; Senior, *Conversations*, I, p. 323; *Lamartine et ses nièces*, p. 186.

62.   A. N., 271 AP 5, C20-29.
63.   Canrobert, *Souvenirs d'un siècle*, I, p. 500; Ollivier, *L'Empire libéral*, II, p. 383; Barante, *Souvenirs*, VII, p. 556. Cf. M. C. M. Simpson, *Letters and Recollections of Julius and Mary Mohl* (London, 1887), p. 69.
64.   Alexandre, *Souvenirs sur Lamartine*, p. 163; J.-I. Mirès, *A Mes Juges: ma vie et mes affaires* Paris, 1861), p. 39. Cf. Lamartine, *Mémoires politiques* in *Oeuvres complètes*, XXXX, pp. 62-5.
65.   A. de Lamartine, *Le Conseiller du peuple*, 3 vols., Paris: administration 85 rue de Richelieu, 1849-51, I, p. 2.
66.   Ibid., I, pp. 16 and 150-2.
67.   R. Gossez, 'Presse Parisienne à destination des ouvriers, 1848-51', *La Presse Ouvrière 1819-1850*, Bibliothèque de la Révolution de 1848, XXIII (1966), p. 169, note 176.
68.   *La France parlementaire*, VI, pp. 41-62, 63-79, 80-2, 83-8.
69.   See *Procès des accusés du 15 mai* (Paris, 1849), and *M. de Lamartine à Bourges. Récit anecdotique* (Bourges, 1869).
70.   *Le Courrier de Saône-et-Loire* (Chalon-sur-Saône), 21 March 1849, p.3.
71.   *Le Journal de Saône-et-Loire*, 2 May 1849.
72.   After Lamartine, the list featured General Thiard, Claude-Louis Mathieu, Augustin Lacroix, Reverchon, Charles Dariot (a Saône-et-Loire representative in the Assembly since June 1848), and Foillard. See *Comité électoral de Mâcon* (Mâcon, 1849); B. N., Le.[70] 1133.
73.   See *Le Courrier de Saône-et-Loire* and *Le Journal de Saône-et-Loire*, 5-9 May 1849.
74.   See Léon Faucher Papers; A. N., 43 AP 1.
75.   See B. N., Fol. Le.[70] 1134.
76.   Goujon, *Le Vignoble de Saône-et-Loire au XIXᵉ siècle*, pp. 323-4.
77.   *Le Courrier de Saône-et-Loire*, 16 May 1849, pp. 1-2.
78.   F. Letessier, 'Lamartine et l'Angevin François Grille (1782-1853)', *Mercure de France*, 1 February 1953, p. 557.
79.   See Lamartine to Dariot, 29 June 1849; Guillemin, *Lamartine. Lettres inédites*, pp. 97-8.
80.   *Le Journal du Loiret* (Orléans), 22 and 24 May 1849.
81.   Ibid., 23, 30 June and 3 July 1849.
82.   He hoped that the Republic would be 'la base élargie de l'ordre, le fondement de la propriété et de la famille, le droit commun sans privilège de date de toutes les opinions qui l'acceptent, en un mot la conservation par la liberté et l'amélioration des droits à acquérir par le respect des droits acquis'; ibid., 3 July 1849, pp. 2-3.
83.   *La Presse du Loiret* (Orléans), 4 July 1849.
84.   Lamartine to the Comité général des opinions modérées, 2 July 1849; ibid., 4 July 1849.
85.   *Le Journal de Saône-et-Loire*, 14 July 1849.
86.   *Le Journal du Loiret*, 24 July 1849; *Le Journal de Saône-et-Loire*, 28 July 1849, p. 2. In simultaneous by-elections Lamartine's candidature was also put forward by left-wing republicans in the Charente-Inférieure (see *Le Glaneur* (Chartres), 1 July 1849), Eure-et-Loire (see *Le Journal de Saône-et-Loire*, 11 July 1849), and Jura (see *Le Patriote jurassien* (Lons-le-Saunier), 27 June – 8 July 1849, and *Franche-Comté et Monts Jura*, August 1926, pp. 144-5), and by moderate republicans in the Seine (see *Le Constitutionnel* (Paris), 27 June 1849) and Vosges (see *Le Patriote de la Meurthe et des Vosges* (Nancy), 1 July 1849, p. 2). Lamartine accepted these nominations, but he neither campaigned nor indicated whether, if elected, he would opt for any of these departments. Conse-

quently his candidature attracted few votes: Charente-Inférieure, 5,846; Eure-et-Loire, 2,837; Jura, 3,328; Seine, 41,661 (Lamartine came twenty-third); Vosges, 6,017. In the Saône-et-Loire by-election caused by his option for the Loiret, he publicly supported the moderate republican Charles Dariot against the left-wing Henry Joly, who defeated Dariot by 28,433 votes to 25,697 (see *Le Journal de Saône-et-Loire*, 15 August 1849).

87. See Biré, *Mes Souvenirs*, pp. 154-6, and *Souvenirs de Frédérick Lemaître* (Paris, 1880), pp. 296-303.

88. *Oeuvres de Emile et Isaac Péreire*, 4 vols. (Paris, 1912-20), IV (1913), p. 3827.

89. A. de Lamartine, *Geneviève, histoire d'une servante*, Paris: Michel Lévy frères, 1851, p. 1.

90. Ibid., pp. 43-68.

91. Chamborant, *Lamartine inconnu*, p. 26.

92. *Correspondance*, VI (1875), p. 383.

93. Ibid., II (1873), pp. 300-2; Lamartine to the baron de Lesseps, 6 January 1833 (unpublished letter, Academy of Mâcon).

94. See W. Sperco, *Lamartine et son domaine en Asie Mineure: lettres et documents inédits* (Paris, 1938), pp. 5-6.

95. J. Michoud, 'Une Correspondance inédite de Lamartine: le livre des familles', *Annales de l'Académie de Mâcon*, third series, XLII (1954-55), p. 21.

96. Lamartine to Dubois, June 1850 (Caplain, *Edouard Dubois*, p. 99), and *Mémoires politiques* in *Oeuvres complètes*, XXXX, p. 361. Cf. Chamborant, *Lamartine inconnu*, p. 28.

97. See *Le Pays*, 14, 22, 23 and 24 August 1851, p. 3.

98. See Lamartine to Dargaud, 16 July 1850; *Correspondance*, VI (1875), pp. 390-2.

99. See Lamartine to Dubois and Circourt, 25 August 1850; *Correspondance*, VI (1875), pp. 409 and 412.

100. Prefect of Saône-et-Loire to the Minister of the Interior, 5 September 1850 (A. N., F[1b] I 166[29]); Castellane, *Journal*, IV, pp. 275-6.

101. *Correspondance*, VI (1875), p. 148; Chamborant, *Lamartine inconnu*, pp. 95-101 and 113; Sperco, *Lamartine et son domaine en Asie Mineure*, pp. 19-21.

102. They included Charles Alexandre, François Aubel, Guichard de Bienassis, Hippolyte Boussin, Léon Bruys d'Ouilly, Auguste Chamborre, Jean-Marie Dargaud, Edouard Dubois, Henri de Lacretelle, Dr Pascal, Charles Rolland, and Louis de Ronchaud; Alexandre, *Souvenirs sur Lamartine*, pp. 241-7.

103. See Lamartine to ?, 14 November 1850 (B. N., nouv. acq. fr., 24839, f. 371), and to Rolland, 27 December 1850 (*Correspondance*, VI (1875), p. 424).

104. On Marianne's role as editor of *Les Nouvelles Confidences* see Alexandre, *Souvenirs sur Lamartine*, pp. 240-1. Part of *Les Nouvelles Confidences* was published separately in *Régina* (1862).

105. Caplain, *Edouard Dubois*, pp. 83 and 86.

106. *Les Foyers du peuple*, 2 vols., Paris: Michel Lévy frères, 1866, II, p. 87. Cf. *Le Conseiller du peuple*, III (1851), pp. 1-17.

107. *Les Foyers du peuple*, II, pp. 147-96.

108. Ibid., II, pp. 197-244.

109. See Alexandre, *Madame de Lamartine*, p. 168, and *Souvenirs sur Lamartine*, pp. 270-1.

110. *Correspondance*, VI (1875), p. 441.

111. See Alexandre, *Souvenirs sur Lamartine*, p. 264; Mirès, *A Mes Juges*, p. 43; Lamartine to A. de La Guéronnière, 8 April 1851 (*Le Pays*, 9 April 1851). *Le Pays* was a daily opposition newspaper founded on 1 January 1849.

112.   Arthur de La Guéronnière had first met Lamartine through Chamborant in 1843 (Chamborant, *Lamartine inconnu*, pp. 63-4) and, as editor of *L'Avenir National*, had backed Lamartine's unsuccessful parliamentary candidature at Limoges in August 1846 (A. Court, 'Une candidature "exotique" de Lamartine', *Travaux du CIEREC de Saint-Etienne*, VII (1974), pp. 39-58).

113.   *Lamartine et ses nièces*, p. 190.

114.   *Le Pays*, 20 April, pp. 1-2, 4 and 12 June, 19 August, and 3 September 1851.

115.   E.g. Lamartine to H. de Lacretelle, 6 September 1851: 'Je défie qu'on sauve la France corps et âme autrement que par la République' (*Correspondance*, VI (1875), p. 431).

116.   *Le Pays*, 8, 10, 12 and 16 September 1851. In 1853 the study was published in book form with the title *Portraits politiques contemporains*.

117.   *Le Pays*, 17 September, 9 October and 4 November 1851; Lamartine to Rolland, 20 October 1851 (*Correspondance*, VI (1875), pp. 438-9).

118.   *Mémoires du comte Horace de Viel-Castel sur le règne de Napoléon III, 1851-1864*, 6 vols. (Paris, 1883-4), I, pp. 209-10.

119.   *Le Pays*, 1 November 1851.

120.   Ibid., 23 and 30 November 1851.

121.   Lacretelle, *Lamartine et ses amis*, pp. 235-7; des Cognets, *La Vie intérieure de Lamartine*, pp. 429-30; *Le Pays*, 22 December 1851.

122.   Alexandre, *Souvenirs sur Lamartine*, p. 310. For the declaration's text see ibid., pp. 305-10.

123.   Lamartine to Mme Duport, 27 October 1852; C. Latreille, *Les Dernières années de Lamartine, 1852-1869* (Paris, 1925), p. 7.

124.   Against his will, Lamartine's candidature was put forward by his friends in various elections. On 29 February 1852 he was defeated in the parliamentary elections for Saône-et-Loire by the comte de Barbentane (21,913 votes to 1,796). He was again defeated by Barbentane on 1 August 1852 in the elections for Saône-et-Loire's *conseil général* in Mâcon Nord (1,455 to 168), and in Mâcon Sud by Ange-Henri Vitallis (1,048 to 431). Lamartine refused an offer of a parliamentary candidature at Le Puys during September 1852 (see F. Bassan, 'Lettres inédites de Lamartine et de sa femme (1835 à 1864)', *Revue des sciences humaines* (Lille), October-December 1969, p. 558). Subsequently, Lamartine was unsuccessful against Vitallis in Mâcon Sud in the *conseil général* elections of 3 June 1855 (1,022 to 76), and against Barbentane in the Saône-et-Loire parliamentary elections of 21 June 1857 (16,950 to 2,373). See Lacomme, *Les Elections et les représentants de Saône-et-Loire depuis 1789*; Lex and Siraud, *Le Conseil général et les conseillers généraux de Saône-et-Loire*.

125.   Lamartine to M. Oddau, April/May 1852; F. Letessier, 'Notes pour la correspondance de Lamartine', *Troisième journées Européennes d'études Lamartiniennes*, p. 425.

126.   See Lamartine to L. Guiraud, 29 December 1852; *Revue d'histoire littéraire de la France*, July-August 1973, p. 663.

127.   *Histoire de la Restauration*, 8 vols., Paris: V. Lecou, Furne et Cie., Pagnerre, 1851-53, I, p. 16.

128.   Ibid., I, p. 393.

129.   Ibid., VII, p. 5.

130.   Ibid., VIII, p. 176.

131.   Ibid., VIII, p. 234.

132.   Lamartine to Bienassis, 17 April 1853 (*Revue des Deux Mondes*, 1 December 1924, p. 633, and H. Guillemin, *Lamartine. Lettres des années sombres, 1853-1867* (Fribourg, 1942), p. 26, where the letter is dated 7 April 1853); Lamartine, *Mémoires politiques* in *Oeuvres complètes*, XXXX, p. 66.

133. Lamartine to Aubel, 30 May 1853; Latreille, *Les Dernières années de Lamartine*, p. 183.

134. See Lamartine to V. de Cessiat, 31 December 1853; *Lamartine et ses nièces*, p. 215.

135. F.-J. comte de Basterot, *Souvenirs d'enfance et de jeunesse* (Paris, 1896), p. 168; Mergier-Bourdeix, *Jules Janin*, II, pp. 434-6; *Nineteenth-Century French Studies*, II, nos. 1 and 2, Fall-Winter 1973-74, p. 21.

136. Alexandre, *Souvenirs sur Lamartine*, p. 362.

137. Des Cognets, *La Vie intérieure de Lamartine*, p. 438; Lacretelle, *Lamartine et ses amis*, pp. 271-80.

138. During a visit to Saint-Point in September 1858 Paul Huet noted Lamartine bought for 10,000 francs land of no obvious value from a peasant in financial difficulties (R. P. Huet, *Paul Huet, 1803-1869, d'après ses notes, sa correspondance, ses contemporains* (Paris, 1911), p. 251).

139. Chamborant, *Lamartine inconnu*, pp. 331-2, and B. H. V. P., Dumesnil Papers, 5705 and 5711. The Society wound itself up on 17 May 1894.

140. See Chamborant, *Lamartine inconnu*, pp. 323-43. Lamartine wanted Dargaud to be the Society's director, but Dargaud refused and suggested Alfred Dumesnil instead (des Cognets, *La Vie intérieure de Lamartine*, p. 26). Alfred Ferdinand Poullain Dumesnil (1821-94) developed a close relationship with Jules Michelet after 1839, and in 1843 married Michelet's daughter Adèle (1824-54). Dargaud knew Michelet very well and through him met Dumesnil. By 1848 Dargaud had introduced Dumesnil to Lamartine. On Dargaud's recommendation, Dumesnil became Lamartine's secretary in April 1853, a post he retained until his resignation in December 1859. See P. Sirven, *Jules Michelet: lettres inédites à Alfred Dumesnil et à Eugène Noel, 1841-1871* (Paris, 1924), and P. Viallaneix, 'Les Services lamartiniens d'Alfred Dumesnil', *Troisième journées Européennes d'études lamartiniennes*, pp. 483-92.

141. See Alexandre, *Madame de Lamartine*, pp. 193 and 201, and *Souvenirs sur Lamartine*, pp. 325 and 334.

142. See F. Delattre, *Dickens et la France. Etude d'une interaction littéraire anglo-française* (Paris, 1927), p. 24; Senior, *Conversations*, I, pp. 174, 264-5 and 315, II, p. 144.

143. H. Malo (ed.), *Mémoires de Madame Dosne, l'égérie de M. Thiers*, 2 vols. (Paris, 1928), I, p. xi.

144. See Nisard, *Souvenirs et notes biographiques*, I, p. 394.

145. Dr. E. Ménière (ed.), *Journal du docteur Prosper Ménière* (Paris, 1903), p. 245; O. Audouard, *Voyage à travers mes souvenirs* (Paris, 1884), p. 250; E. Daudet, *Souvenirs de mon temps* (Paris, 1921), pp. 209-11. Delphine de Girardin died on 29 June 1855. On 30 October 1856 Emile de Girardin married the comtesse de Tieffenbach, Prince Frederick of Nassau's widow.

146. See Ménière, *Journal du docteur Prosper Ménière*, p. 245; Lamartine to Rolland, 15 January 1856, and Dubois, 8 February 1856 (Guillemin, *Lamartine. Lettres des années sombres*, p. 51). Cf. Luppé, *Lamartine*, p. 400.

147. Lamartine to Rolland, 15 January 1856; Guillemin, *Lamartine. Lettres des années sombres*, p. 50.

148. Extracts from *Le Cours familier de littérature* appeared in *Le Siècle* between 2 September 1855 and 6 May 1858. In general see J. B. C. Duboul, *M. de Lamartine et le Cours familier de littérature* (Bordeaux, 1858); J. Gaulmier, 'La Traversée du désert d'Alphonse de Lamartine, à propos du *Cours familier de littérature*', in Viallaneix, *Lamartine. Le Livre du centenaire*, pp. 59-67; M. Hamlet-Metz, *La Critique littéraire de Lamartine* (The Hague, 1974); M. S. Hinrichs, *Le Cours familier de littérature de Lamartine* (Paris, 1930). A biographical index of the work has been prepared by M. P. Marchand, diploma *mémoire*,

Institut National des Techniques de la Documentation, 1970. For an introduction, commentary and notes for entretien XL of *Le Cours familier*, see B. Gavalda, *Lamartine et Mistral* (Paris, 1970).

149.   *Le Cours familier de littérature*, 28 vols. (Paris, 1856-69), I, p. 6.

150.   See Grenier, *Souvenirs littéraires*, p. 23. On Lamartine's article on Musset see Claudin, *Mes Souvenirs*, pp. 195-8.

151.   *Le Cours familier de littérature*, XI, entretien LXVI, p. 422.

152.   Ibid., XX, entretien CXVII, pp. 82, 96-8, 111-12 and 114.

153.   Alexandre, *Souvenirs sur Lamartine*, pp. 338-9. In general see G. Charlier, 'Une campagne publicitaire de Lamartine en Amérique (1856)', *La Revue de France*, 15 August 1934, pp. 655-73, 1 September 1934, pp. 48-64, and *Aspects de Lamartine* (Paris, 1937), pp. 141-78; Lacretelle, *Lamartine et ses amis*, pp. 83-4.

154.   Alexandre, *Souvenirs sur Lamartine*, p. 349; Guillemin, *Lamartine. Lettres des années sombres*, p. 59.

155.   Chamborant, *Lamartine inconnu*, p. 159.

156.   For examples of such letters, see A. N., 271 AP 1, A 7b 33; B. N., nouv. acq. fr., 24638, ff. 292 and 294; Manuscripts Department, University of Nottingham Library, My 2754-6. Cf. *Bulletin de l'Association Guillaume Budé*, January-March 1970, p. 155.

157.   Chamborant, *Lamartine inconnu*, p. 172.

158.   *Le Journal de Saône-et-Loire*, 3 March 1858. Cf. A. Barois, 'Embarras financier de Lamartine: lettres inédites de Lamartine à Armand-Gilbert Le Chevalier, 1856-1859', *Mercure de France*, 1 March 1949, pp. 477-8, and Guillemin, *Lamartine. Lettres des années sombres*, pp. 85-6.

159.   Chamborant, *Lamartine inconnu*, pp. 178-84; Alexandre, *Souvenirs sur Lamartine*, p. 362.

160.   Alexandre, *Madame de Lamartine*, pp. 210-11; Caplain, *Edouard Dubois*, pp. 115-18; *Le Siècle*, 30 March 1858, p. 2. In general see E. Magnien, 'Lamartine et le comité mâconnais de la souscription de 1858', *Annales de l'Académie de Mâcon*, third series, XLV (1960-61), pp. 76-98.

161.   The list included Emile Péreire (director of the Crédit mobilier), the comte de Beaumont, the marquis de La Grange, the comte de Chamborant, the baron Sérurier, Léonor Havin (director of *Le Siècle*), Amédée Renée (director of *Le Constitutionnel* and *Le Pays*), Adolphe Guéroult (editor of *La Presse*), Alexandre Paulin (director of *L'Illustration*), Armand-Gilbert Le Chevalier (editor of *L'Illustration*), Saint-Marc Girardin, Ernest Legouvé, Victor de Laprade, Jules Janin (editor of *Le Journal des Débats*), François Lenormant, Alexandre Dumas, Charles Gosselin, Edmond Texier (editor of *Le Siècle*), Félix Mornand, and Joseph Autran; *Le Siècle*, 1 April 1858, p. 2; Guillemin, *Lamartine. Lettres des années sombres*, pp. 203-5; Ulbach, *Nos Contemporains*, pp. 40-2.

162.   Subscription lists were published in *Le Siècle*, 28 May 1858-16 April 1859, and in *La Presse* after 10 June 1858. For Liszt see D. Ollivier (ed.), *Correspondance de Liszt et de sa fille Madame Emile Ollivier* (Paris, 1936), p. 212.

163.   *The Times*, 29 May 1858, p. 12; *Le Constitutionnel*, 8 April 1858.

164.   Circular no. 16, 4 November 1858; A. N., F¹ᵃ 2084. Cf. Alexandre, *Madame de Lamartine*, p. 238; Chamborant, *Lamartine inconnu*, pp. 193-4.

165.   See D. A. Griffiths, 'Au dossier des "années sombres" d'Alphonse de Lamartine. Lettres inédites de Lamartine à Ernest Legouvé', *Studi francesi* (Turin), no. 25, January-April 1965, p. 79; Chamborant, *Lamartine inconnu*, p. 193; *Le Siècle*, 29 September 1858, p. 3; Guillemin, *Lamartine. Lettres des années sombres*, p. 117.

166.   M.-T. Marchand-Roques, 'Lamartine et un de ses amis', *Mélanges d'histoire littéraire et de bibliographie offerts à Jean Bonnerot* (Paris, 1954),

pp. 295 and 297. Cf. *Mémoires de la Société académique de l'Oise*, XVIII (1901-03), pp. 558-9.

167. Laprade to Alexandre, 31 March 1858; Séchaud, *Lettres inédites de Victor de Laprade à Charles Alexandre*, p. 40.

168. E. Marcotte to ? F. Mornand, 15 November 1858; B. N., nouv. acq. fr., 24328, f. 287. Félix Mornand was the nephew of Dr Pascal of Mâcon. For other documents concerning the Lamartine subscription, see B. N., nouv. acq. fr., 24328, ff. 262-304.

169. Des Cognets, *La Vie intérieure de Lamartine*, pp. 445-6.

170 Ibid., pp. 446-8.

171. *The Saturday Review*, 26 June 1858, pp. 657-8. The article was reprinted in the Catholic newspaper, *L'Univers*, 4 July 1858. For Lamartine's reply see *L'Univers*, 11 July 1858, pp. 1-2. Cf. B. N., nouv. acq. fr., 24633, f. 473, and Guillemin, *Lamartine. Lettres des années sombres*, pp. 105-13.

172. Guillemin, *Lamartine. Lettres des années sombres*, pp. 134-6. Cf. Lamartine to George Kaufmann, 18 November 1859; S. Merton, 'A letter from Lamartine to "Gr. K." ', *Modern Language Notes*, XLIX (1934), pp. 520-1.

173. L. Barthou, 'Sur un manuscrit de Lamartine', *Annales romantiques*, IX, March-April 1912, p. 152; F. Letessier, 'Lamartine et le journaliste Alfred Fonville', *Annales de l'Académie de Mâcon*, third series, LI (1972-73) p. 121.

174. Guillemin, *Lamartine. Lettres des années sombres*, p. 129.

175. Caplain, *Edouard Dubois*, pp. 121-3; Luppé, *Lamartine*, p. 409.

176. Caplain, *Edouard Dubois*, pp. 125-7.

177. *Le Constitutionnel*, 26 September – 2 December 1865. Cf. A. K. Gray, *Teresa, the Story of Byron's Last Mistress* (London, 1948), pp. 319-27.

178. L. de La Brière, *Mes Amis: souvenirs* (Paris, 1891), p. 38; Daudet, *Souvenirs de mon temps*, pp. 209-11.

179. Flaubert, *Correspondance*, IV (1927), pp. 150-1; R. Dumesnil, *Gustave Flaubert, l'homme et l'oeuvre* (Paris, 1932), pp. 229-30.

180. See C. A. Leblond, *Fragments littéraires, précédés d'une lettre de Lamartine à l'auteur* (Pau, 1860), p. 1; Lamartine to the comte Anatole de Montesquiou, 14 May 1855 (B. N., nouv. acq. fr., 15029, f. 242); G. C. Pertus, *Les Echos poétiques* (Pau, 1865), p. v; J. de Marchef-Girard, *Les Femmes, leur passé, leur présent, leur avenir* (Paris, 1860), p. iii; E. V. Garcin, *Léonie, essai d'éducation par le roman* (Paris, 1860), pp. 1-3.

181. *Le Cours familier de littérature*, XI, entretien LXI, p. 18. Cf. Senior, *Conversations*, I, p. 265.

182. Comte de Puymaigre, 'Lamartine. Souvenirs particuliers', *Mémoires de l'Académie de Metz*, 1872-73, p. 188; Chamborant, *Lamartine inconnu*, pp. 246-7; Ollivier, *Journal*, II, p. 82; Séchaud, *Lettres inédites de Victor de Laprade à Charles Alexandre*, p. 80, note 1. See also H. Guillemin, 'Lamartine et les USA: une lettre inédite', *Mercure de France*, 1 March 1949, pp. 466-7.

183. Biré, *Mes Souvenirs*, pp. 297-8; *Mémoires de l'Académie de Metz*, 1872-73, p. 188.

184. Caplain, *Edouard Dubois*, p. 135.

185. Chamborant, *Lamartine inconnu*, p. 208. Cf. Guillemin, *Lamartine. Lettres des années sombres*, p. 150.

186. See Alexandre, *Madame de Lamartine*, pp. 322-4, and *Souvenirs sur Lamartine*, pp. 376-9; Chamborant, *Lamartine inconnu*, pp. 234-5; Lacretelle, *Lamartine et ses amis*, p. 284; Luppé, *Lamartine*, p. 429; Toesca, *Lamartine*, p. 537. For a description of Marianne's funeral see Guillemin, *Lamartine. Lettres des années sombres*, pp. 218-19.

187. See C. Fournet, *Eloge de Lamartine* (Geneva, 1970), pp. 114-28.

188. *La Revue bleue*, 6 October 1934, p. 723; Latreille, *Les Dernières*

années de Lamartine, pp. 213-14; D. H. Carnaham, 'The Financial Difficulties of Lamartine', *Modern Philology*, July 1918, p. 31; Guillemin, *Lamartine. Lettres des années sombres*, pp. 185 and 189; *Revue des Deux Mondes*, 1 March 1961, pp. 139-40.

189. Caplain, *Edouard Dubois*, pp. 122 and 143-4; Luppé, *Lamartine*, p. 437.

190. The Senate approved the Corps législatif's decision on 3 May 1867. See J. Lamber, *Mes Sentiments et nos idées avant 1870* (Paris, 1905), pp. 129-30; Emile Ollivier's report in *La Liberté*, 16 April 1867; Ollivier, *Lamartine, précédé d'une préface sur les incidents qui ont empêché son éloge en séance publique de l'Académie française* (Paris, 1874), pp. 184-208, and *Valentine de Lamartine*, pp. 103-5 and 173-89.

191. See *Annales romantiques*, II (1905), pp. 345-6; J. V. A. duc de Broglie, *Mémoires du duc de Broglie*, 2 vols. (Paris, 1938-41), I, p. 300; *Bulletin de l'Association Guillaume Budé*, June 1965, pp. 253-70; du Camp, *Souvenirs littéraires*, p. 32; Houssaye, *Les Confessions*, I, p. 242; Ollivier, *Journal*, II, p. 312; Ollivier, *Correspondance de Liszt et de sa fille*, pp. 299-300.

192. Des Cognets, *La Vie intérieure de Lamartine*, p. 443.

193. Ollivier, *Valentine de Lamartine*, pp. 116-17.

194. Ibid., p. 117.

195. Alexandre, *Souvenirs sur Lamartine*, p. 393.

196. See ibid., pp. 396-404; Chamborant, *Lamartine inconnu*, p. 284; Grenier, *Souvenirs littéraires*, p. 35; *Lamartine chez lui, souvenirs intimes* (Paris, 1869), pp. 56-69; Ollivier, *Lamartine*, pp. 179-83, and *Valentine de Lamartine*, p. 114, note 1.

197. Latreille, *Les Dernières années de Lamartine*, p. 274, note 1.

CONCLUSION

Poète avant tout, le poète chez lui emporte le député, le politique, l'homme d'Etat. — Cormenin on Lamartine in *Livre des Orateurs*, II (1869), p. 110

C'est la poésie de Lamartine qui sauve la politique de Lamartine. — Barbey d'Aurevilly in *Le XIXe Siècle. Les oeuvres et les hommes*, XI (1889), p. 149

When he died in 1869, it must have seemed that Lamartine as a politician had been an unqualified failure. He had generally failed to influence government policies during Louis-Philippe's reign. He had failed to prevent the insurrection of June 1848 which ended his one brief period in government. The following December his failure in the presidential election had been catastrophic. Thereafter, despite eventual membership of the Corps législatif, his political career was effectively over: it was finally terminated by the *coup d'état* of 1851. Although towards the end of his life Lamartine confessed to have reached a state of 'political atheism',[1] and even at times indicated an admiration for Napoleon III, a Bonapartist dictatorship was repugnant to nearly all his previous principles. Yet, ironically, through eloquently supporting in 1848 the President's election by manhood suffrage, he unwittingly facilitated the creation of the Second Empire.

Lamartine's political career was not, however, one of unrelieved failure. During the July Monarchy he made an important contribution to the movement for a more liberal régime in France; immediately after the February Days he helped prevent the situation in Paris from degenerating into chaos; and he was a moderately successful Minister of Foreign Affairs, though partly because various factors curbed his more ambitious plans. While a member of the Provisional Government, the campaign he had supported for slavery's abolition was crowned with success. He had advocated manhood suffrage, and he duly approved its establishment in 1848. Whether or not he was responsible for its introduction (as he claimed), there is no denying its importance. After 1848 several individuals whom he had undoubtedly influenced achieved political prominence, such as his neighbour Jean-Baptiste Ferrouillat (deputy and then senator for the Var, 1871-1891), Emile Ollivier (deputy 1857-1870 and head of Napoleon III's last government in 1870), and Charles Rolland (deputy and then senator for Saône-et-Loire, 1871-1876). Lamartine also contributed to the developing political tradition which eventually achieved its fullest expression in the French Radical Party, formed a generation after his death. The early Radicals were to share many of his aims and ideals: a belief in rational politics, social progress, law and order, private property, the separation of Church and State, relatively conservative financial and economic policies, and the realisation of Revolutionary *fraternité* by the elimination of class conflict.

Although of limited political influence, Lamartine nonetheless possessed very considerable abilities – even in politics. As a parliamentarian – at least up to 1848 – he was always one of the most prominent and controversial speakers, while *Méditations Poétiques* and the *Histoire des Girondins* were two of the most sensational publications of his generation. He owed his success as a writer to a remarkable facility for literary composition in the Romantic manner. He played on his readers' emotions; he aroused their enthusiasms by the use of colourful imagery and lavish description; he overwhelmed them with words – chosen as much for sound and effect as for precise meaning. His speeches were similarly flamboyant and emotional. Capable of a rhetoric often telling and memorable, displaying an individualistic style that could be extremely effective, he swayed hostile audiences to his own point of view on several vital occasions. But his popular success in both literature and politics depended on the extent to which his emotive appeal and individual style coincided with the mood and sympathies of his audience: such a coincidence was frequently not achieved. Too often he was over-ambitious, too often he failed to understand, and respond to, other people's mentalities.

Lamartine invariably worked with prodigious speed. His later writings were hastily composed to meet the demands of his creditors, but even the *Histoire des Girondins* was written at the rate of fifteen pages a day.[2] Within hours he could assimilate the complicated details of some technical project, and then deliver a speech on the subject in the Chamber of Deputies.[3] The achievement of such speed, however, entailed sacrifices. Lamartine once asked a friend: 'What are you doing there, my friend, with your head in your hands?' – 'I am thinking.' – 'Extraordinary! I never think, my ideas think for me!'[4] Whether this exchange took place or not, Lamartine was certainly not given to original thought, painstaking research, careful analysis or concise argument.

The frantic pace and lack of reflection notwithstanding, Lamartine's stature as a political thinker was by no means negligible. Many of the objects for which he campaigned – the abolition of slavery, the extension of the franchise, the encouragement of popular education, and the alleviation of the sufferings of the poor and unfortunate – were of central importance. His proposed solutions, although usually neither original nor profound, at least revealed more humanity and foresight than those normally advocated by contemporaries of a similar social background. Also, he often appreciated future trends, supporting, for instance, democratic reforms and encouraging railway construction, and believing, like Louis Napoleon, that politicians and governments should be in harmony with the spirit of the times. Sometimes Lamartine displayed an almost uncanny ability to predict the course of future events. To a considerable degree, he foresaw the Revolutions of 1830 and 1848, and Louis Napoleon's *coup d'état* of 1851. His fears of a class war were realised during the Paris Commune; and his anxieties over the building of fortifications round Paris were justified by the events of 1870 and 1871. He even predicted that Algerian fruit, cereals and cheap wine would be dumped on the French market.[5] In his interest in public opinion, concern for a favourable public image, and grasp of the potential of the newspaper press, he seems strikingly modern. He was also remarkable for his dedication to principles. 'A soldier of principle, I fight for principles and not for myself', he once wrote.[6] He was not in politics for money, power or cheap popularity. To uphold a belief he would be prepared to risk his popular standing and political position. With this moral courage went a physical bravery, demonstrated during the Revolution of 1848.[7]

In his private as well as in his public life, Lamartine tried to live up to his high ideals. To employees and neighbouring peasants he was generous and paternalistic. At Saint-Point he freely opened his park to the public.[8] He helped many individuals, most of whom were of no influence or importance. Among those he assisted were his colleague at the French legation in Florence, Joseph Antoir,[9] minor poets and writers such as Baour-Lormian,[10] Charles Lassailly[11] and Armand Lebailly,[12] and Giorgio Mauridès (from whom he had received hospitality while in Bulgaria in August 1833).[13] Lamartine could write generously of a political adversary such as Thiers;[14] and several old opponents eventually became personal friends. Auguste Barthélemy, the writer of a poem in 1831 against his candidature in the Nord, later addressed to him laudatory verses which were published in *Le Conseiller du peuple*.[15] Electoral rivals in Mâcon, such as Pierre Duréault and Léon Bruys d'Ouilly, were converted into staunch supporters. Lamartine had many critics but few implacable enemies. Even Guizot is supposed to have shed a tear when he heard the news of Lamartine's death.[16]

Although rarely hated, Lamartine was often criticised. One criticism, made by hostile commentators such as Odilon Barrot and the comte de Falloux, was that he was merely a poet with the delusion that he was also a politician.[17] He tried very hard to refute such views. He would stress that he attached little importance to his poetic achievements, that poetry had been for him merely a passing phase, and that he was not a poet but a serious and practical man of affairs.[18] He would also assert that no essential conflict existed between the roles of poet and politician. 'Do you know what a great statesman is?' he once asked Ernest Legouvé. 'A great poet . . . in action!'[19] The links between Lamartine's poetry and politics were indeed quite tangible. His poetry had been an invaluable aid to his success in the Paris *salons*, his diplomatic appointment at Naples, his subsequent posting to Florence, and his establishment as a national public figure. Fully aware of this, Lamartine took care to present copies of his published poetry to influential individuals such as Chateaubriand; and clearly he was convinced that through his poetry, as well as his other writings, he could influence public opinion to his own political advantage. Consequently he early acquired a lively interest in publicity. Always very concerned with the critical reception of his poetry, he resented hostile reviews, complained if his poems were ignored, and cultivated favourable reviewers. This interest in publicity encouraged an equally early appreciation of the importance of the newspaper and periodical press: he had individual poems published in newspapers and journals, and seems to have cultivated newspapers which published, and favourably reviewed, his poetry. Similarly, as a politician he avidly followed press coverage of himself, befriended several journalists and extensively used newspapers and journals to publish political statements, articles, and news items about himself or even his wife's charitable activities. In addition, a concern for the sound of words, so pronounced in his poetry, characterised the style of his political speeches and writings; a belief in the need for harmony influenced both his poetry and his social and political thought; and a number of the subjects which interested him as a politician, such as railway construction or the fate of orphans and abandoned children, had, at least so far as he was concerned, a poetic character.

This relationship between poetry and politics was a source of strength as well as of weakness. Poetry launched him on his public career, contributed towards his success as an orator, and helped to give him a Romantic image which, on such occasions as the February Days, could be a major political asset. But in more normal times, because he had first made his reputation as a poet and subsequently written so much poetry, both parliament and public found it difficult to take him seriously. As a worker bluntly put it, having been asked why he was not going to vote for Lamartine in the presidential election: 'M. Lamartine is a poet. We are told that poets cannot cope with public affairs.'[20] He did in fact possess a number of attributes often associated with poets but usually disastrous in politicians: a tendency to absent-mindedness, a certain lack of realism, a weakness for reckless gambles, and a total inability to manage his own finances.

Contemporaries also criticised Lamartine for his excessive *amour-propre*. An American visitor noted in 1850 that a single room of his Paris apartment contained one full-length portrait, three half-length portraits, a bust, two medallions, an engraving, and two or three miniatures — all of Lamartine.[21] A friend who referred to his *gloire*, in an attempt to console him after Marianne's death, is supposed to have received the reply: 'Yes, it is nevertheless sad to be alone in my *gloire*'.[22] Similarly, Lamartine once claimed to have read the poems of Pushkin, at a time when they had not yet been translated into French.[23] His letters as a young man indicate a degree of self-preoccupation extravagant even in an adolescent: he frequently asked friends to perform services for him, while he rarely reciprocated; and he repeatedly complained about his ennui, *mal de foi*, ill-health, social obligations, finances, career expectations, love affairs, and marriage prospects. All the evidence suggests that his self-absorption continued throughout his life — certainly in his numerous writings he was constantly concerned with himself, either directly or indirectly. In addition, from an early age he seems always to have sought, and needed, the adulation of others. He was extremely sensitive about the attitudes towards him of members of his family. The love affairs of his youth can partly be explained by a craving for uncritical admiration. He obviously enjoyed being the centre of attraction in Paris *salons*, and having his poems and writings received with enthusiasm. He delighted in the official honours accorded to him on his Mediterranean travels, relished his short-lived moments of popularity while a deputy, and exulted in the public acclaim that brought him to power in 1848. In his own *salon* in the 1840s he was surrounded by uncritical admirers whose flattery he seemed eagerly to accept.[24] Rarely of outstanding ability or reputation, his closest friends were usually minor figures, distinguished by little except their loyalty and admiration for Lamartine.

As in the case of the links between his poetry and his politics, this vanity and egoism had diverse consequences. Lamartine was determined to prove that he was not a frivolous Romantic — dreamy poet, melancholy lover, perennial traveller — but a man of action and a man of affairs. This helped to give him his ambition and motivation. However, his vanity repelled or exasperated many political colleagues; it made him willing to consider only the most senior posts; it meant that he would tolerate no superior; and it deprived him of the crucial political asset of sound judgement. As a result, he was blind to his own limitations, and he rarely demonstrated a sense of proportion or a sense of humour. His vanity also contributed to his awareness of public opinion and interest in its manipulation. But at the same time it encouraged him to overestimate the political potential of both the spoken and written word, not least his own, and to try to be all things to all people, which resulted in the inconsistencies and contradictions which ultimately discredited him.

Associated with Lamartine's self-preoccupation was a lively imagination. The latter was obviously an essential source of inspiration for his writings, and doubtless contributed to his sensitive approach to human and social problems, but his imagination and egocentricity often led him to disregard the facts. In his poetry he transformed the rather squalid affairs of his youth into sublime romances. In other works he ignored or distorted evidence so as to produce a literary effect or support some historical interpretation. Allegedly he altered his parliamentary speeches for the official record, adding new passages and inserting indications of favourable audience reaction.[25] While Minister of Foreign Affairs he deliberately fed misleading information to the press. Similarly, he refused to take account of the realities of politics. The tenacious adherence to his peculiar notion of personal independence meant that he was not just in opposition, but in virtual isolation, throughout his parliamentary career. A revolutionary situation, his unique political position, and his evolution towards the Left did bring him into power in 1848. But he failed to appreciate that the alliance with Ledru-Rollin would mean political suicide, and that after the June Days his national standing had been destroyed, and would never be restored. This unqualified faith in himself was not limited to politics: as entrepreneur, *vigneron*, landowner, and even architect, he had an overweening confidence in his own expertise. Yet his financial speculations nearly always ended in disaster; his vineyards suffered from a succession of calamities; his wine was frequently sold at a loss;

and his debts compelled the disposal of many of his properties during his lifetime, and of the remainder after his death.[26] As for his architectural pretensions, the *château* of Saint-Point was disfigured by his neo-Gothic extravagances.[27]

A further contemporary criticism of Lamartine was that he was politically inconsistent. Mme de Girardin is supposed to have remarked that Lamartine changed his *idée fixe* too often.[28] Certainly, he appeared to be a legitimist under the Restoration, a supporter and then an opponent of the July Monarchy, a moderate republican and then a radical between February and June 1848, a critic and then an admirer of Napoleon III. His primary concern was often with striking an effect or creating an impression; he was frequently a victim of doubt and indecision; he changed his position on certain questions such as the extent of the parliamentary franchise; and fundamental conflicts and inconsistencies can be found in his thought and actions. He believed in human reason and in human instincts, in the virtues of solitude and in the value of popularity, in the will of Providence and in Rousseau's 'general will', in the omnipresence of God and in the secularisation of education, in the universal application of Christian principles and in the official separation of Church and State. About his objectives he was invariably uncertain: whether to be a poet or a politician, a private individual or a public figure. Yet any failure hurt him deeply. He was convinced of the importance of popularity, eagerly sought it, and found it exhilarating. At the same time he criticised those who courted public favour, was unprepared to sacrifice his principles for his popularity, and attached more importance to his position in the long term than in the immediate future.

Many such inconsistencies can be cited. But changes of political allegiance were not uncommon among Frenchmen at this time; Lamartine believed in progress, and was opposed to any fixed programme or permanent system; he became, up to 1848, consistently more liberal; and there were a number of beliefs and principles he constantly retained. He always tried to preserve his independence. He always supported the institutions of the family and private property. He always believed in personal liberty, some form of political democracy, the ideals of 1789, and their continuing relevance to the development of France. He always remained fully convinced that Christian morality lay at the heart of civilisation, and that the supreme duty of writers and politicians was to make Christian morality the foundation of their societies. It is this idealism which gives an element of nobility to Lamartine's political career, and an element of tragedy to his political failure.

Notes

1. Lamartine to Chamborant, 18 June 1860; Chamborant, *Lamartine inconnu*, p. 200. Cf. Alexandre, *Souvenirs sur Lamartine*, p. 313.
2. Lamartine to Champvans, 29 June 1845; Guillemin, *Lamartine. Lettres inédites*, p. 82.
3. Legouvé, *Lamartine*, pp. 16-17, and *Soixante ans de souvenirs*, II, pp. 362-3.
4. Legouvé, *Lamartine*, p. 36, and *Soixante ans de souvenirs*, II, p. 379.
5. Senior, *Conversations*, I, p. 267.
6. Lamartine to Doisy, 5 October 1842; *Correspondance*, VI (1875), p. 27. Cf. Lamartine to Ronot, 7 March 1843: 'je me suis dévoué dès longtemps à n'être qu'un soldat des idées et de Dieu' (B. M. Mâcon, ms. 107, f. 105; *Correspondance*, VI (1875), p. 60).
7. E.g. see Stern, *Histoire de la Révolution de 1848*, I, p. 228. Cf. *Le Moniteur universel*, 25 February 1848, p. 501.
8. Harris, *Lamartine et le peuple*, pp. 71-2.
9. See Mengin, *Les Manuscrits d'Antoir*.
10. See *La France parlementaire*, IV, pp. 393-4.
11. See A. de Vigny, *Journal d'un poète* (Paris, 1913); Lamartine to Gosselin, 10 September 1834 (*Correspondance générale*, II, p. 62); E. Kaye, *Charles Lassailly, 1806-1843* (Geneva, 1962), pp. 58-9, 127-8, 134.
12. Legouvé, *Soixante ans de souvenirs*, II, pp. 380-1.
13. See H. Bordeaux, 'La Fin du voyage de Lamartine en Orient: lettres inédites', *Revue des Deux Mondes*, 15 January 1926, pp. 358-9.
14. See *Lamartine par lui-même*, p. 308.
15. *Le Conseiller du peuple*, I, pp. 489-94.
16. Lacretelle, *Lamartine et ses amis*, p. 300.
17. Barrot, *Mémoires posthumes*, II, p. 34; Falloux, *Mémoires*, I, p. 312.
18. See Barthélemy, *Souvenirs d'un ancien préfet*, pp. 199-201.
19. Legouvé, *Lamartine*, p. 14.
20. *L'Eclaireur des Pyrénées*, 3 December 1848, p. 2.
21. *Letters of Charles Eliot Norton*, 2 vols (London, 1913), I, p. 66.
22. Marmier, *Journal*, I, p. 316.
23. A. Joubin (ed.), *Journal de Eugène Delacroix*, 3 vols. (Paris, 1960), I, p. 265.
24. See Alton-Shée, *Mes Mémoires*, p. 118, and *Journal de Victor de Balabine*, pp. 108-9.
25. Simpson, *Correspondence and Conversations of Alexis de Tocqueville with Nassau William Senior*, II, p. 166.
26. Lamartine sold the estates of Montculot and Péronne, and three houses in Mâcon: the house at 18 rue des Ursulines (where he was born), the Hôtel d'Ozenay and the Hôtel de Lamartine. After his death Monceau was sold, and is now a holiday home for old age pensioners. Saint-Point was bought by Jean-Pierre Charles de Montherot after Valentine's death (16 May 1894). The present owner is the former's nephew, the comte René de Noblet d'Anglure.
27. See Legouvé, *Lamartine*, p. 8.
28. Estourmel, *Derniers souvenirs*, p. 191. Cf. L. M. de La Haye, vicomte de Cormenin, *Livre des Orateurs*, 2 vols. (Paris, 1869), II, p. 110; Sainte-Beuve, *Cahiers*, I, p. 372.

BIBLIOGRAPHY

A full bibliography listing all the sources used in this book would be very long and largely unnecessary. In the Notes and references an attempt has been made to provide a detailed indication of sources; and a number of relevant bibliographic guides already exist. For an introduction to Lamartine studies see C. Croisille, 'Le Dossier Lamartine', *Romantisme*, I (1971), pp. 230-50. The main guides to printed sources relating to Lamartine are J. Baillou and E. Harris (eds.), *Etat présent des études lamartiniennes* (Paris, 1933), which includes works published up to 1932, and H. Talvart and J. Place (eds.), *Bibliographie des auteurs modernes de langue française*, XI (1952), pp. 23-166, which includes works published up to 1951. Another guide is H. P. Thieme (ed.), *Bibliographie de la littérature française de 1800 à 1930*, II (1933), pp. 34-46. For post-1951 publications see the *Bibliographie de la littérature française du moyen âge à nos jours* (annual), the *Bibliographie annuelle de l'histoire de France* (annual) and the *Revue d'histoire littéraire de la France* (bi-monthly). For recent critical surveys see M.-F. Guyard, 'Etat présent des études lamartiniennes', *L'Information littéraire*, May-June 1961, pp. 93-7, and *Sainte-Beuve Lamartine, colloques 8 novembre 1969* (Société de l'histoire littéraire de la France, 1970), pp. 51-8. Good general bibliographies are to be found in P. Lévêque, *La Bourgogne de la Monarchie de Juillet au Second Empire*, an exhaustive doctoral thesis (Paris IV, 5 vols., 1977) which is now available commercially (Service de reproduction des Thèses, Université de Lille III), and A.-J. Tudesq, *Les Grands notables en France, 1840-1849: étude historique d'une psychologie sociale*, 2 vols. (Paris, 1964). Reference may also be made to my 'Alphonse de Lamartine as a politician and intellectual, 1831-1869', unpublished PhD thesis (London, 1973).

INDEX